STARDOM

Valentino as the bullring urchin at the start of *Blood and Sand*. He always
took pains to differentiate his roles and knew how to use his body, as well
as his wardrobe, in sketching in a character

Stardom

THE HOLLYWOOD PHENOMENON

Alexander Walker

> The Athenians erected a huge statue to
> Æsop and so that everyone might know
> the path to honour lay open to all they
> placed the word 'Slave' on its
> enduring base.
>
> — *Phaedrus*

STEIN AND DAY/*Publishers*/New York

First published in 1970
Copyright © 1970 by Alexander Walker
Library of Congress Catalog Card No. 70-108320
All rights reserved
Printed in the United States of America
Stein and Day/*Publishers*/7 East 48 Street, New York, N.Y. 10017
SBN 8128-1309-X

For Charles Wintour
With respect and affection

CONTENTS

ILLUSTRATIONS

STARDOM

PREFACE

Wherever films are made, stars are made too. Stardom is a characteristic of film industries the world over. But it has always dominated American movies more than those of any other country. Stars laid the basis of the Hollywood film industry; and even now, when Hollywood is in decline, though the name still serves as a handy label, stardom is a hard concept to abandon – even though it may be called 'anti-stardom' by some of the screen's gifted newcomers. By whichever name one chooses to call it, it is the phenomenon discussed in this book.

It is not a comprehensive history of the stars, but an enquiry into the processes by which some stars are made – and the reasons why the end products turn out as they do. The stars treated in detail are ones who facilitate this kind of study and who have had an extraordinary impact on their art, industry and society at large. This is another reason for confining the study to Hollywood – the relevance of the material to things outside Hollywood. European films have a long tradition of expressing the viewpoints of their individual makers; whereas Hollywood movies, until recently anyhow, have generally embodied social and economic forces in a studio-assembled product. (If the *auteur* theory that the director stamps the work can be applied to Hollywood, it is only with the heavy qualification that until lately the Hollywood director has been the hireling of a studio.) Stars in consequence are the direct or indirect reflection of the needs, drives and dreams of American society. And it is against this background that I have examined such phenomena as the emergence of stars, the birth of the 'star system,' the coming of the talkies and the regime of studio rulers: in short, the grandeur and servitude of stardom.

But this is a book of close-ups as well as long-shots. It aims to let the artists be seen not only against the industry and society, but in relation to their films and performances. The central theme is a

13

human one: an attempt to show the star as both a live person and a prepared image and to suggest how the two interact on the screen and off it. Pudovkin in his book on film acting referred to this connection as 'linkage'. 'The image,' he wrote, 'is constructed not only by the intention of the play as a whole, but also by the nature of the actor's self. It is related to himself as an individual personality.'*

The relationship between acting and the star personality makes up the main area of this study. Obviously any conclusions are subjective, in some cases necessarily speculative. Stars' personalities were subjected to many pressures. And the way they were created by studio policies, as well as public prejudices, often took the control and responsibility for them away from their owner. Yet the stars' own films still offer the best chance of seeing how an image builds up as the players' consciousness crystallises it. If I give prominence to actors over directors in analysing this, I can only plead that in my view the current concern with the director attributes too little of the credit to the player. The stars were, after all, the people to whom the public gave their loyalty as human personalities and mythic figures; and we are dealing with a film industry that was based on stars, not directors. Moreover some of the silent stars like Valentino, John Gilbert, Lillian Gish and Douglas Fairbanks Sr. stand in urgent need of reappraisal because their films are seldom seen and their talents poorly appreciated in consequence. It is time to remedy this neglect.

The stars selected for this study are my choices: the omissions are mine, too. It is impossible to include every major Hollywood star and I have preferred to leave out some of those, especially the more modern examples, about whom much, perhaps too much has already been written. I would also refer the reader in search of such great female stars as Clara Bow, Dietrich, Mae West, Harlow, Monroe and others, to my earlier book on the sexual aspects of the movies.†

* *Film Technique and Film Acting*, by V. I. Pudovkin, translated and edited by Ivor Montagu (Memorial Edition: Vision-Mayflower.) pp. 146–7.

† *The Celluloid Sacrifice* (Michael Joseph, London, 1966: Hawthorn Books, New York, 1967. Reprinted in paperback as *Sex in the Movies* (Penguin Books, London and New York: 1968).

With stars as well known as Chaplin and Garbo, I have dealt only with the extraordinary genesis of their star images. For as Pudovkin points out, the relation between screen image and live personality is particularly strong at the beginning of an actor's work. 'This is the period at which emphasis lies on the element of his emotional attitude to the image, his so-called feeling of some aspect of the image that particularly excites him and thereby serves as the essential point of departure of his work on it.'*

With the arrival of the talkies, screen acting loses a lot of its vividness. Its plastic quality vanishes, once the voice does much of the work that previously had to be done by the star's whole body and *persona*. The later chapters consequently put the emphasis on the star's image in relation to society and trace the way in which the gap between player and public has gradually closed with the change in society and the filmgoing audience until the star, or anti-star, becomes barely distinguishable from the fans whose attitudes he sanctions.

Two final points. The date included after the first mention of every important film refers to the year it was shown, not the year it was made, unless the two are the same. A full list of acknowledgements appears at the end, but I must single out four people who made the book possible by showing me many of the less accessible films I have written about: Kevin Brownlow, Philip Jenkinson, Leslie Flint and especially Bohumil Brechja, former curator of the Czechoslovak Film Archive, whose love for the cinema enabled me to see some of Hollywood's richest work at a time when the Russian invasion of Czechoslovakia was oppressing the spirits of himself and his countrymen.

London, January 1970.

* *Pudovkin*, op. cit., pp. 240–1.

PART ONE

INNOCENCE

MRS PICKFORD: 'Would you be very
much against applying for work at the
Biograph Studios?'
MARY: 'Oh no, not that, Mama!'
MRS PICKFORD: 'Well, now it's not what
I want for you either, dear . . . It's only
to tide us over.'
    – From *Sunshine and Shadow,*
      The Autobiography of Mary Pickford

CHAPTER ONE

FROM STAGE
TO SCREEN:
MISS LAWRENCE
AND CO

Stars are born. But most of the cinema's early stars were illegitimate children. They were the offspring of a union between theatrical tradition and technological change which was never officially recognised, much less blessed by those who participated in it. Such dubious parentage had enormous consequences. It helped bring into being the only wholly new art form to be developed this century. But it also created a problem familiar to anyone who has ever been asked to scrutinise a newly-born infant and pinpoint just which of the parents he resembles more. The safe answer is to make none – but wait a little, till he grows up and develops a personality of his own which, happily, will resemble neither side of the family.

With the first film stars, things are not so easily solved. For it is hard to put a date on artistic identity and say with any certainty that the actors and actresses who became film favourites in the early 1900s can now be considered film stars in the modern sense of the term. It would be easier if more of them had recorded their own awareness of what was happening to them as it happened – as the cinema multiplied their images, altered their personalities, projected their uniqueness and forced filmgoers to participate in the collective experience in a way that had more in common with tribal worship, myth and primitive magic. But it would be unrealistic to expect this. Change is not usually seen for what it is until it has taken place. When it takes place inside a human being, it may not be recognised at all.

Memoirs and autobiographies of the stars should be helpful here; but they rarely are, though some offer insights that can be relevant because they are unconscious. All too often, though, they have been composed after, long after, stardom has been recognised by the subjects for what it is – or, disillusioningly, is not. And hindsight has oversimplified the stages in which a star becomes conscious of himself as such. In trying to get at the likelihood of how this happened, and when, it is vital to read events out of the past, not into it.

Film stardom is the almost perfect illustration of McLuhan's thesis that technological innovation begins by re-creating features of the past that it replaces. The course we steer in our cultural progress is determined by the nostalgic reflection in the rear-view mirror. The early American movies offer abundant proof of this, not just on the screen but in the assumptions of the men who made them and in the circumstances in which they were made. The nineteenth-century theatre shaped the new film industry and the people who were to be its stars. It is hard nowadays to grasp just how naturally the bioscope was regarded as the extension of the stage by other less respectable, but prodigiously more lucrative means.

To see these early films as they were seen in their own day probably requires the kind of naïve imagination only available today to sophisticated minds. This is why contemporary screenings of them, even given a pianist in tune with their sentiments, and pardoning the jerky, incorrect speed at which they are usually projected, cannot hope to reproduce their effect on patrons in the early 1900s. Just as painters in the period prior to the discovery of perspective did not need to look for linear truth, so the early film audiences did not need to look for cinematic truth. Neither, at first, did the producers. 'Will you gentlemen never learn,' Charles Pathé told his directors, 'that in the cinema an actor must be photographed so that his feet touch the bottom of the screen and his head the top.' This was proscenium truth. And along with it, at first, went proscenium acting.

It is not true that actors, even in the early silent films, were incapable of subtle pantomime to describe the characters they were playing. It was the director who decided questions like the flamboyance or restraint of his players' gestures; and the first directors naturally regarded a camera as a fixed member of the audience to whom a performance had to be pitched rather more than life-size. Moreover, until the camera got close enough to record the player's own personality, the film star could not emerge from the stage group. The close-up was the first step to this. But even it had stage origins. Without putting too Marxist an interpretation on it, the close-up was the cinema's way of extending to its penurious patrons the privilege of the theatre-goer with his opera glasses. The way it caused actors to lose their feet perhaps pained Charles Pathé, but it opened up the prospect of a wider, finer range of acting; and by isolating and concentrating the player's looks and personality, sometimes unconnected with his or her abilities, it was to be the decisive break with stage convention, the most potent means of establishing an artist's uniqueness and the beginning of the dynamic psychological interplay of the filmgoers' and the film actors' emotions.

D. W. Griffith is usually credited with pioneering the use of the close-up from the time he moved his camera nearer to a couple of actors in an early melodrama called *For Love of Gold* (1908) so as to let what was in their minds register on their faces. As they were playing rogues, what their faces showed was suspicion of each other. Mutual distrust was to persist in the hearts, if not on the faces, of many later stars playing a scene together in close-up: but no doubt audiences in 1908 missed the nice irony of the competitive aspect of the star personality reflected in this early close-up.

Another theatrical feature, the pit orchestra, was soon absorbed into film production with great effect on the acting. Cut down to a violin, cello and portable organ, it moved into the studio to provide mood music and bring the players to the pitch of sorrow or jollity that the story required. The use of music as emotional stimulus began early and lasted late. Griffith imported a violinist into the Biograph Studio in 1909 to 'accompany' Florence Lawrence, the actress known as the 'Biograph Girl', though in general he used music sparingly and preferred the sound of his own melodious voice to rouse artists to concert pitch. Many players, however, developed precise repertoires of their own – signature tunes to introduce their emotions to the camera – and continued to do so when they became stars. The Cadman Indian lyric, 'From the land of the sky-blue water,' was Mary Pickford's favourite stimulant; and when she created the touching scene in front of the mirror in *Stella Maris* (1918), where the poor little skivvy discovers her ugliness for the first time, it was to the strains of Massenet's 'Elégie'.

Sam Goldwyn recalled that during the 1920s, 'my studio became a three-ring band. When I entered it in the morning I ventured from the jazz selections which were tuning up Mabel Normand's comedy to the realm where sad waltzes deepened Pauline Frederick's emotional fervour. The circle was surrounded by the classic themes enfolding Geraldine Farrar.'* Even on as late a film as *The Docks of New York* (1928), made by so sophisticated a director as Josef von Sternberg, a visitor to the set recalled how 'from the darkness behind the big sun-arcs, a violin wailed and a harmonium grunted like a passionate duet between a musical hyena and a melodious wart-hog'.†

A lot of silent film acting was done by ear. Paradoxically it was the arrival of sound that actually imposed silence in the studios. The so-called silent films were made in a babble of noise which was to play an often underestimated part in producing the curiously kinetic quality in much of the acting – a quality that was turned off at the very moment sound was turned on. Live musicians remained a theatrical fixture in cinemas until 1932, the year when talkies finally wiped out the last small orchestra or piano player. The musical scores once specially written for big-budget silent films – and in some cases sent out with the prints, or performed by touring orchestras travelling with the film – were now absorbed into the sound track. Thus mood music was taken out of the actors' hearing in the studios, but still served to cue the filmgoers in on the right emotions they should feel.

Written titles were another way of doing this. They were in essence the theatre's programme notes spliced into the film stock. At first merely identifying 'Place' or 'Time', they soon began

* *Behind the Screen*, by Samuel Goldwyn (George H. Doran Co.), p. 147.
† *Star-Dust in Hollywood*, by Jan and Cora Gordon (George G. Harrap) p. 78.

describing how filmgoers should feel about the action. Gradually they started doing the same about the actors, and the attributes of pathos, courage, gentleness or buffoonery which screen titles conferred on them contributed to turning a stage part into a vehicle for a personality – especially when certain epithets became attached to particular players. It was certainly the sentimentalising description 'Little Mary' that provided an emotional soubriquet for Mary Pickford before audiences were ever made aware of her real name. Stars-to-be were literally 'labelled'. They were the ones who appeared, in stage parlance, 'as known'. Many of them were later to discover the penalties of being so known when they became victims of type-casting. But by then it was usually too late to change the labels.

*   *   *

Mobility played an important part in the environment of the early stars. The stage pattern of travelling stock companies was reproduced in the early film companies. Never again in film history were they to be so mobile as they were between, roughly, 1903 to 1913. Some of them simply had to keep on the move to escape prosecution by Thomas Edison's Motion Pictures Patent Co., founded in 1908, which claimed jurisdiction over every film company or individual then using an unlicensed Edison camera to shoot pictures. Such pirate outfits were numbered in hundreds. Filming for them was a game of hide-and-seek, their camera camouflaged beneath a bed blanket, as the Trust detectives pursued them all over the United States. Out of this diaspora came the founding of modern Hollywood; for some companies went as far afield as California, so as to be near the Mexican border, and laboratory facilities were already set up in a primitive form when more respectable film-makers followed them in the search for reliable sunshine, since expanding production could no longer count on enough dry days and adequate daylight for shooting schedules on the east coast.

At best such enforced mobility promoted a convivial unity among film-makers, giving them a group consciousness that was important when there was as yet no film 'capital'. At worst it added to the disrepute that the cinema earned from the moment of its birth as a back-street entertainment for illiterate patrons, many immigrants among them, who found the screen's lack of language an asset in the easy entertainment they sought. Even those film companies operating safely under Edison licence, and so able to maintain continuity of work at a fixed address, did an enormous amount of hard travelling outside the studio. It saved electricity bills to shoot out of doors. And a scenario could be padded with production values in the shape of striking locations or news events like a fire, a car race or a parade which could be worked into the simple, improvised plots.

And along with the film company on the move travelled a figure familiar in touring stock companies or vaudeville. She was the chaperone who looked after the virtue, and often the harder assets, of the young girls in the troupe. Generally she was their mother. Mobility thus contributed to the prominence of a figure who was frequently to play a preponderant part in shaping the careers of the early stars. The Hollywood matriarch considered herself on a par with the Hollywood producer. Often she was, too. She was not only her daughter's legal guardian for contract purposes, but also her agent, script adviser and early public relations counsellor. Her position was impregnable because the early cinema required its embryo female stars to be and look extremely young: their average age in the 1910 period probably averaged 16 or 17. This was partly due to the fashion set, as we shall see, by the personal predilection of the most influential director of the day, D. W. Griffith; but partly, too, to the crude lighting and make-up which could do little to shield the wrinkles of an ageing 21-year-old against the sharpness of the excellent, custom-made camera lenses then in use. 'I looked older on the films in my first six years in them [1907–13], when we were experimenting with lighting and cameras, than I do now when the mechanics of the screen have been perfected.'* So said Florence Turner, once known as the 'Vitagraph Girl', in 1922. Youth and beauty were assets more essential to films than to the stage. And

* *Photoplay*, July 1924, quoted in 'Unwept, Unhonoured and Unfilmed,' by Frederick James Smith.

in order to get them, one generally had to take Mother too. She stood behind many stars in this early period and in some cases she had a long, profitable reign.

Even in 1922 Sam Goldwyn stipulated, in announcing a talent contest, 'The young woman who wins in the quest for new faces will be given a year's contract . . . sent to the Goldwyn Studios in Culver City, California, with expenses paid and receive a weekly salary that will be sufficient to support herself *with her mother* in comfortable style."* Goldwyn and many other producers privately took a more jaundiced view of having to put up with 'these adhesive relatives . . . generally standing around back of the screen to see that justice is administered.' In the beginning though, they had their value. It was to Mary Pickford's mother that Adolph Zukor very effectively sold the idea of a film career for her daughter. ' "If feature pictures succeed . . . we expect to pay according to the drawing power at the box office",' he told her in 1912. 'Charlotte Pickford was impressed, I could see. She was a very realistic, far-seeing woman. It happened that Mary's stage voice was adequate, but not great. If my thesis held, then Mary, having already proved herself on the screen, had a bright and lucrative future there; a better one than on the stage. *After the Pickford family's years of struggle, it was natural that her mother desperately sought security.* "What salary," Mrs Pickford enquired, "would you consider paying Mary?" '†

Among the players whose mothers energetically, often ruthlessly promoted their careers in early Hollywood were Geraldine Farrar, Clara Kimball Young, Pauline Frederick, Priscilla Dean, Lillian and Dorothy Gish. . . . But Mrs Pickford was the most formidable manager-matriarch of them all. One reason for her power was the astronomical height to which competitive bidding for Mary's services pushed her salary. By 1917 she was getting 350,000 dollars per picture. For inducing Mary to sign with First National for this sum, Mrs Pickford herself picked up a 50,000 dollar bonus; whereupon she showed her own tycoon potential

---

* Ibid., March 1922.
† *The Public Is Never Wrong*, by Adolph Zukor (G. P. Putnam's Sons) pp. 66–7. Italics are the author's.

by offering her son, Jack, who was to become a second-magnitude star, 85,000 dollars per picture to sign with the same releasing company. (Jack declined, preferring the paternal benevolence of Sam Goldwyn.)

This remarkable woman's concentrated drive worked for Mary's greater advancement from the earliest days. 'In the old shabby days of the Biograph Studio,' Sam Goldwyn records, 'her activities, though more limited, were equally pronounced. Every single day she came with Mary to the studio and stayed with her until she left. She watched every move she made. She gave her suggestions about her work. She sat with the faithful make-up box while Mary was on a set. . . . It often took longer to make one of Mary's contracts than it did to make one of Mary's pictures.'* In short the vast economic potential of the movies took the stage-player's mother out of the wings and installed her in the bank.

*   *   *

The kind of protocol and formality found in the better-run touring stock companies, where players lived and worked in close proximity to each other, also shaped relationships in the early film companies. While seniority and talent did determine the distribution of roles, the late Victorian atmosphere stifled for a time the emergence of autocratic personalities. Mother was often left to do the prima-donna fighting for her daughter – while the latter was expected to behave like a lady. Social etiquette, one may presume, smothered star temperament. It was natural, of course, for an eminence like Griffith to impose his own code of conduct on his players through sheer strength of character; and this code did not tolerate 'uppity' conduct. But formality was the rule at other studios, too. 'The courtesy of social address was strictly adhered to by all persons on the set,' Albert E. Smith, one of Vitagraph's executives, recalls. 'We insisted that no matter a person's occupation it was "Mr So-and-So" and "Miss So-and-So", not "Harry" or "John" or "Mary". This was part of a plan to exert every precaution in favour of our young actresses.' And he added, 'While it may have been regarded as an unusual

* Samuel Goldwyn, op. cit., pp. 36–7.

presumption on our part, we nevertheless ordered all couches to be removed from dressing and make-up rooms.'* The proprieties were not always to be so nicely observed inside film studios.

One feature of the stage that the early film companies strenuously resisted carrying over into film-making was the identity of their players. Up to the end of 1909 none of the public and very few of the exhibitors knew the names of artists who were fast becoming box-office favourites. Some were only identified by their exclusive connection with the production company: the 'Biograph Girl', the 'Vitagraph Girl', and so on. Personal identity, the first facet of a star, was concealed from the patrons. But it is wrong to assume that all the pressure for this came from the producers in order to avoid the fate of theatre impresarios harassed by big-name players for correspondingly big salaries. There must have been a willing acquiescence among the film players. For screen acting was regarded for a long time as a considerable come-down in the profession. Linda Arvidson (later Mrs D. W. Griffith) observed about the status of film actors in 1908: 'We were always conscious of the fact that we were in this messy business because everything else had failed – because nobody had seemed to want us, and we just hadn't been able to hang on any longer.'†

Film actors were expected to do menial work besides acting. Norma Talmadge has recalled that when she was a minor artist at Vitagraph 'often a little group of players who were waiting around to be called would assist in the making or mending of costumes. They even helped paint the scenery. . . .'‡ Florence Turner, then one of Vitagraph's most important players, helped with the wardrobe and even looked after the petty cash. The touchy dignity of stage people was easily affronted by such chores. They showed shamefaced reluctance when hard times forced them to take on film work. ' "Would you be very much against applying for work at the Biograph Studios, Gladys?" ' Mrs

* *Two Reels and a Crank*, by Albert E. Smith (Doubleday & Co.) p. 212.
† *When the Movies Were Young*, by Linda Arvidson (Mrs D. W. Griffith) (E. P. Dutton & Co.) p. 54.
‡ Albert E. Smith, op. cit., p. 192.

Pickford said to her daughter Mary one day. (Mary Pickford had been born Gladys Smith.) ' "Oh no, not that, Mama!" – "Well, now it's not what I want for you either, dear. . . . It's only to tide us over".'*

It was indeed demeaning to players with a stage reputation based on the ability to act and speak to have their talents summed up by a film casting manager on looks alone, or to be forced to stand around the edge of the set in the morning trying to catch the director's eye till the order came to 'Get made up' which meant one was hired – three dollars a day for 'mob work', five dollars for a featured part.

Players like Mary Pickford, with months or even a few years of stage experience behind them, naturally hoped to return to the theatre when a suitable play came along. By accepting even part-time work in pictures, they might prejudice their chances. For although the movies continued to be regarded for some years as just a passing craze of the public, they caused enough private apprehension among theatre managers and impresarios with casting rights in the plays they sent on tour for temporary film players not to want to have their presence in the enemy camp publicised by their names on the nickelodeon marquees. The hostility of other stage players had also to be reckoned with. The movies had no 'tradition'. They were a back-street amusement. Above all, they seemed to require no training or talent – certainly no *speaking* talent. It is easy to imagine the huffiness, even ostracism, a stage player would encounter from his own kind if he 'deserted' to films. This attitude lasted till well into the 1912–13 period. Adolph Zukor at that time was negotiating with the theatre producer David Belasco to film the latter's stage hit, *A Good Little Devil,* and he badly wanted the deal to include Mary Pickford who had played a leading role in the stage version after deciding to quit films in 1913 as a result of a row she had had with D. W. Griffith. Belasco told Zukor, ' "Mary was ashamed . . . to come back to me after appearing on the screen. I was looking everywhere for her to play in *A Good Little Devil* when one day she telephoned my assistant to say hello, and aplogised even for that.

* *Sunshine and Shadow*, by Mary Pickford (William Heinemann Ltd) p. 102.

It may be that she prefers not to go back into pictures."* (She did, though, and the stage never saw her again.)

All this indicates that if the film players did not at first get any personal publicity as a matter of policy, there were also sound reasons dissuading them from demanding it as a matter of egotism. Such an attitude, however, was a powerful handicap on emergent stars.

*   *   *

What both sides had to discover was the vast, unsatisfied curiosity of the public about the players. This was the element of 'participation' that, interacting with the 'projection' of the players in the mesmerising atmosphere of darkened halls, was to make the movies so different in kind from any of the older arts. The producers were probably the first to sense it. For nickelodeon exhibitors, ordering a new programme of films from some of the hundred film 'exchanges' that by 1907 were operating in twenty-five key cities, might specify more films with characters whom they had found were popular with their audiences. Lacking names to put to the players, they did what their filmgoers did and referred to them as 'the girl with the curls', or 'the sad-eyed man', or 'the fat guy'. By singling out a striking physical feature of the nameless owner, they endowed it with some of the magic of a totem object. It was a curious reversion to the habit of tribal societies, where the idea of individual identity evolved out of how a person looked or what function he performed. And it presaged the uniqueness of the star whose physical looks, deepening into the personality he or she projected, would invite instant recognition at every appearance and connect with an audience's dreams and aspirations in ways that lay below the level of their awareness.

But in this pre-1909 period the volume, speed and crudity of film production frustrated this subtler interplay. Films were invariably one-reelers, running between nine and ten minutes and often made in a day and dispatched to the cinemas inside a week. The eight-to-ten thousand nickelodeons operating in 1908 showed programmes that lasted from twenty minutes to an hour,

* Adolph Zukor, op. cit., p. 64.

morning to midnight, and often changed them daily. This was another handicap to emergent stars. Not only were they anonymous, but they might not be available for very long when the fans wanted to see them: there was no time for word-of-mouth publicity to build up a following for them. It is doubtful if even the cinema manager had much advance notice of what his programme would be. On the other hand such short shooting schedules and speedy arrival on the screen were splendid conditions for the quick growth of public favourites; and this was a lesson remembered by the first movie moguls, many of whom had owned cinemas or peddled films. They made 'exposure' to the public the first, and almost the only, principle for the creation of their film stars. Familiarity, as they saw it, bred affection.

At this time, though, what it also bred was curiosity. Filmgoers began writing to the studios, well before 1910, asking for the names of their favourites and information about them. Perhaps this proof of the enormous public interest, plus the economic needs of bulk production, contributed to stabilising employment in the stock company set-up at the studios. Florence Turner, an actor's daughter co-opted casually for a scene being shot by a Vitagraph unit on location near her father's seaside cottage in 1906, claimed to be 'the first girl to be permanently engaged by any picture firm'. She was put under contract after only six months of filming – a startling contrast, had any of them noted it, to the time it took stage players to gain a security based on wide public appeal.

But so long as there continued to be a blackout on personal publicity very few public favourites knew their audience or sensed themselves to be stars with a fame that was separate from their employers' company. There were special reasons for the exceptions. John Bunny, the fat man of Vitagraph comedies, was billed under his own name. One reason was the stage reputation he had already made. Another was the significant fact that he brought his own uniqueness, his vast girth, so conspicuously into films that the stories were written around him (and it) from the very first. A leaner comedian might have had to fit himself anonymously into an off-the-peg plot. With Bunny's name on the posters, the fans instantly knew what kind of film it was. Thus the use of a star name to stabilise audience response was known at an early date, though not generally acted on. The reason 'Broncho Billy' Anderson had his name on his Wild West pictures was simpler still: his own company made them. G. M. Anderson, born Max Aronson, after a short-lived career as an outlaw in Edwin S. Porter's film *The Great Train Robbery* (1903), where he was all right on the train but less secure in the saddle, had suggested making a cowboy film for Vitagraph in 1906, but was turned down because that company's starchy boss, Commander Blackton, sympathised with the Fenimore Cooper myth of the noble redskin and felt cowboys to be a common lot of roughnecks. So Anderson produced, wrote and starred in his own westerns, though he undertook the latter chore reluctantly, perhaps recalling his horseback experience four years earlier. The films were enormously popular and he thus became, by accident, the first star to capitalise on his own appeal by being his own producer. He was to have illustrious successors.

*   *   *

Pressure on the film companies to divulge their players' identities increased sharply about 1909. Movie columns began appearing in newspapers around this time: not yet criticism, of course, but interest-arousing news items and gossip. Florence Turner first saw her name on a film poster in May, 1910. Since it was a light-hearted novelty film in which she boxed a round with 'Gentleman Jim' Corbett, it is possible that co-starring with an identifiable celebrity relaxed Vitagraph's guard that it would have to name all its players if it named one. But a more significant solution suggests itself. A few months earlier, in February or March 1910, the 'Biograph Girl' had been publicly named for the first time as Florence Lawrence. For the first time, too, her picture had appeared in a newspaper. The occasion was a report of her 'death' in a hazily specified street accident in New York; and the author of it was almost certainly the independent producer, Carl Laemmle, who then owned Miss Lawrence's services for his 'Imp' Co., though John Drinkwater in the official biography of Laemmle, in 1931, believed that 'the rumour was released from ill-disposed quarters . . . a poor, half-witted ruse, intended in some nebulous way to unsettle the Independent public.'*

The public was indeed 'unsettled'. As a report which appeared not at all coincidentally in the Sunday magazine section of the *St Louis Post-Dispatch* for 6th March 1910, stated, 'deep regret was expressed everywhere. . . . The incident was an awakener to the moving-picture theatre managers of how well-known and how popular their actors had become to the people who sit in the dark night after night . . .' This magazine article, filling a whole inside page, paid good dividends for Laemmle who must be suspected of having inspired it. It dramatised his acquisition of Florence Lawrence and demonstrated the public interest in her: at one stroke he had fortified his financial strength and disconcerted his business rivals. And better was to come. An even bigger publicity coup was made on 20th March 1910, two weeks later, when the same Sunday magazine devoted its entire front page and part of an inside page to Florence Lawrence and included an interview with her, as well as no fewer than seven close-ups and one full-length photograph.† The earlier article had placed Miss Lawrence in a setting described in the heading as 'Heroes and Heroines of Moving Picture Shows.' This one gave her solo billing. The first article contained the paragraph, 'Manufacturers‡ are just beginning to wake to the demand for information by the public of their actors, and are recognising the value of the personalities of their players. They are beginning to print their portraits and names and display them in front of the moving-picture theatres, and it is predicted that the time will come when these actors will command the services of press agents as does any other stellar attraction.' In the circumstances it was not a rash prediction to make. And it was soon fulfilled.

Less than a week later, on 26th March 1910, Florence Lawrence

* *The Life and Adventures of Carl Laemmle,* by John Drinkwater (Heinemann Ltd) p. 133.
   † The full text of this article is given in Appendix Two.
   ‡ The name then in common use for a film producer.

made a personal appearance in, not surprisingly, St Louis.* 'It was,' said John Drinkwater, 'the first time that the film public had been given the opportunity of seeing their favourites in person.' Accompanying her was the young actor King Baggott, also under contract to Laemmle. This was an astute detail; and it may explain why St Louis, besides being a good film-business city with nearly 200 cinemas at this date, was chosen for Miss Lawrence's debut. Baggott was a St Louis actor. Play reviews show that he had had a highly successful season the previous summer, in 1909, in the Suburban Garden Stock Co., before signing with Laemmle. The 'local boy' whose face, name and reputation were already known was thus used to escort and, in a sense, vouch for the girl who up to then had been an intriguing enigma. Various stories persist suggesting that the two players got a riotous reception from St Louis crowds who tore at Miss Lawrence's clothes as if she were a modern pop idol.† Yet it has not been possible to trace any first-hand contemporary report to confirm this. The nearest is one which appeared in *Variety*, datelined St Louis, 30th March and headlined, 'Circusing Picture Star'. It continues: 'Florence Lawrence, the "Imp" company star moving-picture actress, spent two days in St Louis, Saturday and Sunday, and by dint of considerable enterprise her flying visit was made notable. There was a reception at Union Station and short talks at the Gem Theater and the Grand Opera House (which though closed for remodelling was specially opened for the occasion.)' *The Bioscope*, an English trade paper, of 11th April 1910, records that 'by special permission she was photographed by a newspaper man and the picture will be the only one to be permitted except in "Imp" films'.

The absence of lengthy reports does not mean the visit flopped, simply that the days on which it took place, arriving on a Saturday

* Even on a simple fact like this date, there is a conflict of evidence. Terry Ramsaye, the film historian, gives the date of the visit as 2nd April 1910; but the report of it in *Variety*, dated 30th March suggests it was earlier.

† These reports derive, I suspect, from Drinkwater's biography of Laemmle, a very untrustworthy book designed to present the movie tycoon as a candidate for the Nobel Prize.

and leaving on a Sunday, are still notoriously bad days for press men to cover news stories and keep them fresh until Monday. The railroad station reception and the re-opening of the opera house indicate a sizeable event and good publicity management. (The publicity man's presence 'off' is also suggested by the imperious restriction laid down about the photographs, as reported in *The Bioscope:* the desire to control the star's exposure seems to have begun early!)

The St Louis visit heralded, in an early and comparatively restrained form, the public exploitation of film personalities which from this time on was to grow increasingly aggressive. Publicity was a forcing house for the star personality. After the years of docile pseudonymity as such-an-such a company's 'Girl', it would be odd if the exhilarating effect of 'meeting the people' were otherwise. But it also marks the producers' recognition among themselves of the value of exploiting those they owned – and the value they could be to other rival companies, if they were so exploited. Previously, talent had been recognised by individual directors inside the stock-company 'democracy' of the studio; and it was for talent that one studio might 'raid' another, even inside the self-protective companies of the Edison Patent Group, but since anonymity was the rule a purloined player's publicity impact was limited. Even D. W. Griffith cast an acquisitive eye over other companies' players; and in fact he lured Florence Lawrence away from Vitagraph, to become the 'Biograph Girl', by offering her mother, who managed her, twenty-five dollars a week for her services, ten dollars more than she was getting.

But apparently it was one thing for a director to bargain for talent, quite another for the player to try to do a deal. For no sooner was Florence Lawrence well established at Biograph than she unwisely wrote to the Essanay Studios offering them her services in return for a joint contract to include her director husband. Essanay officials promptly reported her presumption back to Biograph and she was dismissed. She found none of the licensed film companies would give her work: this is probably the first recorded instance of film industry blacklisting and it shows the determination of the Patent companies not to let their players get on top of them. So Florence Lawrence was *not* booty carried off by Laemmle, as is often believed, after a raid on Biograph. She had been fired and was about to rejoin a stage stock company when one of Laemmle's directors, who had been at Vitagraph with her, brought her to his chief. So started the build-up for the St Louis 'stunt'. And so, too, started the aggressive element in the boosting of players into personalities.

Publicity provided the fuel for this. It was built into Laemmle's operation right from the start by one of those extraordinary creative accidents common in the early film business. Laemmle had been a small-time haberdasher in Oshkosh, Wisconsin, when he was impelled to quit his job by inspirational literature of the 'get up and go' variety mailed to him by a hustling young Chicago ad man, Robert Cochrane, whose pep was apt to run away with his pen. Guilt, responsibility and interest in the methodical little Laemmle, who had appeared in his office asking what he should do next, all compelled Cochrane to stake him financially – first as exhibitor and distributor, and now film-maker and the chief challenger of the Patent Co. monopoly. It is certain that Bob Cochrane masterminded the exploitation of Florence Lawrence. He had the journalist's instinct for human interest and the ad man's inventiveness for a new sales gimmick. Other companies sold pictures – then Laemmle would sell the people who appeared in them.

Publicity of a belligerent, inflationary and ubiquitous kind was probably the first radical break with the old theatrical conventions that had shaped so much of the early movies; and it was linked with the aggressive selling of a performer who at one stroke had her private identity revealed and made over to a publicity machine that got to work to make it public property. Instead of an advertisement in the local paper and bills outside the theatre where she was appearing, the new film publicity multiplied the presence of a player ten thousand times, wherever mechanical reproduction purveyed her film image, and created a public interest in her personality, earning power, likes and dislikes – things that might have nothing to do with her art.

The first published interview Florence Lawrence gave in the

St Louis Post-Dispatch still saw movie-making in stage terms, and there were references to 'plays', 'footlights' the 'stage director', the 'emotional' rehearsal and the 'mechanical' one, all of which showed the movies still groping for their own vocabulary. But there were also references to her private self, her favourite pastime, horse-riding, reaction to seeing herself on the screen – all of which built her up as a personality. And there were details of her salary, her bundles of fan mail, the sheer number of times her image appeared on a year's output of celluloid (fourteen separate pictures a foot, 14,000 times a week, 4,000,000 times a year) – all of which built up her public power and attached the magic of figures to her name.

Henceforth a screen player was to be marketed for her admirers as a personality, an image and, to an increasingly sinister extent, an object. As a Hollywood star of the next decade put it, 'The fans don't really like us: they like the idea they have of us.' But this was the voice of experience speaking. It is very doubtful if Florence Lawrence on her visit to St Louis found she had difficulty in reconciling the image presented of her with the reality of her own identity, or even noticed any danger in the adulation of crowds who viewed her for what she represented to them. The star had found her audience: but both had some way to go before they found themselves as distinct cinema entities. Florence Lawrence had a successful career under Laemmle, playing the well-bred, girlish, spirited, maidenly yet coquettish idealisation of feminine charms in a variety of photoplays. Inevitably she slipped into being a second-magnitude star as brighter ones rose. An accident compelled her temporary retirement in 1915 and she never really returned. An interviewer tracked her down in 1924 and he recorded a melancholy coda. 'It's very hard at the age of 31,' she said, 'to be left forgotten by an industry you helped so hard to develop.' With this sentiment, too, Florence Lawrence set the pattern for many of her screen successors.

*   *   *

Once Carl Laemmle had breached the anonymity of the players, the Patent companies followed suit, Kalem and Vitagraph first, the rest gradually, except for Biograph which stoically insisted on selling the quality of its pictures, not the personalities of its artists, and even went as far as to put out a roster of its players under false names to placate exhibitors in England where film-goers were demanding to know who was who. Thus Mary Pickford became 'Miss Dorothy Nicholson'; Blanche Sweet, 'Miss Daphne Wayne'; and Mabel Normand, 'Miss Maud Fortescue'. Biograph did not surrender till April 1913, by which time its days of glory were long past.

There is a good reason why Laemmle, and the other independent producers were quicker on the uptake to what the public wanted than the conservative managements of the Patent film firms. The former were showmen, the latter manufacturers. Laemmle and his like had owned cinemas and this had developed their commercial acuteness. They listened to audience reactions, observing the emotional response. The economics of the infant industry were then based on the price per foot of film, but these men saw at first hand that its future lay in the intangibles that made one player more popular than another. With players emerging as the focus of public interest, the movies were becoming an industry oriented towards the consumer, not the producer.

Film-making and film actors began to get prominence in newspapers when cinemas could afford to pay the advertising rates. No very cynical mind is needed to appreciate the fact that newspapers which drew revenue from respectable, well-established theatres were not going to give free publicity to a rival entertainment which, local theatre managers might confide, was proving a threat to their trade. The appearance of news stories in the early 1910s, designed to establish the respectability of the nickelodeons and cater to public interest in their wares, is a sure sign of the film industry's expansion. It was now too popular to ignore – and wealthy enough to pay for attention.

Leading name-players by the end of 1910 were sending auto-graphed photos out to fans. The fan magazine idea started around the same time. Commander Blackton, Vitagraph's manager, had acquired a periodical which the Patent Co.'s members had founded to publicise the stories (not the players) of their productions. *The Motion Picture Story Magazine* publicised only Vitagraph pictures and players so long as it was sold through a cinema box-office. But once news-stands started handling it, gossip about other companies, even the independents, appeared in its pages partly to disguise its partisan origins. A small crop of fan magazines was flourishing by 1912.

The enormous interest now focusing on the players was increased as they started staying on the screen for a longer time. There was not enough room for improvement in the quality of films within the general limit of 1,000 feet, whose action usually proceeded in 100-foot units which the photographer could easily 'cut' inside his camera. Films had to get longer, if they were to get better; but for a long time the companies opposed the idea. One guess is that the accountancy departments found the 1,000-foot units convenient to work with; another is that longer films simply cost more to make; a third might be that the front offices did not want their directors to get more power and hence more money by doing more work. But two- and three-reelers which came to the fore in 1912, broke this rigid pattern. The need for novelty was probably a major cause. But the result was to extend the expressiveness of the medium and allow it to dwell on character and not just incident. And this allowed it, depending on the director's skill, to catch a look or dwell on an emotion that consolidated a player's image. Such films stayed longer in the cinemas; and so the sense of favourite players as 'fixtures' was strengthened, too.

Around the same time an acute shortage of story material was felt. Incredibly the mine had almost been worked out in under ten years. 'Every possible source was ransacked', writes the film historian Lewis Jacobs, 'short stories, poems, plays, operas, popular best-sellers, and classics were condensed into one-reel screen presentations. . . . The adoption of fiction and plays was quickened by the censorship attack which flared up in 1907–8. Producers could feel reasonably certain that material taken from decorous literary works would provide critics with little excuse for further attacks.'*

* *The Rise of the American Film,* by Lewis Jacobs (Harcourt, Brace & Co.) p. 76.

But just when new material was needed for the longer 'features', the free-and-easy pillaging of authors was inhibited by a law case involving the new copyright regulations. The need to pay for material that previously had been freely lifted helped bring the players into even greater prominence since the increased cost of the picture had to show itself in 'production values' – and a saleable personality was more visible than a plot. Even when the latter came from a best-seller, the desire to get full value for the money it cost showed up in the decision to give full value to the players. And once this order of precedence was set, there was to be no reversing it. The industry's boom economy quickly made it possible for producers to pay enormous prices, reaching tens of thousands of dollars, for the screen rights of properties not in the public domain. And as the cost of films rose so did the price of players, no longer anonymous and remote interpreters of a swiftly-made and quickly-forgotten product, but public personalities who were underpinning the popularity of expensive pictures and projecting an interest in themselves outside the confines of a cinema screen. 'The era of the "Star Film" is over', writes the French critic Edgar Morin 'that of the film stars beginning.'*

* *The Stars*, by Edgar Morin (Translantic Book Service), p. 11.

PART TWO
EXPERIENCE

'When her contract expired, she was so
exhausted that she took an extended rest.
Sometime later, in reminiscing, she said a
bit wistfully, "I have often wondered since
if it would not have been better if I had
remained in dear old Brooklyn with
Vitagraph".'

BOSLEY CROWTHER
on Anita Stewart, in
Hollywood Rajah

CHAPTER TWO

GET AHEAD,
GET A STAR:
THE SYSTEM

The American public by 1911 had developed its own screen favourites. But something extra was needed to promote these into modern film stars. A new kind of consciousness, a new kind of confidence. The artists had to feel themselves to belong solely to the movies; and the movies had to learn how to rest their prosperity solidly on the artists.

Popularity and profitability were well in evidence at this date. In 1907 there had been between 2,500 and 3,000 nickelodeons in the country; in 1912 there were over 10,000 and between ten and twenty million filmgoers went regularly. Yet the industry was still labouring under an inferiority complex *vis-à-vis* the legitimate stage, and this was to inhibit its willingness to call its children its own. Until it did so, the honour of being a film star was dubious; the profit in it, restricted. Nothing proves this better than the remarkable experiment that Adolph Zukor entered into in 1912.

Well aware of how minor stage names had gained screen popularity, Zukor, the ex-furrier from Hungary who had turned penny-arcade owner and now distributor, offered a screen career to those who were already big names on the stage. The film historian, Terry Ramsaye, sees this as showing that even at this date 'the motion picture . . . recognised no stars of its own making.'* But it is unlikely that this worried Zukor. What did probably possess his showman's soul was envy of the 'carriage trade' which rolled up to legitimate theatres, but sniffed at nickelodeons as a low-class diversion. By putting eminent stage names into films, he no doubt hoped to dilute the slum tradition – and get such films shown in legitimate theatres at theatre prices.

* *A Million and One Nights*, by Terry Ramsaye (Frank Cass & Co.) p. 621.

The advantages of 'upward trading' were plain to anyone who ever worked in the garment industry – and many of the early cine-moguls did, as cutters, pressers, glovers, etc. – but they were based, too, on Zukor's experience in importing Louis Mercanton's French film, *Queen Elizabeth* (1911), starring Sarah Bernhardt. He paid 35,000 dollars for it: it made him over 80,000 dollars. (It was also four reels long and has been quoted as encouraging Americans to make longer films. This is a slightly exaggerated claim. Quite a number of five-reel American films had been made by 1910, and in 1912 one called *The Christian* was made by Vitagraph in eight reels. But due to exhibitor resistance, they were made so that they could be shown in single, or double, reels on consecutive days or nights. To cut Sarah Bernhardt into nightly slices, however, was unthinkable. Stage fame once again influenced film convention.)

Zukor therefore formed his Famous Players Co., in July, 1912, with the slogan 'Famous Players in Famous Plays', and allied himself with the impresario Daniel Frohman who possessed plays and players but was temporarily short of cash. Their schedule comprised class A films starring stage names in their best-known roles; class B films featuring 'well-known picture players'; and class C films with stock-company reliables. Mary Pickford was only graded class B, though this news was solicitously withheld from her and, presumably, her mother.

Zukor chose his 'famous' recruits with the wiliness of a tempter in some morality play. Minnie Maddern Fiske was lured into *Tess of the D'Urbervilles* (1913) in the hope of 'immortalising' herself like Bernhardt; James O'Neill had been so long 'on the road' playing *The Count of Monte Cristo* that he had not picked up Broadway's snobberies when he came to film it in 1913; James K. Hackett was persuaded into *The Prisoner of Zenda* (1912) by his debts; Lily Langtry, being British, had no anti-film prejudice when she made *His Neighbour's Wife* (1913); and John Barrymore took up a 'couldn't care less' attitude, just as he did when he had his baptism in the talkies some fifteen years later. And Mary Pickford, class B player, repeated her performance in *A Good Little Devil* with producer David Belasco appearing in the prologue – a fact that must have pleased Zukor who repeated his belief that 'if the stage relented the public would follow'.

The public did. But unfortunately for the 'Famous Players' notion, the celebrities it followed were the ordinary picture-players like Mary Pickford. Her film in fact showed up strikingly the flaw in Zukor's plan. 'In *A Good Little Devil*,' wrote one eye-witness, 'the film version used the exceptionally able company which enacted the spoken original . . . Mary Pickford was the only one I believed. . . . Gesture, posture and expression which seemed natural behind the footlights appeared strained and forced on the screen.'*

That Mary Pickford should have excelled as an actress is not surprising: after all, she had had four years under D. W. Griffith's direction before her impulsive, brief return to Belasco and the stage. But there are other reasons why she and the other 'picture-players' proved the drawing personalities. The class A gods and goddesses of Broadway had a maturity in their looks that a camera did not flatter. They also had two careers and tended to look on films as a stop-gap one; whereas the picture players looked on them as their only source of income. The very success of the 'Famous Players' had cut them off from film audiences, for young artists fresh from the versatility of a stock company with an intuitive appreciation of what 'the sticks' wanted were better for stardom.

The psychological consequences of the 'Famous Players' experiment were more important than the economic ones. It did not break down the prejudice against movies among stage folk to any great degree. The middle-class audiences were eventu-ally lured into cinemas by the up-grading in the architecture, not the artists, when the nickelodeons yielded to picture palaces. But the direct comparison with stage actors showed the mysterious superiority of film ones – mysterious because the difference between the two was still not formulated, nor widely understood.

One of Mary Pickford's reasons for quitting Griffith in 1913 was her resentment that he should choose Mae Marsh, a depart-ment-store girl untrained by Mary's stage standards, for the lead

---

* *The House That Shadows Built*, by Will Irwin (Doubleday, Doran & Co., Inc.) p. 183.

in *The Sands of Dee*. Mary was dismayed to see a performance created out of Mae Marsh. By rights, she ought not to have been capable of one – this cinema was a mendacious medium! But once picture players had seen how stage names failed to make the grade, even if they did not quite appreciate why, a consciousness of their power was reinforced. And money sharpened it into a certainty. The stage names had been paid sums far in excess of the film artists. The Triangle Company paid Sir Herbert Beerbohm Tree 100,000 dollars for six months work; but Sir Herbert's status was somewhat diminished when his acting style proved so unacceptable on film that a picture player, Monte Blue, stood in for him in some sequences. Triangle's film artists read the message and demanded fees of Broadway proportions.

The failure of stage names to appeal to the wide public fortified the picture players' identification with this audience – *their* audience. A crystallising moment of stardom seems to happen when a player becomes dramatically aware of the power that he or she wields. It is not quite the same thing as 'popularity'. One can live easily with popularity. The power of stardom strikes home to an artist as a disproportion between *who* he thinks he is and *how* other people think of him. It is bewildering, exhilarating, depressing or terrifying. Chaplin knew he was immensely popular early on in his first year as a Keystone comedian, in 1914, but he did not know his power as a star till 1916 when he took the train from Los Angeles to New York and to his growing astonishment found people standing beside the line as word of his progress preceded him, packing the railroad stations, fêting him at every halt and finally obliging the New York chief of police to beg him to get off at 125th Street, instead of Grand Central, since the crowds waiting there for him could not be contained. On the electric sign in Times Square he read the news, *Chaplin signs with Mutual at six hundred and seventy thousand a year*. 'I stood and read it objectively as though it were about someone else. So much had happened to me, my emotions were spent.'*

The belief that he is 'someone else' is reported as the accompanying emotion by many a star in such circumstances: it is so

* *My Autobiography*, by Charles Chaplin (The Bodley Head) p. 192.

common in film memoirs that it carries conviction as a near-traumatic fact, not an egotistic fantasy. Chaplin's account is particularly dramatic – but then he is Chaplin. But the same kind of consciousness was spreading among film players around 1913. A great number of factors were persuading them that they were different people from stage players – that by virtue of the medium they worked in, they wielded a different kind of power.

Ironically it took her brief return to the stage to prove this to Mary Pickford. For as James Card, the film historian and curator, has suggested, she first had the nature of her fame and future brought dramatically home to her by the audiences which packed the theatre and thronged the stage door not to see a Belasco leading lady, but the ex-Biograph film star. As an emotional response, it was different in kind and fervour from that which greeted stage celebrities. It was close and personal, yet dissociated and mob-like. It radiated love, yet turned the loved-one into an object. It derived from a star's uniqueness, but was diffused by her ubiquity. Many of those who felt it around this time must have been struck by the disproportion it showed between their personal assessment of their talents and the public's response to them. But they were not long in making the adjustment.

* * *

Money helped close the gap. It is no accident that stardom arrived almost at the same time as the star acquired great economic power. Once players got a sense of their worth, they were not slow in putting a price on it. And this price became the main means of transforming film-making from a growing business to a mass production industry.

It could never have happened this way in the theatre. Stage actors and vaudeville artists had a slow, uncertain climb to popularity and financial power. The numbers of stage stars were limited, their appearances restricted, the profits low and the risks great. But the cinema could mechanically record an artist's performance and repeat it endlessly, cheaply, simultaneously in many places at once. The movies annihilated time and place, the great deterrents to investing in the talents of a stage artist.

Moreover, a film star could be given the sense of permanence beloved of bankers. He or she could be transferred on to emulsified film stock and packed into an easily portable can and serve as collateral for a bank loan. The human being was made economically viable by being turned into a negotiable object. Film-makers who often had little ready cash in their accounts could nevertheless set a value on a human personality with reasonable assurance of getting a financier to underwrite it. And by vying with each other to inflate its worth, they could achieve their own economic aggrandisement. Star salaries from the very first came to have a significance not entirely financial. High fees were taken to be proof of unique talents. Because a star was paid so much, or was said to be paid it, she must be worth it. Money created its own charisma in an industry that was short on certainties but well provided with shibboleths. In the early days the men who had such talents under contract to them profited from the 'evidence' of power that the equation created; and the people owning the talents profited in their turn from the mystic aura of being 'worth' such colossal amounts of money.

Of course this contained a fatal contradiction that has harassed the industry throughout its history. For the fiction that 'price' in some way equalled 'worth' was to prove a distinctly one-sided advantage: useful to a producer when he could make it reflect his own worth but a cause of recurring conflict when his stars presumed to use it to boost their price.

The new stars at first seemed to command all the power. The fees they demanded, given the value of money half a century ago, put some of today's superstars in the shade. Escalation was unbelievably rapid. Adolph Zukor paid Mary Pickford 500 dollars a week in 1912, which was doubled to 1,000 dollars a week in February, 1914, doubled again to 2,000 dollars a week in November, 1914, doubled yet again to 4,000 dollars a week in March, 1915. Fifteen months' later he was paying her 10,000 dollars a week – and a year later she was making pictures for First National, the distributing company formed by exhibitors, for

Florence Lawrence, one of the first film stars to be known to her fans by name as well as sight. The mark at the top corner suggests the photo was one sent out by American Biograph when it re-released her old films after she had gained fame as another company's star. Ironically, Biograph had refused to allow her name to be revealed while she was acting under their banner

Lillian Gish had a gift for inventing small-scale imaginative effects, many of them deriving from the idea of motherhood. In *Broken Blossoms*, paying a young slum girl, she falls asleep with a rag doll, its arm adroitly arranged to stick into her cheek like an importunate baby's (*Frame enlargement*)

Lillian Gish's embattled rancher's wife in *The Wind* glances apprehensively through the sand-caked cabin window . . .

. . . where the unending wind in Victor Seastrom's film is scouring the top of the grave in which . . .

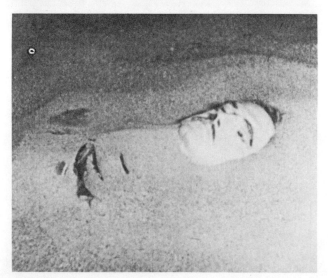

. . . she has buried the assailant she shot in defence of her virtue. As more of his body is exposed, it seems . . .

. . . he is rising from the dead to invade her home again. Gish watches with mounting derangement on her face . . .

. . . which, one writer said, 'required only a breeze to whip it into change'. Now at storm-pitch, it shows hysteria . . .

. . . as the door is forced open. But the hand that falls on her shoulder is no corpse's – only her husband (*Frame enlargements*)

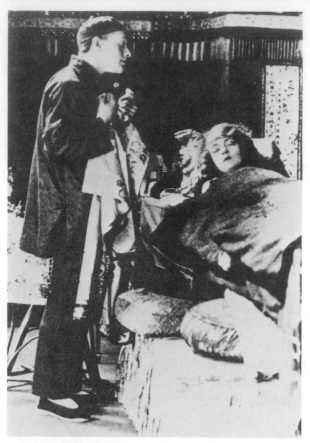

Richard Barthelmess, as the Chinaman in *Broken Blossoms*, chastely contemplates the orphan girl he is sheltering. D. W. Griffith's mesmerising direction sank the actor's personality unrecognisably into a statuesque image – though a rubber band under the skull-cap did its part, too, in pulling the face tight and achieving an Oriental effect without too much make-up

(Frame enlargement)

Another kind of innocence: *Tol'able David*, made two years after *Broken Blossoms*, turned Barthelmess into a star in his own right as the homely American boy who wants his mother to be proud of him. This sentiment stayed box-office for a generation. David was the Gentile relative of Al Jolson's Jazz Singer and the country cousin of Mickey Rooney's Andy Hardy

350,000 dollars each.* Chaplin's popularity was so colossal that Terry Ramsaye could write without exaggeration that whoever controlled him in 1915 virtually controlled the film industry.

The business from 1913 on resembled a battle of serpents with one company entwining another, swallowing its rivals or tying itself into knots. With the old Patent Co. monopoly growing financially weaker compared with the more aggressive independents – it was declared illegal after 1917 – stars were no longer simply a way of gaining the trade's confidence in one's product, but a means of disconcerting one's rivals by disrupting their distribution deals. 'Raiding' reached its height around 1916. The huge fees that top players commanded, plus the high investment in publicising them, finally broke down the old stock-company notion of loyalty. Vitagraph, for example, was probably one of the best organised and wealthiest studios at this date, but up to then it had never had a contract with any of its leading players. 'A handshake or a word was sufficient,' Albert E. Smith recalled. Written contracts did not become company policy till 1916 'when gestures towards Vitagraph's established stars became numerous and serious. . . . Contracts were now a studio's lifeline.'†

Even that lifeline was tenuous. In 1916 the name of Clara Kimball Young went up in lights in New York City – perhaps the first time such a sign had been used away from a theatre marquee – announcing that her next picture would be distributed by Lewis J. Selznick who had placed the ex-Vitagraph star under contract to him, with her own corporation, in order to disrupt the deals his rival, Adolph Zukor, had done with distributors. These now found they could get Clara Kimball Young pictures singly without having a block of inferior films forced on them. Zukor eventually had to move in on Selznick through an embrace of interests. Too late, Selznick found it was a death clasp.

If a star's power could break producers, it could also make

* An interesting sidelight is thrown on the huge salary Zukor paid Mary Pickford by the law suit brought against her by an agent a few years later, which revealed that Famous Players had also agreed to pay her income tax while she was under contract to them, though the Government had subsequently regarded this payment as an addition to her salary.

† Albert E. Smith, op. cit., p. 210.

them. To acquire a star was to acquire instant capital – the stuff on which a business could be built. In the earlier decade 'rogue' film-makers had done their worst to get hold of one of Edison's cameras: now they went after a human patent in the shape of someone else's star.

When Louis B. Mayer's eye settled on Anita Stewart in 1917 she was under contract to Vitagraph where her salary of 1,000 dollars a week, plus ten per cent of the profits, and a guaranteed 127,000 dollars a year, put her into the top earning brackets. She was then aged 22 or 23. Her speciality was the quality of athletic gentility that allowed her to show vim and virtue in the face of the train smashes, car crashes and shipwrecks which made her films popular. Since short contracts were then customary, stars of her celebrity were physically guarded by their studios; and Mayer, by this time a small-time distributor in the Boston area with a background in the scrap-metal business, probably made an indirect approach through the star's mother and her own vanity. His biographer, Bosley Crowther, has shown he was well equipped for this by virtue of an ethnic respect for matriarchal figures and a sure instinct for flattery that paid off with impressionable women. He fostered the star's ego by setting up a production company in her own name – which had the advantage of making her into a legal entity, harder for anyone else to pursue. But Vitagraph fought Mayer for re-possession of their star and a settlement was reached only when an accident would have put her out of filming until her contract had legally expired. The court had found against her claim that the stories and directors supplied by Vitagraph were unsuited to her art. This set an important precedent that studios were later to use against rebellious stars. And such experiences may well have confirmed Mayer in the 'strong management' policy he gave Metro-Goldwyn-Mayer from its inception.

He produced Anita Stewart's first film in studios in Brooklyn and had another film under way in California, where he now moved himself, before the first had been shown in New York. Anita Stewart effectively built his business – and paid for it. 'When her contract expired,' Crowther records, 'she was so exhausted' – after making fifteen pictures in three years – 'that she took an extended rest. Some time later, in reminiscing, she said a bit wistfully, "I have often wondered since if it would have been better if I had remained in dear old Brooklyn with Vitagraph" '* If Mayer ever had any similar doubts, they have gone unrecorded.

*   *   *

To say that if stars had not existed at this time, it would have been necessary to invent them is only to understate the truth. Where stars did not exist, they *were* invented. The exhibitor and producer, William Fox, seeking a way to put an edge on his product, created a star of his own – Theda Bara. He thus established the practice of the prefabricated personality and gave a thrust to the cynicism that took an early hold on the industry. For Theda Bara's importance, apart from giving the word 'vamp' a local and lurid habitation, lies in the fact that having no previous reputation of any note on the screen, she had one created for her off-screen as an intriguing public personality. Her real name was Theodosia Goodman, a tailor's demure daughter from Cincinnati.

Fox's publicity department remodelled every part of her into the image of a sex siren, beginning with her name. 'Theda Bara' is generally held to have been an anagram created out of the evocative words 'death' and 'Arab'. But the more probable solution is the reverse one. 'Death' and 'Arab' are likely to have been evolved out of the shortened version of the star's family name – 'Theda' is after all a contraction for 'Theodosia' and 'Bara' for a family tie with the Barangers on her mother's side – by some anagramatically-minded Fox publicist who let the words suggest the rest of the exotic campaign built up around her. Born in Egypt, child of a sheik and a princess, weaned on serpents' blood, given in mystic marriage to the Sphynx, fought over by nomadic tribesmen, clairvoyant and insatiably lustful: the emphasis was put heavily on her supernatural powers since Fox cast her in a role in the film *A Fool There Was* (1915) which entirely consisted of her mesmerising and then ruining a succes-

* *Hollywood Rajah, The Life and Times of Louis B. Mayer,* by Bosley Crowther Holt, Rinehart & Winston) p. 78.

sion of besotted lovers – such an unbroken run of successes needed a reason that neither the film nor her performance could suggest.

The publicity tour she made in 1914, complete with the baleful props of a *femme fatale*, took place well before the film was seen. It proved two things. One was that film stars could be made without necessarily having to make films. Bara was the earliest in a long and still continuing line of newsworthy women – among them pin-ups, model girls, première starlettes and celebrities generally known for being, well, generally known – who have flourished by using the attributes of stardom as a substitute for it. Her difference is of course that once her film was seen, and sensationally received by audiences who still stood in awe of sinful love but were growing sneakily curious about sex appeal, the pre-publicity instantly confirmed her star status.

Moreover her public image transferred itself to her screen image so strongly that life did not seem to ape art so much as transfuse it. Few of her fans can have been deceived for long – and her vamp soon became a laughing-stock – but right into her retirement years later she kept meeting people who expressed surprise that she was 'human after all', so well had Fox established her supernatural origins. She also found to her dismay how the star image could stick to its owner, so that even when she played non-vamp parts the public came expecting the old brazen allure. Theda Bara's exotic heyday was brief – but long enough for her to learn how small the difference was between being a favourite of the public – and its captive.

*   *   *

The enormous emphasis now put on the stars was not to everyone's taste. Directors in general resented and feared it. Whereas the producers had quickly learned how to use stars to fortify their economic power, directors saw the risk that stars would whittle down *their* artistic power. To have to build a picture around a star was an affront to the autocratic temperament of some, the democratic ways of working of others. One can doubt if two of the greatest names of the time, Cecil B. de Mille and D. W. Griffith, really welcomed stars. De Mille in fact leaves no room for doubt. He profoundly mistrusted stars all his life, even though he fondly nurtured the talents of Gloria Swanson, Bebe Daniels, Leatrice Joy and others. 'Believing in 1917, as I still do,' he wrote in his autobiography with the defensive touchiness characteristic of the whole book, 'that the story a film has to tell is the one all-important element in it, I believed then, and still do, that great pictures can be made without "name" stars.'*

De Mille and Griffith were strongly affected in this outlook by their early stage ambitions. De Mille, a frustrated playwright turned film director, naturally stressed the quality of the story, not the stars. Griffith, a frustrated actor who had been pressured into directing films, was always on guard against the *prima donna* concept of a star player. Neither man basically sympathised with the developing star system, for it went against the grain of their formative experience in stock companies where players could be used interchangeably in parts great and small. But many far less autocratic directors submitted grudgingly to the new prominence of players receiving larger salaries and vastly more publicity than they did. And the self-awareness of the stars posed new problems in directing them. A tension was introduced into the creative relationship. The director who wanted to make a masterpiece now had to reckon with the stars who wanted to keep their public's approval. Stars had to be on the alert, to estimate how much good a picture might do their reputation – and how much risk they ran from an uncompromising director.

Once they acknowledged the primacy of the star, the movies left themselves exposed to all the frightening consequences which could follow from any situation ruled not by reason or business sense, but the most extreme and irrational varieties of human behaviour. Only an industry based on stardom could have survived; and only as film stars could many of its workers have held down a job or indeed found a place in society.

But the stars, too, found themselves under pressure from the start. In order to completely assimilate them into the star *system*,

* *The Autobiography of Cecil B. de Mille* (W. H. Allen Co.) p. 170.

the method evolved to stabilise production and give a continuity of appeal to the product, the appearance, personality and to a great extent the performance of each star had to be standardised from picture to picture. In this way the public would know what to expect from its favourites. At the same time publicity about them, their pictures, activities and offscreen characteristics – and in this respect the establishment of Hollywood as an exotic *and permanent* background played an enormous role – could be employed to provoke curiosity, stimulate expectation and keep filmgoers coming back again and again. Participation in the players' identities thus took root at the same time and in the same soil as the star system.

But just as the creation of stars had a built-in economic conflict between the salary-conscious film idols and the cost-conscious film-makers, the creation of the star system had a built-in human conflict. The producers' energies were devoted to standardising the appeal of their stars; the ego and artistic drives of the stars were bent on demonstrating their individualism, range of talent and capacity to change their established images. Hollywood from the start was one vast ironic contradiction. When the gods who assembled it finally lay down to rest, they must have laughed in their sleep.

*   *   *

By 1914, as Lewis Jacobs said, 'the movie business was at a turning point in its development'. The feature-length film established itself 'with a suddenness and finality that startled even its own backers'. Two picture palaces, seating 5,000 people between them, opened on Broadway in this year and their success freed capital from the Wall Street banks and finance houses which had been held back till such theatres' futures looked assured. Stars were given tremendous impetus by this event. Since it was now possible simply to go along to such places and see which gods and goddesses were packing the temples, star-building and studio raiding increased enormously. Long films tied stars up for more working days: since they were seen less often on the screen, they had to be kept more constantly in the mind. Publicity got a fillip.

Art kept pace with industry. Between 1914 and 1917 film technique grew rapidly more sophisticated. And in the screen's advantage lay the star's enhancement. A critic who saw Mary Pickford in *Tess of the Storm Country*, in 1914, saw a film that was still influenced by the swift-packed action of the one- and two-reel movies which had to condense a lengthy, complicated novel. He commented: '[It] never gives Mary Pickford a real chance to impress her personality upon her audience. When she pleads, she rushes into the scene like the victim of a "chase" picture, throws herself abruptly on her knees, delivers a set of whirlwind gestures, rushes out. So confused and complicated is the action that none of the intelligent party with whom I witnessed the film could afterwards make a synopsis.'*

Within a space of time so swift that it seems more a matter of months than years, the specialisation of film crafts – scripting, camerawork, lighting – had opened the way for the audience to enter into a new relationship with the personality on the screen. Photography which previously had merely recorded a performance was now able to shape one due to the advance in lighting. Another critic who saw Mary Pickford in *A Romance of the Redwoods* in 1917, commented on the star's new expressiveness: 'Light becomes atmosphere instead of illumination. Coming naturally from some window, lamp, a doorway, it illuminates the centre of the picture and the people standing there with a glow that in intensity, in volume, or in variety of sources has some quality expressive of the emotion of the scene. . . . Under a small, single source of light, the walls of the cabin and the faces of the actors are filled with strong shadows to match the terror of the episode enacted.'†

It was a sure sign that stars had come to stay when they started insisting on the same lighting photographers for their pictures. Photography quickly became the star's own way of standardising her appeal – and also protecting her career against unsympathetic directors. From very early days Mary Pickford relied on Charles Rosher, Norma Talmadge on Tony Gaudio, while Corinne

* Will Irwin, op cit., p. 226
† *Behind the Screen*, by Kenneth Macgowan (Delacorte Press) pp. 169–70.

Griffith had a contract clause giving her first call on John Seitz. Two of the pioneer cameramen, Fred J. Balshofer and Arthur C. Miller, have given a precise account in *One Reel a Week* which shows how film lighting kept step with the exploration of film acting. So did story- and scenario-writing which instead of condensing events now expanded a character. So did editing which instead of simply making the action logical now helped to make a personality apparent.

By the last half of the decade all the technical and economic conditions were present for the emergence of the great star prototypes. What must now be examined, as well as conjecture and criticism permit, are the human elements – the ways in which some of these early stars shaped their own art and reputations, or had others shape them for them.

PART THREE

DEDICATION

'Happiness Must Be Earned.'
– Moral in *The Thief of Bagdad*

CHAPTER THREE

THEIR MASTER'S
VOICE:
D. W. GRIFFITH

Along with the new cinema came a new ideal in American woman-
hood. The female star whom it brought into fashion was small,
very feminine, soulful or child-like, yet vigorous, energetic,
resilient and, above all, young. The reigning beauties of the
American stage had been Junoesque types like Lillian Russell, the
Floradora Sextet and the Irene Brent chorus-girls, or Katherine
Elkins, the statuesque showgirl who became Mrs John Jacob
Astor. With the movies one seems to be among a totally new
brand of feminine charm – certainly a new dietary ideal – typified
by Mary Pickford, Mae Marsh, Blanche Sweet, Marian Leonard
and Lillian and Dorothy Gish, just to mention an outstanding few.

Credit for establishing the strain rightly goes to D. W. Griffith –
and his predilection suggests how, from early on, the movies were
a unique medium for making one's fantasies flesh. For such girls
existed in Griffith's imagination long before he ever met them and
was able to offer them work. He was by birth a Kentuckian, by
upbringing and education a romantic. The South's traditionally
chivalrous attitude towards women was reinforced by a literary
bias, formed in class and the family reading-circle, in favour of the
English Victorian poets like Browning and Tennyson and the
romantic novelists who either repressed sexuality or else refined
it to the idealised degree that convention permitted. His outlook
strongly influenced him in the selection of poems and plays for
filming when he gained authority at Biograph and, as Lewis
Jacobs and others have noted, it also affected his recruitment of
players – though not quite for the sentimental reasons that his
own statements might suggest at a first glance.

'When I consider a young woman as a stellar possibility,'

he stated in 1923, 'I always ask myself: Does she come near suggesting the idealised heroine of life? . . . The girl, to have the real germ of stardom, must suggest – at least in a sketchy way – the vaguely conscious ideals of every man. Again, she must suggest – and this is equally important – the attributes most women desire.'* It does not require a very cynical mind to appreciate that spiritual appeal here coincides very helpfully with box-office appeal. For stars must ideally be able to focus the desires of both the sexes or, at the very least, not attract the disregard or hostility of one of them.

This mingling of the softly romantic and the severely practical is entirely characteristic of Griffith. In fact it suggests the clue to his temperament, for it is a very Celtic combination of gifts and Griffith probably owed more to his Celtic ancestry than his Southern upbringing. His resemblances to other Celts are striking. It is not just his tumultuous, epic imagination which recalls the work of the artist Frank Brangyn, whose giant canvases and murals are organised on the scale and with much of the saga-like inspiration of Griffith's films *The Birth of a Nation* (1915) and *Intolerance* (1917); but when both men falter, they fall into precisely the same Celtic sentimentality. Then again Griffith's voice and manner of speaking, which was so important in directing his players, recall the peculiar talents employed by two of his Celtic contemporaries in a quite different field. It was said of Lloyd George, the Welsh statesman, and Briand, the Breton-born French one, that they could cast a spell over audiences by the cadence and tonality they gave their respective languages. We shall return to the way Griffith used his voice to cast a spell over his players; but it seems quite likely that inherited characteristics of the kind indicated enabled him to employ the same bewitching instrument of language for hard practical ends. Indeed he, too, had quite a touch of the calculating politician in him.

In declaring what he looked for in an actress, he said: 'I am inclined to favour beginners. They come untrammelled by so-called techniques, by theories, by preconceived ideas. I prefer the young woman who has to support herself and possibly her

* *Photoplay*, August 1923.

mother.* Of necessity she will work hard. Again, I prefer the nervous type. I never engage a newcomer who applies for work without showing at least a sign or two of nervousness. If she is calm, she has no imagination.'

Sensitive, suggestible, industrious, obedient – this is not just the make-up of a performer, but of a *protégée*. There is already an air of dependence and dedication about successful applicants. But there must be something more. 'To me, the ideal type for feminine stardom has nothing of the flesh, nothing of the note of sensuousness.† My pictures reveal the type I mean. Commentators have called it the *spirituelle* type. But there is a method in my madness. . . . The voluptuous type, blossoming into the full-blown one, cannot endure. The years show their stamp too clearly. The other type . . . ah, that is different.'‡

*   *   *

Griffith's sentimental preferences were perfectly suited to the sophisticated equipment in use even at this early date. The camerawork, as has already been observed, had its origins in Victorian craft photography; and the lenses employed were as good as any the cinema was to develop for several decades. A face had to be youthful to withstand their scrutiny – Lillian Gish recalls that Griffith once had to return a baby which had been borrowed from an orphanage for a scene and ask for a younger looking one. He must have discovered very quickly how strongly filmgoers identified with the slips of girls in his pictures and the Victorian stories involving them. It is worth emphasising that the sentimentality of the plots, which jars today, was then very much a fact of life for nickelodeon audiences from the back streets or immigrant ghettos where drunkenness bred brutish parents, long-lost offspring were the common price of having to leave one's homeland, and the dying babies of melodrama had their statistical reality in the infant mortality rate.

* Note how Griffith unconsciously does away with the need to cope with the girl's father.

† Mary Pickford, spotted by Griffith when casting the lead in *Pippa Passes*, later lost the part because he thought she had grown too plump.

‡ *Photoplay*, August 1923.

Technically a pioneer of cinema techniques, Griffith belonged temperamentally to the tradition of the autocratic actor-manager. He had had to give up any ambition he had for filling this role in the theatre when Biograph, after engaging him as an actor, had pressed him into service as a director; but his speedy success gave him total control over those who now did the acting for him. And it was Griffith's genius in the human and technical sides of the art which gave Biograph its outstanding lead over the early studios so long as he remained there.

Yet a studio under Griffith's control must have been an emotionally strained place to work in: this is the other side of the artistic perfection some of its stars achieved. Preferring new-comers who showed 'a sign or two of nervousness', Griffith seems not to have been averse to maintaining a touch or two of insecurity among the established players. Since he did not sympathise with the idea of any fixed stars he had a way, Linda Arvidson, who later became his wife, recalled, 'of not letting an actor get all worked up about himself. When that seemed imminent, new talent would suddenly appear on the scene to play "leads" for two or three weeks so that the importance of the regular could simmer down a bit.'* And Lillian Gish, many years after she had left Biograph and Griffith, said, 'Of course, we never knew whether we would finally play the parts we rehearsed in the actual picture – Mr Griffith never told you what you were doing till the last minute.' (That 'of course' is a measure of how much Griffith's domination of them was accepted by his players.)

The need to have replacements handy to rub home a lesson in humility probably contributed to perpetuating the 'Griffith type' in the studio's company; but it can hardly have helped his players' ease of mind to know how interchangeable or dispensable they were. We know that Mary Pickford quit Griffith in pique because he had assigned the lead in *The Sands of Dee* to Mae Marsh. And Anita Loos, one of Griffith's closest assistants in the 1914 period, has gone as far as to imply that Bobby Harron, the Bio-graph messenger boy whom Griffith had picked out and promoted to screen parts requiring a gentle, slightly wistful masculinity, had

* Linda Arvidson, op. cit., pp. 174–5.

a motive for suicide in the director's preference for another *protégé*, Richard Barthelmess, 'who was allotted roles which previously would have gone to Harron.'* Bobby Harron was found shot in his New York hotel in September, 1920 on the very eve of the East Coast *première* of *Way Down East* in which Barthelmess had one of his greatest successes.

The dependence of his players on him was probably reinforced by one curious feature that almost all of the inner ring had in common. They came from homes where a mother or grandmother had been the breadwinner or family support. Death, divorce or desertion had deprived them of their fathers at an early age. Mary Pickford's father was killed in an accident when she was five; Mae Marsh's father died when she was four; the mother of Lillian and Dorothy Gish was deserted by her husband when they were four or five; Blanche Sweet's father deserted his wife when she was one year old and after her mother's death a year later at the age of only 19, the child was reared by her grandmother, a 57-year-old divorcee. Without insisting too much on this factor, it is worth bearing in mind when considering the girls' passionate devotion to a strong, stern father-figure like Griffith and the zeal they showed to please him and win his favours by a piece of acting that he would commend. 'Anything he told me to do, I did,' said Blanche Sweet. '*Anything* to win his praises.'

Competition for roles, emotional insecurity and professional jealousies: these are ruthless ways in which to keep players at artistic pitch. Beneath the porcelain exteriors of Griffith's stars there must have been wills of steel. On the set he allowed no lapse of attention or deviation from the desired effect once it had been achieved. In the achievement must have lain a great deal of the satisfaction for both parties; and it is the heights that this achievement reached which excuse Griffith's imperious and sometimes physically rough nature. (In quarrels with him, Mary Pickford occasionally found herself rudely pushed aside and once even knocked down.)

Sam Goldwyn speaks of Griffith possessing 'the hypnotic baton of Svengali'. The comparison is banal, but just. Griffith seldom

* *A Girl Like I,* by Anita Loos (Hamish Hamilton) p. 95.

used a script, but rehearsed the scenes of every story in sequence till each fitted smoothly into the next. And to get a player in the right mood, he used a single musical instrument – his voice. Everyone who heard it speaks with awe of its power. 'He remains calm and quiet,' wrote Allene Talmey, one of the sharpest (and often wittiest) Hollywood observers, '[his] amazing voice cutting through all the noise around him. It is deep and slow and grave. . . . It is a voice to mould phrases, like recitations. . . . If the scene is an intimate one, it is directed with Mr Griffith drawn close, his face a dimmed mirror to guide the cast. Promptings form on his lips and die. "Come quicker, not quite so much support, good enough, and once again please." '*

In addition to the feeling for language which he may have inherited, Griffith must certainly have been impressed with the power of the voice to induce emotion from the family readings from the Bible, Shakespeare and the poets which were given almost nightly during his boyhood by his father, a former Confederate colonel nicknamed 'Thunder Jake'. A striking example of the director's own vocal magnetism is reported by an eyewitness during the filming of an old-time evangelist meeting in *True-Heart Susie* (1919). According to this spectator, 'the director had engaged an evangelist . . . but somehow the crowd of extras remained cold and unmoved. The scene threatened to collapse, when Griffith took the evangelist's place on the platform and began to preach. He kept his place on the platform for an hour and obtained the most valuable shots of religious fervour ever filmed.'† One of Griffith's actors, Harry Carr, testifies vividly to the power of this oral *rapport:* 'D.W. knows just the moment an actor is spiritually reaching out for a lifeline. At that moment he will speak the lines for them. "Go to hell!" he will yell as the hero is defying the villain. It is wonderful to see the effect of this on the actor. It is just like an experienced jockey letting a horse feel the touch of his hand on the rein.'

The 'voice over' method of guiding a player was, of course,

* *Doug and Mary and Others*, by Allene Talmey (Macy-Masius.) p. 97.
† *Photoplay*, May 1923: 'What Makes Them Cry', by Frederick James Smith.

possible only as long as the films were silent. It cannot be too strongly emphasised that silence permitted the great bond of the human voice to exist between director and players right up to the talkies – whereupon sound immediately became the great barrier and acting lost much of its continuous plastic quality, the feeling of a performance being moulded vocally as well as emotionally and of people being kept at full stretch throughout by a presence that was just out of camera range. Griffith's finest films convey the feeling that if Billy Bitzer's camera moved an inch beyond the action it would pick up that sombre-suited eminence with his wigwam hat, lofty brow, hawk-like nose and trumpet nostrils pressing his face as near the caged emotions as he dared.

*   *   *

Of course these techniques had their other side: they were exhausting, dictatorial, restrictive. The gratitude and devotion that Griffith's stars later expressed for him were not unmixed by a tone of relief when they temporarily eluded his control or escaped from it for good. 'You know that scene in the closet,' said Lillian Gish in 1957, some thirty-eight years after she had played it in *Broken Blossoms* (1919) when I spin round and round in turn as Donald Crisp is trying to open the door to beat me and kill me. I worked that out for myself, and never told Griffith about what I was doing.' (The secretive pride, slight guilt and rare omission of the respectful 'Mr' Griffith make such a confidence sound like a declaration of revolt.) 'You see, if I had told him, he'd have made me rehearse it over and over again; and that would have spoiled it. It had to be spontaneous – the hysterical terror of a child.'*

Griffith's sensitive girls learned perfectionism, but sometimes at the expense of self-expression. When Sam Goldwyn asked Mary Pickford how she had ever brought herself to take final leave of her mentor, her reply was illuminating: 'I felt I was getting to be a machine under Mr Griffith. . . . I made up my mind to see if I could really do anything by myself.' Mary's second, and this time final break with Griffith came early in her career, in

* Conversation with Lillian Gish,' *Sight and Sound*, Winter, 1957–8.

1912, and her artistry, business sense and, above all, power-base in the affections of her fans established her self-sufficiency so solidly that one hardly thinks of her as a Griffith *protégée*. She soon discovered that she could do *everything* by herself whereas Griffith, by contrast, fatally lacked his pupil's economic hard-headedness.*

But the image of Mary that blossomed into 'America's Sweet-heart' contains a tragic irony not altogether unconnected with her break with Griffith. For it is a mistake to think that Griffith pro-moted the later Pickford image of curlylocked childhood: on the contrary, although she joined Biograph as a child of 16, he fre-quently cast her for parts a little older than her real age and much older than her worldly experience. Her looks were apparently a good deal darker in those days and Griffith felt that her high cheekbones gave her a good face for playing Latin American beauties, redskin maidens and young squaws. 'She played many character parts with her hair smacked straight back,' says Linda Arvidson, 'and she did young wives with her hair in a "bun" on the top of her head to make her look tall and married.'† Curls and Mary Pickford were not yet inseparable in the public's mind, though the quick way in which they did catch on as a hair style whenever she wore them in a film demonstrates the early power of their appeal.

The point is that at the very moment when Mary Pickford left Griffith she was versed in playing young women and ready to come of age – she was then 19 or 20 – in parts that would have given full scope to her adult emotions. Instead she went to

* One sidelight in this context that reveals, in a superficial yet totally convincing way, the unsentimental business side to Mary Pickford that protected her artistic independence is contributed by Herbert Howe, *Photoplay*'s chief show-business columnist, in a laconic report on the star and her husband Douglas Fairbanks Sr. ' "I have only 300 billboards for the New York showings of *Rosita*," she said. "Do you think that enough? I wanted 500. I think billboards very important in the advertising campaign. Douglas, how many billboards have you for *The Thief of Bagdad*?" ... "I've got 50 billboards," said Doug. "The first of the year is a long time off." "You need to reserve billboards a long time off," was Mary's pert rejoinder.' – *Photoplay*, January 1924.

† Linda Arvidson, op. cit., p. 168.

Adolph Zukor and soon found herself playing parts that required her to look and act like a child again.* The first child waif she played was in *Rags* (1915) and as late as *Little Annie Rooney* (1925) she was playing a slum kid of 12 when she herself was aged 32.

The powers of inventive imagination which enabled her to remain within the mind as well as the body of a child also helped her play such parts better than any other actress of her generation and win immense public affection the world over.

But the price she had to pay for it petrified her artistry; for the same loving public simply would not allow her to grow up and play mature parts till it was psychologically too late for her to make the adjustment. Having the early burden of looking after her younger brother and sister robbed Mary Pickford of her childhood; being required to continue her childhood by other means after she left Griffith deprived her of her career as a mature artist.

Of course what would have happened had she stayed with Griffith can only be speculation: she would quite likely have prospered as an actress, but the temperaments of master and pupil were probably too inflexible to make for an easy *human* relationship. She retained, however, the creative self-confidence that Griffith instilled into her, whereas others who tried the temperature of the outside world shrivelled up without his protection. One of them was Blanche Sweet, whom Sam Goldwyn lured away for 2,000 dollars a week against the 85 dollars she was getting from Griffith. Her tempter later reflected ruefully on 'Griffith actresses . . . [who] find that they cannot perform in another environment.'

But no such reproach can be levelled against the actress who became the supreme exponent of Griffith's art and techniques. She not only survived the inevitable break with him; but she transcended all that he had taught her through the degree of dedication she showed to the cinema. She is that very rare fusion of qualities, the star who is also a pure actress. Her name is Lillian Gish.

* For a fuller discussion of the consequences of this the reader is referred to my book *The Celluloid Sacrifice* (Michael Joseph, 1966; New York, Hawthorn, 1967: reissued as *Sex in the Movies,* London & New York, Penguin Books, 1968).

CHAPTER FOUR

ALL FOR ART:
LILLIAN GISH

Silent stars have paid a heavy price for so many of their films being lost or in poor repair or simply being out of popular circulation for a long time. Those who have not gone out of memory have gone out of focus. They have become names by which to label a period, rather than strikingly individual identities. Their styles of acting have been confused. And stars who were simply close contemporaries are often spoken about as if they had been historical replicas.

Lillian Gish has suffered badly in this respect. She is invariably linked with Mary Pickford; but the resemblances in their careers, of which the chief was having D. W. Griffith as their mentor, are far less important than the differences. A principal one suggests itself right away. One can approach Mary Pickford's art through any number of significant events in her life; but Lillian Gish seems to have had no life outside her art. Mary Pickford would have fitted well into a Dickens novel: one would have wished to reserve Lillian Gish for Henry James. Pickford had an early, immense and essentially popular success which drew its strength from the urban working classes whose daily load Mary's screen pranks and resilient outlook invariably lightened. Gish was vastly successful, too, but hers was a more rarified and, as Griffith would say, *spirituelle* contact with her public. Pickford was the penny whistle that could sound cheerful in adversity; Gish was the flute that specialised in laments. Pickford was born to suffer and overcome in her films, Gish to suffer and be crushed. Pickford's acting was a reaction to the world around her. Gish's acting always seemed to be striving towards some ideal partly because the roles she played supremely well had their creative source in motherhood or chastity, both of which are ideal states.

68

Both stars of course were tough. Mary's toughness showed in a self-reliant realism that lies never very far below the sentimental surface of her roles. Lillian's toughness was marvellously at variance with the fragility of her looks, but it was there. And physically there, too, otherwise she would not have survived exposure in below-zero weather for the ice-floe rescue in *Way Down East* when Griffith considerately put an oil stove under his camera to stop it from freezing up but periodically had to halt the filming in order to defrost his star.

But besides dedication, Gish had a moral sternness towards her work that as she grew older drew her sympathies and some of her later roles close to the kind of pioneer stubbornness which expresses a lost American ideal. It is hard to think of another actress who could have turned on the Haitian police bullies when they assault her and her husband in *The Comedians* (1967) with the same force of hereditary indignation behind her – as if it was not just an outrage against her person, but against her patriotism. Not that Gish would have been confined by any role as narrow as, say, a Daughter of the American Revolution – not while the candidature for the Mother of the American Revolution remained unfilled.

It is easier to categorise Lillian Gish in the most recent stretches of her long career because the pale, frail, wistful *protégée* of Griffith's day looks so insubstantial. The silent-film historian, Edward Wagenknecht, spoke the truth when he said that the effect Gish makes is 'virtually to blot out the flesh'. To which one must immediately add that she knew the value of getting outside help in doing so. To photograph *Broken Blossoms,* for instance, she brought Henry Sartov to the Griffith studio – her contract gave her this power – and Sartov made use of the soft-focus photography which was still an impressive novelty in 1919. It is the effect he creates by filming her through a layer of gauze which adds an insubstantial dimension to her little London waif who is befriended by a Chinaman and beaten to death by her brutish step-father. What would have been cameo-sharp in a more corporeal conception now seems to be created out of Limehouse mist. Yet it retains uncanny clarity of pain and pity, because Gish is an artist to her literal fingertips. She works in the miniature emotions that go with the small bodies and delicate features of Griffith's preferred type of actress. She works at the extremities of her physique, so that the child's fluttering excitement in *Broken Blossoms* as her fingers reach to touch the gorgeous Oriental robe the Chinaman is offering her is like that of a nervous butterfly.

*   *   *

It comes as no surprise that Griffith's advice to Lillian Gish on acting was to study small animals and birds. (To Pickford, his advice was, study small children.) Neither Freud nor Jung needs to be called in to interpret her performance: just watching her movements reveals the inner message. She has the same concentrated sense of *presence* that a small pet engenders in its cramped world of hutch or cage, where every eye-blink or feather-flick is a miniscule disturbance relaying an emotion to the outside world. If that world is filled with some impending catastrophe prepared by God or man, then the disparity between the scale of the peril and its effect on the victim becomes itself piteous – and this was generally the case in her films for Griffith.

Her looks assisted her enormously. She had very precisely defined lips, the upper one of which fit like a long lid over the much smaller lower one and increased the wistfulness of her features. Her eyes have always had the effect of a baby's – they seem disproportionately large for the face they are set in. (They are large even by the ophthalmic effects obtained inadvertently in the silent movies where the studio's Klieg lights made the players stare and often forced them to drop out for a few days with eye strain, though fortunately the result in front of the cameras was simply to expose the whites and make the sufferers look more soulful and romantic than migrainy.) Lillian and her younger sister Dorothy were unlike in temperament; but when the pair of them starred together as the sisters who are wrenched apart by the French Revolution in *Orphans of the Storm* (1921) they were so alike in looks that some filmgoers got a sensation of parallax vision. Now twin-like looks give a slightly mysterious air of 'apartness' to those who share them; and it was this which must

have marked out the little Gishes when they sallied forth, dressed
alike, with their mother to the Biograph Studios in 1912 in order
to renew acquaintance with a childhood friend, Gladys Smith,
whom they had seen in one of the company's films. Gladys
turned out to be 'Mary Pickford' – and she introduced them to
Griffith. One can only guess at the favourable effect which two of
his *spirituelle* types must have had on him when they appeared in
duplicate. He engaged them and immediately tied a blue ribbon
round Lillian and a red one round Dorothy so as to tell them apart.

Behind them lay several years in touring stock companies
which their mother had joined at the suggestion of a theatrical
lodger when her husband deserted her. She had found that the
popular melodramas gave plenty of employment to children, too,
who were often required to play identical roles to the ones in
which life had stranded them. It is easy to underestimate the
conviction brought to these catastrophe-laden chronicles, on both
sides of the footlights.

Griffith had his favourites at Biograph and could play them
mischieviously against each other. But where acting was concerned, all that mattered was art; and his judgment was in-
corruptible. Dorothy Gish he described as apter at picking up his
intention than Lillian, 'quicker to follow it, more easily satisfied
with the result'. Lillian, though, 'sought to realise an ideal'. And
so, of course, did he. This was the inspirational bond between
them from the very beginning; but there must have been others
to produce those astonishing results on the screen. Love was one,
though translated into respect and devotion. Literature was
probably another. The values that both held dear had been
shaped by the poetic strain in American letters, the tradition of
Whitman, Longfellow, Greenleaf Whittier and Nathaniel Hawthorne. This was part of Griffith's sentimental education and
Lillian's classroom one. She was much better read than Pickford
or the Talmadges, Constance and Norma, whose choice of
stories for filming when they eventually turned independent
producers betrays an early shaping by *Peg's Own Paper*. (Not that
this was a handicap, just the contrary: their tastes were the same
as their public's.) Lillian's retort is well known when Louis B.

Mayer expressed doubt, in 1926, that the film censor would be agreeable to a screen version of *The Scarlet Letter* in which she wished to play Hester Prynne, the deserted wife who bears the child of a sinful pastor. 'It is a classic in every American classroom,' she declared warmly, putting Hawthorne's literary status before her own purity rating although in fact it was the latter which won the censor's approval for the project.

Literature shaped Griffith's film aspirations as well. The device for linking the four parallel plots in *Intolerance* apparently occurred to him in a flash of inspiration after reading Whitman's lines 'out of the cradle endlessly rocking, uniter of here and hereafter'. But it was the acute perception he had of Gish's nature which caused him to cast her, in spite of other roles in the film open to her, as Whitman's eternal mother, rocking the cradle of humanity, her face linking the stories, binding together the ages of intolerance. The posture of a mother with her child is not simply an emblematic one for Lillian Gish: it is a concept running through acting, even in the most maudlin plots, like a current of pure emotion.

Part of her Limehouse waif's loneliness in *Broken Blossoms* comes from her isolation from both motherhood and childhood. Her own mother in the film is dead. A child-ridden neighbour warns her against the burdens of marriage. The local prostitutes warn her against sex. In fact her age in the film is oddly indeterminate. Griffith's own characteristically lachrymose subtitle refers to 'the child with tear-stained face', but her interpretation has more subtlety and ambiguity than this. First seen sidling along a wharf with a ragged shawl, holes in her stockings and a hat with an absurdly wide brim which enhances the woebegone effect, she creeps home with dread in her step and a stoop that makes her look all of 50 years old. It sounds like a compilation of tear-jerking tricks and tatters, but that is not how it looks. James Agate, who was no easy touch for any player trying to ape Sarah Bernhardt, expressed his astonishment that Lillian Gish in *Broken Blossoms* 'should give the world an exact image of the great actress in her far-off youth'.*

* *Around Cinemas*, by James Agate (Home & Van Thal) p. 22.

Pickford in the same part might have felt the need to invent some comic business – like the scrubbing brushes she uses as skates in her own film *Through the Back Door* (1921) – to relieve the harshness of life. Gish, typically, uses gestures that accentuate it. And again and again she falls back on childhood for her emotional inspiration and technique. Ordered to smile by her bullying ex-pugilist step-father, she inserts two fingers in her mouth, baby-like, to push her lips up into a temporary smile of strained wistfulness. This effect she devised herself, to Griffith's intense delight, and it is repeated at the end of the film as the breath leaves her broken body. It is an emotional shorthand sign : it packs a world of pathos into a minute dimension. Gish anticipates, and brilliantly avoids, sentimental banality; so that when she takes to bed the doll that the 'yellow man', played by Richard Barthelmess, has given her, one of its sawdust-filled arms pushes into her cheek like the finger of an importunate baby. Again the effect is 'arranged', but the arrangement is the product of flawless instinct.

Even when one is well aware of Gish's technique, her effects generally succeed brilliantly, because the intensity behind them is so genuinely experienced. The baptism of her dead baby in *Way Down East* was apparently so affecting that the real father of the infant who had been borrowed for the scene was overcome while watching her on the set. She could produce such moments *en passant,* too, not just as part of a set-piece. In *The Scarlet Letter* her baby falls ill and she goes for help. Casually yet touchingly, and without making it seem a conscious gesture, she moves two chairs with clothes hung on the backs of them between the baby in bed and the cottage door – to shield it from draughts while she is away. Gish has also instant recourse to motherhood in scenes to which it is not precisely applicable, yet is emotionally apposite. A love scene with Joseph Schildkraut in *Orphans of the Storm* leaves an afterglow of rapture. Then, abruptly, she turns to a rocking chair and, as she pushes it, her thoughts are clearly several leaps ahead of marriage and already on maternity. Gish tucks moments like these meticulously into scenes, like fuses, and primes them emotionally.

*   *   *

It is right to emphasise such small moments in her art, for Gish's performances under Griffith are usually remembered for the big ones of emotional crescendo. He matched her climaxes to the destructive power of man or nature. A master of screen counterpoint, he sensed the effect of making this frail-looking girl a victim of overwhelmingly cruel destiny from the minute she appears on the screen looking, ominously, too gentle for the world's pain. It is on record that Gish knew precisely how to produce her trauma effect. 'It is expressed,' she once said clinically, 'by the arm from the elbow to the fingers and depends entirely on rhythm – the gradual quickening of movement up to the pitch desired.' But this merely proves she appreciated that, in screen acting, less is more. As Allene Talmey put it, 'her face required only a breeze to whip it into change whereas others of her craft dealt exclusively with typhoons'.*

Yet when a dramatic typhoon does engulf Gish her carefully graduated loss of reason, the way she dissolves into hysteria or madness, never loses its human proportions, while the intensity expressed belies the effect of a time-and-motion study which her own dispassionate analysis of it suggests. When she shuts herself in a closet to escape from her step-father in *Broken Blossoms* she creates great eddies of claustrophobic panic not by pounding on the wall, but by the more disturbing means of whirling round and round. Just as a body immersed in water displaces its own volume of liquid, Gish uses space to displace her hysteria.

Her features change alarmingly under stress like the moment in *Hearts of the World* (1918) when, in one uninterrupted shot, she loses her reason beside the dead body of her mother, a war victim. First she kisses her, tilts back her head with the mouth open in a silent shout of grief, then suddenly snaps her mouth shut, lets her facial spasms die away into a mask of immobile incomprehension, and finally stares unseeingly straight into the camera. The carry-over effect of dislocated sanity is shattering enough to lend conviction to a plot that calls on Lillian to wander distractedly through a battlefield bombardment clutching her bridal gown and to spend what was to have been her wedding

* Allene Talmey, op. cit., p. 68.

night beside her badly wounded *fiancé* whom she takes for dead. After witnessing such a pathetic demonstration of madness one understands why Tennessee Williams wrote *Portrait of a Madonna,* an early draft of *A Streetcar Named Desire,* especially for Lillian Gish. Her screen personality exhibits a lot of the same desperate lyricism as Blanche Dubois: insanity and the effect of blunt reality on too unprotected a sensibility is the fate that threatens both women.

But one area of life that Gish did not touch in her apprenticeship to Griffith, which lasted till 1921 when she followed the consequences of her stardom and went to work with other directors, was the sexual one. Perhaps it fitted Griffith's temperament not to explore it with her, even though his unfortunate racist outlook, the product of his Kentucky upbringing, which made him equate colour with lust, imparted one highly disturbing moment to *Broken Blossoms.* Gish has run away from home and is sleeping in the house of the Chinaman who has offered her sanctuary. At this point Barthelmess's eyes are shown in huge close-up as he draws near the girl's bed, followed by a medium shot of his head craning forward in a more than fond contemplation of her body. Then, abruptly, he kisses the Oriental robe he has given her – and the subtitle, 'His love remains pure', clinches one's relief.

Two years later, when Griffith made *Dream Street* (1921), another London slum story, the Chinaman in it possessed a somewhat less pure passion. However the girl who rejects his offer of marriage and denounces him to the police with a smug, 'After this, you leave white girls alone', was played by Carol Dempster, a cooler *protégée* than Gish. Griffith's sentimental romanticism also probably deterred him from the sexual realism that de Mille was exploring as early as 1917 in *The Cheat* where yet another Oriental makes a faithless white society woman part of his personal property by branding her. Fortunately Gish's sensitivity is so complete that one never questions whether her Griffith heroines are at the age of sexual awareness or not. She interiorises love and in the process purifies it.

Nevertheless such abstention may have reinforced certain puritan aspects of her art that began to obtrude into the sentimental penumbra of films she made for other directors. The extent of her devotion to Griffith can be guessed at from the extent to which she had underpriced herself compared with what other stars were getting. She had made *Orphans of the Storm* for 1,000 dollars a week which Griffith ultimately found he could not afford to pay her. Once their ways parted, Gish assumed many of Griffith's powers: the power to vet a director's appointment, approve the script and rehearse the whole film in advance as Griffith's training had taught her. Her betrayed wife in *Romola* (1924: directed by Henry King) and her nun in *The White Sister* (1924: also by King) whose 'dead' lover returns to try and claim her back from the convent, have passages where Gish's emotional stress breaks prismatically across her face with the old Griffith magic; but it is not just the lack of her master's voice which makes them appear slightly more self-regarding exercises. The latter film owes its warmth to Ronald Colman as the sailor lover. Gish's rejection of worldly happiness with him in favour of the veil is meticulously played. But devoutness does not become her quite so well as defencelessness.

King Vidor in his autobiography, *A Tree Is a Tree,* has given perhaps the most authoritative and insight-filled version of what it was like to work with a Griffith *protégée* of Gish's lustre. He pays a slightly mixed tribute to her insistence on exhaustively – and exhaustingly – rehearsing every scene in the film, in this case *La Bohème* (1926), on an empty set with imaginary doors, windows and dressing mirrors. Even more illuminatingly, he recounts the masochistic lengths she was prepared to go to for Mimi's death scene, turning up to shoot it with 'lips curled outwards ... parched with dryness. ... She said in syllables hardly audible that she had succeeded in removing all saliva from her mouth by not drinking any liquid for three days, and by keeping cotton pads between her teeth and gums in her sleep.'*

Impressed though he was by such artistic commitment, Vidor was disconcerted by her conception of the love affair between Mimi and Rudolph, played by John Gilbert who was then near the peak of his romantic fame. 'Miss Gish,' Vidor writes, '. . . be-

* *A Tree Is a Tree,* by King Vidor (Harcourt, Brace & Co.) p. 132.

lieved that the two lovers should never be shown in physical contact. She argued that if we photographed their lips coming together in a kiss, a great amount of suppressed emotion would be dissipated. She was convinced that if we avoided this moment a surge of suppressed romance would be built up. . . . She suggested love scenes in which the two lovers were always separated by space . . . Jack (Gilbert), of course, had been exploited as the 'Great Lover'. How was he to live up to this reputation?'*

Gish apparently carried this chaste conception into her off-screen hours, too, playing the unapproachable virgin to Vidor and Gilbert. It is all evidence of how thoroughly Griffith's training made her immerse herself in a part; but the result was that parts of *La Bohème* had to be re-shot, on the orders of M-G-M's production chief, Irving Thalberg, so as to 'bridge the gap' between Gish and Gilbert. The experience of acting with so pains-taking a player was particularly frustrating to Gilbert. He worked on mood and spontaneity, Gish on rehearsal and repetition. He later described *La Bohème* as 'artistic and delicate, but never believable'.

*   *   *

About this time, the mid-1920s, Lillian Gish's critics were starting to pick and scratch at her performances. 'Griffith man-nerisms', is a reiterated phrase. 'Gish is . . . a technician', said James R. Quirk, whose editorial thunder in *Photoplay*, the most powerful of the film magazines, was dreaded by the stars. 'Exam-ining (her) characterisations, you find that she achieves greatness of effect through a single plane of emotion – namely, hysteria.'† Louise Brooks, a sharp observer of Hollywood politics from inside the stars' compound, even believed there was a conspiracy between the fan magazines and M-G-M to bring down Gish's prestige and market price – she was then getting, according to Quirk, 8,000 dollars a week. The truth is probably not that her skill was any less, but that her sensitive virgin type was looking outmoded against the social and moral freedoms of the 1920s and

* Ibid., p. 130.
† *Photoplay*, March 1926, 'The Enigma of the Screen' by James R. Quirk.

in comparison with the new screen image embodied by the up-and-coming Greta Garbo of the modern, neurotic woman whose sexual inclinations caused suffering wherever they led her, but whose own spiritual suffering went a long way to mitigate the disapproval of the screen's official and lay censorship groups.

It is against this background that Gish's determination to film the censorship-prone theme of *The Scarlet Letter* has to be seen. She requested Victor Seastrom to direct it; and in this, too, showed her instincts were right. She felt that the Swedish-born director would have an affinity with Hawthorne's colonial Puritans and their God-fearing, life-denying repression of sexuality. Many years later, though, she added another reason: '[Seastrom] was himself an excellent actor, the best who has ever directed me.'* This provides an important clue to her art. Gish was the type of star who makes acting into a 'dialogue' with her director. Not necessarily a spoken dialogue, though in the case of Griffith it was all of that, a matter of talking the performances out of the cast as they had evolved the film together in rehearsal and then encouraging them vocally to give something beyond the call of craftsmanship when in front of the camera. The radar that thus flowed between them was that of actors, even though one of the actors was now called a director. Seastrom had been an actor, too, an incomparably better one than Griffith would have made: see his majestic performance in Ingmar Bergman's *Wild Straw-berries* (1958), as the aged scientist whose boyhood memories humanise him and rejuvenate him, as if a spring had spouted out of a tombstone. Charles Laughton was another 'excellent actor' and Gish gave the best performance of her career in the Talkies when he directed her in *The Night of the Hunter* (1955) – and for the same reason. It was actor 'talking' to actor.

And yet *The Scarlet Letter*, in spite of Seastrom, remains an obstinately Griffith-type movie. The Swede's sympathy with the subject is plain to see in the tender pearliness of the woodland lighting when Gish and the pastor, played by Lars Hanson, come face to face; and the sense of budding passion is present in the couple's discovery of their sexuality. But censorship reduced the

* *Films in Review*, May 1960, quoted by Charles Turner.

sex to a shot of the knickers, which Gish has been washing when she meets the minister, now abandoned on a bush. And the theme of persecuted motherhood is obviously so congenial to Gish's talents – and depicted by her so lovingly, in the manner of a practical Madonna – that one guesses the erotic would never have been prominent in the film anyhow.

But there is one astonishing moment which shows what might have been. Gish and the minister decide to face up to the community's wrath and ripping the scarlet letter 'A' (for 'Adultress') off her dress and the constricting bonnet off her head, she lets a waterfall of long hair cascade over her face and is invested with a sudden, illicit intensity. A second later her child's hand comes up into the frame and winsomely sticks the scarlet 'A' on to her bosom again – but one has glimpsed another of those vivid Gish transfigurations, from Puritan maid to Pre-Raphaelite siren.

Though *The Scarlet Letter* was an immense popular success, it is far below the power and art of Gish's second film with Seastrom – *The Wind* (1928). This is her finest film. It is among the greatest in the silent cinema. And it is the first in which Lillian Gish's virginal heroine is shown facing up to the sexual realities of life. She plays a girl from the lush green fields of Griffith's Kentucky who arrives in the twilight region of barren Texas where a great wind constantly scours a landscape that is now definitely Seastrom's country. (The whole film is thus a remarkable transitional metaphor for its actress.) The wind never lets up, not for a single scene and though unheard, it is always 'there'. Intending only to visit a childhood friend, Gish is forced by the man's careworn wife who is jealous of her girlish freshness into marriage with a rancher – Lars Hanson again. Seastrom turns Griffith's familiar drama of the elements inside out, so that the wind becomes an interior, alien force in the characters' lives. The newly-wed girl's first night orchestrates her sexual apprehension with gritty billows rattling against the bedroom door; and when her frustrated husband bursts through it and embraces her she wipes his kiss off like a smear of dirt that the wind has blown in. But the *bravura* climax comes when Gish is left alone in the buffeted ranch and its walls take on a queasy, subjective roll and swell as she feels it, and her sanity, being shaken to pieces. A traveller man, resting there from an injury, attacks her. She flees out into the storm, but runs smack up against an invisible wall of wind. It hurls her back into her rapist's arms. The bucking white stallion of Indian myth kicks up its heels in the clouds – a symbol of the unbridled libido. And Gish, in desperation, shoots her assailant. She buries him in the sand, but then with mounting derangement in her features sees the wind exposing the body till the man's face lies on the top of the dune like a death mask.

Seastrom wanted a tragic ending, presumably Gish's death. But M-G-M forced a happier one on him – husband and wife reunited and bravely facing windward. Fortunately it is pictorially bold enough to look like a fit conclusion and not a forced compromise. And Gish's fearless stance presages the pioneer fortitude she later went in for in films like *Duel in the Sun* (1946), *The Night of the Hunter* and *The Unforgiven* (1959), the John Huston western in which she played a classical sonata on a concert grand in defiance of a redskin scalping party. It is as if by coming through the trauma of imperilled virginity in *The Wind* she had somehow braced her screen image. For by dealing exclusively with the girl's sexual predicament the film forced Gish into an unflinching characterisation far more realistic and sustained than any she had ever attempted.

It is astonishing that the film did not make more of an impact at the time. Studio politics may be involved here. Louise Brooks has noted that although she was filming at the same time at M-G-M, she hardly heard of the remarkable picture in production next door. Perhaps M-G-M compared what Gish cost on the payroll with what Garbo was bringing in at the box-office – and knew which to let slide. Joseph Schenck placed Gish in 1925 in the second rank of stars rated by earning power along with Ramon Novarro, John Gilbert, Keaton, Norma Shearer and Corinne Griffith. This seems good company, but 'her drawing power is equal to first-rank players' – Fairbanks, Chaplin, Pickford, Swanson and Norma Talmadge – 'in big films, not in small ones.'* The very psychological profundity of *The Wind* which put

* Joseph Schenck, quoted in *Photoplay*, January 1926.

it ahead of its time caused it to lack the box-office expansiveness which 'big films' had built into them. The wind, after all, was an invisible production value!

Gish successfully made the switch to sound movies, picking a version of Molnar's play *The Swan*, about the cool princess who is thawed by love. After that the Broadway stage claimed more and more of her time and talent – one guesses that she found more seriousness towards acting here than in the Hollywood regime of the 1930s. For the truth is that Lillian Gish approached acting the way some other women approach the veil. It was a semi-mystical vocation that exacted total dedication.

Such a star does not usually acquire, much less seek out the amplifying dimension of scandal and sensation in her private life to dramatise her public image. The alleged breach of promise suit brought against Gish in the mid-1920s by an importunate producer who was himself married at the time is an odd episode and probably had to do with contracts other than the marriage one. It was so out of character that it neither blemished nor burnished her reputation. She has never married and she has never retired. 'Perhaps much is lost in selecting an acting career,' she once reflected. '[You must] not be swayed from the path which leads to your desired goal. You must live with the story you are going to appear in from the moment the scenario goes into the writing until the time it is completed, breathing with the character until you leave it.'

The echo one hears in this is Griffith. When he shaped Gish, the greatest of his stars, he showed the age he belonged to by putting duty and obedience high on the list of desirable virtues. Once learnt, these never left her. The stars who followed her had drive and determination which sprang from the will to succeed. But somehow, as if an era had begun and ended in Gish, these were never the same as her ideals. They sprang from the will to serve.

CHAPTER FIVE

ALL-AMERICAN
BOY:
A NOTE ON
BARTHELMESS

The close personal and working relationship which D. W. Griffith maintained with his young actresses has tended to squeeze his young actors to the side of the picture. But Richard Barthelmess deserves attention. He is not only a good case of someone who began at the height of his power, at full imaginative stretch as an actor, and continued at a somewhat lower but still significant level as a star; but he set a pattern in American heroes which persisted, with different stars, in different films, until well into the 1930s and even the 1940s. It is open to doubt if he was an artist of much original inspiration, but he had a gift for taking direction in a way that made it look as if he was. Through his performances some of the best acting in silent films has survived – and hence some of the best direction.

If Lillian Gish is the unforgettable sensation of *Broken Blossoms,* Barthelmess is its unexpected revelation. Over fifty years later his lonely Chinaman, cut off from home by the Limehouse fogs, is as modern an image of isolation as one could fear to meet in a refugee camp. It is so mesmerising that one could suspect *the actor* has been mesmerised: one watches him as one watches a person who has temporarily been dissociated from his conscious control of his body and made to perform functions and assume states not usually within his competence or sympathies. There may be some truth in this impression, too, for Griffith *was* a mesmerising presence. Moreover he began rehearsals for *Broken Blossoms* without anyone definitely cast for the part of the Chinaman who befriends Gish's little waif; and a veteran actor called George Fawcett stood in temporarily. Barthelmess is said to have watched closely as Fawcett elaborated the part under Griffith's instruction; and when he was finally cast, this is how he played it, too. Performances 'created' by a group in this way are rare in Hollywood cinema: but they are the end result of much of Stanislavsky's teaching and the affection of Russian film directors for Griffith's cinema might very well be extended to the way his best players embodied, however innocently, the principles of their own Soviet stage master.

Broken Blossoms was filmed, complete, in eighteen days. Such concentration has kept everyone in it at full emotional stretch, but Barthelmess has benefited particularly. He might have gone on hunger strike for those eighteen days, his Chinaman has such an unearthly sense of self-containment: the semi-mystical sense associated with confinement and deprivation. It recalls Gandhi and indeed is close to the Mahatma in the way the impassive features are the visible passport to a pacifist temperament. The film opens in the Orient as a statuesque Barthelmess receives the blessing of a Buddhist before his journey; and Griffith's close-ups lay great stress on the quiet face and eyelids that look too heavy to be kept open. His face takes on the fixed lines of a brass rubbing against the softer-focused London mists enveloping it. The character's gentleness has to be expressed by gestures that have the digital economy of a conversation between the deaf and dumb, which in turn helps the spiritual configuration so that when Barthelmess intervenes in a sailors' brawl and holds up an admonishing finger, it is with the restraint of a saint.

The Limehouse scenes show the director's creative liaison with the player even more strikingly where Barthelmess hunches himself up against the alien cold with one foot planted against a wall in a posture suggesting an act of martyrdom with the victim's limb contracted in a spasm of suffering. (A similarly illuminating touch occurs when the Chinaman shoots the brutal step-father and Donald Crisp's dying rictus jerks him into the weaving, ducking posture of the pugilist he once was.) Barthelmess's scenes with Lillian Gish have a poetic reticence – the Oriental's glances of love and compassion are angular ones, like stolen looks. It is a wonderful conception of a character – its inner and outer renderings unite to enrich its significance and compel belief.

*   *   *

But stardom has to be created in the image of the actor – presumed or real. It rarely collects round the image of the character, unless this is one repeated from picture to picture, like Karloff's monster, in which case the character eventually takes over. Barthelmess had sunk his own characteristics untraceably into the Chinaman and, in spite of a variety of parts as a half-breed Mexican, a drunken beach bum and a roving sailor, he had to wait for the hugely popular *Way Down East* to bring out the characteristics henceforth associated with *him* – the good-hearted, uncomplicated, rural American boy whose story combined a tenderly awkward profession of love with the gallant rescue of Lillian Gish from the drifting ice floes.

He quit Griffith and acting on the logic of a film that had brought him stardom in a wholly American image, and in an indigenously American setting, he set up his own production company, with Henry King to direct him, and made *Tol'able David* (1921). The film was an immense success. Incorporating an affection for a rural America that was still a reality to many, and a nostalgic memory to most, it proved the vast, continuing film audience for simpler heroes than the Valentino type who was then in fashion. *Tol'able David*'s very lack of fashion, like the cut of country clothes, was part of his durability: he was built to last. Perhaps the spread of the motor-car and the tarred road ironically assisted the film's widespread appeal by bringing the farming communities out to see it at the small-town cinemas.

From then on, Barthelmess *was* David, the grassroots boy with a cast-iron conscience, a love for his mother and a sense of duty as clearly spelled out as any lesson in McGuffey's *Reader*. Mother worship was a potent feature of *Tol'able David*'s popularity (just as it was an additional quantity in the appeal of the first really popular talkie, *The Jazz Singer,* six years later).* It is the simple

* Both films might figure on the graph suggested by Leslie Fiedler showing the Judaization of American culture: for Tol'able David turns into Jack Rabinowitz of *The Jazz Singer* as surely as Huckleberry Finn becomes Augie March, and rather more quickly. The fact that *Tol'able David* is based on a story by Joseph Hergesheimer, but deals with Christian worry, while Jack Rabinowitz takes on the less Semitic stage name of 'Jack Robin' sets a nice puzzle in ethnic disentanglement.

story of a farm boy trying to prove himself a man and having to save the mail wagon from being robbed after a terrific do-or-die fight before he gets more than a 'tol'able, David, jest tol'able' measure of approval from his fond but firm parent. Barthelmess catches very skilfully the gawky uncertainties of American adolescence – he was 25 at the time – but what makes his performance disturbingly memorable is the amount of worrying that the boy does. David just *has* to be a success in his mother's eyes. Barthelmess's own physique assists the impression powerfully, for his shortish neck keeps David continually bowed down as if by the load on his conscience. The superhuman fight at the end is the timely release of the super ego in action. *Tol'able David* has undertones that make for uneasy viewing: but for the same reason its impact has been better preserved than if it had been simply a rural comedy-drama.

Barthelmess inevitably found himself typed by the part and its principal attributes, innocence and conscience, and as the 1920s lost their own innocence he knew which way he had to move. His roles were variations on the theme of David's sense of duty, or the need to prove oneself, or redeem oneself, or even bear an intol'able burden of guilt like the draft-dodging boxer in *The Patent-Leather Kid* (1926), the squadron commander who sends his flyers to their death in *The Dawn Patrol* (1930), or the pilot in *Only Angels Have Wings* (1939) who once baled out with the only parachute and left his buddy to die – not to mention the sharecropper boy in *The Cabin in the Cotton* (1932) who was all set to improve his lot till he let his conscience doze off one hot Southern afternoon and got seduced by Bette Davis. 'I have become,' Barthelmess said wryly in 1932, 'the screen's champion underdog.' Yet he was remembered for the role that crystallised his star personality, Tol'able David, the all-American boy of a gentler generation.

Parts of David were re-distributed among the screen heroes who succeeded Barthelmess in public favour, though without ever displacing him from public affection. John Gilbert inherited his battling tenacity; James Stewart, his country gaucheness; Henry Fonda, his uncontaminated Americanism; Gary Cooper, his weight of conscience. The hero that Barthelmess represented in David was a boy of manly ways and simple virtues, who took the side of right through instinct and upbringing, who accepted a job determined to stick at it and make good, who looked bashfully at girls but loved the one he set his heart on. There was probably no room in such a characterisation for him ever again to equal the skill with which he had depicted the Chinaman in *Broken Blossoms*. But it touched the nation's unconscious; and the image of stalwart virtue it epitomised hung on to screen heroes long after the innocent America that bred Tol'able David had become part of folk-lore.

CHAPTER SIX

A DIFFICULT
BIRTH:
SENNETT
v. CHAPLIN

Hollywood grew up by a process of accretion. It was never planned as a film capital: it just expanded haphazardly on the outskirts of the small city of Los Angeles as studios, large and small, huddled together for convenience and the profitable sharing of natural advantages like the scenery and industrial facilities like the printing laboratories. The sunlight factor has probably been over emphasised: there are many reports of the day's shooting having to cease prematurely because of Pacific coast fog. Lighting, anyhow, made sunlight unnecessary after, say, 1918, though the fact that studios continued to be built with glass roofs is a tribute to the lotus-eating ambience that California created around its new immigrants. The safety factor has already been referred to – and some recent memoirs have revealed how the handiness of the Mexican border was used not simply to defeat pursuit by the Edison detectives bent on confiscating equipment being used by unlicensed film-makers: one studio as early as 1912 had to rush some of its stars to safety over the border so as to avoid a likely morals charge. Griffith took a Biograph troupe to Los Angeles for the winter of 1910–11 and settled there just over a year later.

The stage tradition that players on tour were paid a consolation allowance for leaving home persisted for a time in film-making. This helped in a small way to make Hollywood popular. But the fashion factor eventually did more: film actors, a notably caste-ridden people, soon considered it 'smart' to voyage far afield and their sense of 'apartness' was ultimately enshrined in actual territorial separation from the legitimate stage and indeed from the rest of America.

The land distance had immense consequences for the film industry. Philip French has acutely analysed how the incessant power tug-of-war between the West Coast, where the studios were, and the East Coast, where the money was, shaped the entire film-making process.* Distance, too, came to be built into the ritual of stardom – at least in the days before air transport was commonplace. The celebrity's descent off the express at Pasadena, or her personal appearances at railroad halts, resembled a royal progress. In a few cases the adulation that the stars encountered *en route* gave them their first taste of the immense popular power they could wield. Distance also had solid advantages for the early film units. It lent enchantment to their often shaky finances. It was convenient and sometimes essential to pay West Coast actors with cheques drawn on East Coast banks. The four or five days it took a cheque to travel overland across the States gave the home office in New York time to fatten the account.

By 1913 there were about sixty studios located on the West Coast as against forty-seven in the East, though to put these figures in perspective it has to be remembered that many of the operations were small, perhaps one-man affairs. A 'studio' was simply a film-making compound akin to the stockaded camps thrown up by the pioneers on the trek west. Nevertheless just because they were small enough to be bossed by a single dominant personality they were fast-working and prolific enough to throw up stars with the energy of the oil gushers beginning to prickle the surrounding hills.

The Keystone Studio, opened by Mack Sennett in 1912, is one of the most celebrated examples of one-man rule – and it is the one that concerns us here. For it was a studio that one man built in his own image to turn out films formed by his own tastes and starring comedians built to his own specifications. In all of which Keystone functioned with incomparable inventiveness and efficiency – until the arrival of a new talent whose creative personality, ways of working and sense of what was comic challenged the boss's at every crank of the camera. Two supremely independent wills met head on when Mack Sennett engaged Charlie

* *The Movie Moguls*, by Philip French (Weidenfeld & Nicolson).

Chaplin. If Griffith represents the unquestioned supremacy of the star-maker over his stars, then Chaplin represents the compulsive revolt of the individual against the system. He was a star formed against the grain of the studio.

*   *   *

Keystone was a comedy compound akin in its concentration of means upon ends to the company towns that mined ore, dug coal or felled lumber. It took its style from its Irish-Canadian boss, Mack Sennett, an ex-actor from Griffith's Biograph days, and a man whose earthy, sardonic, exuberant, cruel and caustic nature seems to have been parcelled out among the comedians he recruited. Sennett's view of his fellow men was generally low – and the particular relationship he had with actors simply confirmed it. His business policy was dictated, like the salaries he paid, by his East Coast bosses who comprised an ex-bookmaker and an ex-streetcar conductor who had boasted that he made one penny for himself out of every five for the transport company.

Where Sennett came into his own was as a creator of comedy who operated from the gut, not the soul. His eye appreciated physical abnormality; and there was more of this around in the days before dietary habits, social change and a new generation literally bred out of existence, or at least ready availability, the idiosyncratic physiques and looks of nineteenth-century American and immigrant stock. The Keystone comedians, from the fat but fast-moving Roscoe Arbuckle to the cross-eyed Ben Turpin and the Moloch-sized Mack Swain, exist in outline with the strength of a cartoonist's broad, heartless nib. Their bodies are made for assault and battery, their defects for mockery and burlesque. The numerous circuses and acrobatic acts in vaudeville were a good training ground: so, it was rumoured, were the public mental asylums.

Only on women as temptingly lovely as Mabel Normand did Sennett rest a softer eye. His book of memoirs, *King of Comedy*,* catches a curious Calibanesque note of pathos when he speaks of

* *King of Comedy*, by Mack Sennett as told to Cameron Shipp (Garden City New York, Doubleday & Co., Inc.).

his unrequited love for Mabel. She occupied the same slightly privileged place in Keystone comedies as she did in Sennett's affections. For some of the comics, working as Mabel's co-star or even under her direction had to be a tactful business. Various actors' memoirs hint that to flirt with Mabel off screen, or to cross her on the set, was a quick way out of Sennett's employment.

His own memoirs are most revealing for a peculiar reason. One can hear him speak through the printed text. The book is described 'as told to Cameron Shipp' – and it is just that. Sennett's technique of improvising his films through initial gag conferences made him an easy, vivid talker. What he said to Mr Shipp was taken down in shorthand and on tape. And although the book was edited for publication, large parts of it retain the rhythm at which Sennett habitually functioned. It is a rhythm that duplicates in many respects the tempo of his comedies. It is vivid, funny, fast and furious – a graphic depiction of the world's madness in accelerated motion.

Speed was indeed the essence of his films. Most of the comedies were built around the idea of a crazy chase; and the Keystone stars' personalities had to be instantly recognisable. This was another advantage of their anatomical oddity: speed in flight simply left no time for interior characterisation. One passage in Sennett's book shows particularly well how the studio style was set by the man himself. Appropriately enough, it describes a chase. Sennett has been caught with a pretty blonde by her jealous lover ('greasy, overdressed and agile': Keystone characteristics of villainy.) The man produces a razor. Sennett grabs a chair. What follows is pure Keystone:

'He lunged. I parried in *seconde*. His blade nicked a rung. As I went back *en garde* he attacked again. I parried in *carte* and made a *riposte* that missed his head by an inch. He came in more cautiously next time, feinted, thrust and slashed in almost one continuous movement. I believe I ran the gamut, parrying from *primo* to *octavo*. Then I threw my weapon at his feet and departed. While the greasy man disentangled himself I went down stairs six at a time. He came close behind, shrilling curses. Now I could have broken that razor duellist into two twisted pieces with my hands. I could have picked him up and put him on a mantelpiece. But the sheen of that razor, wagged by that supple wrist, terrified me. I fled out of the house and up the street, and that angry man came right behind me, shrieking. He pursued me for eight blocks before Canadian stamina won out. As I saw him collapse against a building, I went up an alley and into a bar where I bought a drink and paid ready cash. "To the chair," I toasted. "Now that's a handy tool!" '*

There one has a perfect one-reel Keystone comedy-melodrama, moving at the speed of flight, and equipped with a surefire laughter-getting sub-title for the fade-out: 'To the chair. . . . Now that's a handy tool!' Sennett used his own built-in speedometer to check on the funny side of life. But he also derived his most celebrated screen innovations from the industrial rhythm of the times. The Keystone Cops, the custard pies and the bathing belles duplicate the mass production techniques that were beginning to revolutionise the consumer industries. The numbers and uniformity of cops, pies and girls which make them so funny on sight or impact also make them into products that can be repeated precisely and endlessly once the conveyor belt of the comedy factory had been laid down. If the Keystone comics represent grotesque departures from the norm, the cops, pies and girls are standardised approximations to it. By interacting, they create the distinctive Keystone havoc. But together or apart, they need something else to complete them – and that is an apprehension of the larger human comedy to which they belong.

Sennett may have set the tone at Keystone; but whether or not he was ever really pleased to acknowledge it, and he usually maintained a scoffing disbelief when the notion was put to him, the traditions that he and his comics established in Hollywood soil had seeded themselves from a much more distant time and place. For just as the early cinema reproduced the theatre it sprang from, Sennett's studio re-invented the characteristics of the art form it belonged to, the Italian *commedia dell' arte*. Everything that happened inside the Keystone corral is an extraordinary

* Ibid., pp. 37–8.

example of how a naïve art can be carried like a bacillus and reproduce itself far from its source and period.

*   *   *

For reasons not hard to see, the *commedia dell' arte* was the silent cinema of its day – a day that lasted for most of three centuries in western Europe. Its audiences had no need to know the language of the Campagna di Roma since the playlets they witnessed relied on mime and action.

But the resemblances between the *commedia* and the Keystone styles are more precise than this. Both believed in improvisation: in the beginning, at least, Sennett never used a script. In both the stars caught in any predicament resorted to slapstick. In both the stars developed treasured bits of 'business', *lazzi* in the *commedia* vocabulary, pratfalls, slow burns, double takes and '108s' or backward somersaults in Keystone lingo. In both the stars never took liberties in altering their roles, though they were free to add diverting incongruities. (Since the Keystone comics were living caricatures already, this took some doing and may explain the studio's fondness for burlesquing the box-office hits of other film companies which thus provided familiar characters with ready-made incongruities.)

Players performing as Harlequin, Pantaloon, The Doctor, The Captain, etc., wore masks in the *commedia*. The Keystone comics got the same effect in a more homely way with their own mugs. But masks (or mugs) had one purpose which is true of all stars and especially comic ones. 'People in general,' wrote Pierre Louis Duchartre, author of the classic work on the *commedia dell' arte*, 'prefer the well-known actor in the type of role he has played a thousand times to a new face and personality to which they must grow accustomed. The mask, then, is one of the best and simplest ways of giving an illusion of permanency to a favourite character.'* The Keystone comics' mugs (or masks) also facilitated their capers. Since they were already funny through looks alone – and a well-aimed custard pie became simply an additive to per-

* *The Italian Comedy*, by Pierre Louis Duchartre (Dover Publications, Inc.) p. 41.

sonality – they could concentrate on the plastic acrobatics of their bodies. The ability to 'take a fall' was the first thing Sennett looked for when he went talent spotting. The *commedia* and Keystone troupes not only radiated great energy because each man could devise 'business' that best suited his particular talent, but they also promoted the self-protective kind of unity or group loyalty which comes from each man knowing where his partner was weakest. A Keystone newcomer who did something better than anyone else in the group threatened the existing order almost physically – and the reprisals taken on him by his peers tended to be physical, too, in the shape of painful practical jokes. The latent hostility these contained could be passed off plausibly as the horseplay one would expect in a comedy studio.

One such newcomer was engaged by Sennett in 1913 and the fellow arrived to start work in December of the same year. He was the 24-year-old Charlie Chaplin; and almost from the beginning he unwittingly committed the offence, for such it seemed, of not just being *better* than some of the established comics, but of being *different* from all of them.

That Chaplin came to work at Keystone at all was the result of Sennett's first misconception about him. He was engaged by mistake. Sennett got the man he wanted all right, but then discovered he was not the comedian he had taken him to be. For when Keystone's chief first clapped eyes on Chaplin he was doing a vaudeville sketch called 'A Night in an English Music Hall' (Sennett remembers it as 'a London Music Hall') with Fred Karno's troupe in New York. Chaplin played an aged drunk in a box who got himself mixed up with the show on stage. Due to Chaplin's make-up, Sennett took him to be at least twenty years older than he was. He also took him to be a good man at 'taking a fall', the vital test for a Keystone recruit. (Presumably Chaplin's act included him falling out of the box on to the stage, though neither his own memoirs nor Sennett's explicitly recall this.) Now most of the other Keystone comics were men in their forties and when Sennett had suddenly to look for a replacement for Ford Sterling, his ace comedian who was quitting for more cash elsewhere than Keystone's top rate of 250 dollars a week, Chaplin's apparent age and acrobatic adroitness seemed to qualify him to take Sterling's place. He could not have been hired for worse reasons.

But what were the reasons *Chaplin* had for accepting? The salary of 125 dollars a week, twice his Karno paypacket, was one of them. Yet he later admitted that the movies had held little attraction for him, in particular the Keystone comedies which he found 'a crude deluge of rough and tumble [justified by] a pretty, dark-eyed girl named Mabel Normand who . . . weaved in and out of them.'* Such was his unvoiced view of his future employer. What alone made him agree to work for Keystone was the publicity value: 'A year at that racket and I could return to vaudeville an international star.'†

But the significant part of Chaplin's cynicism is his dislike from the beginning of the Sennett comedies' tempo; and this is not simply due to a partisan affection for Karno as against Keystone. It was part of Chaplin's very metabolism. It went back to the feeling of personal inadequacy which his first contact with American life had given him. 'It was an ordeal to go into a restaurant and order something because of my English accent – *and the fact that I spoke slowly*. So many spoke in a rapid, clipped way that I felt uncomfortable for fear that I might stutter and waste their time. I was alien to this slick tempo.'‡

It was the same 'slick tempo' that was also part of Sennett's metabolism. The two men clashed from the start, though in a wary, reconnoitring way as they scouted each other's field of comedy. Chaplin particularly hated the Keystone 'chase'. His brand of mime required him to move at his own pace. His self-consciousness in the first few weeks at Keystone was acute, though fortunately his suppleness in joint and limb enabled him literally to find his feet while he tried to find his form. This took longer.

*   *   *

Even the physical proportions of his rival comics must have depressed Chaplin. He could hardly have shared the star dressing-

* Charles Chaplin, op. cit., p. 146.
† Ibid.
‡ Ibid., p. 125, italics are the author's.

room with a six-footer like Ford Sterling, or the 285-pound Fatty Arbuckle, without it strengthening his conviction of not belonging. He also had to find a character suitable for the screen, a medium totally new to him, since Sennett had (rightly, one suspects) vetoed Chaplin's stage rig-out, which sometimes included a large red nose, as being meaningless for American filmgoers.

Chaplin's discomfort was increased by his own creative nature. For what his account of these times makes plain is that he is a pragmatist, not a conceptual artist. The significance of something he does, the *artistic* significance, becomes apparent to him only after he has done it, felt its effect on himself and possibly witnessed it on others. It is extraordinary, for example, that he should only have discovered his power of pathos when he saw tears in the eyes of an actress who was watching him on the set. To that instant, he wrote, 'I can trace the first prompting of desire to add another dimension to my films besides that of comedy.'* Again the first feeling he had of complete artistic self-reliance is also traceable to a single specific act that he could recall with perfect clarity fifty years later: 'If nobody made me an offer I would go into business for myself. . . . I remember the exact moment that feeling was born. *I was signing a requisition chit against the studio wall.*'†

Chaplin is the kind of artist who uses his physical senses to investigate himself and invent his art. His imagination is set racing by a sudden glimpse of himself, almost as if an *alter ego* had split off without a second's notice and permitted the owner to get his bearings on himself. The self-realisation that first occurs when a film actor sees himself on the screen is coupled with just such an alienating jolt to the possessor of the image up there in the darkness behaving independently and living a surrogate existence. When Chaplin first saw his image on a screen at Keystone he was, according to Chester Conklin, 'all bowled over. "It cawn't be me. Is that possible? How extr'ordinary. Is it really me?" he said.'‡ But once he had undergone the shock of recog-

* Ibid., p. 164.
† Ibid., p. 170, italics are the author's.
‡ Mack Sennett, op. cit., p. 153.

nition it was like an induction coil plunged into his artistic consciousness. And when he took full command of his comedies a few years later he developed, to an obsessive degree, the technique of having himself filmed while endlessly rehearsing and elaborating often minor pieces of mime. (Today's instant replay would have been a great gift to him then.) One guesses that at the moment he first saw himself on the viewing-room screen at Keystone the publicity value he had initially seen in the movies was superseded by a personality awareness that was far more mysterious and exciting than he had ever conceived.

Inanimate objects also helped Chaplin make 'contact' with himself as an artist. This may be partly a legacy from working alongside jugglers and acrobats in the English music-hall and developing something of their sensory proficiency. Perfect control of plates, balls or billiard cues is, after all, one way of asserting one's 'self'. Chaplin's way was more complex. Instead of apparently charging the inanimate objects with energy, he transformed their very personalities. What he extended to them during the comic metamorphosis they underwent in his hands came from the increasing sense of knowing himself which they facilitated.

Laughter is said to derive from the disruption of expectations: Chaplinesque comedy certainly derives from the disruption of function. Even as a child, playing inside a cat's skin in *Cinderella*, at the London Hippodrome, he had experienced the power of this when he substituted canine characteristics for his feline ones: 'After smelling the dog, I smelt the proscenium, then I lifted my leg. The audience roared – possibly because the gesture was uncatlike.'* The same source of inspiration produced the marvellous 'metamorphosis' gags in the later Chaplin films, like the alarm clock in *The Pawnbroker* (1916) on which he performs an appendectomy, or the stewed boots in *The Gold Rush* (1925) which assume the properties of spaghetti and fish.

Such extraordinary faculties were latent in Chaplin when he arrived at Keystone. They might have remained that way in the unsympathetic ambience. Some of the comics were merely sceptical that this little Englishman could teach them anything.

* Charles Chaplin, op. cit., p. 40.

Others like Henry Lehrman, who directed Chaplin's first film, *Making a Living* (1914), were actively hostile. Lehrman deliberately cut the film in the editing so as to sabotage every gag of Chaplin's. (Lehrman was to follow Ford Sterling from Keystone, as his director for another company, which may have been another reason for showing Sterling's replacement to bad advantage.)

Plainly Chaplin needed some sympathetic refuge – and he found it in the distinctive costume of the Tramp. It is hard to imagine a more appropriate disguise than this costume which instantly shielded Chaplin from the professional scepticism around him and ultimately became an expression of the world's larger adversity. Every item of the Tramp's wardrobe came off the back or out of the closet of some other Keystone comic. The baggy pants were Fatty Arbuckle's, the shabby-genteel cutaway coat was Charlie Avery's, the bowler hat belonged to Arbuckle's father-in-law, and the boots were Ford Sterling's – thus Chaplin stepped literally into the shoes of the comic he had been hired to replace. He added the tiny moustache – it was actually larger to begin with – as a gesture to Mack Sennett's worry about his not looking old enough. The springy walking cane was the antenna of a comic genius whose inspiration was stimulated by touch and who knew the value of extending his reach. Borrowing bits and pieces from other actors was of course commonplace in studios like Keystone; but given the circumstances of Chaplin's arrival, and his own ultra-sensitive nature, it seems probable that such sympathetic borrowings from his colleagues may have had the unconscious aim of neutralising their antipathies. One thing is sure: no sooner were they on his back than he had a new identity.

Out of contact with the inanimate items of wardrobe, Chaplin drew his inspiration. It came all at once, complete and detailed. Where before there had been an artistic blank, there was now an individual identity, a character history, even a *curriculum vitae*. It was Chaplin speaking, but speaking about someone else. 'The moment I was dressed, the clothes and the make-up made me feel the person he was. I began to know him, and by the time I walked on to the stage he was fully born. When I confronted Sennett, I assumed the character. . . . I began to explain [him]. "You know this fellow is many-sided, a tramp, a gentleman, a poet, a dreamer, a lonely fellow, always hopeful of romance and adventure. He would have you believe he is a scientist, a musician, a duke, a polo-player. However, he is not above picking up a cigarette-butt or robbing a baby of its candy. And, of course, if the occasion warrants it, he will kick a lady in the rear – but only in extreme anger.'*

*   *   *

The first film in which the Tramp met his public was *Kid Auto Races at Venice* (1914) into which he packed an enormous amount of anarchy by obstructing the police and getting in the way of drivers in a children's car race in the Californian coast resort of Venice. Astonishingly, Chaplin's memoirs make absolutely no mention of the film. The reason may be because it was again directed by his 'enemy', Henry Lehrman. In any case the Tramp's cavorting is brief and crude and, apart from his funny waddling walk, Chaplin evidently found no great inspiration in the race-track location. The film was not long enough to develop a story, such as that in *Gentlemen of Nerve* which he made in October, 1914, and a mime could not do much with a speeding racing car except take a fall.

Chaplin himself probably dates the Tramp's 'birth' on a film set from *Mabel's Strange Predicament* (1914), a film starring Mabel Normand which was about to be shot at the very moment he invented his character. 'All right,' said Sennett, when Chaplin had finished his introductory spiel about his new character, 'get out on the set and see what you can do.' Had the cameras been turning when Chaplin did a characteristic funny scene, getting mixed up with hotel guests, raising his bowler to the ladies and falling over the spitoon, this film would have had the distinction of incorporating the first appearance of the Tramp and in a much more inventive mood than in *Kid Auto Races at Venice*. Chaplin's memoirs in fact leave it uncertain whether or not the act he improvised there and then on the set of *Mabel's Strange Predicament*

* Ibid., p. 154.

was being filmed. He simply states that the scene ran to seventy-five feet, instead of the usual ten feet, which could lead one to assume that a kind of extended 'screen test' was being made for the new character. Sennett's memoirs do not quite clear up the point. 'Chaplin,' he told him, 'you do exactly what you're doing now in your next picture. Remember to do it in that get-up.'

The 'next picture' was *Kid Auto Races at Venice*, which was released two days before *Mabel's Strange Predicament*, on 7th February, but which could easily have been shot after the latter picture since it was half the length and could be done in one afternoon at the races. This is perhaps a point of interest only to historians; but it is worth referring to since it exemplifies the confusion that often surrounds quite factual matters throughout the cinema's history. One is indebted to Kevin Brownlow for clearing the matter up by publishing an interview with Chester Conklin who refers to Chaplin doing his Tramp routine on the set on *Mabel's Strange Predicament* and then adds, 'Sennett stood back of the crowd and watched. Finally, he went up to Charlie and said, "Listen, do what you've been doing *when we shoot the picture* with Mabel and Chester." Well, of course, it wound up that he stole the picture from us.'* Regretfully, then, one has to acknowledge the right of *Kid Auto Races at Venice* to be regarded as the first appearance of the Tramp in a film.

Chaplin has never mentioned going to see it in a cinema; but he does give an account of watching the Tramp's antics in *Mabel's Strange Predicament*, all seventy-five feet of them and for the first time not cut to pieces as in Lehrman's films with him. Chaplin found that the cinema audience received his amusing business in the hotel lobby in cold silence and only began laughing at him towards the end. This uncomfortable lesson taught him the importance of giving people a face and personality they were used to seeing – the very same point made by Duchartre in his remarks on the *commedia*'s use of masks. Chaplin's previous stint in the music hall had accustomed him to playing a variety of parts; his

* *The Parade's Gone By* by Kevin Brownlow (Knopf), p. 498. Italics are the author's.

brief film experience convinced him that henceforth he must play essentially one part. Everything seemed to strengthen the Tramp's welcome.

But there were still formidable difficulties. To begin with, he had to slow down Keystone's typically hotfoot pace. The camera had to wait upon Chaplin. And the editing of the films had to take its cue not from the length of exposed film stock, but from the Tramp's inward thoughts and fancies as outwardly manifested in the delicate hints of Chaplin's mime.

The Tramp's character development was even trickier. Chaplin's pragmatic way of working meant he could only take new artistic bearings after experimenting – and his scope to experiment was limited. Keystone had hired him to replace Ford Sterling, which often meant playing the 'heavy' in the comedies, as an aggressive ladies man, an undesired suitor, a lodger who flirts with the proprietor's wife, a nob who forces himself on the maid, a jealous rival in love, a villainous sporting type, a trouble-making boxing referee and, on any possible occasion, a gent who is too fond of the bottle. His vices were the ones that Keystone tradition sanctioned: adultery, intemperance, venality and cruelty. Chaplin was being forced even in the stories he made up for the films he directed to view life as Mack Sennett saw it – a world in which it paid to be dour, suspicious, belligerent, lustful and quite ready to strike the first blow.

But Chaplin had some formidable compensations. One was the speed at which his fame spread. He did not have to wait around to be recognised – he was spotted from the start. After his very first film *The Moving Picture World* hailed him as 'a comedian . . . who acts like one of Nature's naturals'. After he had been only five or six times on the screen in as many weeks, and in parts that hardly lasted as many minutes, the film trade papers were full of references to 'the sensation of the year', 'one of the most popular comedians in the world', 'an entirely new variety of screen clown'.

This last remark is the significant one. As well as a 'natural,' Chaplin was an 'original'. Americans had seen nothing like him on the screen before. His Tramp was not the American hobo, nor was he the English gent: but he was suspended between the two in a way that was to give him immense mobility between a variety of social roles without sacrificing human characteristics which remained basically the same from part to part. And as well as being funny in a new cinematic way, outstandingly so against the Keystone tradition and comedy tempo, his physicality was extraordinarily vivid. His personality formed around him with amazing definition the moment his body went into motion.

Yet although Sennett knew Chaplin was a novelty, he did not yet know he was box-office. The 3,000 miles between the West Coast studios and the East Coast accountants meant that the star's commercial value was first apparent to people who had nothing directly to do with film-making. Chaplin was about to be fired by Sennett for being unwilling to 'take direction' – actually for being unwilling to take Mabel Normand's direction – when the order arrived from New York to turn out more Chaplin pictures as fast as possible.

Chaplin made thirty-five films in his first year at Keystone. When the Essanay Studio offered him 1,250 dollars a week at the time his contract expired with Sennett, he waited for a counter-bid and when it did not come, he left and went to work at Essanay as star and director of his own films. (He had directed about twenty of his Keystone pictures.) Why Keystone let him go is still a mystery. Chaplin gave the simplest explanation when he said that Sennett could not pay him enough – but this in turn needs some explaining. The likeliest reason is that the money men in New York realised that if they paid Chaplin his market value – which was huge – they would be inflating every comic's salary at Keystone and establishing a star system in what was still in many ways a stock-company one.

One sees now that this was incredibly short-sighted of them. But at this time, 1914, the Keystone executives' way of doing business took no account of star appeal but was based on the old notion of selling film prints at so much a foot, usually ten cents, no matter which of the comics was in the film. They did put up their asking price by an extra cent, which would have allowed them to meet Chaplin's price had they wished, or at least pay him more than he was getting, and when the distributors refused to pay the increase they let him go. As Terry Ramsaye said, they were businessmen, but not showmen.

* * *

It is harder to guess at what Sennett's feelings were over the loss of Chaplin. Confidence had made Chaplin stubborn. Directing himself in Keystone pictures had reinforced the sense he had of being different from the other comics. He had tasted the heady power of pathos, an emotion that no one before had ever any call for at this studio. He had begun to scale down the Tramp's caricature vices into credible traits of personality. Poetry and humour, both motivated by the mime that metamorphosed the nature of inanimate objects, had begun taking over the Tramp like some benign spirit and flashing out at moments in the comedies – like that in *Twenty Minutes of Love* (1914) when he relieves his amorous frustrations by tenderly embracing a tree, or in *His Prehistoric Past* (1914) when he plucks some hair off his bear's skin and stuffs it into his Stone Age pipe. Sennett must have realised that here was a nature that could not be corralled in Keystone without growing fractious and rebellious.

It is likely also that with Chaplin's self-awareness growing apace, the clown got into the need of explaining himself and what he was after to a man temperamentally unsympathetic – as his memoirs show – to looking for weighty psychology in such comic standbys as a funny walk or a kick in the rear. High on his list of comic priorities for keeping in business Sennett put 'the downfall of pretension'; and he may have sensed just enough 'pretension' in Chaplin's search for self-expression to resent it or consider it a bad risk at the box-office. He later remarked sarcastically that 'giving an actor, any actor, world-wide fame is like hanging a Ph.D. on him'. It was hardly necessary to identify whom he had in mind.

The compulsion Chaplin felt to explore himself by directing the Tramp – 'the two overlap, yet neither contains the other', as Isabel Quigly accurately remarks* – can best be judged from his dismissive remark about *Tillie's Punctured Romance* (1914). It was

* *Charlie Chaplin, Early Comedies*, by Isabel Quigly (Studio Vista/Dutton).

almost his last Keystone picture. It was made in six reels and has considerable importance as the first American feature comedy. It was a tremendous hit and, according to Sennett, was the film that really made other producers run after Chaplin with contracts. But Sennett, not Chaplin, directed it. And Chaplin appeared in it not as Charlie the Tramp, but as a heartless city slicker who fleeces a girl out of her savings. 'It was pleasant working with Marie [Dressler],' says Chaplin in his autobiography, 'but I did not think the picture had much merit. I was more than happy to get back to directing myself.'*

In this curt dismissal one sees the change in Chaplin since the marvellous moment when the Tramp had crystallised in his consciousness. From being a physical performer making muscles, joints and limbs do the work for him through inventive mime, he had become a mental and moral philosopher whose most compelling study was himself. He must henceforth protect his autonomy. In short he had evolved beyond the resources and, to a great extent, the sympathies of Mack Sennett.

In this respect he is an odd, inexplicable recapitulation of the character he most closely resembles in the *commedia dell' arte* tradition. For Harlequin, too, started off as the youngest member of the family whose acting, as one critic put it, 'was nothing but a continual play of extravagant tricks, violent movements, and outrageous rogueries . . . at once insolent, mocking, inept, clownish and exceptionally ribald. . . . I believe that he was exceptionally agile . . . and I might confidently add that he was a proficient tumbler.' But Harlequin's individuality asserted itself as those who played him discovered his *esprit:* a process that sitting back, watching oneself on the screen and directing oneself on the set must have speeded up in Chaplin and thus compressed centuries of received tradition into months of visual invention.

The result in each case was so extraordinarily similar that one can best sum up the genesis of Chaplin's stardom among the Keystone comics by simply quoting a note on his earlier ancestor: 'Although his companions were types drawn from society in general and subsequently standardised, the subtle and foolish

* Charles Chaplin, op. cit., p. 168.

Arlechino . . . seems a strange personification of the fancy. He embodies a whole gamut of the imagination, now delicate, now offensive, comic or melancholy, sometimes lashed into a frenzy of madness . . . the unwitting and unrecognised creator of a new form of poetry.'* For Chaplin, of course, strike out the word 'unrecognised'.

* Duchartre, op. cit., pp. 133–4.

CHAPTER SEVEN

JOY THROUGH STRENGTH: DOUGLAS FAIRBANKS SR.

The world for Douglas Fairbanks Sr was not a stage, it was a gym. It was a God-given environment for a fellow's setting-up exercises. Hollywood may have seemed so alluring to him in the winter of 1915 when he was a Broadway actor, and known as a decent, reliable, good-natured type of guy, simply because California was an ideal place to lead an outdoor life. What had the movies to offer compared with the sun for most of the year and a swim every day of the year? Well, a friend pointed out tentatively, they had 104,000 dollars a year to offer him for acting in them. 'Yes,' replied Fairbanks, 'but the movies . . .!' He went to Hollywood in the spring of that year with a stage actor's typical disdain for the film industry.

Possibly he also looked on the movies as a slightly shameful way for a man, a real man that is, to make a living. If so, he was the forerunner of later stars, also reared in a rough, male world, natural Jack Londons who had learnt to rough it and like it in a string of jobs or trades, and for whom posing for a camera was akin to taking a scoop out of a jar of skin cream. Not a manly act. Their response was apt to be one of calculated cynicism or contempt in case the grips caught them acting, *really acting*, at some off-moment in a scene; or else an extreme and costly (to others) aptitude for making trouble throughout the picture; or perhaps even a penchant for masochistic roles in which they found fulfilment through suffering and growled a refusal when the services of a stand-in were tendered.

But Doug Fairbanks, like the age he lived in, was altogether simpler. Doug conquered acting through virility. In fact he threw acting away as if it were a rather cissified preoccupation and instead let the parts of him that were above suspicion, his muscles and his physique, do the work for him. Only of course, as Doug did it, it did not look at all like work. In that lay his early charm and instantaneous popularity. In some ways he was more of a conjuror than an acrobat, for Doug's tricks produced surprise without exertion. He began with the stuff of ordinary athletics and ended with the feats of a *chanson de geste*. In that perhaps lay his later folly and the thing that makes us retrospectively mistrust him. Around all this exertion he accumulated a philosophy which was conceived as a way of looking at the absurdities of life and manners but somehow evolved into being propaganda for the kind of life that Doug himself revered. The strenuous life. In that lay his greatest self-deception and maybe even a measure of his own mortality.

Fairbanks was born into a middle-class family. His father was a lawyer. This fairly comfortable background, as David Robinson has noted,* distinguished him from most other Hollywood actors of the time. Even more important, he was an urban type who was thoroughly at home in the city. He had been to Harvard (for three months anyhow) and had tried the Stock Exchange (for hardly longer) and the hardwear business; and despite some time spent bumming around Europe with three football players who had crossed with him on the same cattle boat, these middle-class city characteristics stuck to him so that the neat, natty clothes, the double-breasted suit and waistcoat and Homburg he wears in many of his early films suggest the fast-moving, confident, optimistic, city go-getter – a sort of Rotarian on springs.

His youthful inability to apply himself to anything was no handicap when he drifted into stage acting – perhaps the reverse. His restiveness came over the footlights as a mood that buoyed up the part and on occasion even the play, though Kenneth Macgowan recorded that 'when I saw him on the stage, I was annoyed by his bouncing breeziness. His exuberance seemed overbearing . . .'.† It was this infectiousness, not any athletic

---

* *Hollywood in the Twenties*, by David Robinson (Zwemmer/Barnes).
† Kenneth Macgowan, op. cit., p. 192.

stunts he did, which persuaded Henry Aitken to sign him to a Hollywood contract. Aitken was president of the Triangle Film Corporation which had been formed in mid-1915 to weld the talents of Mack Sennett, D. W. Griffith and Thomas Ince into one company that could, in theory, supply a twice-weekly change of programme throughout the year to all exhibitors signing up with it.

Griffith took against Fairbanks from the start. Not surprisingly. For Fairbanks could not 'act' as Griffith understood the term and he could not slow himself down to Griffith's tempo. Even in those early days, an acquaintance noted, 'enthusiasm swings out from him, whirling ideas as on a pin wheel. So excited is his speech that the words are flying out in the irregular rhythm of a woman beating a rug.'* Griffith wanted performers he could modulate, not manics like Doug. He suggested Sennett might find a place for him among his comics.

*   *   *

Instead it was a Triangle director, John Emerson, who took a chance on the 31-year-old Fairbanks, mainly because he felt he might be able to put over the somewhat sophisticated satire of the young scenarist Anita Loos whose ideas looked good on paper and read amusingly in wittily pointed sub-titles, but needed an interpreter to carry them visually into action on the screen. To Anita Loos's talent for social satire Doug owed his development in the extremely unlikely role of a social satirist. Of course like any healthy extrovert of the era he had been 'against bunk' from the start.

Miss Loos added a vast range of other things for him to be against. Miss Loos had a disturbing gift for this. Her autobiography, *A Girl Like I*, written many years later, reads like a merciless autopsy of the period. Each personality's weakness, vanity or physical shortcoming is recorded wittily but just a shade too appreciatively – like a palmist relishing a catastrophe she has spotted in some client's line of fate. But her attacks on the fads and affections of American life at the time she became Doug's

* Allene Talmey, op. cit., p. 301.

mentor and began to write his screenplays have an unvindictive vigour.

The subjects that both of them treated are astonishingly varied: the new rich, Coué-ism, vegetarian addicts (after eating at home on 'greens', Doug slopes off to the diner for a steak), the craze for getting publicity (getting his picture in the papers is the new American boy's way of proving himself), Anglophilia, the mania for success (inventing the two-hump hat-pin qualifies Doug to marry the daughter of the man who made his millions out of the one-hump hat-pin), hemanship out west contrasted with eastern effeteness, the power of positive thinking (exemplified by a villain who puts the hex on Doug by negative thinking), hypochondriacs, and the petty snobberies of America's aristocracy of trade (a 'beer baronness' is snubbed by her haughty sisters with the rebuke, 'Madam, *we're* distillers').

Fairbanks was extremely fortunate in finding Anita Loos to take care of the social satire while he took care of the physical gags. Their films together gave him a topical relevance that he might not have found in conventional adventures, however high he leaped. They identified him very closely with popular feeling at a time which Alistair Cooke has called 'a difficult [one] in American history, when the U.S. was keeping a precarious neutrality in the European war ... Douglas Fairbanks appeared to know all the answers and know them without pretending to be anything more than "an all-round chap, just a regular American".'* He was consequently able 'to leave his admirers with the feeling that they were manfully facing the times rather than escaping from them'.

But Fairbanks the national idol only emerged after Doug the natural athlete had captivated audiences; not long after, though, since he turned out a film every six to eight weeks in these early years and by 1917 was famous enough to have a mountain peak named after him.

The fame of the later costume spectacles has largely eclipsed the attractive freshness of these early comedies. This is a matter

* *Douglas Fairbanks: The Making of a Screen Character*, by Alistair Cooke (Museum of Modern Art Film Library Series, No. 2) p. 16.

for great regret. For filmgoers who only know Doug from clips of *The Black Pirate* (1926), *Robin Hood* (1922) or *The Thief of Bagdad* (1924) certainly do not know the altogether more winning qualities that made him enjoyed, admired and emulated in the pre-1920 period. His face without its familiar moustache looks squarer, but more boyish and less beefy. His movements are suppler than they appear in the over-trained physique of the later years. Above all the fact that he performs acrobatics on the commonplace objects of daily life and does not need a ninety-foot castle wall, a galleon's rigging or an 'Arabian Nights' staircase to flex his muscles only makes his simpler tricks that much more winning. They can be related to the experience of ordinary – i.e. non-Olympic – members of the human race.

The braggadocio is absent from this young Doug. He does the jumping, vaulting and climbing almost absent-mindedly – not with the 'look at me' flamboyance of the later movies. He uses gymnastics to describe the comic disproportion between an end and a means, a threat and a response. Where ordinary folk might simply cross the street to avoid an unlucky black cat, Doug takes the vertical way of eluding fate – up a drainpipe, still in his city suit and black homburg, and then, with one twist over the balcony, safe into the office. At his best he has the ease of a skier: his velocity annihilates the cautious pauses of more pedestrian travel.

His grace is surprisingly demonstrated in the nightmare sequence in *When the Clouds Roll By* (1919) where he is chased by the food he has eaten at dinner and in slow motion hardly seems to touch the ground. He knows how to enhance a joke by refusing to admit to its existence. Determined to get married in *The Matrimaniac* (1916) he escapes from those pursuing him out of a top-floor window, tightrope-walks along a double line of telegraph wires up to the linesman at the top of the post, asks to be plugged in to the jail where his *fiancée* and a clergyman are being held and, once he has been put through, bellows down to the earthbound mortals snapping around the base of the post as he squats aloft amid the wires, 'Quiet down there, I'm getting married by proxy.'

The motto Doug acts on always seems to be, 'Never go round an obstacle if you can jump over it'. His usual way of sitting down on a chair or park bench is by doing a standing jump over the back of it, often while immersed in a book or a newspaper. The apparent effortlessness of this confers on him total power over the things in his environment. This was a great part of Doug's star image. He expresses his exuberance through things. And unlike Harold Lloyd and other comedians, he is offered no resistance. Things are 'for' Doug, not 'against' him. Overcome by his confidence in his physical prowess, inanimate objects suspend their traditional malevolence. Thus the early Doug is often seen at his best in small actions. One applauds the timing of the big set-piece, such as Doug swinging off and on to a succession of moving vehicles in *American Aristocracy* (1916), just catching each one at the last possible split-second. But one admires even more Doug climbing a fence in the same film. He seems to switch off the power of gravity: a second later, Al Parker, as the villain, makes heavy work of the same manoeuvre.

At such moments Doug's demonstration of grace approaches the quality of a moral ideal. It is true that such a hero's life is a continuous obstacle race and 'Do It the Hard Way' ought to have been one of the hortatory slogans which he later became so fond of punching over to the youth of America. But when Doug does it, it never looks hard. His physical feats in the early comedies are all within the competence of the common man or at least his son, the common boy, provided he has trained himself to the same pitch as Doug.

*　　*　　*

It is true that in some of these films there are ominous signs of the unbridled extrovert to come. It is especially noticeable, and unlikeable, when Doug limbers up on people, not things. In *Manhattan Madness* (1916), fresh from the west, he floors all the namby-pamby easterners in his New York club by the force of his back-slapping welcome. Servants are particularly exposed. One's sense of discomfort is increased by the sight of Doug inflicting his exuberance on those in no position to hit back as he makes the butler in *Wild and Woolly* (1917) caper about while the young master fires six-guns at his toes, or does chin-ups in *American Aristocracy* while his valet is trying to tie his cravat and ends by winding his legs round the man in an excess of prehensile pep.

Fairbanks in such moments uses people as if they were things – his he-man is closely related to the bully. It is no surprise that he had a fondness for practical jokes that often discomforted visitors to Pickfair. The jape was enhanced if it involved some contest of strength. A favourite one was seeing who could stay under water longest in the Pickfair pool, and many a visitor seeing Doug and his pugilist cronies lying supine on the bottom of the pool must have imagined a multiple disaster.

It is hard to say precisely when Doug began caricaturing features of himself rather than satirising aspects of society. But by the time of his marriage to Mary Pickford, in 1920, he was well set up as a virility symbol and apostle of physical fitness. His private life was just as strenuous, and as strenuously publicised, as his screen career. 'Doug knocks off work at 5 p.m.,' it was reported in 1919, 'then starts his training schedule, wrestling with Bull Montana, boxing three rounds with Spike Robinson, running a mile in 6 mins. 15 secs., followed by a dip in the pool.'

The fact that the Pickford-Fairbanks marriage involved their both going through the hazards of a double divorce, yet left their careers intact in public affection, proves how iron-clad were their respective screen images of decency and sweetness. Doug was valuable to the Hollywood Establishment at a time when morals, off screen and on, were under attack. He was such an obvious Good Influence. (Walt Disney served the same purpose in the subsequent decades.) It was 'safe' for visiting Royalty and lesser V.I.P.s to pay official calls on Doug and Mary whose clean, popular and profitable entertainments burnished the industry's image. Doug's gymnasium on the United Artists lot was the Disneyland of its day. The various majesties and highnesses who made diplomatic visits there to show they were in touch with the American people found a host who was himself treated like royalty when he went abroad. Doug's cronies were like a court circle starring with him in his film stunts and generally keeping the adrenalin flowing through him. Doug did not drink or smoke and he preached such abstinence in his pep talks. He associated himself strenuously – how else? – with the cause of youth, once he had been given the notion by flattering newspaper editorials and the awards of civic bodies.

Not that his sincerity need be doubted. Doug had a lot of the evangelist in his make-up and his films show an increasingly heavy strain of moral didacticism as he took to supervising every aspect of them. Alistair Cooke has noted how Fairbanks used 'the West', the great outdoors, as 'a source of natural virtue . . . a perfect formula for throwing off little satires which turned, under the impact of the West, into energetic sermons.'* But even city-bound comedies have their share of sermonising. It is quite Griffith-like when the hero's fantasy presents him at a black moment in *When the Clouds Roll By* with a little morality tableau accompanied by the subtitle 'Out of Despair spring Worry and Jealousy, the arch-enemies of Reason.' It works like a tonic on Doug. Wise counsels are tucked into the costume spectacles like Rotary pins on a doublet. Apart from the twinkling stars at the end of *The Thief of Bagdad* which remind us that 'Happiness Must Be Earned,' *Don Q, Son of Zorro* (1925) promises that 'Truth crushed to earth will rise again' and adds for the benefit of the generation that was still brought up on home-baking, 'if you have the yeast to make it rise.' *Whistle and Hoe – Sing As We Go!* was the typical title of one of several books that Fairbanks wrote (or had ghosted) to add to his reputation as a homespun Socrates and cheer-leader of the nation. And when Hollywood's top stars took part in a coast-to-coast radio hook-up at the end of the 1920s, mainly to prove the suitability of their voices for the talkies by saying things highly characteristic of themselves, Doug knew what was expected of him. He announced that he would address – 'the youth of America'.

*   *   *

Public identification of himself with Good Causes naturally amplified his stardom. It also provided an outlet for emotions and ambitions that had outgrown the early comedy satires. The

* Ibid., p. 19.

profits these films had made and the celebrity they had brought him convinced Doug – as Chaplin and Mary Pickford had been convinced – that in order to safeguard himself from being exploited and to re-direct the profits into his own pockets he needed to be his own producer. This power he obtained when he, Chaplin, Mary Pickford and D. W. Griffith formed United Artists, their own production-distribution company, in 1919.

On a man of Fairbanks's nature, who saw life in terms of physical exertions and records to be broken, the effects of the move were not long in showing themselves. He finished *The Mollycoddle* (1920), a typical comedy about a Riviera ne'er-do-well regenerated by a spell in the American west, and said goodbye to the contemporary world in his films. It had become too small to hold him. He needed a wider stage and larger gestures and he found them in films that were costume spectacles of ever-increasing cost and magnificence. Hollywood was just then about to embark on an unprecedented spending spree as one company after another went in for super-productions. But Doug's blockbusters are peculiarly related to Doug's vision of himself. He gradually fell victim to an affliction that could be called elephantiasis of the creative spirit – the curse of unrestrained bigness. Richard Schickel, writing of the first fine careless rapture that his early films had so effortlessly achieved, said: 'If . . . the basic concern of Americans is not with end product, but with process, then it was at the moment of these improvisations that Fairbanks achieved greatness in our eyes.'* This is a shrewd distinction. For what condemns most of the costume spectacles that Doug's company proceeded to make is their over-elaborateness as end products.

The armies of period historians, costume designers, special effects men and art directors whom Doug recruited, some of them even imported from Europe to guarantee the authenticity of their workmanship, do not support their leader so much as swamp him. He is submerged by detail, dwarfed by production values. He built the biggest castle set in Hollywood for *Robin Hood* and at

* *The Stars*, by Richard Schickel and Allen Hurlburt (Bonanza Books) p. 36.

first sight it looks impressive, especially the castle hall with its staircase spiralling up a colossal pillar like the track of a giant snail. But then he only uses it for a couple of memorable bits of acrobatic hyperbole: Doug leaping for the rising drawbridge and swinging up into the sky with it, or the famous moment when he slides down a fold in the wall tapestry by means of a hidden delivery chute. But these *are moments* in an over-decorated bore of a film that makes a slow tour of the Middle Ages replete with didactic titles, pompous pageantry and fustian dialogue titles. Where once he danced on air, Doug now stands on ceremony. One gratefully clutches at the unintentionally 'camp' spectacle of the Merry Men behaving, well, 'merrily' as if Isadora Duncan were their leader. For all its fairy-tale sets, and despite some patently faked magic effects, *The Thief of Bagdad* is glum evidence of how Doug's overweening pursuit of 'art' simply improved the scenery into magnificence and dwindled himself into insignificance. The moral uplift that used to come so joyously out of the pep and dash of the early films now has to be spelled out literally in the sky-writing of the final starry maxim.

The Black Pirate (1926) is probably an exception. This is partly because the scenery is mostly afloat, in the shape of superbly designed Spanish galleons, and thus at least moves; and partly because Doug's fiery exuberance is bottled explosively into the cramped deck space, companion-ways and cabins. And the same film also contains two of Doug's finest stunts. In the first he climbs to the mast top and then, digging his dagger into the centre of the huge sail, slides down the canvas as the blade cleaves it in two – obviously the dagger had an invisible counterweight to balance his body, but the effect is a beautiful blend of grace and cheek. The other occurs as Doug is being hauled vertically up the side of the ship by his men as if he were on a human elevator while the camera, which probably *was* on an elevator, duplicates the hydraulic zest of the movement exactly.

It must be admitted that such jaundiced views of these spectacles were not shared by Doug's mass following. They vastly enhanced his popularity. Everything was on a rising tide of super-abundance and Fairbanks caught the tide in masterful fashion.

Robin Hood cost, it was said, 900,000 dollars and by the time publicity and other costs had been added to the budget of *The Thief of Bagdad* it was a 2,000,000 dollars production. But both made millions. Moreover they were films without moral reproach, as Bosley Crowther has noted (though his sharp eye did catch Doug's penis 'outcropping' his silken pantaloons in *The Thief of Bagdad*) and for maintaining this oasis of reliable purity amidst the 'roaring twenties' he got the vote of millions of filmgoers and their families.

But one has to judge Fairbanks as an artist as well as a 'good example' – and he is terribly vulnerable. It is even painful to see the unconscious athlete taking second place to a self-conscious narcissist, for this diminishes him spiritually. It is the difference between an acrobat and a muscle-builder. Fairbanks always betrayed the acrobat's impatience never to stand still, but by the time he made one of his late films, *The Gaucho* (1928), he had contracted the show-off's impulse to do anything. Though intended as a burlesque of its bandit hero's operatic ways, Doug's bits of braggadocio do not cut smoothly into this intention except in a few surprise gags like the one where he appears to run fifteen feet up the parabola of a palm tree before needing to use his hands to assist his ascent. But throughout the film he continually picks a fight with objects which he once made into allies, so that every time he lights up he fights a duel with the match, subdues the cigarette before putting it between his lips and then has to reach round the back of his neck when removing the cigarette to exhale and put a wrestler's lock on it.

*   *   *

Mary Pickford appears briefly in *The Gaucho* as a Divine Vision with a penny sparkler throwing a halo effect around her. (She performed for nothing, lest it be thought she played bit parts for money.) The only other time she and Doug appeared together in a film was *The Taming of the Shrew* (1928), a movie made when their marriage was breaking up and during which, as Mary Pickford tells it, Fairbanks was surly towards her and un-cooperative in doing retakes in which the camera favoured her. Yet their per-

formances as Petruchio and Katharine show few signs of having
suffered because of this off-camera mismating.

Fairbanks in fact makes an excellent shrew-tamer – the discipline of having to speak Shakespeare, for it was his first talkie, has
tamed *him* to some degree. And if he sweeps a woman bodily off
her feet there is now a dramatic reason for it that goes well beyond the caveman exhibitionism of a similar habit in *The Gaucho*.
But Fairbanks was 45 when the film came out and encroaching
age was proving an embittering experience for a man who had
invested so heavily in youth. The economic realities of the
American Depression took the steam-kettle whistling off his lips
and cost him the converts he had made for the strenuous life while
the Stock Market was rising. The later Doug used to speak sourly
of American boyhood going to the bad.

His own dedication to physical fitness even played Doug an
unfair trick in the end if Anita Loos's account of his approaching
death is to be believed. For it was certainly a monstrous irony
that Doug should over-exercise himself to the point where the
circulation of his body was being impeded. He died in 1939
largely, it would appear, from being muscle-bound. He had been
the dashing embodiment in his time of a very American ideal that
found immense favour and brought him spectacular stardom; but
in the end his body betrayed him, subverting him almost from
within. He had stopped making pictures five years earlier. But
earlier still an event had taken place which symbolised the end of
his reign – indeed the end of a movie era.

The old gymnasium on the United Artists lot where he had
held court over the years was dismantled and turned into a more
democratic establishment altogether – a dressing-room for extras.
And so vanished the place where Doug played leapfrog with
Babe Ruth, traded punches with Jack Dempsey and Gene
Tunney (who surely pulled theirs, just a little), where he ran races
with Joey Hay, where the Duke of Sutherland lay on his rubbing
bench, the King of Siam rode on his mechanical horse, the Duke
of Alba crossed foils with him, Conan Doyle used his punch bag,
Prince George of England wrestled with him, Lord Louis
Mountbatten looked on at a game of basket-ball and where of

course Prince William of Sweden did his Swedish exercises.

No one was left to inherit all this and initiate other eminent personages into the lesson of joy through strength, no one felt up to it after Doug departed. After all, a certain rank and style are needed to be able to challenge a champ, coach a king or cheer on the nation. And Doug Fairbanks, whatever his other failings, had earned both and found happiness.

PART FOUR
EXTRAVAGANCE

'Oh, the parties we used to have!'
— GLORIA SWANSON

CHAPTER EIGHT

MAKE MONEY, SPEND PASSION: GLORIA AND POLA

It is not simply distance away in time which makes the 1920s seem so exotic a decade in Hollywood. Nor is it the disenchantment with screen illusion which the talkies brought that now makes the silent stars appear as extravagant creatures living in a play-world of incredible affluence and instant gratification – a kind of overspill area from the make-believe they indulged in on the screen. The truth is that Hollywood life often did 'ape' art. What looks in retrospect like a fantasy existence was more often than not simply the economic and social fact of stardom at this time in Hollywood. 'In those days,' Gloria Swanson later recalled, 'the public wanted us to live like kings and queens. So we did – and why not? We were in love with life. We were making more money than we ever dreamed existed and there was no reason to believe that it would ever stop.'*

This is not nostalgia speaking: it is merely the truth. Stars were never again to be so well rewarded, and at the same time so free from restraint, as in the early years of the 1920s. The star system which had created them was in the ascendant, while the studio system which was to curb their power had not yet been fully formed. Hollywood itself was a multiplicity of small units: producer-directors who signed up talent for their pictures, or stars who owned their own studios and produced and distributed their own movies, or stars who freelanced from film to film at escalating prices, or studio heads who paid their stars percentages of a film plus a salary. The variety of deals that were available was not to become possible again till the economic break-up of Hollywood in the mid-1950s.

*Gloria Swanson, quoted by De Witt Bodeen in *Films in Review*, April 1965.

There was certainly exploitation of talent, even abuse of it, in the 1920s. Whenever a star who suddenly acquired fame was caught in a weak bargaining position through ignorance or lack of foresight, like Valentino, the film-studio chiefs were swift and ruthless in taking advantage of him. But the sheer availability of choice open to the stars in the shape of producers, directors, properties, etc., prevented the brutal disciplining of talent which became the practice in the 1930s. In 1924, for example, there were still nineteen studios listed in the Hollywood directory: in 1935 there were only eight. The early 1920s was a time of flux, conflict and cannibalism as the businessmen fought each other for control of production and distribution backed by the huge funds which Wall Street was now prepared to pour into an industry whose gross revenue in 1920 totalled 800 million dollars, more than the thirteen largest rubber companies put together. High finance fed the appetites of the producers. And the stars fed off them.

This was the time when Hollywood stars started to become millionaires. Income tax then amounted to less than one per cent of the first 20,000 dollars. As far as stars were concerned the only law they were subject to, at least up to the mid-1920s, was 'the law of undiminishing returns'. The only important qualification that needs to be made about the astronomical fees many of them were paid is that, in cases where the stars were producers of their own pictures, the fees were meant to cover the cost of the production. Even so, it was a munificent deal. A self-obsessed perfectionist like Chaplin might spend months working on his films, so that their immediate profit to him is hard to assess because the cost of them is unknown – although the ultimate profit was bound to be enormous since he owned the films outright.

But Chaplin was the brilliant exception. Other stars with good business sense could calculate the profit to them before the camera started cranking. Norma Talmadge made eight films for First National, in 1919, for which she was paid a lump sum of 1,280,000 dollars, or 160,000 dollars per film. The average cost of the films was a little over 100,000 dollars. In 1920 she got an even more lucrative deal, agreeing to produce twelve films at 350,000 dollars each plus a percentage of the net profits. The average cost of each film worked out at 200,000 dollars. Her sister Constance also made twelve films for First National in 1920 and was paid 300,000 dollars for each and presumably did not work at a loss. Even relatively minor star-producers made fortunes. Anita Stewart, the star whom Louis B. Mayer had used as his economic *entrée* to big-time production in 1917, was still big enough in the early 1920s to command 90,000 dollars for producing and starring in a film; and by the time her First National contract expired in 1925 it had brought her at least 720,000 dollars.

The earning power of salaried artists who had become stars in the previous decade lasted well into the 1920s. Mabel Normand in 1923 was paid 70,000 dollars a film by Mack Sennett. Thomas Meighan, Dorothy Dalton and Alice Brady were making 5,000 dollars a week at the same time. Richard Barthelmess and Lillian Gish were getting between 7,000 and 10,000 dollars a week, plus a percentage of the profits for releasing their films through First National. Pola Negri had barely landed in America in 1922 before Paramount was paying her 2,500 dollars a week. Agnes Ayres, who had co-starred with Valentino in *The Sheik* (1921), was getting 3,000 dollars a week at the same time. Nazimova, the Russian star, was probably the highest-paid Hollywood actress of the period: at her height, she was said to be getting 13,000 dollars a week from Metro. Yet even this was overtaken. Gloria Swanson had been getting 3,500 dollars a week from Paramount in 1923, rising to 5,000 dollars in 1925 and then to 6,500 dollars in 1926. At this stage she showed an impatience to produce her own pictures for she had heard that W. S. Hart, the cowboy star, had got 2,225,000 dollars in two years out of nine of his films. Adolph Zukor offered Swanson a rise to 15,000 dollars a week to remain at Paramount. She still demurred. It was increased to the colossal sum of 900,000 dollars for three pictures a year, plus half of the net profits. But convinced that her future lay in production, she formed her own company backed by Joseph P. Kennedy's millions – only to encounter in Erich von Stroheim, the director of her abortive *Queen Kelly* (1928), a man whose talent for extravagant consumption outran her own.

*   *   *

The profits made on these stars' pictures were immense. But there came a time when the sheer number of cinemas available for showing them in had reached saturation point. It became impossible to squeeze enough extra money out of the box-office to sustain the soaring cost of production. By the end of 1923 the cost had reached – and in some notorious cases crossed – the danger line between profit and loss. (In Hollywood's lexicon 'loss' was defined sometimes as a profit that was not big enough or quick enough.) 'When a picture costs a million dollars, or a million and a half, there is no possibility of making big money with it, or even getting fair return on the investment,' a *Photoplay* editorial warned in January 1924.

By this date *The Ten Commandments* had cost near two million dollars; *Scaramouche* (1923), 850,000 dollars; *The Courtship of Miles Standish* (1923), 650,000 dollars; *The Hunchback of Notre Dame* (1923), close to a million dollars; and *Robin Hood*, nearly 900,000 dollars. Some of these expensive films were not getting a quick release, and therefore not starting to earn money, because litigation between distributors was snarling up the usual pattern of play-offs.

When a backlash began to mobilise itself in the industry, it hit the most conspicuous objects of envy and blame – the stars. 'Producers are again inveighing against the high salaries of stars,' wrote James R. Quirk in *Photoplay*, 'but again they have only themselves to blame. Instead of casting actors according to their fitness for roles, producers have been engaging them for their "names" – which are supposed to aid the box-office, but which, as a matter of fact, mean little. . . . With very few exceptions producers are afraid to take a chance on a beginner. They engage the players by their price tags. . . . Big business firms take young men and educate them to the business. Thus they are not compelled to pay exorbitant salaries through shortage of capable men. In contrast, motion picture producers have taken the easiest way – and have to pay the price.'*

* *Photoplay*, January, 1924. (The editorial by Quirk would have been reflecting opinion in the fall of 1923, since *Photoplay* had a three-month deadline.)

This criticism came at a time when foreign films were seriously cutting into the profitability of the home-made product – the post-war prejudice against Germany, and things German, had largely expired and German films in particular were proving tough competitors. Moreover the rash of scandals connected with Fatty Arbuckle and others had triggered off accusations of immorality against the movie industry in general and thus further impaired its self-confidence. Paramount had to suspend operations for ten weeks at the end of 1923 so as to bring production costs back to what was reasonable; Universal, too, shut down for some weeks; Metro had only one company working on a film and so had Sam Goldwyn, while numerous independent producers were announcing lay-offs of indefinite duration. For the first time the Hollywood system felt shaky. But it was only a temporary shudder. The Wall Street financiers stepped in to protect their investments; and the results were some mergers of studios, the appearance of 'supervisors' who tried to take away much of the directors' independence, and the laying down of the assembly-belt system for turning out 'formula' pictures whose cost, popularity and profit were all calculable in advance.

The most ominous thing about the new order that thus began to arise was the resentment against the stars which had been built into it. Producers who had done as much to precipitate the crisis by their own greed found it expedient to put the blame on the inordinate demands of the conspicuous movie stars. 'Names' were more necessary than ever to help sell the movies; but more than ever they were regarded as necessary evils. The conflict between 'strong' management and individual egos really began to show itself from 1924 onwards until the talkies put a weapon into the hands of the producers for cutting down the power of the stars by calling into question the adequacy of their voices.

For the moment, however, the growing discipline inside the studios was concealed by the extravagance and exoticism of the life it was possible for the stars to lead outside. Audiences, as Gloria Swanson said, wanted their stars to be extraordinary creatures – and they were. In keeping with the baroque movie palaces that were rising up, incorporating fantasies in the shape of frescoes from the Arabian Nights or motifs from Babylon, Old Cathay and Seville, the life led by the stars seemed a product of the romantic imagination. Their salaries provided the means for unrestraint in every part of it.

It was only after the Arbuckle scandal, and the widespread adoption of morality clauses in contracts, that notoriety became a heavy liability rather than the asset which Leo Rosten observed it to be in his classic study of the movie colony.* Rosten found evidence that the producers even encouraged conspicuous consumption by their stars in the way of cars, clothes, houses and never-ending parties, not only because the ostentatious confidence thus manifested was 'good for the industry', but because it was a way of reducing the economic independence of those with vast amounts of money to spend. Stars were encouraged to overspend so as to put themselves in debt. Sometimes their principal creditor was also their agent – and a reputation would be put into receivership unless its owner did as he was told.

Spending also boosted the ego in a world where insecurity induced moods of excessive elation and depression; while in a world of status-conscious artists, spending was one way of defending prestige. Rosten has suggested that it also showed 'a striking resemblance to the spending of gamblers or those who obtained money by means which precipitated guilt on themselves. Spending becomes a mechanism by which one part of the personality pays off another.'† The fantasy element of the films was extended into the favourite after-hours past-time of an enclosed society like Hollywood, which at this time had to amuse itself in absence of a commercial night life. Costume balls were the main way of doing so. Stars who spent their working lives playing roles seemingly could not exist without the same sort of stimulus in their social lives. Perhaps it was a relief to dress up in a role which one was not being forced to play; perhaps it was a way of playing roles which one might not get the chance to play in films.

* *Hollywood: The Movie Colony, The Movie Makers,* by Leo G. Rosten (Harcourt, Brace & Co.).

† Leo G. Rosten, op. cit., p. 104.

Whatever the reasons, fancy dress was appropriate wear for the fantasy people in need of continual entertainment themselves. Perhaps it was more fun than seeing each other's pictures.*

*   *   *

The emphasis on material goods and fun living, which made Hollywood appear such a festive place in the 1920s, was characteristic of the wider American society. The screen both reflected and stimulated the way of life made possible by the tide of postwar prosperity, in which the luxuries of comfortable living were openly pursued, and sex was freely discussed by most and readily practised by some. The way the stars behaved on and off screen made them objects of the wish-fulfilment drives of such a society. As some of the following accounts reveal, life did not stop at aping art – it transfused it, so that it was hard to tell what was fantasy and what was fact. The most characteristic attribute of stardom in the 1920s was the belief, held by millions in a far more passionate way than in any following decade, that the stars were in real life the same exotic creatures that they appeared to be on the screen.

Gloria Swanson was the chief representative of this glamorous illusion. Even the syllables of her name, rich and indolent, exuded the feeling of extravagance. She herself was perfectly prepared to live up to the fiction: money gave her the means, stardom the incentive, publicity the apparatus. And she acquiesced in the creation of her myth, even helped it along by the life she led in her heyday, because 'the public didn't want the truth and I shouldn't have bothered giving it to them'.†

In retrospect at any rate, she has been able to smile a trifle cynically at the sumptuousness of the 'private' life she was reported to be enjoying: the 100,000-dollar New York penthouse, the 25-acre estate on the Hudson, the perfumed elevator in her apartment block, the gold-backed mirror that slid aside to reveal a movie screen. . . . Publicity in the 1920s had worked up a head of

* See Appendix Three for a characteristic account of such a function.
† Gloria Swanson, quoted by De Witt Bodeen in *Films in Review*, April 1965.

steam that could present a personality through the strength alone of its owner's material affluence. 'What imagination they had,' Swanson said forty years later. But it would have been astonishing at the time if the public had not regarded her films as representative of the total environment she inhabited. It was largely due to Cecil B. DeMille that she was projected as a way of life for people to follow with fascination, as well as a personality for them to pay to see in a de Mille film.

In his pre-Biblical period, roughly from 1919 to 1924, DeMille was a master of bourgeois display: 'a showman,' Lewis Jacobs calls him, '[who] flourished at a time when showmanship was the nation's way of life.' It is no accident that the bathroom and the bedroom, the two places where display and luxury of an intimate, sensuous kind could be achieved within the realms of a filmgoer's experience or aspirations, became the main showcases for Gloria Swanson. DeMille had picked her out after she had done a brief stint as a Mack Sennett comedienne and groomed and gowned her into the salesgirl's and housewife's dream of high fashion and 'new' morals.

Her ritualised *levée* at the start of *Male and Female* (1919) contains all the voluptuous display and social enviousness in which her fans vicariously participated. The film is a skilful adaptation of J. M. Barrie's play *The Admirable Crichton* about the English earl's family who find the butler is their moral superior when they are all shipwrecked on a desert island. Before Swanson is even seen as the earl's daughter, DeMille has let material display tell all about her. Buckled shoes placed ready for the blacking-brush outside her bedroom door intimate her modishness; the camera peeking appropriately through the keyhole catches a suggestive flash of discarded lingerie; the peacock-feathered background of the sub-title that next appears clinches her character; and then she can be revealed under the bedclothes, her hip so disposed by her overnight slumbers as to give a sensuous, serpentine convexity to the silk bedspread.

Preparations for her bath are prefaced by a sub-title – 'Why shouldn't the bedroom express as much art as the drawing-room?' – which is DeMille establishing justification. The still

Valentino's famous entrance as the impetuous gaucho in *The Four Horsemen of the Apocalypse* has eclipsed the sophisticated ladies' man he plays throughout the rest of the film. His experience as a professional dancer gave him a natural grace and delicacy in the love scenes with Alice Terry which no other American male star came near to matching. He sometimes looks as if he were about to partner her in a fox-trot, not seduce her

Moran of the Lady Letty, a modern-dress Valentino film, proved his skill at playing an outdoor type. But it did not succeed in its aim of overcoming the resentment of male film-goers who envied his style of seductive blandishment – a talent hardly obscured by his proficiency at swabbing the deck

Valentino flexes his muscles at the morning *levée* in *Monsieur Beaucaire*. But film-goers, observing the primping noble plucking his eyebrows on the left, wondered what their Great Lover was doing in such unmanly company

Frustration: John Gilbert, the screen's Great Lover, found that Lillian Gish in *La Boheme* had her own notions on love. She thought their lips should never touch or else a great amount of suppressed emotion would be dissipated

Compensation: Greta Garbo in *Flesh and the Devil* was Gilbert's most seductive co-star. Physical touch gave their scenes together an erotic friction unmatched on the screen up to then. They also made love lying down, an audacious notion in films in 1927

Her white mask looks like a sulky rash against her own white face . . . the tired look that would make another woman seem merely apathetic gives her a yearning tenseness. This is Greta Garbo as she appeared in the opening scenes of *The Temptress*, her only Hollywood film to be part-directed by her friend and mentor, Mauritz Stiller. Stiller was fired from the picture, but he had given Hollywood the fully-realised Garbo. (*Frame enlargement*)

invisible Swanson has the way prepared for her by maids getting her tub and douche ready, busily displaying outsize bottles of bath-crystals, king-size powder puffs, etc., and then tipping rose-scented toilet-water into the shower cistern. Now Gloria rises. She lets her bed-wrap slide off her shoulders while the maids raise a towel to precisely exclude the intervening gap of bare flesh, though her buttocks make titillating little bumps in the material before she steps down into the coloured water of a sunken tub and, later, crushes a freshly delivered bouquet of roses against her lips while the shower cascades down round her.

DeMille's social dramas propagated the idea that romance after marriage is essential to keep the union happy. But frequently it is the romance of husband or wife with someone else on which the emphasis is placed. After a suitable period with this third party the dowdy wife left at home had learnt her lesson and smartened herself up, or the neglectful husband deserted by his spouse had realised his mistake and was ready to prove his affections. Everyone could be united again.

DeMille gave Hollywood the ethic that a moral ending makes good every immoral lapse. The fashionable gowns and luxurious *décor* were essential parts of the theme, so were all the smart hair styles and lavish toilets of Gloria Swanson. Money had to be spent and seen to be spent if matrimony was to be portrayed as a state of perpetual seduction. 'The most gorgeously sensual film of the month,' a contemporary critic wrote of *Why Change Your Wife?* (1920) in tones of reluctant praise. 'In decoration, the most costly; in physical allure, the most fascinating; in effect, the most immoral. Mr DeMille and his studio associates know that the "moral" they have tacked on to the picture – that, in effect, every married man prefers an extravagant playmate-wife, dressed like a harlot, to a little homebody who has achieved sewing spectacles and a reading lamp – is not true of normal husbands anywhere in the world . . . But there is enough hidden truth in it to make a lot of husbands and wives unhappy.'*

This was the allure that settled around Swanson. She was invariably the 'playmate-wife', not the 'other woman'. She was

* *Photoplay*, April 1920.

among the first film stars to be seen off-screen in the fashions designed for her films. From DeMille, too, she acquired a taste for expensive living. She has often recalled how he made up to her for the fright she got from a lion in the flashback-to-Babylon scene in *Male and Female* by offering her a choice of a heap of jewellery – 'I picked out a gold-mesh evening bag with an emerald clasp and immediately felt better.'

At the height of her stardom she was obliged by contract always to appear in public dressed in the height of fashion. Her yearly clothes bill for personal and professional wear was said to exceed that of any other star: fur coats, 25,000 dollars; other wraps, 10,000 dollars; gowns, 50,000 dollars; stockings, 9,000 dollars; shoes, 5,000 dollars; perfumes, 6,000 dollars; lingerie, 10,000 dollars; purses, 5,000 dollars; head-dresses, 5,000 dollars. True or false – and the likelihood is in favour of the former – the important thing about such publicity is that it was believed.

The aura of fascination that surrounded Swanson was increased by an emphasis on waste. This was summed up well in the studio's description of her as 'The second woman to earn a million' – Pickford had been the first – 'and the first to spend it.' And other figures not strictly financial soon attached themselves to her – the number of times she got married. The acquisition of fresh husbands, though based on a wry self-confessed lack of judgment about men, seemed in her fans' eyes to endow her with a love life that was an extension of her screen life. (These were also the days when stars' marriages, like that of Rod La Rocque to Vilma Banky, began to be studio-managed so as to create a ferment of curiosity which would boost the newly-weds' box-office receipts.)

The third of Swanson's five marriages, to Henri, Marquis de la Falaise de Coudraye, who had been interpreter on her French-made film *Madame Sans-Gene* (1926), gave her the asset of a genuine title in a status-ridden industry and inspired the famous telegram to her Hollywood studio: 'AM ARRIVING WITH THE MARQUIS TOMORROW STOP PLEASE ARRANGE OVATION'. Not that there was any need. The audience at the picture's Hollywood *première* arose spontaneously to sing *Home, Sweet Home,* while the new marquise, wearing silver lamé and a fortune in diamonds, enjoyed the last luxurious thought of the superstar – 'What's left?'

*   *   *

What was left was the subtle actress underneath all this top dressing. It is unfortunate that few of the large number of films made by Swanson in the 1920s are easily available today: some, like *Madame Sans-Gene*, are apparently lost for good. But enough remain to indicate that she was far more than a glamorous clothes-horse.

Part of Swanson's uniqueness lay in her appearance; and she was shrewdly assisted in projecting it by the English romantic novelist Elinor Glyn – who was also to perform a similar service for Rudolph Valentino. Madame Glyn, as she liked to be known, saw a golden chance in early Hollywood to use her own reputation as a counsellor on love in order to underwrite the reputations of the stars, like Swanson, whom she made her protégés. The eyes in particular were the features of the star in which Madame Glyn placed most importance. For a screen test she would get the players to cover all of their faces but the eyes and express emotion through them alone. 'If they cannot do it, it means they are not thinking their parts and I have no further use for them.'* Swanson passed this scrutiny. '[She has] perhaps the loveliest eyes I have ever seen. They are strange eyes, not altogether occidental, which gives them their charm – blue eyes, a little up at the corners and the lashes half an inch long. . . . This is the bond between us, perhaps; we both have up-at-the-corner Slavonic eyes.'†

Allowing for the mystical bond – a common Glyn discovery – both parties also had a good business eye. Swanson let Madame Glyn sponsor her appeal; and although it aroused some amusement in the film colony to be known as a Glyn-approved star, it did one no harm at all outside Hollywood. And stripped of its showmanship, the Glyn technique was perfectly in accord with the way a movie camera could photograph what was going on

---

* *Picturegoer*, April 1930.
† *Photoplay*, June 1921.

behind a player's eyes. As Clarence Brown was often to say of Garbo, she did not need to alter her face to express her change of emotion: the change in her eyes did it all.

But Swanson's eyes were only part of her art. Her body, small (5 ft 4 in.) but perfectly proportioned, retained its comedienne's training: its reflexes were quick and detailed and easily adaptable to impersonations of other types, even other film stars as is wickedly apparent when Swanson, as Norma Desmond in *Sunset Boulevard* (1950), goes into her Charlie Chaplin routine.

There is a persistent story that at one time Chaplin turned Swanson down as his regular co-star in his early comedies. It sounds very likely. In a comedy film of her own like *Manhandled* (1924), where she plays a little shopgirl out to have herself a ball while her boy-friend is out of town, Swanson reveals a slapstick inventiveness that might have been too close to Chaplin's own for his comfort. The opening scene in a jam-packed subway train, with Gloria battered by commuters but giving better than she gets, has the indiarubber resilience of great clowning: her flesh is bruised, her spirit is unmarked. She has a mischievousness reminiscent of Dorothy Gish, Lillian's sister, but even more of a hard-boiled tomboy than Dorothy in her famous role as the Little Disturber in *Hearts of the World*.

Swanson is vulgar in the way Chaplin used to be before the Little Fellow could afford the price of a poetic soul. Even in a film like *Queen Kelly*, which carries a full charge of von Stroheim's perverse eroticism in its story of a mad sovereign's furious jealousy over her little rival in love (Swanson), she contrives to keep her Chaplinesque streak untainted by her director's darker penchants – even when both come together in a scene. The moment when her knickers fall down in front of the passing Prince, that's Chaplin: the moment her knickers are flung into the rude nobleman's face, that's von Stroheim.

Swanson's reputation as a glamour queen overshadowed her gifts as a comedienne. And both have been overtaken by a curious fate. For when Gloria Swanson played Norma Desmond in *Sunset Boulevard* many filmgoers and even critics made the mistake of assuming that the tragic figure of the silent-era movie idol, living like a forgotten star whose mind is now as echoing as her own cracked and empty swimming pool, somehow bore a resemblance to her own life and career. Of course it did nothing of the sort. What Swanson acts – and acts impeccably and without a second's worth of sympathetic softening up – is a pastiche of a period style and a parody of a star type. Neither belonged to the real Gloria Swanson.

Her gestures are all the melodramatic exaggerated ones which people who have never laid eyes on a silent film imagine to be typical of the era. She constantly poses as if in front of an invisible camera set-up. Significantly the word 'camera' is the only one that gets through to her in her state of mental shock after shooting her lover-gigolo – for it speaks directly to her star ego. Even her dialogue is lifted out of the sub-title on a silent movie: 'There are no other guests, just you and me. Do you think I want to share this night with other people?'

It is true that amid the nostalgia being force-fed into the film there are facts that fit Swanson's career perfectly: the gates of Paramount, which was *her* studio, and the appearance of Cecil B. de Mille who was *her* director and even addresses Norma as 'young-fellow' which was his nickname for Gloria. But the parallel stops there. The myth of stardom in Billy Wilder's film has to end in tragedy because the film's conception of Hollywood is that of a machine that eats its creations: one of the very first newsreel vans to dash up to 10086, Sunset Boulevard after Norma's crime has made the headlines comes from Paramount Pictures!

In fact the only part of Gloria Swanson in which Norma Desmond has a share is the afterglow of stardom – but it is this very quality which confers a plausibility on the part and ironically results in a transfer of its fictional characteristics to the performer.

The casting, as Billy Wilder accurately calculated, is enough to lead to a confusion of image and reality, very much in the same way that Swanson's career on and off screen made it hard to know where the one left off and the other began. But only someone who had achieved both the image and reality of stardom, and survived both, could have succeeded in dazzling our perceptions so extravagantly.

*   *   *

The box-office recession and the production standstill that occurred briefly but alarmingly in 1923 coincided with Hollywood's awareness of a competitor on its own territory – the European film industry. Left for dead after the first world war, Europe's film industry was now more advanced and inventive an art form than the American one which had lost its freshness by its dependence on formula films and increasingly highly priced stars to retain its audience. 'The producers,' wrote James Quirk in a *Photoplay* editorial, 'do not seem able to abandon their pattern idea of making pictures and selecting stars. . . . First it was the out-and-out vampire. . . . Then it was the almost-naked bathing beauty. . . . Now it is the good woman with so-called sex appeal: that is, one who plays the part of a good woman, but gives the impression that she isn't too good.'*

The speeded-up drive for new and hence cheaper stars extended Hollywood's reach to Europe where its purchasing power made it possible to offer salaries that were alluring by Continental standards, though economical by American ones, to the very directors and stars whose imported films were cutting into the time available for showing the Hollywood product on the home screens. From 1923–4 onwards Hollywood was invaded by European talents, particularly from Germany and Sweden where the native film industry was almost crippled by the raids of American talent scouts.

By early 1926 the 'foreign legion' was strongly enough entrenched in Hollywood to earn the resentment of some of the old residents. 'Where three years ago a foreign star was a novelty, a foreign director a curiosity, today they are almost a menace, so rapidly are they arriving and so closely do they stick together.'† Such directors as Lubitsch from Germany, Seastrom and Stiller from Sweden, and Benjamin Christiansen from Denmark brought new techniques and sophistication to their made-in-Hollywood films; and the stars who came along with them, or in their wake, added the spice of novelty to the American staple. Paul Kohner, the Austrian-born Czech who had been made Universal's casting

* Ibid., March 1923.
† Ibid., July, 1926.

director, declared that foreign artists 'had more background than the Americans and, besides, will work cheaper'.

But many of them also had a quality of exoticism that was lacking in the Hollywood stars. Pola Negri was among the first to make sensational use of this. Imported by Paramount in 1922, she represented the resurrected vamp who had been killed off by the ludicrous exaggeration of her which Theda Bara had been pushed into giving and by the pretentious artiness which had cost Nazimova her American following. Negri, who was the daughter of a Polish nobleman, arrived in Hollywood with a refreshingly different reputation made through her German films which had already been seen by the American public and which conveyed her unrestrained temperament in an unblushingly direct and passionate way. In other words, 'she was not yet "camera-wise",' as Max Vinder put it in *Photoplay*. She let herself go 'and she didn't care a damn whether the emotion made her look pretty or ugly. She delivered the goods.'*

American opinion of the time concurred. Reviewing *Du Barry* (Germany, 1919: presented as *Passion* in the United States, 1920) a writer in the *New York Times* wrote: 'She is lovely in many scenes, it is true, but some of her features are not beautiful and she makes no apparent effort to pose becomingly without regard to the meaning of her performance. She is expressive. That is her charm. She makes Du Barry real, as fascinating as she has to be, with as much of the appearance of dignity as she must have on occasion, and as contemptible and cowardly as she was. She actually wins sympathy for a woman who cannot at any time be admired. It is an achievement.'†

At the time this film was shown in America the photographic innovations which Lillian Gish had set in motion with Henry Sartov's atmospheric soft-focus treatment of her in *Broken Blossoms* were having a thoroughly banal effect on screen acting, especially feminine screen acting. 'The fad became so overdone,' writes the veteran photographer Arthur C. Miller, 'that at times it was virtually impossible to identify the performer on the screen, but

* Ibid., May 1922.
† The *New York Times*, 13th December 1920.

the feminine stars demanded it.'* And Max Vinder confirms that, 'The (established favourites) were beginning to sicken the public by their insistence on looking pretty at all times. Too many close-ups, too many left profiles, too many soft focusings: it was all of the same school. The cameraman was prettifying the screen to death, and the stars liked him for it. In *Passion* the photography was dull, the lighting was flat, there were few close-ups of Negri. She, with her wide, intelligent forehead, and her big, restless eyes, her unascetic mouth, dashed about from one scene to another, and went through all sorts of emotional changes. . . . From the point of view of absolute art, her Du Barry was not wonderful. But it got the audience in America all worked up, just as they got aroused by Al Jolson or Billy Sunday or anybody else who put his heart into his job.'†

The impact that Negri made on America in *Carmen* (1919), which Lubitsch directed in Germany, was even more sensational. Though her operatic intensity knows no let-up, she is in other ways astonishingly realistic. A flesh-and-blood vitality dances over her soiled gipsy face – nothing in the least self-conscious about it. Her incredibly supple body avoids the langorous poses of the hothouse vamp – this is a wild, open-air creature with no time for the gauzy cobwebs of her soft-focused American sisters.

Once in Hollywood, though, Negri made certain elementary mistakes. The first was the mistake of taking herself seriously in a self-made society that was tolerant of its own pretensions and maintained its own snobberies, but resented the ill-concealed superiority of a 'foreigner' with a genuine claim to rank and title. Negri gained initial advantage as the challenger from her well-publicised feud with Gloria Swanson – though Swanson's withdrawal to Paramount's Astoria Studio, on Long Island, was due to a wish to be nearer New York society than further from Negri's competition.

The exotic attitudes that Negri struck off screen also cost her a lot of public patience. She did not behave in an 'American way'. Instead of spending money, like Swanson, she spent passion.

* Balshofer and Miller, op. cit., p. 150.
† 'She Delivered the Goods,' by Max Vinder, *Photoplay*, May 1922.

Instead of giving the public a feeling they were part of her glamorous life, she gave the columnists cause for mockery at her extravagant gestures. When she made her dash across the continent to be at Valentino's death-bed, claiming they were passionately in love with each other, the cynical Press called it a stunt. Perhaps Negri's fatal mistake was to let America suspect that she had no sense of humour where her own exotic image was concerned. She and Swanson were both fairly small women, but one could never imagine Negri replying, as Gloria did, when a fan panted out how excited she was to meet the famous Miss Swanson at last: 'And I bet you were surprised at the little runt you found.'*

She had the initial misfortune to make her first American film, *Bella Donna* (1923), when Hollywood was coming under fire from moralists alarmed by the William Desmond Taylor murder and the Wallace Reid drugs scandal. Negri's *femme fatale* was toned down to allay these apprehensions. But the process also toned down her spontaneity. 'She seems determined,' said one critic, 'to be a good woman, even if she dies of *ennui*. They have taken the passion flower and made it into a poinsettia.' However, she fitted well into the light, sexy, suave satires which Lubitsch guessed would appeal to American tastes. *Forbidden Paradise* (1924) institutionalised the vamp's power by transforming her into Catherine the Great, commanding her guardsmen to accept her favours or be executed.

It was Lubitsch who supplied the sense of sophisticated humour to the Negri personality on the screen, in the moment, for instance, when trying to kiss her lieutenant and finding herself shorter than he, she slyly moves a small stool into place with her foot so as to be able to reach him. Another sophisticated director, Mauritz Stiller, directing her in *Hotel Imperial* (1926), could employ his Swedish sense of inner psychology to bring out wit or other subtleties in her performance. But in other hands, she fared less well. Her natural exoticism was not easily adaptable to the 'modern' psychology of what Lewis Jacobs referred to as 'the restless, driven, over-sexed' heroine of the later 1920s.

* *The Parade's Gone By*, by Kevin Brownlow (Knopf) p. 372.

Negri risked becoming a type whose appeal was for the unsophisticated filmgoers. *Woman of the World* (1926), directed by Mal St Clair, solved the problem by giving in to it. It placed her literally among the hicks as a European countess paying a visit to her in-laws (Chester Conklin, of all people!) in a one-horse mid-west town. It is a film that very clearly reveals Negri's strength and weakness.

The opening on the Riviera is splendidly Grand Vampish, the star cutting an exotic figure with her glossy black hair licked into the effect of a bather's skull-cap, her eyebrows quivering like wire struts supporting a full-moon face, and a veritable branch of orchids on her shoulder as if she had just swung down on a jungle creeper, trailing the foliage with her, in time to catch her lover with another woman. Negri's old gipsy abandon was always connected with the pain she inflicted on her men. Now it lingers on in a mannerism, as at first she fondles her faithless lover's cheek and then whips a stinging slap on to it.

She is in her element when she gets to Main Street America and tames the local D.A., who wants to run her out of town, with a worldly smile that shades into an enticing one and a bold parrying movement of her vamp-sized cigarette holder. Negri's type was not satisfied with anything short of infatuation from her man, but the impression grows as the film progresses that the type is being sent up. The clapboard homestead of the Chester Conklins gives the appearance, as it is meant to, of course, of the wrong back-cloth being let down for scenes in which she makes her involuntary lover light her sin-tipped cigarette, or grope for a slipper under her hammock while she entwines her fingers in his hair and plants a kiss brazenly in his ear-drum. Negri's successful projection of herself depended on her keeping the whip hand, which is exactly what she does by giving the D.A. a bull-whipping in the end.

It is true that she keeps her dignity and can muster a baleful power. (She objected, on obvious grounds, to the casting of a comic like Conklin.) But while the film never makes her look ridiculous, which is a considerable victory on her part, it does something worse. It makes her look *passée*. It leaves her exoticism

stranded in a hick town; and the analogy with her Hollywood
career is hard to resist. She waited till 1931 before tackling a
talkie and then chose *A Woman Commands*, a kind of Zenda story
with music which tried to re-create the witty sophistication of
Forbidden Paradise, but fell indeterminately between the high-
caste style of Czarist circles and the low comedy tempo of *opéra-
bouffe*. Negri as a cabaret singer sang two verses of a torch song
and 'is disclosed with a heavy foreign accent', as one reviewer
himself disclosed, surely belatedly, though he added 'that is no
detriment in a picture of foreign atmosphere'. But 'foreign
atmosphere' and much else that was exotic, including the passionate
heroine, was on its way out long before the talkies. For the new
breed of female star who was to dominate the screen for the last
half of the 1920s needed no bull whip to muster her male victims.
And she inflicted as much suffering on herself as she did on
others. The greatest representative of this class was Greta Garbo.

CHAPTER NINE

THE NEW TYPE:
GARBO

It is a sure sign that a new type of film star has arrived when reviewers are forced to compare her with an old type. That the comparison is made at all is evidence of her impact; a little later will come evidence of her individuality; and then of her uniqueness. Greta Garbo telescoped all three stages into one with her first American film, *The Torrent* (1926).

'The find of the year,' is a phrase so often repeated in contemporary reviews that it would sound suspiciously like studio propaganda were it not backed up by the reviewers' sharp sense of revelation – which is not contradicted by the comparisons they made. 'An excellent and attractive actress with a surprising propensity for looking like Carol Dempster, Norma Talmadge, ZaSu Pitts and Gloria Swanson in turn,' wrote Richard Watts Jr, in the *New York Herald Tribune*, and added, 'This does not mean she lacks a manner of her own, however'; while a critic in *Pictures* declared that 'she possesses that which heretofore has only been laid at the door of Pola Negri – fire, animation, abandon'; and Laurence Hall, in *Motion Pictures,* said that 'she suggests a composite picture of a dozen of our best-known stars. . . . She is not so much an actress as she is endowed with individuality and magnetism.'

There is a feeling here of critics who are excited, but still searching for the right words. We now know the words they were after, for we know what Garbo became, but anyone looking at *The Torrent* today might be forgiven for questioning what the excitement was about. It makes very uneasy viewing; for although there are certainly many Garbos on view in it, their fusion into *the* Garbo of the later films is so sketchily achieved that one has a niggling doubt whether, back in 1926, one would have been as prophetic and perspicacious as Messrs Watts, Hall and all the other unidentified writers who cried, in variations of *Variety*'s verdict, 'Hail this girl, for she'll get over.'

What *The Torrent* shows in retrospect is that M-G-M, which had imported the actress and her director and mentor Mauritz Stiller from Sweden, had absolutely no idea how to use Garbo, or even what type she was. Accordingly they took a stunningly maudlin novelette about a peasant girl who turns into a *prima donna* and by altering the character, and hence Garbo's type, every ten minutes hoped to solve their problem by seeing what would click. Garbo by turns is a mawkish sweetheart, a scornful vamp, an embittered lover, a great artist behaving with *noblesse oblige* to a humble cabaret player, a woman of the world toting a cigarette-holder and hobnobbing with kings, and ultimately a fatalistic beauty wedded to her vocation.

It is a solution achieved at the expense of artistry, credibility and continuity in which even the photography is altered like a signature tune as Garbo runs the gamut of established star types. No wonder Stiller was reported to have flown into a violent rage, and the rest of the Swedish colony sympathised with Garbo on the premature end to her American career. Though good critics, they proved poor prophets. And yet what can the impact have been? – what can the American public have seen in this disjointed debut?

Well, there was certainly the surprise of seeing a Swedish import convey Latin passion so convincingly, if briefly and intermittently. While Garbo's third M-G-M film, *Flesh and the Devil* (1927), is the one generally remembered for its 'horizontal' love scenes – an audacious position to assume in public at this period – there is a fleeting scene in *The Torrent* that fits Garbo and Riccardo Cortez together in a supine embrace with almost jigsaw neatness: it is still voluptuous and must at the time have seemed even more vivid.

And there are moments that anticipate the later Garbo when she had assumed command of a scene. Her *prima donna* entering her limousine at the end, adored and envied by the crowds but bereft of love and resigned to 'dying a bachelor', prefigures

Queen Christina; and her vertical collapse, straight down out of the frame, when she hears Cortez has called off their marriage duplicates the feeling that Camille leaves at a similar moment – not simply that her legs have given way, but that the earth has opened.

Garbo herself, quite innocently, probably elucidated the sensation of her American debut when she wrote home in a pessimistic note to a friend: 'They don't have a type like me out here, so if I can't learn to act they'll soon tire of me, I expect.'* She was indeed a new type: a fact that was missed by Hollywood's other Swedish actors, to whom, of course, she would not have been a new type. They tended to put their homeland's dedication to acting before Hollywood's concentration on personality. Hence their dire prophecies after *The Torrent*.

Where Garbo's 'type' registered so effectively on the awareness of American filmgoers was in her physical proportions and the way she used them. Even Monta Bell's insipid direction could not hide the moments when the parts of Garbo's square-shouldered, flat-chested, long-legged body shifted into sensuous adjustment to each other as she moved and relayed a liberated, animal will quite unfamiliar in Hollywood-made pictures.

It is not *The Torrent*, but Garbo's next film, *The Temptress* (1926), which shows this at its clearest. And it is this film that clinched her career: for M-G-M allowed seven months to go by between the two films, a very long time to keep 'the find of the year' off the screen, whereas *Flesh and the Devil* was rushed into the cinemas less than three months after *The Temptress*'s *première*. The reason is obvious: M-G-M were now sure of what they had got and knew both the nature and the value of the prize.

*   *   *

The irony is that the man who did most to reveal it to them, Mauritz Stiller, was abruptly prevented from having anything more to do professionally with Garbo or the studio. Stiller had begun directing *The Temptress,* but had finished less than a quarter of it when he was pitched off the picture and replaced by Fred

* Quoted in *Garbo,* by Fritiof Billquist (Arthur Barker) p. 78.

Niblo who had made *Ben-Hur* the year before. Stiller was sacked because it was said he worked too slowly and could not get on with the film's nominal star, Antonio Moreno.

The enforced separation of the actress from the director who had discovered her, tutored her and turned her into his own Pre-Raphaelite ideal of 'supersensual, spiritual and mystic' woman-hood probably did more than any other event to turn Garbo into the remote, obdurate and mistrustful star she soon became. The severance of Pygmalion from his Galatea, just when he has learnt to animate her, has an anguish that probably only Garbo can understand. The only consolation for Stiller were the opening sequences of the film which he directed; for they reveal the completely realised and magical Garbo.

She plays an unhappily married woman whose misfortune is to have every man she meets – a banker, a dam builder, a South American bandit – fall wildly in love with her against her will. Stiller's part of the film is set at a *bal masqué* in Paris and opens abruptly, dramatically, with Garbo in a *loge* spurning her banker lover and fleeing from him. The thin, tall, tubular, supple extent of her body is the first striking thing seen. She darts about on business-like legs. She resembles a white exclamation mark. Her white domino mask set against her own white face looks like a sulky rash.

What one notices next is an extraordinary feature of Garbo's that runs right through her silent movies but vanishes in her talkies: the tired, strained look in her face. It would make any other actress seem apathetic, listless, even anaemic. (In Garbo's case it was probably due to the unromantic fact that, ordered by M-G-M to get her weight down, she over-dieted and kept on doing so until the studio's medical advisers put her on to more balanced fare towards the end of the 1920s.) But her washed-out weariness in this and other early films only gives her a yearning tenseness that increases her sex appeal. It plays dramatically against the nymphomaniac compulsion when she comes to grips with Moreno. The famous Garbo grip of the woman in love who reaches first is displayed with all its disturbing ambiguities. She always seems to be leaning against Moreno looking for support.

Not that she is any tender vine. On the contrary. The pressure of her grip signifies that given time she will dominate the host plant. No actress, before or since, has combined the masculine and feminine wills so tightly into one embrace.

For Garbo love was intense and physical right from the start. She places a little flurry of kisses on Moreno's cheek, then masks his eyes with her hand as she plants a longer one on his face, blotting the vision of her out of his sight while she leaves him with a final touch of the lips. The last glimpse he has is a haunting one of a phosphorescent, perpendicular Garbo – the angularity of her movements makes this the only word – moving off through a prismatic scattering of moonlight in a woodland shot that shows Stiller's native genius for placing figures in romantic relation to light and landscape.

The rest of *The Temptress* is Fred Niblo's work. The effect is immediately to coarsen Garbo. Instead of getting at the psychological truth of her character, she looks as if she is now being directed to play that character as a type – in this case, a Pola Negri type. From what Niblo said when he directed Nita Naldi in *Blood and Sand* (1922), five years earlier, one suspects that he saw Garbo as an 'imitative' rather than 'creative' actress. Niblo had acted out Naldi's scenes for her in the Rudolph Valentino film 'so that she might see exactly how it was going to look . . . then even if her emotions had not been entirely awakened to the scene, her understanding would enable her to present it perfectly.'* It is likely that being compelled to work at speed and having a star who was suffering from the shock of separation from her mentor-director, Niblo felt obliged to use this technique on Garbo. (The fact that her slight knowledge of English placed him at a disadvantage to Stiller may also account for the lack of *rapport* between actress and director.) Instead of acting from behind the eyes, she is now pressed into some bad hand-me-down gestures that belong to the early vamp, so that her reactions to the whip fight between Moreno and the Argentine bandit which are meant to signal alarm might do equally well to serve at tennis. She was never again to have such a crude conception forced on her.

* *Photoplay*, November 1923.

M-G-M may have thrown Stiller out, but it was his vision of Garbo that they kept.

Garbo was valued by M-G-M because her artistic nature allowed her to commit sin without outraging the moralists. She never stopped causing men to suffer, but the suffering she herself experienced sanctioned her sexuality. Moreover, she sinned out of weakness. The old bold vamp had sinned out of principle. Garbo's weakness turned into a destructive force in film after film, but the moralists found it hard to blame a woman who was in possession of more subtle drives than she was able to control. 'She becomes a symbol of sexual appeal rather than any particular bad woman,' wrote a National Board of Review critic at the time of *Flesh and the Devil*.

She presented an imperfect human being – hence a far more credible one than the vamp whose eyes flashed out her brand of fully-fashioned evil as if they were twin sky-signs. Garbo with a speaking voice was a much more complete actress, but even in the silent era she projected an image that made unequalled use of the metaphysics of personality and the mechanics of art.

✻   ✻   ✻

She had the great good fortune to come on to the Hollywood screen at the start of a period of superlative photography. Panchromatic film stock had been perfected in 1924 and was in general commercial use by the following year. It allowed the sensitive style of acting imported from Europe to register on film in a naturalistic way. It facilitated emotional subtlety and the projection of psychological truth.

There were two provisos. The subtlety and truth had to be there in the first place – and the studio lighting had to complement both, it had to be benign. Garbo from the very first found a photographer who ensured it was practically beatific. William Daniels lit and photographed nineteen of her twenty-four silent and sound movies at M-G-M, at the worst protecting her, at the best transfiguring her.

Daniels found the right light for every state of mind, something no exposure meter could measure. His lighting often said things that dialogue could not. It was he who put a minute light bulb in the tip of John Gilbert's cigarette for the impalpable effect its glow would give the two lovers in *Flesh and the Devil:* and he again who lit the happy woodland interludes between dangerous spy missions in *The Mysterious Lady* (1928) so that the luminosity dissolves the treacherous real world into a hazy haven where love can call a truce in the war. In those 'neutral' moments in Garbo's acting when she expresses absolutely nothing, it is Daniel's art which projects the mood on to her face, in the way, for example, that the rain's pattern on the window pane suggests her lack of feeling through its vitreous reflection. All this is not to diminish Garbo's own art. But in view of the 'divinity' sometimes claimed for her, it is salutary to remember that her performances are the product of collaboration with human agents – and even electric light bulbs.

Half the secret of her visible art is the way she used her body. Garbo has a great length of leg between kneecap and pelvis and it gives her movements a piston-like quality, a steely directness surprisingly at variance in many of the silent films with the rest of her withdrawn self. She cannot take six steps without making it look like the start of a hike. By all the laws of motion, it should not coalesce into anything more romantic. But the grace one discovers in athletes who are filmed in slow motion, one sees in Garbo at normal speed. Each movement has its matching emotion timed by an instinctive stop-watch and then edited smoothly together in performance.

When Gilbert first meets her in *Flesh and the Devil* and breaks a flower off from her bouquet, she looks at him with surprise, tolerant amusement, a sudden rush of modesty, then smells the flowers and freezes into mystery as her carriage pulls away – and all in one unbroken 'take'. The romantic line of her performance in this film changes into modern shorthand for her part as the 'Lost Generation' heroine of *A Woman of Affairs* (1929: Hollywood's version of *The Green Hat*). The lipstick quickly applied, the cigarette sharply exhaled, the green hat whipped off behind the wheel of her Hispano-Suiza so as to feel in direct contact with wind and life – each action is executed as if there might be no time left for completing it.

As well as altering the tempo of her body, Garbo appears able to vary the volume of it to suit the scene. Reacting to the puppyish charm of young Lew Ayres in *The Kiss* (1929), she is buoyant, radiant, pounds lighter spiritually and physically – and then the gravity is restored as the heavier weight of the doomed affair with her older lover confronts her. Just as her voice in the talkies was a marvellous instrument for testing the emotional strength of each line she spoke, her body in the silent films becomes a way of displacing its own emotional weight.

The coaching Mauritz Stiller gave Garbo must have refined the senses of a woman whom one feels to have been an instinctual 'Method' actress long before the word became modish, and generally misapplied, in New York and Hollywood. Stanislavsky could have worked as fruitfully from Garbo as he did from the great stage artists whose performances he analysed and codified for the use of his actors. 'Objectification' or the art of relating emotionally to physical objects, is a classic Method exercise and one that Garbo had at her finger-tips. For her sense of touch guided her to emotional illumination the way it did Chaplin to comic inventiveness. 'Things' did for her what Braille does for the blind. The furniture-touching sequence in *Queen Christina* (1933), where she goes around the bedroom she and her lover have slept in, touching objects and endowing them with significance, is an often-quoted example. But her silent films are as rich in these transmutation effects, especially the ones directed by Clarence Brown.

Brown's *rapport* with some of his stars seems to have been like that of a water diviner to the source of supply: a baffling but persuasive way of bringing forth what he sensed in them. *A Woman of Affairs* has the hallucinatory moment when John Gilbert visits a hospital to comfort the sick Garbo, but reports that she does not know him. As he and his wife are standing in the corridor, Garbo suddenly appears at her bedroom door, advances on the bouquet he has brought – seeing only it, everything else is unfocused – and taking the flowers in her arms she presses them to her and plunges her face deep into them like a woman with her lover, drawing new strength from them and letting them add a pathetic dimension to her unfulfilled affair – for as she carries the bouquet back to her hospital bed, pressed close against her cheek, it uncannily assumes the significance of a new-born baby.

In *Flesh and the Devil* she turns the communion cup round so as to drink from the same place as her lover's lips – and a holy rite is subtly exchanged for a sensual act. Her studio's delight must have been boundless when it was appreciated how the star's sensory perceptions could defeat or deflect the censor's disapproval of a scene like this by rendering its particular sin almost intangible.

Garbo embodied eroticism more intensely than any other star of the period. In adulterous love scenes she is nearly always granted the dominant position. Gilbert's head in *Flesh and the Devil* lies on her lap, with her arm encircling it and the physical posture suggesting his enslavement. The spirituality of her looks leaves one unprepared for, and hence intrigued by, the ruthless-ness of her love-making. Her arms encircle, her hands clutch, giving a physical thrust to her passion. She rubs her cheek against the man's as if to set a current passing between them. Even in her lighter, modern roles she leads with her physique the way a model girl 'sells' her body, not the clothes on it. And in the high-romantic ones there is always the tiredness on her face. Perhaps she needs sleep, one thinks, before she needs to sleep with a man. Or perhaps to a tragic nature like hers, passion is a form of oppression. One certainly never suspects it may all be due to a poor diet! But just as normal people turn calories into energy, Garbo at this time is able to turn the lack of them into love-sickness.

Even stranger is the effect that usually appears when the love affair is hopeless and two little coiled springs of concern contract her brows. On any normal person it would be migraine. But Garbo raises it to a higher plane and makes it look like remorse. There was always a small but hard core of critics in the 1920s who professed to see no art in Garbo: one suspects it must have contained the healthy eaters and the headache sufferers!

Once or twice, especially at the beginning, Garbo released such a heavy erotic charge in her films that M-G-M felt compelled to add 'happy' endings, or at least 'moral' ones, to appease the censors. While she was permitted to turn streetwalker as a result of her experiences in *The Temptress,* only European audiences were made aware of it: the Babbits of Main Street saw her re-united with Moreno in the American version – with a chaperone in tow, too. Clarence Brown wanted *Flesh and the Devil* to end with Garbo falling through the ice and the two men whose friendship she has come between shaking hands again. M-G-M insisted on his taking the story to an unwarrantedly 'happy' conclusion, with Gilbert making up to a 'nice' new girl and frisking beside her couch while his aunt's knitting wool, which he has been holding, unravels out behind him. Such endings were best left to Mary Pickford.* Needless to say, Garbo's sexuality makes a mockery of them.

'If they want me to talk, I'll talk,' Garbo said in an interview in 1929. 'I'd love to act in a talking picture when they are better, but the ones I have seen are awful.' When she did talk, she had no trouble – though her performance in *Anna Christie* (1930) grows noticeably more confident as the film goes on. But paradoxically Garbo is more accessible in her silent films than in her talkies. Speech broadens the range of her effects, but adds a dimension of remoteness to her. It renders her, if possible, more unique. One cannot project one's own interpretation of how the silent image might sound on to the talking Garbo. Moreover when she found her voice, she retreated more and more from her public as if to compensate for the communication that the spoken word un-fortunately enforced! Her writers, too, learned to use the complex resonances of her voice to build up the mood of the film: it was easy to calculate in advance the effect of dialogue passages once one was familiar with the tone and pitch in which she would speak them. Perhaps this is why her talkies grew more and more saturated with fateful pessimism till it became possible to mount a whole publicity campaign on the very opposite characteristic – 'Garbo Laughs' – as if this were something alien to her, although

* When the film was presented a few years ago at the Paris Cinémathèque, a friend of Brown's suggested successfully that the story should be ended where its director had wished.

the young wife aboard ship at the start of *Wild Orchids* (1929) could hardly be merrier even if her laughter could not be heard at this date.

It was around the same time that silent-filmgoers began to see the Garbo myth transferred to the characters she played, so that her off-screen mystery 'justified' the roles. There must have been a thrill of recognition in seeing a solitary Garbo in gumboots and slicker giving the brush off to a stranger as she trudges through the rain in *The Single Standard* (1929) while the sub-title flashes up, 'I am walking alone because I want to be alone.'

The myth eventually enriched but confused the art that Garbo demonstrated in acting. And this is why the silent films made in the first four years of her Hollywood career are so valuable. Belonging to an earlier time than the calculated and lavish 'vehicles' of the sound era, they enable one to see Garbo before the myth had quite shrouded her and to marvel at the extraordinary nature of this star and the effects she could produce – even if the source of both finally proves elusive.

CHAPTER TEN

ENTER THE
GREAT LOVER:
VALENTINO

The problem with Rudolph Valentino is trying to see the artist behind the man. The man has been over-exposed in nearly every area of his life except his films. The fascination he still exerts on today's generation seems indeed to be in inverse proportion to the knowledge people have of his work. For like all stars whose appeal is sexual, the nature of the man commands more immediate speculation than the achievement of the artist.

While an article published in 1968 in a highly reputable English newspaper did not manage to mention as much as the title of a single picture he made, it nevertheless contained the unequivocal statement that he had been impotent. One hardly needs to add that no evidence for this was offered, nor could any have been. But that such a charge was made at all tells one a lot about the present-day attitude to Valentino. It is no longer enough to suggest that a public idol has feet of clay; other and more vital parts of him are involved in the exposure. And in a period when people are noticeably unsure where their own sexuality lies, Valentino offers a tempting target for mockery and suspicion based on the belief that a man who had such public power over women may have been somewhat less than a man in his private life. For many people, it is a consoling possibility.

Fairbanks was protected from such a charge, now as then, partly because his virility was expressed through muscle-power, and such areas are open to inspection, and partly because he was no actor and for safety's sake remained a resolutely asexual lover where screen romance was concerned. Fairbanks never aroused male jealousies. Valentino did and even in his own short career of barely seven years experienced a backlash from this quarter which culminated in the notorious allegation that he was having a deleterious effect on American masculinity. But the word 'American' is the key one here, not 'masculinity' – and in any case the Chicago newspaper article that made the charge was almost defensively masculine itself.

It is true that Valentino had a passive streak in his character. That is probably why he was able to take all the adulation lavished on him in such a calm way. And it may have dictated to some extent his two marriages to women, the actress Jean Acker and the more complex Natacha Rambova (otherwise Winifred Hudnut, the cosmetics heiress), who had stronger wills and more possessive natures than he. But this again hardly justifies a charge of 'impotence'. Nor is it likely that what drew millions of women to him were negative qualities such as those exhibited by a modern romantic hero like Marcello Mastroianni with his air of a lethargic Lothario nursing some disability that needs feminine care, intuition and tenderness to heal it and restore him to the state where he can give satisfaction in return.

Valentino was typed from the very first – in a phrase that later pained his national sensitivities – as a 'Latin lover', the kind of charmer who takes immediate advantage of a woman in circumstances that (for her at least) prove compromising. But this tag is quite insufficient to describe the appeal that Valentino actually exerted on the screen. It leaves out subtleties that made him a star of more variety than is usually acknowledged. And it completely fails to explain why the Latin lover, as he created him, was acceptable to himself as well as being desirable to women. For Valentino was by no means the first or only Latin lover on the pre-1920 Hollywood screen. The character was so commonplace in the adultery dramas that sprang up in the post-war permissiveness that it had become a stereotype long before he was heard of. The novelty of Valentino is that he was the first Latin lover to make an impact that was audacious, original, liberating yet fundamentally reassuring for millions of women.

It is always the first impact that should be examined in seeking the reasons for someone's rise to stardom. With Valentino one is lucky. This impact can be isolated in one film which simultaneously established his characteristics and fixed his reputation. Before he made *The Four Horsemen of the Apocalypse* (1920) he had simply been the male support in films featuring female stars of fading appeal. After he made it, he was a national phenomenon.

One does not appreciate, until one sees the film *in toto* and not simply in its better known excerpts, how much it is centred on Valentino. Its reputation today is as an anti-war film and undoubtedly in its time it had this harrowing pull for the generation who had survived the 1914–18 conflict. Films that glorified war heroics started dropping dead at the U.S. box-office once the armistice had sounded. But *The Four Horsemen of the Apocalypse* struck a note of majestic disillusion that reverberated sympathetically down the 1920s.

And yet its romantic interest, lodged in the personality of Valentino, is unmistakably built up into the main feature by a director, Rex Ingram, shrewd enough to recognise the new quality this little-known actor was giving in a supporting role and to expand it into the film's star part. The film is for the greater part of its length a story of Bohemian love and smart seduction among the pre-war international café society. Here lies a great deal of its fascination – and almost all of Valentino's. To understand him it is essential to try and see him as he was first seen by the audiences at the film. Obviously one cannot do so with complete certainty. But perhaps one can convey a feeling of the discovery that the original filmgoers experienced by presenting the following notes which were made during the first screening of what is considered to be a complete print of *The Four Horsemen of the Apocalypse*.

*   *   *

Valentino plays Julio, the playboy grandson of a rich Latin-American cattle king. He is introduced into the film about ten minutes after its start and remains one of the central characters, and the whole embodiment of its love interest, till about ten minutes before the end, when he is shot in no man's land by one of his German cousins and subsequently appears in a vision admonishing his mistress, played by Alice Terry, not to desert her war-blinded husband.

Impact of Valentino's first appearance in the film is increased because the child whose birth is announced in the prologue is not shown growing up – but appears, suddenly, as Valentino in close-up. Striking regularity of his features under the gaucho hat that at first hides his glossy hair. Teeth clenched determinedly on a cigar, smoke puffed resolutely out of nostrils – like a stud stallion on a frosty morning. V. decides to cut in on a couple dancing the tango. Saunters over, hand on hip, tapping the man meaningfully, gazing unambiguously at the girl, his right eyelid quivering and giving a ladykilling look to the whole approach. Suddenly beats the man to the floor with his stock whip and takes over the girl, guiding her into a lazy tango, both of them sagging sensuously then darting back and forth impulsively. Ends by pressing his mouth over hers like a suction cup. It is a very deliberately 'staged' debut – nothing leads up to it, but V. is *there* in all his gaucho aggressiveness, perhaps reacting to director – one seems to hear Ingram calling out guidance – a shade too deliberately, but nonetheless making instantaneous impact. NOTE how V. modulates his romantic approach to reflect the character of the girl he is making love to – a very varied kind of romancer, contrary to the all-at-one-fell-swoop popular reputation. His patent-leather hair first revealed in death-bed scene when he removes his sombrero as he stoops to kiss lips of dead grandfather. Emphasises astonishing symmetry of his face. Totally unAmerican.

Scene shifts to Paris where V's side of the family have returned. Screen title setting the period speaks of 'debauches in Montmartre' where V. is a dilettante artist, but expectations are lessened when his favourite mode of debauchery is identified as 'tango teas'. V. first seen in smock at easel, cigarette dangling loosely as he daubs at painting of three not unduly clad but far from naked women. Later V. wheedles money out of his mother. NOTE the extreme delicacy of the little movements he slips into the rather unsubtle purpose of such a scene – the split-second flutter of his fingers as he chucks his mother lovingly under the chin. NOTE the whites of his eyes revealed as Terry comes to call. Then a restaurant scene, chic, twenty-ish, with title 'The world was dancing – Paris had succumbed to the mad rhythm of the Argentine tango'. V., dressed in fashionably cut suit, at table with Terry – both the objects of gossip. NOTE how he languidly sights down his nose, eyelids lowered, as he talks, the delicate movements as he takes the bud vase that Terry has just smelled and breathes in its perfume as if her fragrance had been transferred to the petals. Asks her to his studio. 'I promise to be good,' he adds. 'You promise?' she asks. V. gives a quick little look direct at the camera, as if taking us into collusion with him before he nods assent. NOTE his way of pressing the woman's hand back as he kisses her and the way his cheeks suck in ever so slightly as he again raises her hand to his lips.

Scene in V.'s studio. Helps Terry off with her wet shoes. NOTE his playful quick pat at her stockinged feet, his raising two fingers with almost feminine Chaplin-esque gestures as he pours out the tea. NOTE again how V. expresses the playful gentleness of his love, kissing the sugar lump before he drops it into her cup, transferring a kiss by his finger-tips to her lips as if putting the stamp on some *billet doux*. NOTE how his glossy hair flattened to the skull matches the highlights in his shoes, emphasising the bandbox neatness of his physique. Terry's husband, accompanied by V's father, disturb them. NOTE V's skill at freezing into semi-operatic pose of guilty lover and yet, by his innate poise, making it seem natural when the scene is little more than a tableau of discovered lovers. V. now drops out of the story as 1914 war breaks out. Reappears in a scene at Lourdes as a rather callow looking non-combatant in smart grey suit, Homburg, black tie with pearl pin and gloves – Alice Terry is a nurse whose latest patient is her blinded husband. For his sake she rejects V's advances. V. decides to enlist, is reconciled with his father and is next seen in battledress with a week's growth on his chin. NOTE how it removes the smoothness of his skin and makes one realise what an asset that olive-skin sleek cheek is to his personality. V's death is never shown, only the two cousins on opposite sides highlighted with drawn pistols in the glare of the flare over no-man's-land. Then V. appears in a vision to Terry, urging her to stay with her husband. Film ends with a symbolic encounter between the relatives of the fallen and the figure who throughout the film has personified Prophecy behind them a rolling hillside spiky with grave crosses.

The first thing such a summary conveys is how stunningly *The Four Horsemen of the Apocalypse* is constructed to display a wide, absorbing variety of its star's personality facets. He is the focus of over half a dozen big scenes; none of them repeats the emotional mood of the others. There is (1) the opening scene on the dance floor with its *aggressive sexuality*; (2) the scene where he *romances* his mistress in a chic *thé-dansant:* (3) the *seduction* scene in his artist's studio; (4) the scene of *adulterous discovery* by the lady's husband; (5) a *rejection* scene where she opts for marriage and atonement; (6) the *reconciliation* with his father and (7) the *do-and-*

die heroism in the trenches. If certainly not the earliest, this is the most successful example of a film constructed to display and promote its leading actor. There is evidence that Rex Ingram went about this very deliberately when he saw how perfect Valentino was as Julio. 'When we came to rehearsing the tango, "Rudy" did so well that I made up my mind to expand this phase of the story. I did this by means of a sequence in a Universal picture I had made some years before. The sequences showed an adventurous youth going into a Bowery dive and taking the dancer after he had first floored her partner. Bone and marrow, I transferred this action to South America – yet only a few of my wise Universal friends recognised it. This bit of acting not in the book gave Valentino a chance for one of his showiest bits of work. I rehearsed it very carefully for three days right on the set, and I think the result shows it.'*

The result in fact shows more. Ingram was a director who worked for the incandescent moment, the flash when an actor's personality ignited; and he supervised the editing of sequences with this in mind.† The whole tango scene not only has great deliberateness in its aim and action, but the editing makes Valentino's debut into a series of dynamic poses. In fact the states of posing and reposing, and the ability to be at home in each, constituted a large part of Valentino's appeal for this director.

This becomes clearer if one looks at the film Valentino had appeared in the year before and the effect of it on the woman who first brought him to Ingram's notice. She was June Mathis who scripted *The Four Horsemen of the Apocalypse* and urged Ingram to give the Julio part to this actor who by then had three or four not

* Samuel Goldwyn, op. cit., pp. 188–9.

† Ingram's methods were revealingly reported in *Photoplay* by Herbert Howe who observed him directing Valentino's successor in Ingram's affections, Ramon Novarro, in *Scaramouche* (1923): 'He lashed him through 12 rehearsals and then, when he seemed utterly despairing, he turned to me with the explanation, "Isn't that boy a wonder? He's the greatest actor on the screen – I've never seen anyone like him." – "But you drove him through twelve rehearsals," I remonstrated – "Yes, but did you notice that I had the camera grinding all the time? I'll use his most spontaneous moments." ' Howe concluded that Ingram 'has an instinct for the vibratory key of an individual.' – *Photoplay*, November 1923.

very notable films behind him. Here again we are lucky. June
Mathis has recorded which of these films made her sure he was
the man for the part and although she does not spell out her
reasons they may be deduced from a film that fortunately still
exists, *Eyes of Youth*, directed by Albert Parker, starring Clara
Kimball Young and released in November, 1919, in which
Valentino plays a 'cabaret parasite', hired to compromise the
heroine by luring her to a road-house with the tale of an accident
where her husband can discover them both.

It is a trite tale, but already Valentino has an elegance, an
enormous delicacy in his movements utterly in character with
Julio's, but unlike those of any other American film actors at the
time. He guides the shocked Mrs Young into a chair, helps her
off with her shawl with the light, deliberate motions of a practised
seducer, pours himself a drink with complete mastery of the
intimate situation and stifles her cry of help in a way that is
economical yet determined and not nearly so melodramatic as the
fade-out view of his victim hanging on to the door for support.
What makes such villainy so un-American is not just its Latin-
ness, it is the grace, suppleness and poise behind it all moving
together with perfect methodicalness. For Valentino brought on
to the screen the qualities he then used to earn his living off it –
those of a professional dancer.

He was a very good dancer, too. He partnered Bonny Glass
when Clifton Webb dropped out of the act. They performed in
smart restaurants like the Ritz; and later on, when Valentino was
a star, but feuding with his studio and barred from appearing in
anyone else's films, it was again to exhibition dancing that he
turned to keep himself before the public.

But much earlier than his partnership with Bonny Glass he
had supported himself as a taxi dancer, a far lower class of
employment and one that grated against the family pride, as well
as the peculiarly Italian sense of 'honour', which he had brought
with him as an immigrant to America. Dressed with slightly too
much elegance, he had to be at the beck and call of the smart or
'fast' women for whom the *thé-dansant* and the tango provided
both a post-war craze and a permissiveness not to be found in the

hard-liquor bars before Prohibition. It meant Valentino had to make himself agreeable to this ever-changing clientèle of women who came alone or in couples; he had to be well groomed and easily disposed towards the kind of seductive flirtatiousness on the dance floor that gigolos practised for profit in other places. He was playing a masquerade before he ever got into films. While it gave him a public ease with women, it also made him treat their sex with a certain reserve. There is a parallel here with Greta Garbo's early experience as a lather-girl in a back-street barber's in Stockholm, where the work gave her insights into the male sex that later enabled her to be attractive to them on the screen yet keep her distance off it.

However strongly dance-hall convention sanctioned it, living off women was repugnant to Valentino and when desperately short of money he hesitated before taking any film role involving it. Yet his professional poise, learnt on the dance floor, kept imposing its own redeeming grace on even the darkest-dyed character he played. If June Mathis ever saw another pre-*Apocalypse* film of his, *Stolen Moments* (1920), it must have confirmed the impression he made in *Eyes of Youth*. Though cast as a Brazilian scoundrel with a thickish moustache, he gestures his pretty victim into his private apartments as if preparing to partner her in a dance, not seduce her. Kissing a girl, he bears down on her using his body like a counter-weight in some dance step. And even when pretty heavily accoutred in top hat, tail coat and cane as a society blackmailer, he has the professional dancer's manner of carrying his clothes, not being oppressed by them. One reviewer even made a point of his grooming, commenting on how out of character it was for an American (*sic*) leading man to look so immaculate. Probably this was among the characteristics which made American males mistrust and grow jealous of Valentino as his fame was reinforced by the impression he made on their womenfolk.

The Four Horsemen of the Apocalypse allowed all these characteristics full play, for the first time under a director able consciously to display and project them. And the film's story added a quality of romantic sincerity not in the parasites and blackmailers he had previously played. He was still a menace to women – this was important. But the heartlessness had gone. Women who saw the film just when they were beginning to throw off their own social conventions could rest secure in the belief that there was still one convention which they and this exotic seducer would respect – the convention of true love. The revolt against the American male involved submitting oneself to an attractively un-American male – but how nice to know that he would love and cherish them as well as before, and maybe better. And indeed obey them into the bargain. The slave bracelets that Valentino's second wife, Natacha Rambova, clamped affectionately round her husband's biceps aroused the mockery of other men, but significantly they did nothing to impair Valentino's appeal with their wives and girl-friends.

But the full extent of this was unsuspected by the Metro Film Co. at the time they released *The Four Horsemen of the Apocalypse* – until the box-office told them they had made the most successful film of 1921. Even then they did not really attribute it to the fact that it starred one of the decade's unique personalities. By the time they did believe their own publicity, Valentino had left Metro after being refused a pay rise – he was getting 450 dollars a week – and had bound himself to Paramount.

Perhaps Metro thought of him as a one-shot phenomenon. It is a not uncommon result of the cynicism with which a studio goes about the business of star-making. Probably Ingram grew resentful of what he regarded as the disproportionate interest being taken in a relative 'unknown' who was assuming responsibility for the film's success which this touchy director felt belonged to himself. Years later he called Valentino 'just a good-looking lucky guy who copped a sensational role and a good cameraman'.*

He directed him in one more film for Metro, *The Conquering Power* (1921), based on Balzac's *Eugénie Grandet,* and then, as if to prove how stars owed everything to their creators, he took another beginner called Ramon Samaniegas and turned him into Ramon Novarro. But in the meantime Valentino had made *The*

* *Photoplay,* November 1923.

Sheik (1921) – and had assured his fame and life tenure on the Latin Lover prototype.

*   *   *

The Sheik, both as book and film, is a most successful example of fantasy projection. The idea of an Arab chieftain being the hero is a vital part of this. For it suggests polygamy and so intensifies the male-ness of the man who abducts and rapes Lady Diana Mayo in the desert. At the same time the desert setting makes the confrontation between the two even more concentrated than would have been the case in a location where other women were to be found – significantly Ahmed Ben Hassan does not maintain a harem, though enjoying the potency that comes from such a traditional part of Arab life. Consequently each reader of Edith Maude Hull's novel, or each filmgoer, saw herself as 'the only woman'.

The exoticism of sex in a tent with a man, who took it for granted that his victim knew what it was all about and would soon let her reluctance be overcome, consummated the thoroughly modern American woman's revolt against the conventional manners and men of her own country. Moreover the story ended happily – even legally! There was additional reinsurance in the revelation that the Sheik turns out to be a Scottish earl – who had been found as a baby in the desert. This effectively removed any objection to mixed blood that publishers, or film-makers, might have to fear and substituted the far more commercially viable notion of blue blood. Nevertheless the fact that hardly any of those who fell under the book's spell remembered the Sheik as the Earl of Glencaryll shows how substantially this aristocratic fantasy was eclipsed by the more barbaric one; and the film, beyond identifying the hero as definitely white and putting him in Western dress for the last scene, does not insist on it either.

From all these factors Valentino immediately profited once he stepped into the part. The film was released in October–November, 1921, and caught the full beneficial force of public interest in Valentino that had been building up since *The Four Horsemen of*

A teaser poster put out for
The Gaucho in 1928. It
captures better than any
film still the braggadocio of
the later Doug.

Clark Gable was cast as a
minister of religion in *Polly
of the Circus*, in 1931, one of
the films he made before his
image, as the guy who
makes his women take to
rough treatment, finally
crystallised. The star of the
film was Marion Davies, but
cinema managers gave Gable
top billing and his studio
sooned learned the danger of
letting their new property
co-star with actresses of
fading popularity

Pola Negri: a vamp felt unarmed without a cigarette

the Apocalypse had opened in March. The fact that in *The Sheik* he acted with nothing like the sensitivity he gained from Ingram in the earlier film was something that hardly mattered – except to Valentino who came to loathe the film for the poor camera angles and comic-strip make-up that often gives him a pop-eyed appearance.

What mattered to filmgoers was the air of menace-in-action that he radiated so masculinely. Scooping Lady Diana off her horse and on to his, he barks, 'Lie still, you little fool.' Back in his tent the victim, played by Agnes Ayres, demands, 'Why have you brought me here?' and draws the sardonic reply, 'Are you not woman enough to know?' Eyeing her riding breeches with a frown of disapproval, he has her change into a dress – an act intended to force her femininity back on a woman who has earlier been described as 'beautiful, unconventional, spurning love as a weakness.'

Part of Valentino's effect on the emancipated woman was, paradoxically, to make her feel more womanly by submitting herself to his spell. *The Sheik* dramatises this without subtlety: it even opens in the slave market with Valentino eyeing the females for sale. But its crudity is part and parcel of its power. Valentino's masculinity is continually boosted in the film: in the boast he makes as the lady threatens to take the clean way out and kill herself, 'If I choose, I can make you love me,' accompanied by a grin the size of a melon slice; and even in the cigarettes he smokes which gain a phallic overemphasis from the length of the holder he affects. It is this implement, hardly in the nomadic Arab tradition, which Lady Diana sees violating the combs and brooches on her dressing table when she awakes. But this pregnant bit of still life is allowed to do duty for the rape which never happens. The seducer who could be trusted to act like a gentleman tips Valentino's appeal even more firmly towards his female followers. True love makes it sure and marriage makes it a contract.

'I am afraid I shall make the devil of a husband,' says the Sheik at the end in a line that, fortunately, filmgoers' memories have not recorded, preferring to enshrine as a camp catch-phrase of the

1920s the bride's reply, 'I am not afraid with your arms around me, Ahmed, my desert lover, MY SHEIK.'

What the American woman wanted her husband to be to her was a constant lover. Perhaps this was another reason why American males resented the female hero-worship of Valentino which grew to uncontrollable pitch after the release of *The Sheik*. The man who is continually willing and able to gratify a woman is a frustrating exemplar for homelier types of male to emulate. It is no accident that Valentino at this time received the patronage of an immensely influential woman who shared this view and also had the power to propagate it for her own enrichment throughout two continents. Elinor Glyn, the Edwardian romantic novelist already referred to, authoress of *Three Weeks* and other once-daring books, had turned herself into a sort of twentieth-century Eleanor of Aquitaine, a philosopher of love. She had arrived in Hollywood in 1920 as part of the drive then on to recruit famous authors to write screenplays and, more important in Hollywood's view, allow their reputations to be used to shelter the studios from the wave of criticism that their more lubricious product was attracting throughout the country.

The exotic colony was tolerant of Madame Glyn's pretensions to endow it with her own social graces and romantic attitudes: it was also shrewd enough to recognise in her a superb showman and calculate that if she could sell Hollywood stars as well as she could sell herself then she was worth cultivating. Her success in promoting Clara Bow as the 'It' Girl of the mid-1920s was her greatest triumph. She also 'supervised' some film productions of her own and other people's books, though her insistence on preserving the niceties of social etiquette produced petrified results. She was surest when on more Delphic territory than a movie set, such as the divining of which stars had sex appeal. But she was hard to please.

'American men in those days could not make love,' she wrote in her autobiography. 'Not even the leading actors. . . . One after another screen tests of handsome young American film stars were shown to me for approval, but in every case I considered that the performances were lamentable.'* One infers from her memoirs that Valentino was an exception to this because he was so un-American. But one human phenomenon can quickly scent another human phenomenon coming down wind; and assigned to script Valentino's next Paramount picture, *Beyond the Rocks* (1922), Madame Glyn set out to make propaganda for him on and off screen.

She is reliably said to have taught him the arch little trick of kissing the palm of a lady's hand, instead of the back. And she ghosted some of the articles that appeared under his name, like the one entitled 'Woman and Love' in *Photoplay*, March 1922.† The piece of propaganda for romance echoes with Glyn-isms. Parts of it sound like a woman writing advice for other women. For example: 'The most difficult thing in the world is to make a man love you when he sees you every day.' Other parts reprimand 'the modern American (who) tries to destroy romance. Either it must be marriage or it must be ugly scandal.' And though an aphorism like 'The tragedy of age is not that one grows old, but that one's heart stays young' is plainly masculine in sentiment, one is less sure about the adage that 'nothing interferes with romance like restlessness'.

Other parts of the article skilfully combine the Glyn ideal of romance with the Valentino reputation for menace: 'It is the woman who decides whether she finds you charming. It is only after you have won her love that you dare be master. One can always be kind to a woman one cares nothing about – and to a woman by whom one is attracted. But only cruel to a woman one loves or has loved.' This article and other pieces, as well as interviews he gave, committed Valentino even more firmly to the romantic ethic – in public anyhow.

In private life Valentino probably found romance a fatiguing concept. Apart from such legal mix-ups, like his semi-comic arrest on a bigamy charge for attempting to marry Natacha

* *Romantic Adventure: The Autobiography of Elinor Glyn* (Ivor Nicholson & Watson) p. 299.
† Information supplied to the author by Margot, Lady Davson – Elinor Glyn's daughter.

Rambova before his divorce from Jean Acker had been made final, the off-screen Valentino led a life that is marvellously without scandal of the type that might have been expected to cling to a romantic lover acting on his own precepts. He was not a noticeably pious man: his boyhood in Castellaneta, in Southern Italy, made him resent the authority of the priest and relatives whom his devout widowed mother was forced to call on to curb his constant disobedience. But even Italians who dream of a romantic existence, or *especially* such ones, as Professor Barzini's well-known study of his countrymen shows, find it hard to throw off entirely the typical Italian passion for *sistemazione* – for comfort and security. '*Poets maudits* and *avant-garde* writers, painters and film directors, who shock the world with their daring, often marry good cooks and good housekeepers . . .'*

Valentino's two marriages, neither of which turned out romantically satisfying for him, make one suspect a strong temptation to *sistemare* existed under the romantic attitudes he was compelled to strike publicly. Unfortunately the film business rarely fosters orderly lives among the people it makes into stars. Valentino was no exception.

*   *   *

It was soon after the enormous receipts of *The Sheik* began coming in – it made over three million dollars – that Valentino began to claim that Paramount was exploiting him. He was then getting 1,200 dollars a week, but other stars were getting many times this: Mary Miles Minter, 8,000 dollars; Norma Talmadge, 10,000 dollars; William Farnum, 10,000 dollars; even Thomas Meighan, the sort of solid, dependable American male whom Valentino had displaced as the chief romantic interest, was making 5,000 dollars a week.

Out of resentment at the profits he was not sharing in, he began piling up huge bills for automobiles, jewellery, clothes, a new mansion and genuine Spanish and Moorish artefacts to be used in the film *Blood and Sand*. It seems like a punitive campaign against his studio; and there are countless other cases like it up

* *The Italians* by Luigi Barzini (Hamish Hamilton) p. 114.

to the present time since conspicuous extravagance is the commonest way a discontented star finds to hit back at a studio. The studio, of course, may often encourage the debts in the first place so as to make its star more of a dependant.

Valentino also started demanding artistic control of his films, in which he was encouraged by Natacha Rambova, a woman with a very real flair for theatrical design but no sense of cinema. Paramount first noted the danger signs when he insisted that *Blood and Sand* be made in Spain to ensure its realism: the studio held firm and it was not. Then came the bills for all the imported Moorish furnishings and matador trappings he hoped to use in it. Such insistence on 'authenticity' is often found in stars whose work or career leaves them with a sense of incompleteness. When a star has gained fame and money the next step is usually a more or less direct attempt to prove that he or she is worth the fame or money.

Personal prestige or artistic fulfilment is now behind the drive, but the ways the star expresses his need for them result in a high casualty rate, in quarrels with the studio over scripts, directors, sets or costumes, psychic strains and stresses which widen the occupational split between the world of reality and the stars' world of illusion, and, inevitably, gathering money troubles that allow power to pass from the beleagured star to the studio that owns him. Both parties are in a state of siege, the studio offering financial inducements while the star holds out for ego satisfactions.

Paramount tried offering Valentino an immense rise to 7,000 dollars a week if he would give up his claim to artistic control. He refused and towards the end of 1922 was suspended from work, and the pay-roll, while the dispute went to court. During the following months Valentino lived on star capital. He appealed to his mass public directly. He and his wife made nation-wide tours, judging beauty contests or giving exhibition dancing while tactfully advertising the products of the face-cream company that was footing the bills. He collaborated on his autobiography. He put his name to *Day Dreams*, a volume of swooning poetry said to be inspired by psychic communication, though this confused many who had taken the initial 'G.S.' at the end of one rhapsody to stand for Gloria Swanson. (Actually the sender was George Sand.)

It was during this period that the charges of indolence, effeteness and being under a woman's domination began collecting around Valentino. He always maintained they were inspired by an embittered studio which could not use his services and wanted to write down his market price in case anyone else managed to do so. Given the latent sadism of a film studio, which finds relief for its own cynicism and self-contempt in humiliating the very stars it has made, the charge has a ring of probability.

Valentino attacked Paramount at press conferences, or from the public stage, for trying to depict him as 'a wan, pale and beardless youth, leisurely reclining on downy sofas, supported by silken pillows and wickedly smoking sheikishly perfumed cigarettes'. At the same time he reiterated his wish to return to work and make 'good pictures'. In an open letter addressed to 'the American public' he wrote: 'I say today that if this company will permit the writer and director in whom I have such confidence to have the last word on pictures in which I appear and run them story length, if they will give me the contract I thought they explained to me I was getting in the first place, I will go back to work.'*

When at last he did go back, in late 1923, all his points had been won, including a salary of 7,500 dollars a week and artistic control over his new film *Monsieur Beaucaire* (1924). It was quite a victory. But it had one risk which in his euphoria he may have overlooked: his claim to be a creative artist now placed him in opposition to the vogue that had made him a sensation and sustained him through the months of 'exile'. He wanted to modify the image of the sultry lover in which he had been typecast by the studio; but he found that his performance, especially in as self-consciously arty a comeback film as *Monsieur Beaucaire,* suffered from the even more absolute type-casting of the public. The film did disappointing business. It was as if the old image had detached itself from the star who owned it and had won its own legion of admirers.

The phenomenon of the star who is of consuming interest

* *Photoplay*, January, 1923.

everywhere except at the box-office of his latest film was thus brought home to Valentino and Paramount. He made one more film for the studio, *A Sainted Devil* (1924), which significantly returned to Argentine adventure; and then after appearing for an independent producer in an unsuitable modern story, *Cobra* (1925), his services (but specifically *not* his wife's) were bought by Joseph Schenck, head of United Artists. Schenck guaranteed him 520,000 dollars a year plus 40 per cent of the profits of his pictures. High pay. But the price exacted was a retreat to the 'image' – as a Russian Robin Hood-type in Clarence Brown's *The Eagle* (1925) and then, in the last film he made, as *The Son of the Sheik* (1926).

*   *   *

Yet the word 'image' is only a convenient way of defining a star's outline. Within the image of Valentino there was an actor of considerable variety of impersonation. His performance as Monsieur Beaucaire, for example, in a story about a parasitic courtier under Louis XV who proves his virility to himself, differs, bodily as well as in detail, from all the earlier Valentinos.

At the risk of damaging his public image he subtly underscores the effeteness of the wasp-waisted dandy first seen with two beauty spots on his cheek doing a stiffly elegant dance at a court masque or languidly strumming an absurdly outsize, six-foot-long lute. Valentino's *levée* is a limp mockery meant to show the debilitating effect of letting one's servants live one's life for one. It succeeds perhaps too well, in spite of the sight of him throwing out his bare chest while he waits to be dressed and flexing the muscles bunched thickly round his upper arms and collar-bone. Many a filmgoer expecting a Fairbanks type of swashbuckler must have wondered what the virile lover was doing holding a *tête-à-tête* with a preening male queen who takes out a vanity box, puts on lipstick and delicately plucks his eyebrows. Yet Valentino bravely preserves a minute consistency in his foppish interpretation, forever posing as if a court painter, and not a camera, had an eye on him, and employing a walking cane like a spindly third leg on which he swivels with studied weariness.

Even in love he is passive: the victim of an arranged marriage.

Not till he is taunted with no longer being a man does his latent virility come out of hiding and he runs off to England to out-fence, out-gamble and out-love all-comers. Unfortunately for him and the film this release of energy seems to come after hours of Sidney Olcott's tableauesque direction (probably itself under the direction of Natacha Rambova) and too late to efface the fans' memory of the ex-Sheik in a silvery marcelled wig with a ring on every finger of his hand. James R. Quirk put his editorial finger accurately on the reason why the film failed to please when he declared that 'except for one or two situations in which he puts on rattling good sword fights, the old spark disappears. [Valentino] doesn't look a bit dangerous to women. . . .' The truth of this judgment, should serve to emphasise how unselfishly the star had assumed the anti-Valentino aspects of the part and committed himself to it with such sincerity that, to judge from his lip movements, he is speaking some of the silent 'dialogue' in French to help his interpretation of the character.

Valentino's skill in using his body to differentiate his roles has also been underpraised. His matador in *Blood and Sand* is an elegant dragon-fly in the ring, but outside it remains basically the bullring urchin who is first spied grinning behind the barricade and under an un-Valentino mop of curls. The actor subtly suggests the clumsiness of the peasant elevated by fame above his station. In the seduction scene he hardly knows where to put his hands – they seem to have been specially enlarged for the part! In *Moran of the Lady Letty* (1922), a modern tale of a socialite who is hijacked while still in his week-end sailor's rig and put to work aboard a clipper, the rolling gait that Valentino assumes so convincingly after weeks at sea follows him back on to dry land at the end of the film as a guarantee of his permanent redemption from playboy ways. He really thinks the role through. His light-bodied grace is always at the command of his light-hearted disposition: both give his films plenty of slyly humorous moments.

In *The Eagle* he is on his knees enduring some Imperial endearment from Louise Dresser's heavily upholstered Russian empress; and as she pats his head with rapturously closed eyes, Valentino sidles boyishly out from under her palm so that she strokes the air for a hilarious second or two before realising the object of her pursuit is no longer there. It is done with the relish of a puppet suddenly showing an independent will and cutting its own strings. The emotional projection of a mime was always available to Valentino. He shows sorrow at his father's deathbed in *The Eagle* with such gentleness that his hand hovers just a millimetre above the dying man's temples – the body need not be there at all, for this gentle gesture suggests everything about it. He has a ballet dancer's hidden strength always on call: watch him lift a woman, like a dancing partner, in one easy hoist from ground to horseback. Fairbanks would have made a he-man show of it.

The range of lovers that Valentino played has been unfairly overshadowed by his two best-known roles as Julio and the Sheik. He could be exceedingly winning in a non-ladykilling way, plucking Dorothy Dalton's sleeve in *Moran of the Lady Letty* like a puppy attracting its mistress's attention and kissing her ever so tenderly while his *fiancée* from the San Francisco smart set glides by on her yacht a mile away with her new lover.

This film was shot on location, largely with natural lighting; and Valentino wearing hardly any make-up, cutting a deliberately virile figure in singlet and bellbottoms, throwing punches and taking them, gives one of his most attractive performances. The picture, however did poorly. Its star put the blame on its modern story and henceforth was to prefer costume parts. But again the likelihood is that the public did not find Valentino sexually menacing enough. He had to be cruel before they would permit him to be kind.

One senses the tensions this set up in his choice of later parts and in the way his writers drew on his off-screen reputation and the gathering myth of his fatal fascination. *Blood and Sand* is not so much a love story as a career story in which the women who threaten to come between him and his dedication to the arena bring out his callous side – and only then his repentant lover side. Instead of vamping a woman on the dance floor as she tilts her lips up expectantly, he curls his own lip and spurns her with the cry, 'I hate all women . . .'. Instead of a bold abduction, as in *The*

Sheik, there is an arch seduction in which a badly miscast Nita Naldi – the lady in Ibanez's novel was a blonde who attracted the dark-skinned matador by her contrasting allure – does a dated Theda Bara routine on Valentino till he spins her away from him with the cry, 'Snake! One minute I love you – the next I hate you!' The strong-weak man ends up asking forgiveness with his head resting on her lap – real passion he reserves for the bullring, just as the main assignation he keeps is not with a woman but with death.

Death and suffering were important parts of Valentino's stardom. He could be killed off at the end of a film and his fans sensed it sealed some romantic pact he had made with life – as well as putting him beyond any screen vamp's lifetime grasp. The last film he made, *The Son of the Sheik*, is not only the coda of his career but also shows the remarkable extreme to which his ambivalent love-hate appeal could be pushed. Less famous than *The Sheik* it is in every way an advance on the simple eroticism of the earlier film. Most of it is devoted not to passionate love-making, but to passionate hate. Instead of abducting an emancipated English girl and winning her back to feminine ways, Valentino, who plays both father and son and excels as his own peppery patriarch, this time carries off a dancing girl to take revenge on her for betraying him to a gang of thieves.

Nearly every look he fixes on Vilma Banky underlines his intention to humiliate and rape her. The camera takes his subjective viewpoint as he advances into a gigantic close-up of her frightened eyes and drives her backwards towards a bed like a dog cornering a sheep. His kisses are blows, not caresses; and only his father's nick-of-time arrival averts the girl's rape. The son's character is in fact an amalgam of the *two* sons in Edith M. Hull's sequel to *The Sheik*. But in placing the accent on sado-eroticism, Valentino and his writers plainly calculated where his fans' gratification lay. The fashion he had started had carried the Latin Lover to the extreme.

Personal reasons may account in part for the purgative zeal Valentino brought to the part. When he was first offered the role of the Sheik's offspring he had not been sure that it was far enough away from the brand-mark image the earlier film had stamped on him. But once in it, it took possession of him. At this very moment he had just gained his freedom from Natacha Rambova; and the sense of relief he felt, which he expressed by ordering all traces of her to be cleared out of his Hollywood home, Falcon Lair, followed him into the making of the kind of film which so little appealed to Mme Rambova's artistic pretensions.

Released a few weeks before his death from a ruptured ulcer, *The Son of the Sheik* gave Valentino's reputation the definitiveness of an obituary notice. It is not surprising that his death should have touched off mass hysteria. The myth of a fatal lover which he had helped promote into a period phenomenon, sustained by publicity and many imitators, now rushed back to its original source in his dying body intensified by the very real sense of fatality the event engendered. Only one event could have transcended it – if Valentino had almost, but not quite died. Like some more recent film stars similarly stricken in sensational circumstances at the height of their careers, and then reviving, or even returning from the state known medically as 'death', such a brush with mortality would have rendered him that little bit more immortal.

He was to enjoy only the next best thing – 'returning' in the form of spirit messages received by mediums almost before he was in his grave. It was not quite so consoling a substitute for stardom, perhaps, as the one Joseph Schenck, had prudently provided for by insuring Valentino's life for a million dollars.

Yet one has to conclude, unsentimentally and with the advantage of hindsight, that it was probably a good time to go. American womanhood, to whom Valentino had revealed the excitement of love-making, was already beginning to turn away from the foreign model and back to the home-grown American male. They were not, though, the same shy backwoods boys, the brotherly sorts and dependable types represented by Barthelmess, Wallace Reid or Thomas Meighan. Whether or not American men admitted it they had been affected by Valentino's frank revelling in his own sexuality. The appearance of a new American male star who could play the ardent lover without embarrassment restored the ordinary man's confidence in what he had previously mocked through mistrust or jealousy. And the ordinary man's wife found it refreshing, even exciting to discover in her own husband or at any rate, a more accessible male type than Valentino, all the flattering attentions that once seemed only to go with a Latin name. There was nothing Latin in the ancestry of the new star John Gilbert. All the same Gilbert knew – and being a generous man often acknowledged it – the darkly glamorous Italian youth to whose example he owed much of his own success. And anyway stardom is not a matter of nomenclature, but of attitude. 'Who are you, my lord? I do not know your name,' the dancing girl enquires of the sheik she has met in the temple ruins. 'I am he who loves you,' comes the answer with splendid certainty. 'Is not that enough?'

It was. It is.

CHAPTER ELEVEN

EXIT THE
GREAT LOVER:
JOHN GILBERT

Whenever people blame the eclipse of some of the great stars of the 1920s on the coming of the talkies, the name of John Gilbert is the one most often mentioned. There he was, the story goes, the outstanding male star of his day, the screen's Great Lover, the successor to Valentino, with Greta Garbo as his co-star, being paid 10,000 dollars a week, 250,000 dollars a picture, with a contract that guaranteed him 1,000,000 dollars in two years, in short the pride and a great part of the profit of Metro-Goldwyn-Mayer. And then, suddenly, without an interval, without even a warning, he was utterly ruined, finished, dead. Worse still, he was utterly ridiculous. For when he opened his mouth to speak in his first talkie, people laughed.

A Great Lover had no need to be a great actor. He could rise above bad scripts. He could even live down bad pictures. What he could not recover from was the embarrassment of finding he had a voice just that fatal note too high to match the impression of dazzling virility which had been projected from the silent screen. A humiliated and increasingly desperate man, Gilbert still showed up for work as his contract specified to claim his 10,000 dollars a week, only to find that his peculiarly ironic fate brought out the latent malevolence of a film studio where the public's favourite stars may be privately loathed by some of those who helped to make them. Drink, doubt, remorse and an early death complete the popular version of John Gilbert's downfall.

It all has such an awesome appropriateness to the Hollywood myth of overnight fame and sudden ruin that one almost resists casting doubt on it. The mere fact that 'talking', an ability so commonplace among the mass of ordinary folk that they hardly think of it as they do it, could menace the wealth and privilege of stars like Gilbert seems a nemesis that could have been designed for no other race of mortals.

But the generally accepted view of John Gilbert's eclipse does need to be challenged – if only to put into perspective the man's extraordinary popularity and the peculiar power that his stardom gave him in the film industry at the time. His voice did play a part in his downfall. But it is by no means proven that it played the major part.

The accepted version of Gilbert's downfall has perplexities and inconsistencies which warrant close enquiry. For example why was Gilbert not give a voice test when his studio offered him the colossal fee of 250,000 dollars per picture at the end of 1928, by which date it was clear that the talkies were there to stay and stars were almost standing in line to have judgment passed on their speaking abilities? And if Gilbert's voice caused people to fall about with mirth when they first heard him speak in *His Glorious Night* (1929), why is it hardly distinguishable in most of the films he subsequently made from the acceptable light tenor voice of many a Hollywood star in the 1930s? And why especially was a man whom M-G-M- judged to have 'no voice' in 1929 to be found co-starring with M-G-M's greatest star, Greta Garbo, in *Queen Christina* as late as 1934? 'There is a mystery in you,' says Gilbert to her in that film. It is time to turn the implied question in his direction.

The first thing to understand about John Gilbert is that he was a romantic by conviction. Valentino had been one by adoption. What Gilbert envied in the Italian-born star – 'the ease with which he wore his crown' – was in reality the reserve of a man who never quite identified with his own divinity. Valentino holds something of himself back from his fans; John Gilbert gives all of himself generously to *his* fans. For him it was the supreme kind of love affair. '*The Merry Widow* was finished,' he once wrote in tones that reproduce, with only the slightest catch of modesty, the sense of his impending stardom, 'I became a famous personage. Everywhere I went I heard whispers and gasps, in acknowledgment of my presence. "There's JOHN GILBERT!" "Hello,

Jack!" "Oh, John!" The whole thing became too fantastic for me to comprehend. Acting, the very thing which I had been fighting and ridiculing for seven years, had brought me success, riches and renown. I was a great motion-picture star. Well, I'll be damned!'* A year later with the enormous success of *The Big Parade* (1926) there is not even the conscious self-deprecation – the commitment is total. 'When I returned to my hotel, I sent for the morning newspapers and got drunk all over again, reading the reviews of the picture. No such adjectives had ever been used to describe a movie. I sat for hours crying and thrilling to the printed phrases. Then I staggered to bed and slept round the clock. I had sounded the depths and reached the peak of emotional excitement.'†

What sounds throughout this confession is not studied conceit, but goggling incredulity – the lady has accepted his favours and found them good! Well, bully for her! It was this temperamental boyishness, this emotional un-formedness, this absolute ability to yield to his feelings as he put them down on paper or panted them out on the screen which gave John Gilbert his romantic dash and self-charging energy. It matched his screen looks to perfection: his smile, his broad forehead with its crown of curly hair, his eyes whose mascara make-up provided a hypnotic darkness against which the whites flashed like phosphorus, and especially his wide-wide grin and cocky chin. It is the romantic look American-style as opposed to the romantic look Valentino-style. Gallantry is the word, rather than seduction. It is that of the pirate of romantic fiction, not the gigolo of the ballroom floor.

*   *   *

There is another vital difference between John Gilbert and Rudolph Valentino. Gilbert could appeal to women without alienating the men in the audience. The exotic style which Valentino had set in love-making had been the perfect response to the emancipated American woman's need to express her revolt, yet remain essentially a woman. But it left her husband or boy-friend feeling like a country yokel. He was unable to compete in

* *Photoplay*, September 1928.
† Ibid.

its refinements – even perhaps unwilling to make such a fuss over a woman. Gilbert in contrast, established a *camaraderie* between himself and the American male. He looked such an all-round good sport to begin with – 'the ideal companion for a hunting trip', a writer said of him. Without evincing any lack of sincerity or ardour, he took short cuts through the intricacies of wooing devised by Valentino which looked more natural and manly to male filmgoers.

Gilbert in other words did not leave them feeling outclassed. And the unabashed romanticism with which he displayed these qualities won him the male's approval and emulation at just the moment when the female, deprived of Valentino by his death, was beginning to hanker for a new kind of dash and fire in her male film idols. Gilbert made it available. He and Ronald Colman, whose star was rising around the same time, set a pattern in wholesome strength and manly romanticism which typified the American screen manner and was passed on to many of the male stars in the following decade.

Let Gilbert swerve from this image at any time in his silent-film career and he was liable to sharp rebuke from reviewers. For a change he played "an egotistical panderer' in Tod Browning's *The Show* (1927), a carnival tale set in Hungary, and at once incurred the wrath of critics. *Variety*'s reviewer echoed others when he predicted, 'It will undoubtedly hurt his general popularity with women, for while he is a great lover there is nothing romantic in the character, it being a sordid type of role which tends to degrade.'* Though the writer's fears proved groundless, they illustrate how strongly Gilbert's image was linked in the popular imagination to one type of character.

Gilbert's real name was John Pringle. His father had been a stock-company actor-manager and the boy had quit the stage at an early age with a view to becoming a film director. He was actually assisting director Maurice Tourneur when the multi-millionaire Jules Brulatour who held the controlling interest in the Eastman Kodak Company, bought up his contract with Tourneur and signed him at the age of 23 to a five-year contract,

* *Variety*, 19th March, 1927.

at 1,500 dollars a week plus half the profits, to direct films that would glorify Brulatour's *protégée* Hope Hampton. (Tourneur had refused to direct her.) Gilbert's first film nearly ruined her career – he was apparently hopeless without Tourneur – and it is entirely typical of his ingrained romanticism that being in love with Leatrice Joy, who was 3,000 miles away in California at the time, he simply tore up his contract and fled west so as to pursue the romance by less costly means than the long-distance telephone. Money troubles forced him back into screen acting.

Gilbert always affected to despise acting. And this, too, ties in with his impulsively romantic temperament. His personality lit up during the first few takes of a scene when he was keyed up to the highest pitch of interest or excitement. Subsequent takes were never as good. The trouble this caused when he co-starred with a painstaking actress like Lillian Gish have already been mentioned. Quite likely the sheer physical intensity that Gilbert put into his silent acting was in part to blame for his voice trouble in the early talkies. To relax his body, and hence his voice, while playing passionate scenes was contrary to Gilbert's nature as well as his craft.

When he was matched with an actress like Greta Garbo in *Flesh and the Devil,* who answered him flash for flash, then the effect on them both was practically incandescent. This film about a friendship between two men which is interrupted by a *femme fatale* still conveys a conviction in the sexual attraction that two people feel for each other which is very rare in the American cinema. The love scenes between Gilbert and Garbo were audacious at the time, 1927, because they were among the first to be filmed with both the man and the woman lying down; but there also seems to be a genuine erotic friction between Garbo and Gilbert going on in which they bring each other up to pitch. It is one of the few films where two completely clothed people generate sexual desire through physical contiguity – and almost the only one that makes one believe the old publicity ruse that the stars were in love off screen, too.

Gilbert's restless eyes, seeking Garbo out in the ballroom, are answered by her lips yearning automatically upwards towards his as he takes her into a dance. Outside in the garden she insinuates herself around the creepers. Her eyes are downcast one moment, flashing lustrously the next. The garden greenery, reflecting light in every leaf, lends an impalpably erotic ambiance to the encounter. Gilbert even makes one sense the dryness in his throat, especially at the flare-up of the match as he lights the cigarette Garbo has transferred from her lips to his; and its glowing tip pulsates like an emotional indicator illuminating more than physical surfaces.

*   *   *

Gilbert was not an easy actor to work with. The romantic temperament is a shallow one, but it can be very stubborn. Like many other stars he did not know what was good for him and at first resisted concepts and suggestions which ultimately repaid him a hundred-fold; though his frank admission of how wrong he had been, coupled with child-like delight at how right others were, gave him an attractive if ingenuous honesty.

His feuds with directors like King Vidor or Erich von Stroheim tended to be temperamental flare-ups followed by a drink and pledges of life-long friendship. Their direction of him also had to cope with the fact that as a one-time director himself, however unsuccessful, he would come to the film with fixed ideas about it: to break down his conceptions, they often had to play upon the other side of him, the actor's suggestibility. Fortunately for them, Gilbert was extremely impressionable. Once fired by someone else's notion, he seized it and improvised on it.

Vidor had not wanted to cast him at first as the down-to-earth doughboy in the World War One film, *The Big Parade*, because he thought he had too smooth an image; but Irving Thalberg, M-G-M's production chief, insisted on it. So Vidor cunningly created a character and then persuaded Gilbert to live it. 'I decided he would use no make-up and wear an ill-fitting uniform. Dirty finger-nails and a sweaty, begrimed face were to take the place of perfectly made-up skin texture. Jack rebelled, as I knew he would. He was well on his way to being established as the

'Great Lover' and it wasn't fair to change his character when his career after all these years was fully in the ascendancy.'* But starting on the outside was just the way to reach the inside of a romantic enthusiast. Gilbert took over the role and filled it with pure feeling – 'moment after moment of just goin' in and doin' it,' he later wrote. 'The shell-hole scene with the German soldier boy. The only thing known about it being "Jim offers him a cigarette," and when it was over Vidor's question, "Do you think you slapped him too many times?" and my hysterical reply, "God, no. I felt it." And his, "If you felt it, it's right." '†

The film historian Lewis Jacobs is possibly right, too, when he criticises *The Big Parade*, despite its phenomenal success, for being 'based in sentimentality'. But it hits the right emotions, if perhaps for the wrong reasons, and Gilbert is true from start to finish, the embodiment of Ordinary Man in uniform. He found working with Vidor that romance need not always be in the intense and capitalised state of the Great Lover. Provided his feelings were right, he could pass as naturally into a good-humoured flirtation with Renée Adorée's peasant girl. This is what makes Gilbert's romantic image so viable. Ultimately the test lay in himself – in what he felt. And only when he was forced to give voice to his feelings was he struck with self-doubt.

Yet there is always something disturbing about an actor who is 'possessed' by his roles to the extent that John Gilbert was. He carried his love-affair with love into his private life in ways that might be merely thought playful were it not for all the other unstable traits in his personality – all of which left him so vulnerable when tragedy struck. His dedication to romance was even advertised in the very names he gave to the numerous boats he owned. His schooner was called *The Temptress:* his motor-boat, *The Vampire:* his sail boat, *The Harpie:* and his dinghy, *The Witch.*

King Vidor had ample chance to observe how difficult Gilbert found it to keep his personality independent of his screen image. He tells an extraordinary anecdote in his memoirs about discovering Bea Lillie's car upside down on the road and tracing the

* King Vidor, op. cit., p. 105.
† *Photoplay*, September 1928.

'victim' to Gilbert's near-by home where he found Miss Lillie on a settee, apparently unhurt, while Gilbert 'dressed in blue brocaded silk dressing gown . . . his hair profusely greased with a white silk shirt open at the neck' kept sobbing over her, 'Iris March must not die.' 'Iris March' was the heroine of Michael Arlen's novel *The Green Hat* whose last defiant gesture against society was to crash her Hispano-Suiza into a tree. Gilbert had just starred with Garbo in the film version entitled *A Woman of Affairs*. 'The paths he followed in his daily life were greatly influenced by the parts that some scriptwriter had written for him,' Vidor adds in explanation. 'When he began to read the publicity emanating from the studio which dubbed him the "Great Lover", his behaviour in real life began to change accordingly. . . . Whatever role he was playing, he literally contrived to live it off screen.'*

Reconstructing the real world in terms of the fantasy one is among the commonest occupational ailments of film stardom. It seems to have been particularly prevalent in the 1920s. It is significant that Hollywood exoticism flourished before the realistic impact of the talkies killed quite a lot of the fantasy themes of the silent cinema, or left American stars unsuited to play them, and before the Depression at the end of the era wiped out the fabulous salaries that made it temptingly practicable to turn a film star's life into an extension of the movies that he or she made. The dizziness of freedom which their star status gave them, or appeared to do, is the particular characteristic of Hollywood idols in this decade. Only elemental wills resisted it: weak heads like Gilbert's were utterly turned by it. 'If his next assignment were a dashing Cossack,' Vidor says, 'Jack would have Russian servants in his household and guests would be entertained with a balalaika orchestra while they were served vodka and caviar.'†

The heightened intensity of this kind of life had its feedback to the movies that Gilbert made. In *The Cossacks* (1928), made at the height of his popularity (and in which Clarence Brown took a

* King Vidor, op. cit., p. 134.
† Ibid., p. 134.

hand even though the credits state that George Hill was director),*
Gilbert gives one of his most flamboyant performances. The degree
of stimulation he exhibits is almost alarming. Every flicker of
expression is on a chivalric scale. As a Cossack's playboy son who
proves himself a man by giving his (secretly gratified) father a
drubbing, enduring ferocious torture and and choking the life
out of his enemies almost as passionately as he bullies the love
out of his women, Gilbert shakes off virility as a dog might shake
off drops of water on regaining a river bank. If the film were a
talkie, the part would be played in a continual bellow. The sight
of such unnatural stimulation makes one think of someone under
the influence of narcotics. But if Gilbert is drugged by anything,
it is the style of stardom he lived on and off screen. He has become 'high' on romance.

*   *   *

After *The Cossacks* Gilbert made one more silent film, *A
Woman of Affairs*, but the accent of interest in it is now on Garbo;
their love scenes have little of the previous fire and ardour,
perhaps because their off-screen affair had also cooled. Then
came the first film in which Gilbert's voice was heard. It was not
His Glorious Night but an early all-star movie, *Hollywood Revue*
(1929), designed to prove that M-G-M stars were accomplished
'talkers'. Most of the stars on the M-G-M roster did little self-
contained acts. Gilbert and 'the gracious Norma Shearer', as the
introduction called her, chose to do for their 'turn' the balcony
scene from *Romeo and Juliet*.

This is where the mystery of John Gilbert begins. For although
his voice is light and certainly high-pitched, it seems quite unlikely to have aroused the derision that greeted *His Glorious
Night*. Indeed there are no reports that it did when *Hollywood
Revue* was shown. One reason may have been the tolerance that
filmgoers extended to the sound in general in *Hollywood Revue*: it
was on disc and even a sound engineer like Douglas Shearer,
brother of the gracious Norma and head of M-G-M's sound

* Information supplied by Kevin Brownlow from conversations with
Clarence Brown.

department, was cutting his teeth as well as his discs in these early months. Added to which the sound had to be reproduced in cinemas that were, for the most part, pitifully inexperienced or equipped to cope with the talkies.

But another reason has to do with the sequence itself. In it the stars first do the Shakespeare extract straight. Then a voice calls 'Cut!' and one sees Lionel Barrymore in the director's chair. 'How was it, Lionel?' Gilbert asks. Barrymore signifies approval in such florid terms that Gilbert cracks, 'I never know whether he's quoting or directing.' At this point a cable arrives from New York indicating the East Coast's anxiety over the 'art' sequence they have just 'filmed' and suggesting some changes to make it less highbrow. 'Call it "The Necker" ' is one of them. 'Make it modern, pep it up, don't change a thing but the main title and the dialogue.' So Gilbert and Shearer launch into a modern version of the balcony scene. Revamped dialogue like 'Julie baby . . . you're the cream in my Mocha and Java, the berries in my pie,' indicates the crudity of the joke; but what is noticeable, too, is the way Gilbert's voice grows more and more relaxed as the scene takes on the tone of running gag. In colloquial comedy like this, he feels, he *sounds*, once again at ease.

There is nothing for audiences to laugh at except the burlesque; and his higher pitch in the 'serious' balcony scene at the start of the sequence may have escaped unfavourable notice at the time because it is the 'sacred' text of Shakespeare that Gilbert is quoting and until told, in effect, 'You may now laugh,' audiences treated such a cultural recital with respect. When he came to make *His Glorious Night* he had no such protection.

No one apparently appreciated the risk of putting Gilbert into a romantic film like *His Glorious Night*, based on Molnar's play *Olympia,* in which the element that had never counted for anything in his earlier films, romantic dialogue, would now be predominant. What had been forgotten during the silent era was not the art of speech, but the ability to evaluate the effect of what was spoken. Moreover *His Glorious Night* had been rushed through production in four weeks; for M-G-M had first put Gilbert into a Tolstoy adaptation, *Redemption,* which so shocked him when he heard his voice reproduced that he begged the studio to shelve it.

Ironically when it was released a year later, in 1930, it was judged in a far more kindly fashion than *His Glorious Night*, which tends to confirm that the words put into Gilbert's mouth in the latter film damned him far more effectively than the tones in which he pronounced them. After seeing *His Glorious Night*, *Variety*'s reviewer opened his notice with words that are said to have turned Gilbert ashen when he read them: 'A few more talker productions like this and John Gilbert will be able to change places with Harry Langdon. His prowess at love-making which has held the stones breathless takes on a comedy aspect in *His Glorious Night* that gets [them] tittering at first and then laughing outright at the very first ring of the couple of dozen "I love you" phrases designed to climax . . . the thrill in the Gilbert lines. The theme is trite at best. And the dialogue, while aiming for most of the time at irony in the Continental manner, is inane.'* But the same writer added significantly, 'Gilbert presents a voice passable when it does not have to work into a crescendo.'

Sequences of the film, when viewed today, bear out this judgment. Though the sound has deteriorated, Gilbert's voice only goes shrill when his passionate declarations key him up to abnormal pitch: elsewhere he is quite 'passable', at any rate vocally. But his performance suffers from an undeniable loss of magic that has nothing to do with the quality of his voice, but derives from a loss of conviction in his playing.

What really broke Gilbert's romantic spell was the nature of the sound cinema itself. Speech made some of the most potent archetypes of the silent movies into obsolete caricatures almost overnight – and the 'Great Lover' was the earliest casualty. So long as he had no voice, the 'Great Lover' existed inside the romantic imagination of every filmgoer. The same applied to the passionate sentiments he was supposed to be uttering: they were only 'heard' by filmgoers with the inward ear. But the talkies individualised him. Speech forced him out into the open to stand competition from reality. It put a distance between him and the

* *Variety*, 9th October 1929.

audience that brought a critical perspective into play. Whereas one could have said previously, to paraphrase Pascal, that 'the heart has its reasons that the ear knows nothing of', henceforth the ear grew embarrassed at hearing the heart's outpourings.

One reaction to embarrassment is laughter; and Gilbert was only one among many film stars who found their audiences taking refuge in uneasy titters when the already high-flown lovers' dialogue was made even more absurd by the silent-picture pantomime that still accompanied it. This unsynchronised style was something that most stars quickly learned to put right – but the fate of the 'Great Lover' was the lesson from which they learned.

The very novelty of hearing love declared in so many words in a public cinema seems to have had an effect on audiences, for a short period at least, similar to that of hearing four-letter words spoken openly on a public stage many years later. It was one of shock and embarrassment. A *Variety* reporter writing three weeks after the New York *première* of *His Glorious Night* noted: 'Not only has Gilbert received the bird lately, but all the other male screen players who specialise in romance. Charles Farrell in *Sunny Side Up* (1929) draws many a giggle for his mush stuff. In the silents, when a lover could whisper like a ventriloquist, lips apart and unmoving, and roll his eyes occasionally preparatory to the clinch and the kiss, it looked pretty natural and was tolerable. The build-up to the kissing now makes a gag of the kissers. When the kiss is with serious intent, the laughs are out of order. . . . [But it seems] the only kind of love stuff received as intended since the advent of the talkers is the comedy love scene. The screen comics are becoming the kissing lovers and the heavy lovers, comedians.'

Sound reproduction in cinemas equipped for the talkies was still imperfect enough to give the 'Great Lover' a rough time. 'The usual kiss, delivered with the usual smack, sounds like an explosion. For that reason clinch scenes in the early talkers had them rolling in the aisles . . . but suitable or not, the kissers are getting laughs where they don't belong. Soft pedal on dialogue in romantic love scenes in the future. Hereafter the saccharine stuff will be put over in pantomime. The order has gone out since audiences gave the razz to the romantic chatter in John Gilbert's *His Glorious Night*. Studios have found that the . . . big he-man pulling the soft patter won't be taken seriously. Someone in the audience titters and it's all off. Hereafter the love passages will be suggested with the romantic note carried by properly pitched music. Metro, the first to learn by experience, is leading the way. Others follow suit for their own protection.'*

Other contemporary reports bear out the same audience reactions. *Photoplay* commented: 'As the Talkies grow to maturity, one terrible, tragic fact has been learned. Love scenes that were tender and impressive in the silent days now get the succulent and vulgar raspberry in dialogue. John Gilbert has been a victim. The same amorous technique that made Jack adored and famous in the dear old days is inclined to raise a storm of titters in the new.'†

Evidence of this kind helps dispel the belief that Gilbert's ruin was entirely on account of his voice. It certainly did not help. But the really fatal element was the matter of passion, not pitch.

*   *   *

Nevertheless, it is extremely relevant to ask why John Gilbert was never given a voice test, especially when M-G-M at the end of 1928 was preparing to sign him to a new contract of quite fabulous proportions. It is an amazing neglect, if indeed it is a 'neglect' at all. Certain evidence exists which suggests that it was not: that, on the contrary, it was connected with one of the strangest deals in Hollywood history in which John Gilbert was almost certainly an innocent party.

This deal concerned nothing less than the sale of the vast M-G-M empire to one of its greatest rivals. Details of it are still a matter of controversy, but the general plan is now fairly well established. Late in the autumn of 1928 Nicholas Schenck then president of Loew's Inc., the East Coast end of M-G-M, secretly canvassed a group of stockholders with a view to selling a controlling interest in M-G-M to the producer William Fox for the

* Ibid., 30th October 1929.
† *Photoplay*, January 1930.

sum of 50 million dollars. Those whose power base was in the Hollywood studio, in particular Louis B. Mayer, Irving Thalberg and J. Robert Rubin,* were to be kept in the dark until the public announcement in March 1929, since they did not own any sizeable holdings in Loew's Inc. But Loew's Inc. needed to be sure that it could also 'sell' the M-G-M stars to Fox, otherwise the deal lost a lot of its allure.

Lon Chaney, Ramon Novarro, Marion Davies, Garbo, Joan Crawford and others were all safe under contracts of a reasonable duration, but John Gilbert's contract had just over a year to run and he was talking of going over to United Artists whose president was Nicholas Schenck's brother Joseph. It was also probable that if the deal with Fox fell through, Loew's Inc. and United Artists would form a producing combine, dropping Louis B. Mayer but retaining Irving Thalberg as production chief. Either way, it was essential to 'secure' a superstar like Gilbert so as to use him in the bargaining with Fox or United Artists.

Consequently Gilbert was offered a contract of unprecedented terms, drawn up in December 1928, for four pictures, two a year, at 250,000 dollars per picture. In addition he got the right to approve his co-stars, certain discretion over the choice of stories and directors, an elaborate new dressing-room which was built at a cost of 30,000 dollars, and the right to have his affairs handled independently of the studio by his personal manager, the powerful Harry Edington who had come over to this side of the business from M-G-M's accounts department bringing much inside know-how with him.† Mayer had nothing to do with these terms: they were agreed between Gilbert and Nicholas Schenck. As for giving Gilbert a voice test, even if Schenck had thought it prudent he was scarcely in a position to insist on one while courting a star whose signature he needed so badly.

Ultimately the deal fell through. In fact the financial risks which Fox accepted while negotiations were still on, coupled with an

* Rubin was Mayer's lawyer and the man who had negotiated the signing of Anita Stewart which had set Mayer up in business.

† Edington was also Garbo's manager and helped manufacture much of her myth, including the solo billing of her as 'Garbo' in the manner of 'Bernhardt' or 'Duse'.

accident which put him out of action for several vital weeks, contributed to his own bankruptcy. Relations between Mayer and Schenck dropped to freezing point. And the only gainer in the bizarre affair seemed to be Gilbert who was left holding a contract for one of the highest fees ever paid to a film star – and an iron-clad contract, too. It could not be broken by the studio. In his need for speed Schenck had been forced to forego the usual option clauses.

So much can be established with reasonable certainty; where speculation begins is how such manoeuvring may have harmed Gilbert's relationship with Mayer. For here the actor had made a grave mistake. By doing his own deal direct with Nicholas Schenck, he had shown his independence of the man who was head of the studio. If the risks in this needed underlining, the *Variety* headline of 19th December 1928, obliged. 'LOUIS MAYER LEAVING M-G-M IN MARCH,' it announced, 'WITH JACK GILBERT REMAINING AS ITS FILM STAR.'

The first statement, though it proved incorrect, was distinctly ominous at the time. But much worse was the linking of Mayer's name with Gilbert's in the same report. It rubbed a painful lesson in, publicly, so far as Mayer was concerned. It implied that a film star was more important than a film magnate – that the head of the studio could be done without, but not an employee whose career he had shaped. Mayer was a dangerous man to slight. Along with vast power he combined a vindictive nature. He is known to have ruined several stars' careers for perverse personal reasons usually connected with some real or imaginary offence to his own ego or outlook. Bosley Crowther's biography of him, *Hollywood Rajah*, reveals the reverence in which he held things dear to his family and his religion. No one trespassed here with impunity.

Yet here, too, Gilbert had apparently already offended him. '. . . Shortly after they made *The Big Parade,*' writes Crowther, 'Gilbert was telling Mayer his life story and casually remarked he believed his mother was a whore. "What's that you say?" Mayer hollered. "I said my mother was a whore," Gilbert replied. This horrified Mayer so profoundly that he leaped on Gilbert in violent wrath and was pounding the astonished actor when associates pulled them apart. Ever after, the innocent Gilbert was held in scorn by Mayer.'*

This was probably the relationship between the two when Mayer met William Fox in New York while the Fox-Loew's deal was still on. Fox, too, disliked Gilbert. He had fired him some years earlier because he took objection to the shape of his nose – it had a slight bulbous tendency, which Gilbert's moustache had been specifically grown to counter-balance. Fox made it plain that he was displeased about Gilbert's new million-dollar contract; and Mayer, who had not been party to the making of it, whole-heartedly agreed with him. Fox is then reported to have said to Mayer, 'I'll tell you how to get rid of him. Give him a couple of bad parts. That'll make him mad.'† But it seems that Mayer rejected this suggestion on the spot. He probably appreciated that while 'a couple of bad parts' would indeed make Gilbert mad, at a quarter of a million dollars apiece they might also make M-G-M bankrupt. Mayer was a good hater, but he was a business-man first: he did not strike others until they were in no position to hurt him. His feelings must have been mixed indeed some months later when the star who had threatened to eclipse him at his own studio was personally humiliated and had his commercial value written down overnight when he made his first talkie.

Even so, he may have reckoned, Gilbert was still enormously popular, stars like him had a fanatically loyal public, and Mayer was committed to pay him a quarter of a million dollars a picture. ...A desperate attempt was now made to redeem Gilbert's reputation by recasting his image. Irving Thalberg realised, perhaps even before Gilbert did, that sound had turned the 'Great Lover' archetype into an antique. So Gilbert in his next film, *Way for a Sailor* (1930) was accordingly cast as a hard-boiled, hard-drinking mariner who takes his loves lightly. Reviewers generally found that 'his voice shows great improvement'. But some evidence of the trouble this had taken is provided by the film being booked into the Capitol Theater, New York, and withdrawn no fewer than three times, partly because of censorship differences,

* Bosley Crowther, op. cit., p. 145.
† Ibid., p. 145.

but mainly because of difficulties at the studio in manipulating the microphone to give Gilbert's voice more bass.

But if he was judged 'okay for sound', the new image was less well received. 'This can't be considered complete ruination for Gilbert,' the *Variety* reviewer wrote. 'His voice isn't at all bad. . . . His diction merely doesn't suit a hard-boiled sailor character. But the voice in the film sounds suitable for the element in which Gilbert belongs, drawing-room material minus the heavy love stuff. Metro's attempt to make him into a rough guy, of the Mc-Laglen type, appears a case of bad judgment.'* The opinion was endorsed by the box-office receipts.

The impact of all this on Gilbert was shattering. Hitherto his insecurity about his real role in life had been masked by the zest with which he threw himself into playing the part of a romantic on and off screen. Now that this no longer worked, he was left virtually without an identity. He had suffered one of the worst rebuffs a man could – his very masculinity had been mocked. The fact that it was his wife, Ina Claire, who now took it on herself to give him voice lessons while pursuing her own successful acting career was more a cause for aggravation than comfort. And money only rubbed in the awful irony without salving it. There he was being paid (or about to be paid†) a fantastic fee per picture and around the studio he was, at best, an object of pity – at worst, one of vindictive satisfaction.

He knew he had made an enemy of Mayer. He knew he depended on Thalberg to help him create a new image. He was made to feel that he needed a new voice – and this seemed to depend on Thalberg's brother-in-law, Douglas Shearer, in M-G-M's sound department. And all the time the new male stars of the 1930s – Gable, Tracy, Fredric March, Cooper – were beginning to assert themselves and challenge his tottering supremacy as the screen's leading male idol. Gilbert gradually withdrew into moroseness and intemperance.

One can appreciate in retrospect that his salvation might have

* *Variety*, 17th December 1930.
† It has not been possible to fix with accuracy exactly when Gilbert's new contract came into operation.

been possible in the light, slightly cynical comedy of the Lubitsch type which would have put few strains on his passions, and hence his vocal powers, and perhaps even made capital out of casting him against the kind of lover he had made celebrated. But Lubitsch was over at Paramount and Gilbert was bound to M-G-M by that golden contract.

The trouble with the films M-G-M assigned him to was not that they were poorly made. They had good directors like Mervyn LeRoy, John S. Robertson, and first-rate scriptwriters, like Leonore Coffee and Gene Markey; but as films they simply did not command enough public interest to be sure of more than modest box-office success, and probably not even that sometimes. His voice was judged perfectly all right in most cases. In an off-beat role like that in *The Phantom of Paris* (1931), where he played a Houdini-ish magician who solves a crime by passing as a double for the murderer, he was able to profit from the cynical and embittered temperament that was now the dominant one in his off-screen life. Critics found him 'far more forceful than he has been since sound made him speak'.*

But this film was followed by a potboiler, *West of Broadway* (1932), which did not even open at Loew's main cinema, but at a neighbourhood 'grind' theatre on 83rd Street – a sure sign for the star of his falling appeal. The film is obviously the work of a man who is now living out his contract; and Gilbert himself declared on a visit to London, a few months before its *première*, that his remaining M-G-M films would be 'lemons', adding that it was always so when a star's contract was not being renewed. But this is perhaps not the whole truth about the film. It shows internal evidence of having had to accommodate features of Gilbert's personal life that would have made any studio think him a bad bet. He plays a millionaire who marries a girl while intoxicated and spends much of the remainder of the film drinking heavily. Gilbert gives a suspiciously good impersonation of a drunk. 'That's the only thing the picture doesn't exaggerate,' said one trade critic with an edge of inside knowledge to his notice. His voice was, again, judged to be quite satisfactory.

* Ibid., 15th November 1931.

The next film Gilbert made was even more illuminating. He wrote the story of *Downstairs* (1932) himself and it co-starred his new wife, Virginia Bruce, and himself as 'Mr and Mrs John Gilbert'. (The billing was unofficial and designed to help its box-office appeal.) The film is extraordinarily bitter in tone and shows a disenchantment with all that had made Gilbert a star in his romantic heyday. *Variety*'s chief reviewer opened his notice in a way that might have been mistaken for an obituary. 'John Gilbert, who used to be a scenario writer himself, must have known what he was about when he didn't do right by himself in this script. . . . Maybe [he] figured that, since among his "used-to-be's" could be included the scintillation of a passionate screen favourite, he [would] make his "ex"-career 100 per cent by fashioning a story such as this for himself. Anyone knowing Gilbert may well appreciate this trend of thought.'*

It is certainly true that Gilbert's role, which is that of an unscrupulous chauffeur in a baron's household who elopes with the butler's bride, is the reversal of all his romantic attributes; he goes in for blackmail, conmanship and double-crossing. Yet as acting goes, it is a very satisfactory piece of work. Von Stroheim might have fashioned exactly this kind of image for him in the early days had Thalberg approved of the commercial wisdom of turning romanticism inside out to show its shabby lining. But it is also possible that Gilbert was trying to re-cast his own appeal more in the cynical image of Clark Gable who had now established what a huge following there was for a star who treated women roughly and made them like it. In one respect, though, *Variety* was right: the film did no business at all. The public could not see Gilbert as Gable.

By this time Gilbert and Louis B. Mayer were not on speaking terms. The star resolutely reported for work at the studio, lest his absence provided a cause for cancelling or disputing the contract under which he was still paid 10,000 dollars a week. If some reports are to be believed, he was made to suffer numerous petty humiliations: the gateman, it was said, sometimes failed to recognise him or a new staffer would pointedly enquire what his

* Ibid., 11th October 1932.

business was. After one more feature, the expiry of his contract mercifully ended what had become essentially a self-destructive relationship with M-G-M.

*   *   *

Yet barely a year later M-G-M was being forced to take John Gilbert back on the payroll and co-star him with the studio's most prestigious actress, Greta Garbo. The truth is that Garbo had demanded Gilbert as her leading man for *Queen Christina* (1933). The studio had been appalled at the thought of a has-been playing love scenes with its top female star. But Garbo was adamant. The reason why she requested Gilbert was as simple as it was rare in the movies – loyalty. It was Gilbert who had got Garbo her first big break by approving her as his co-star in *Flesh and the Devil,* in 1926, and offering no objection to her receiving equal billing in the picture. She now gracefully 'sent back the lift'.

The studio had wanted John Barrymore for the part of the Spanish ambassador in *Queen Christina.** Garbo did not approve him. Nils Asther and Fredric March were also rejected. The shortage of the 'Great Lover' type in the new decade is shown by the necessity M-G-M was then put to – of testing a relative 'unknown', Laurence Olivier. Rouben Mamoulian, who directed the film, has described how he persuaded Garbo to do a screen test – an unheard of chore for her at this time – in order to see how the young Olivier withstood her presence. It is perhaps not surprising that, with Garbo's heart set on Gilbert, Olivier found her coldly unhelpful. Gilbert got the part – but paid a humiliating price.

Just how humiliating came to light in 1934 when he began a suit against M-G-M for declaratory relief from the contract which he had had to sign before being cast with Garbo. It had provided that the studio might use his services for three films a year, as actor and director, at the fee of 20,000 dollars per picture – less than one tenth of his star salary – but it did not stipulate that M-G-M would in fact do so. It also gave the studio the right to

* Information supplied by Rouben Mamoulian.

Gilbert's services for one year with options for six additional years – but again it did not provide for specific employment or for payment in the event that M-G-M would elect not to use his services as actor or director. An agreement like this could have had only one aim – to ensure that the studio got the advantage of any miraculous come-back that Gilbert might have pulled off in his co-starring role with Garbo.

As it turned out, the precaution was unnecessary. The film puts the accent of romantic interest entirely on Garbo, though Gilbert plays a gallant second to her. The hours of agony which, according to Rouben Mamoulian, were consumed on the set in calming his nerves and keeping his vocal tones steady hardly show up at all in his performance. It was rumoured that M-G-M had used a double for his voice; and in some scenes, particularly when Gilbert first meets Garbo in the snow-bound inn, his vocal strength seems excessive when matched against his lip movements, though this may just be due to re-looping of the dialogue after the scene had been shot – a common enough necessity in movies. Mamoulian denies knowledge of anyone dubbing for Gilbert. All one can say is that it would not have been surprising if M-G-M's anxiety to protect the studio's investment in the film, and Garbo, had made them secretly resort to this subterfuge. One cannot be sure.

There is one rather remote, though interesting sidelight. On or around 3rd January, 1934, just a week or two after *Queen Christina's* New York *première*, one Herman Cline, aged 28, the son of a Los Angeles chief of detectives, was killed when he fell, or jumped, from the window of a hotel in Denver. In an obituary note which appeared in a film trade periodical, Cline was said to have dubbed the voice of John Gilbert in some of the actor's films. No further details have become available – except one which throws no light on the dubbing but only an eerie irony on Cline's death. It occurred a few hours after he had had to break off his night-club act – because his voice had cracked.

John Gilbert made his last film at Columbia Studios, then known as 'The Home of Fallen Stars'. He played a character in *The Captain Hates the Sea* (1934) who closely resembled what he himself had by now become: a burnt-out, self-loathing, ex-Hollywood talent, a writer in this case who goes on a sea cruise to help him lay off the bottle and begin a new book. And Gilbert acts the part well. Lewis Milestone directed the film, an extraordinary assembly of cut-price stars including The Three Stooges, which steers a zig-zag course between being a poor man's *Grand Hotel* and a floating *Dinner at Eight*.

Gilbert was drinking heavily throughout the shooting, and his very slightly swaying stance in scene after scene conveys the unsettling feeling that he is not just acting drunk, though his voice comes through unslurred and dryly cynical. In place of the old romantic fire he had developed a raffish Errol Flynn-ish charm. With his slightly fuller face he could almost pass for Flynn's double. The picture ends with his wife collecting him on the quay-side when the cruise ship docks again. 'Did you stop drinking?' she asks him. – 'No.' – 'Did you start your book?' she asks. – 'No,' he answers again. And that was the last heard on the screen from John Gilbert.

He died from a heart attack a few months after the film was released. He had been drinking even more heavily and was having psychiatric help. Adela Rogers St John has reported meeting him in an agitated state, swearing he was going to kill Louis B. Mayer, for whom he had developed a pathological hatred, and then shoot himself. It was a sad, though not entirely a dishonourable way for a 'Great Lover' to go; and in his last film he even manages to make a bitter jest about it. For surely Gilbert must have savoured, and may even have inspired, the irony of the moment in *The Captain Hates the Sea* when the writer unpacks his cabin trunk and finds that his wife has bought him a new suit for the voyage – a rather flashy 'ice cream' suit for tropical wear which reminds him of his palmier days in Beverly Hills. Gilbert eyes it hollowly for a second, then puts it back in the trunk; and with an undertone of contempt for all it now represents to him, he quips, 'I know I lived in Hollywood, but after all you got to remember I came from Chicago.'

For a man whom the talkies supposedly ruined, he managed to have a caustic last word.

CHAPTER TWELVE

RULES OF CONDUCT: THE ROLE OF SCANDAL

Scandal has been one of the greatest of Hollywood myths. The belief in its power to besmirch reputations, and hence jeopardise the investments that had been made in the talents and personalities of the owners, persisted in Hollywood from the early 1920s until well into the 1950s. The period spans almost precisely those years when film stars were turning their independence over to the studios in return for systematised stardom as part of the production machine and a continually inflating scale of salaries and mode of living.

The need to live a moral life in public, or, at any rate, to appear to do so, was built into the economy of the film industry at a very early date. 'Mary Miles Minter,' said a report in 1919, 'has signed a three-an-a-half years contract with the Realart Company, a corporation [behind which] is Adolph Zukor of Paramount. . . . She will, for the term of her contract, receive 1,300,000 dollars. The pictures are to be divided into four groups of five; for the first five, 50,000 dollars each. For the second five, 70,000 dollars each, and the third five, 80,000 dollars each. But the most interesting part is that this contract is alleged to concern itself with the star's intimate life and mode of living. She is not to become a "public figure" except in the ways that the Zukor evangelists direct. She can be interviewed seldom, if ever – except as a part of the said evangelism. She must be seen very little in public, if at all. She is to be a real "home body" and have an existence only in her work. *And she must not marry.*'*

This arrangement shows two trends very clearly. One is the

* *Photoplay*, September 1919.

assumption of the right to control an artist's whole life as if her personal life were simply an extension of her public one, and especially in the emotional or sexual areas which might conflict with the public image of the star. The other trend is the mistrust of the press. The dependence on newspapers and magazines to project favourable images of their stars has only been exceeded by Hollywood's own anxiety to protect the latter from the unfavourable attentions of writers and reporters. The tremendous real-money investment a star represented once he or she had become the centre of the 'star system' is again the reason for such an attitude. The apprehension of scandal in this way, and the counter-measures taken to cover it up or neutralise it, all contributed to the phenomenon of Hollywood stardom.

The sheer concentration of stars in one place made them particularly vulnerable to scandal hunters – but also to studio surveillance. Blackmail in these circumstances was not limited to the means used by an outsider to extort money from a star who had been detected offending against the moral code of society: it could be used, and was, as a weapon by the studio which invoked morality clauses in contracts to make a 'difficult' star fall into line. With the 1930s and the widespread establishment of the iniquitous system whereby time lost during a star's contract period, through indiscipline or indiscretion, was added on to the term of the contract and might continue to be added on indefinitely, the threat of 'moral turpitude' became a rod that was permanently kept in the studio closet.

Something called 'verbal turpitude' made its appearance in 1932 following a magazine interview in which Tallulah Bankhead stated that she could have a love affair with any man an hour after meeting him. The Hays Office, the industry's own self-regulatory organisation, appealed to all major newspapers and magazines not to reprint the offending part of the interview – and the star, editor and reporter concerned all received the studio's stern rebuke and threat of reprisals. When Miss Bankhead quit Hollywood soon afterwards to return to the stage, her studio had no regrets at all. Her notoriety had constantly imperilled the career Hollywood wished to carve out for her.

Things were easier, however, at the start of the 1920s. Censorship had not yet been institutionalised in the shape of the Hays Office or the Motion Picture Production Code or the Roman Catholic Legion of Decency. Nor had the magnetic pull of the star concept drawn reporters to the film capital in such numbers as followed the coming of the talkies and the move west of Broadway talent which brought along many of its own camp followers among the columnists. By the end of 1931 it was estimated that there were 300 reporters in Hollywood, covering about 150 screen names or less, and including eighty foreign correspondents. In 1921, on the other hand, it would have been surprising to find more than a dozen directly accredited Hollywood correspondents.

In a rough way one can check the increase of press interest and pressure by observing how Hollywood social life altered during the decade. For the stars at the beginning of it generally benefited from the Pollyanna attitude that the fan magazines took towards them. They were presented as glamorous yet virtuous, privileged yet homely, extremely rich yet essentially ordinary folk. They were better, in fact, than ordinary folk. 'I have never known anyone losing caste for any personal action or opinion yet,' wrote one influential observer, clinching such broadmindedness by adding, 'Even that part of the colony that is happily married and lives more like the rest of the world, subscribes to this *esprit de corps*.'*

A Hollywood topography published at this time reinforced the notion of the stars as just plain folks. If it is to be believed – and the important thing is that, for a number of years, it was – many stars lived their public lives in nowhere more sensational than the flourishing tearooms, like Kitty's Come-On Inn ('the most popular . . . frequented by Viola Dana, Colleen Moore, with Wally Reid at the piano'), or Marion's ('. . . its phonograph, all the latest records, and the best devil cake and real Chinese tea. Antonio Moreno a frequenter.')

Permissible 'bohemia' was represented in this slightly Watteau-esque ambience, accepted as real by many millions of fans, by the Laurel Canyon colony of odd, tumbledown little

* Ibid., May 1921.

houses where the 'extra' girls had made their homes, keeping on
their camera make-up during the day, smoking incessantly,
wearing their hair bobbed and going bare-headed even in the
rain. Moral welfare for these bare-heads was strenuously dis-
pensed at the Studio Club, founded by various 'women of
standing' in the film colony such as Mrs William de Mille and Mrs
Jesse Lasky, with a screen celebrity playing hostess every Sunday.
'Margery Daw, Doug's leading lady, at the phonograph, a
divertissement on the ukulele by Carmel Myers . . . accompanied by
Constance Talmadge on a "sublimated sophietucker" of the latest
jazz tune, while Margaret Loomis – lately a South Sea Island belle
for Sessue Hayakawa – taps her toe in time.'*

This extraordinary impression of moral protectiveness and
gentility had of course some basis in reality: it was a hangover
from the days of the theatrical stock companies. It survived visibly
for several years in the posed and flattering studio-portraits of the
stars that fan magazines used, for the portable and intrusive
'candid' camera did not come into general deployment for nearly
a decade.

* * *

But Hollywood was indeed like a small town in many of its
attitudes. Scandal did not begin to manifest itself so long as many
of its celebrities lived in one or two hotels. It emerged as a force
to be reckoned with about the same time as the stars' inflated
salaries enabled them to live a 'private life' in style. By 1921 the
bungalow court, consisting of eight or ten houses grouped round
a bit of greenery, had begun to scatter the celebrities in a way that
facilitated permissive behaviour. The move into private homes
that followed in the next few years is cited by one of the residents,
Anita Loos, as the beginning of 'the film capital's mass mis-
behaviour'.

Linked with this perhaps is the spread of night spots, which
suggests that the stars were already feeling the hot breath of the
columnists and needed to escape from their easily accessible
concentration in a few central and public restaurants. The Malibu
beach colony came into existence at the end of the 1920s just so

* Ibid., May 1921.

that the stars would play, drink and otherwise amuse themselves out of the sight and hearing of gossip columnists – or so they hoped. The same reason partially accounts for the dearth of any genuine social life that might relieve the pressures of stardom. (Other factors, though, played a preponderant part in this, including the way the stars' screen ratings dictated their guest lists and the habit of working long hours in the days before unions tightened their grip.)

On the other hand conspicuous consumption grew rapidly in Hollywood in keeping with the spiralling cost of films in the mid-1920s; and this display of material wealth and mode of life in the days when servants were plentiful gradually eroded the 'ordinary folks' image of the stars; while the scandals which broke in the early 1920s replaced the fans' naïve curiosity with a kind of envious cynicism. Apathy, too, played a part.

For by 1926 signs of a box-office decline began to be felt. The public had grown jaded by feature films which had become standardised in plot and routine in the telling. It needed to have its appetite whetted. One means was to be the talkies; another was the creative use of scandal and sensation.

Fan magazines had probably been feeling the public listlessness, too, and this may account for the disenchanted, even hostile attitude many of them began manifesting towards the stars in the late 1920s. For the first time the stars were expressly pictured as 'victims'. Resentment of their luxury was barely concealed in articles that expressed pity for their condition. *Photoplay* reminded its readers of the penalties some of the stars had paid, how scandal, temperament, broken marriages, type-casting, premature fame, public fickleness and, yes, even bad pictures had consigned many of them to oblivion. Ruth Waterbury rehashed old scandals in an article entitled 'Underworld of Hollywood'. ('Its symbol is the flapper. Its lure – gold. Its trade – gin and sex.') And Adela Rogers St John, a very influential show-business columnist, drew enormous readership response with a *Photoplay* series, in 1927, based on fictionalised but, she claimed, real-life cases of aspiring stars entitled 'Hollywood: Port of Missing Girls.'

The studios reacted to the new trend with pained apprehension.

Their concern was still linked with the fear of censorship that might be imposed on them by Federal legislation. What increased it was the threat by religious and civic bodies to boycott the box-office: a threat that could be applied in a very real way and in a very short time. No studio was anxious to take the risk of defying such critics. Yet the likelihood is that while the pressure groups made their protests felt in the jittery front office, the fans simply went on lining up at the box-office. In other words the studio obsession with 'respectability' was a less realistic reaction than the fans' appetite for 'sensationalism'.

But Hollywood never had the courage of its transgressions whether they were actual or imputed. It welcomed a certain degree of sensation, but ran for cover if it looked like hurting. Two examples can be quoted which show the ways in which the producers tried to guard or salvage star reputations. One concerns Cecil B. DeMille, the other Clara Bow.

The de Mille case history reveals nothing less than an attempt to hold human nature in check for seven years. It came to light in June, 1927, when Dorothy Cumming, who had played the Madonna in DeMille's religious epic, *The King of Kings* (1927), sued her husband for divorce. Lawyers stated that under a contract signed with DeMille the previous year she must so regulate her personal life for seven years that not the slightest reflection might be cast on her character 'thereby to prevent any degrading or besmirching of the role she was about to play'. The contract spelled out the reason, and the penalties, in some detail. It stated that 'because the people of the Christian faith are sensitive concerning their faith and are anxious that no reflection, direct or indirect, be cast upon Christ or his Mother in particular, during the seven years designated as "the life" of *The King of Kings,* Miss Cumming must conduct herself with the regard to public convention and morals, and at all times must observe and act in entire accord with strict Christian conduct and behaviour.' Such pieties were not unconnected with more worldly considerations – as was the case in most DeMille productions. Miss Cumming was also prohibited from working for any other producer till her seven years were up.

It was contended – successfully as it turned out – that a clause like this inserted in a film star's contract was an infringement of personal liberty. It is probably a minor and slightly extreme case, though similar considerations applied as late as 1965, when Max von Sydow was cast as Christ in *The Greatest Story Ever Told* and had to agree to forego press interviews and live an extremely circumspect life, as regards smoking, drinking, etc., at least until shooting on the film was finished. The Cumming case shows not only the ingrained fear of scandal, but also the desire that there should be no 'conflict of images' where a star was concerned. The public in other words should accept that the star's characteristics, as real person or screen image, were not irreconcilably crossed.

It is true that an actress playing a sacred role in a religious epic was a rather special case of this kind, and her image was best served by retiring the public side of it into virtual obscurity, but an example of what happens when public and screen images come into collision has occurred more recently when Ingrid Bergman's name was linked sensationally with the Italian director Roberto Rossellini. Publicity and the parts she played had persuaded her fans that Miss Bergman was a star in whom romance ran strong but pure. Her settled home life had seemed to bear this out. When she shattered the image people felt they had been deceived. An attempt was made to re-adjust her image to reality by the lurid publicity surrounding her appearance in Rossellini's film *Stromboli* (1949); but it was some years before a star part, bolstered by a publicity campaign which stressed the irresistible nature of human passions, was found in which she could mollify her public. Ironically it was the part of Anastasia, a woman seeking to regain her reputation and identity.

But where the star's off-screen life appears to transfuse her screen image, or vice versa, then however embarrassing it may be for the studio which has her under contract, her box-office reputation is rarely harmed and can even be enhanced. Elizabeth Taylor is one star whose off-screen life and temperament have many similarities with the roles she plays. When the public sense this, it confers a mythical quality on even her worst films. But of course she is a modern star, bound to no studio, who has profited by the permissiveness prevalent in films and society.

One of the nearest ancestors of her inside an earlier, traditional Hollywood is Clara Bow, the 'It' Girl of the 1920s, whose perpetual readiness for wild parties, flirtatious offers, assorted experience and disregard for convention made her the idol of the flappers. Her off-screen life was indeed an extension of her movies: in both she showed an appetite for emotional gratification that left the ensuing messes to be cleared up as best they could. Life, though, was not so tidily co-operative as her scriptwriters: and Paramount had prudently inserted a morality clause in her contract guaranteeing her a 500,000 dollar bonus at the expiration of it if she did not 'run wild' too publicly.

Towards the end of the 1920s, however, she was involved in several scandals including an alienation suit which cost her studio a reported 30,000 dollars to settle and lost Clara her bribe for good behaviour. This was followed almost at once by bad publicity as the result of a visit to a Nevada casino where Clara had dropped 14,000 dollars and paid it off in cheques which she had later had stopped. The cumulative publicity, including an unfounded report that the star had entertained Al Capone in her dressing room, thoroughly alarmed the Hays Office.

A somewhat desperate studio took what was then a novel line in rehabilitating their star, for Clara's contract had too many months left to run to make it attractive to drop her. Much of the publicity was the sort that could not be denied, consequently it was capitalised on. Clara's image was recast to conform with the heightened interest that the public were taking in her. Her new film, *No Limit*, was given a more pointed gambling angle and the flirtatious thoughtlessness that often seemed to redeem Clara's provocativeness in other films was toned down. The studio in short made the best of a bad job by absorbing her real reputation into her screen image.

One helpful side-effect was derived from public cynicism. Accustomed by this time to studio-managed publicity for the stars, some filmgoers simply decided that the gambling scandal was a stunt, too.

*   *   *

It is exceedingly doubtful if any star has ever been ruined solely by scandal, for a studio has ample techniques at its command, if the will is there, to save the sinner and rehabilitate the outcast. But sometimes the will has faltered. It was especially shaky in the days when the Hollywood tycoons, with memories of their recent immigrant past clinging to them, feared that scandal might bring them into conflict with an older, more confident way of life to which they themselves aspired. The making of distinctly American movies was for many of them a passport to the new society – a way of integrating themselves into it despite the race and class prejudices that still existed, even in Hollywood, towards the founders of the major new industry of the twentieth century. The fear did not dwindle till a new, assured generation of film-makers took control and the industry itself was made a less obvious target by the dissolution of the studio system from the mid-1950s onward. Such a lingering apprehension can be traced back to the traumatic shocks that the industry sustained in the early 1920s just when it had passed from being a big business into a mass production entity.

Each of these scandals has been exhaustively examined. Some of those who featured prominently in at least one of them are still alive and it is doubtful if anything more can be prudently added to the story at this time. But the internal industry politics in another of them deserve fuller attention than they have got to date: for they throw interesting light on the damage it was feared that scandal could do to the industry and those who ran it.

One of these sensations occurred in 1923 when it was revealed that Wallace Reid, a star of the decent, 'upright' breed with a large following, had been a drug addict. Since the news did not break till after his death it hardly affected his career; but from Hollywood's viewpoint even the posthumous consequences were grave since they showed that racketeers were flourishing in the film colony, pushing heroin and cocaine among the stars.

Defensive action was necessary, so the valour of Reid's personal fight against addiction was emphasised in an attempt to play down the wider implications. His widow even appeared in a film, *Human Wreckage* (1923), dealing with the physical and moral breakdown of a narcotics victim, a young lawyer in this case, who is brought to ruin and death. How he fought the habit, aided by a faithful wife, was the theme. (An interesting sidelight was the *Caligari*-inspired décor intended to give an addict's eye-view of the world.) The film certainly deflected the public response to the Reid scandal from one of outrage at the moral delinquency of the film colony to one of compassion for the widow and family of a gallant but weak young star.

A less happy solution had been found the previous year to the still unsolved murder of the film director William Desmond Taylor. Taylor himself was scarcely a household name; but two top stars, Mabel Normand and Mary Miles Minter, were implicated in the police enquiries apparently because they were among the last people to see Taylor alive on the night of his killing. The personal publicity which the actresses received was hardly helpful to their careers and entirely unwelcomed by their studios; but this alone cannot be blamed for their gradual eclipse in the following years. Ill health and bad pictures were more mundane reasons than a front-page scandal.

But for awesome finality and long-term implications neither of these notorious events can compare with the tragedy of Fatty Arbuckle who was at the height of his fame as a screen comedian when he suddenly had to face a manslaughter charge. It arose out of a party he gave on 5th September, 1921, in a San Francisco hotel, at which a small-part actress, Virginia Rappe, died of 'internal injuries'. There is no doubt that Arbuckle's excessive weight which made him so funny as the screen's fat man rendered him poor service in these changed circumstances. It made him into a monster of lust in the public's imagination; and though he was acquitted after two trials, his screen career was ruined and the films of his which were awaiting release when the scandal broke were destined never to be shown.

As Will Hays, Hollywood's overseer of morals and public relations, put it sanctimoniously in his memoirs, 'the two men who *deserve the credit* for that decision are Joseph N. Schenck, who had Arbuckle under contract, and Adolph Zukor, of Paramount, who had been producing the latest Arbuckle comedies.'* For a time Arbuckle was blacklisted; and though this was eventually ended his face was never again seen in a star role on the screen. He found individual champions among Hollywood directors and a few executives, but the industry chiefs, far from forgiving him, maintained their attitude to him with a hostility that seems disproportionate to the offence until one examines events which had taken place prior to the major scandal.

One of these events is distantly related to it, the other directly: both sealed Arbuckle's permanent expulsion. The former scandal came to light on July 12, 1921, when an action was brought by the Attorney-General of Massachussets for the removal from office of the District Attorney of Middlesex County, Mass. It was alleged that he had accepted bribes not to proceed against some prominent motion-picture people involved in what had proved to be an embarrassing and costly affair four years before, in 1917, when a dinner had been held on March 6, in a Boston hotel, in honour of Fatty Arbuckle. The dinner guests had later adjourned to Brownie Kennedy's road-house at Mishawn Manor where the bill for the night, including one item relating to the entertaining of twelve girls, came to 1,050 dollars.

Less than two months later, a film executive called Hiram Abrams received a hint from none other than James Curley, Mayor of Boston, that some of the girls had lodged complaints. The huge sum of 100,000 dollars was quickly raised by some badly scared film magnates. These facts emerged during the Attorney General's action and a report of this hearing in the *New York Times* of 17th July, 1921, suggests what the purpose was behind this sum of money. 'The deposition of Adolph Zukor, the New York motion picture magnate, who was present at the Mishawn Manor party, was read to the court. Mr Zukor said in his deposition that he had made two payments of 25,000 dollars each to Hiram Abrams, one for himself and the other for Jesse Lasky. He said he understood the money was to be paid to prevent

* *The Memoirs of Will Hays* (Doubleday) p. 360.

publicity and to shield certain persons in Boston, whose names he was unable to give.'*

Referring with some reticence to this case, for he was writing just five years after it, Terry Ramsaye said: 'The affair and its revelations had some internal bearing on personal politics and grudges within the motion-picture industry. . . . [It] added to the velocity of gossip and ill-will against the . . . industry.'† Arbuckle could hardly be blamed for the way in which his earlier indiscretions, and those of other film names, had come to light. But the proximity of such an embarrassing case to his own grave scandal, two months later, must have caused a rueful association in the minds of his employers who had been linked with his name not only in the court reports touching on the 1917 affair, but by all the publicity that their own studios had given the star and his pictures.

The other event on which reaction to the Arbuckle scandal hinged had concerned Hollywood's present rather than its (hopefully) buried past. Carl Laemmle, head of Universal, had invited fourteen of the most important film censors from the eastern states to pay a visit to Hollywood in August 1921. They came by special train and they stayed at the best hotel with all expenses paid: an arrangement that in at least one of their home-town papers, the *Kansas City Star,* prompted sharp criticism.

Laemmle had indeed a vested interest in making the visit an agreeable one. He wanted to show the censors a print of Erich von Stroheim's film, *Foolish Wives,* which had just been completed at a cost of a million dollars and was intended to be the first Universal production to have its première on Broadway. Laemmle anticipated censorship trouble and wished, if possible, to forestall or soften it by winning the goodwill of the censors and seeking their advice so that the film could be cut, sub-titled and, if need be, re-shot in parts to accord with their views.

But there was a more general reason why Hollywood welcomed its powerful visitors. The film colony wanted to prove how wholesome it was, despite what the guests might have heard, and

* The *New York Times,* 27th July, 1921.
† Terry Ramsaye, op. cit., p. 807.

how ill-founded all the scandal was about the wild, hedonistic lives its stars led. So the hospitality laid on for the censors included all the other studios besides Universal and reached a climax at a reception given by von Stroheim at the Sunset Inn and attended by so many stars that the guests were nearly injured in the crush to do them honour. A contemporary report noted the presence of Mabel Normand, Antonio Moreno, Nazimova, Valentino, Bebe Daniels, Colleen Moore and many others; and it added, 'Roscoe Arbuckle was host at a big table and did his damndest to hand the censors plenty of laughs.'

Just a few weeks later the unhappy Arbuckle was not giving anyone a cause for mirth. When the scandal broke the censors felt they had been taken in by Hollywood duplicity and that all the reports about its scandalous sub-life were true. Laemmle saw all the advantage he had hoped for from the visit vanish, for *Foolish Wives* was not released till the following year and then parts of it were heavily cut by some censors. And Hollywood in general had it brought directly home to them that if scandal could ruin a star, then a star also had the capacity to ruin the commercial as well as the moral integrity of the industry.

Universal immediately issued an announcement that it had inserted a morality clause into all present and future contracts with its stars. The clause said in effect that any actor or actress who committed an act tending to offend the community or outrage public morals and decency would be given five days' notice of the cancellation of his or her contract. Other studios gradually followed suit and together they demonstrated their sense of fear and outrage by completing the ruin of Arbuckle, even after he had been legally acquitted, by permanently enforcing his banishment from the screen.

That he had been the victim of his own weaknesses is indisputable. But, ordinarily, this would not have been enough to justify such ferocious ostracism. It is also true that he had been the victim of circumstances brought about by the cumulative effect of two scandals, with certain damaging similarities, which had emerged publicly within weeks of each other, plus the calamitous effect on the aura of goodwill that the censors' visit had been intended to create for the film industry. This alone would certainly have earned Arbuckle the enmity of the mighty. But he had been guilty of something even worse – and it was this that ultimately proved fatal. Hollywood might have been prepared in the long run to look charitably on a man who was victim of his own moral shortcomings. What its leaders never felt able to pardon was a man whose misconduct had forced *them* into the invidious position of having to pose as public moralists.

Arbuckle returned to vaudeville, which had a more tolerant attitude to transgressors as well as a sturdier tradition of individualism than Hollywood. But he found the film capital's summary judgment hard to shake off. One pitiable episode occurred in 1924 during his one-week vaudeville engagement at Long Beach, California, where the local association of church ministers petitioned the city council to have his appearance cancelled. The wretched ex-film star came in person before the council to plead that he was in debt to the tune of 184,000 dollars, caused by the cost of defending himself at his trials. One is glad to record that the majority of the council sided with him.

Hollywood later allowed him to return and direct minor comedies under an assumed name, but until his death, in 1932, Fatty Arbuckle remained an uncomfortable reminder of Hollywood martyrdom – and Hollywood hypocrisy.

PART FIVE
SERVITUDE

' "But don't forget you can have
actors talk," Sam [Warner] broke in.
' "Who the hell wants to hear actors
talk?" Harry [Warner] asked testily.'
   – From *My First Hundred Years
   in Hollywood*, by Jack L. Warner

CHAPTER THIRTEEN

SOUND BARRIER:
STARS AND
THE TALKIES

One of the most extraordinary tests to which Hollywood's top
stars ever submitted took place on 29th March, 1928, in Mary
Pickford's bungalow on the United Artists lot. The doors were
locked: not even United Artists executives were allowed to enter.
But gathered inside, in a mood of increasing nervousness, were
the leading names on the studio roster, every one of them world-
famous. There was Mary Pickford herself and her husband,
Douglas Fairbanks Sr, Charlie Chaplin, Norma Talmadge,
Dolores Del Rio, Gloria Swanson, John Barrymore and the
director D. W. Griffith.

They were gathered to talk to the listening American public
over the radio in a programme sponsored by The Dodge Brothers
Hour and arranged by none other than the president of United
Artists, Joseph Schenck. Such a Big Broadcast was costing
250,000 dollars. The illustrious cast were being paid 50,000
dollars, divided equally between them: a sum that some of them
spent at their dressmakers' in a week. But the value of the occasion
was infinitely greater. It was designed to prove to millions of
fans that their idols had voices, *speaking* voices, good enough to
meet the challenge of the talkies.

The published programme suggests that all of them – as Max
Beerbohm once remarked about other great historical personages
in a stage direction – did things highly characteristic of themselves. Fairbanks acted as compère and also addressed the youth
of America. Mary Pickford 'talked intimately' to women. Norma
Talmadge discussed fashions and their effect on films. Dolores
Del Rio sang *Ramona*, which happily happened to be the theme
song of her current film. Gloria Swanson discussed the possibili-

ties of girls gatecrashing Hollywood. John Barrymore did a
soliloquy from *Hamlet*. And D. W. Griffith discussed 'love in all
its phases, eschewing the sex angle completely'.

The voices from 'the broadcasting chamber', as well as being
received on home radios, were relayed to audiences in cinemas
across the country. Sad to say, the results were not completely
favourable. Possibly the half-hour introduction given by the
president of Dodge Motors in favour of his product did not strike
the desired note of easy informality. But there were also suspicions,
fostered by reporters resentful of being locked out of the studio,
that all had not been above board in Miss Pickford's bungalow.
It was suspected that a professional singer had stood in for
Dolores Del Rio. Norma Talmadge was accused of having someone else give the fashion talk for her; and this was generally
believed since she was notoriously speechless at public events.

The stars' own reactions varied. At one extreme Chaplin confessed he had 'nearly died of mike fright' and it only strengthened
his resistance to using his voice in films. At the other John
Barrymore appeared totally indifferent to the whole thing. 'I
don't take this radio thing seriously,' he said. Very few of the
other stars in Hollywood were so sanguine about having to
undergo a voice test; for 1928 was the year when something akin
to panic manifested itself in the film colony.

'For the first time,' Adolphe Menjou later wrote, 'movie actors
were conscious of their vocal chords.' By adding an ear to an eye,
as Marshall McLuhan interpreted it, talking pictures did more
than revolutionise an industry: they threw into turmoil, for a
short-lived but shattering period, the mutually dependent
relationship between the stars and the studios. The economic dislocation which has chiefly attracted the attention of historians
was a human one, too. We can scarcely appreciate, simply by
looking back at it today, the extent or degree of the disorientation
many of the stars suffered through finding themselves no longer
the focus of the film industry's present concern and possible
future. So little was understood about talking pictures – or 'the
talkers' as the trade papers called them for several years – that
anything was probable.

Those who should have been the best informed were full of the worst predictions. Roy Pomeroy, who was in charge of sound research at Paramount, said in mid-1928 that 'one year will be required to photograph a feature picture accompanied by a complete dialogue duly recorded by a sound track.' 'Another thing that will have to be worked with for perfect results,' he went on, 'is the moving from long shots to close-ups and the proper adjustment of voices for the dialogue ... while in the matter of speech between two persons in a "two shot", it is necessary to permit an appreciable lapse of time between the end of the remarks of one of them and the beginning of the other's, so that the audience may follow the change and have an opportunity to realise the shift of emphasis.'*

The wildest 'scare stories' were printed and believed. 'Film stars are coming to the fade-out,' one paper predicted and went on to imagine such an Apocalypse that one almost suspects it may have been inspired by the studios to make their stars shake in their buskins. 'Talking pictures will push out the beautiful but dumb and others of both sexes who have depended upon their faces or vogue with the fans. ... Talent is becoming supreme. ... Now it is a case of actors being fitted to the pictures. In the legit.' – i.e. the stage – 'this is called "casting" and the same theory is coming into the Hollywood studios. ... The star system dominating the picture industry since its inception is about to be tagged for the junk heap. ... One of the most prominent producing companies will allow its options to lapse on nearly half the stars now under its banner. ... Total eclipse of many old-time favourites seems inevitable.'†

'THIRTY-THREE PER CENT OF FILM ACTORS ARE OUT,' was another headline. The report estimated that production had declined by half in Hollywood. It quoted an unidentified director who said, 'After all these years everything is swept away in a moment. It means that we all have to start from the beginning again. Past reputations will count for nothing.' It added, 'despite the reports that strictly picture stars' – as distinct from stage stars from

* *Variety*, 9th May 1928.
† Ibid., 28th November 1928.

Broadway – 'may be trained for dialogue films, it is improbable except in special cases.'*

Though this now seems the height of exaggeration, the effect of it, and of dozens of reports like it, induced a feeling among Hollywood stars that the plague was indeed within the walls. Fear was everywhere: the fear that they would have to learn new techniques. In this, of course, they were right, though few of the techniques were as bizarre or humiliating as the thin electric wires which Lionel Barrymore attached to concealed parts of his stars' anatomies while directing *Madame X* (1929) so that he could signal instructions to them, since of course he could no longer use his voice during the shooting.

The stars feared that henceforth their talent would be assessed not by directors, but by the new sound engineers most of whom were initially drawn from the ranks of radio and telephone technicians. These men who had been paid, on average, 200 dollars weekly in their old jobs now drew 750 dollars and up; and in the early months of sound they had considerable power to aid or frustrate a star who was taking a voice test. (They also had power to declare many 'takes' abortive, and in 1928 the sale of negative stock was double that of the previous year. Since overall production declined, it is clear how costly it was for directors to learn from their mistakes.) Above all, what the stars and featured players feared was the front office's lack of interest in them. If they received no command to take a voice test, it was interpreted as a brush-off.

Much of this fear again proved groundless. It was probably due to the fact that the front office was as usual, immersed in the economics of the change-over from silence to sound and dis-regarded the human strains and stresses it was causing. In many cases the more insecure the talkies made these highly-priced and troublesome people feel, the better a front office liked it,

*   *   *

The economics of the switch-over were certainly crushing, An industry which had grown to a value of 65 million dollars

* Ibid., 10th October 1928.

in fifteen years had spent 24 million dollars *in eight months* – from June 1928, to February 1929 – and was bracing itself to invest another 13 million dollars before the end of the year. Sound had, however, brought some natural economies.

Silent-film titlers were first in the dole queue; 55,000 fewer extras were placed by Central Casting in 1928; the end of the studio orchestras which had been used to induce the appropriate mood among the stars was foreseen in the fall of the same year as studios equipped themselves with playback systems and amplifiers; and the number of sets built for a talkie fell from an average of twenty or twenty-two in the silent days to about seven or eight. Even so, the cost of a talkie was estimated in 1928 to be 125 per cent above that of a silent film.

The burgeoning complexities of the technical side added to the anxieties of accountants and stars: more than forty synchronous sound systems were registered in the first six months of sound and more than fifty non-synchronous systems. A poor recording could – and, as we shall see, did – harm stars' reputations. A poor reproduction in the cinema carried the same risk; and the problems of manufacturing and installing these, and training projectionists in their use, were daunting. According to Gilbert Seldes, fourteen to fifteen cinemas a month were converted for sound in 1927. By mid-1928 more than 220 cinemas were showing talkies, by the end of the year over 1,000, and by the end of 1929 some four times this number. But as late as 1929 it was estimated that 'sound annoyance' conditions still existed in 75 per cent of the cinemas wired for the talkies.

Until well into 1929 silent versions of talkies remained a headache for studio chiefs and stars; because so long as many cinemas were not wired for sound, the studios were reluctant to abandon the silent movies. Some people forecast that they would be made side by side. And in August, 1928, new contracts were announced governing the studio practice of filming each picture *in toto* as a silent one and then calling the actors back to add dialogue to those scenes which needed them. Such extra work was now to be regarded as a 'retake', which meant that although the stars were not paid for making a second sound version of the film, they were generously permitted to look for new employment after the completion of the silent version. It all added to their confusion and fear.

Everywhere the demand was for actors who could talk. The technological confusion and competitive panic bred a quite irrational atmosphere in which the silent stars who had been without voices on the screen found themselves in some cases regarded as natural mutes! A fever of voice-testing was going on 3,000 miles away on Broadway, whose actors were definitely known to have voices, in order to find star names from the stage who were fluent in dialogue and might replace those on the screen. Fox, Warner and Paramount were all testing stage players in New York. 'Talker tests are being made blind and under cover by all the companies. . . . When stars are recognised by the crews, orders are issued that the thing mustn't leak. . . . Wholly satisfactory tested people become in immediate demand. There are not enough of them so far . . . for the producer making the test to chance other producers getting to them first.'*

The raid on Broadway talent – stage directors, dialogue coaches, as well as stars – reached such proportions in the mid-1928 to mid-1929 period that it seriously threatened the new 1929 theatre season: film studio contracts calling on stage artists to report for filming upon thirty to sixty days' notice impeded the casting of stage plays and disrupted those in production. One New York producer of musicals abandoned his show planned for May 1929, because he could not find a choreographer anywhere – 'all the ablest ones were in talking pictures on the Coast'. Song writers were scarce for the same reason; so were stage directors who were at first 'doubled up' with film directors.

Some Broadway impresarios were forecasting in 1929 that their salvation lay in Hollywood moving in and acquiring control of their theatres. This was even happening in some cases. 'An offer nowadays for a picture firm to bankroll a stage producer is very common, if the stage producer's record warrants the investment. The talker intent is to have a stage play put on that could be easily adaptable to the dialogue (picture). It could go through a

* Ibid., 18th July 1928.

two-in-one production of a stage-screen play with what the motion-picture people say could be accomplished almost with a single effort. It would also achieve the elevation of the dialogue picture to class heights.'*

Such a view, though naïve in retrospect, looked perilously practicable at the time to the silent film stars; and the experiment accounted for the surfeit of talk in stagey films which character- ised some of the early talkies for a short period. Adolphe Menjou has left a very candid and perceptive account of what it was like to be a silent film star at this period. 'I was a silent film actor, so nobody thought I could act in talkies. The biggest Paramount stars were being replaced by stars from the stage; they knew how to talk. Tommy Meighan, who had been the highest-paid actor in the business, was finished; Gloria Swanson, the highest-paid actress, was on the way out. The studio had paid off Emil Jan- nings. . . . Maurice Chevalier was the new hope of Paramount; he not only spoke English, but also sang. I was in the last year of my contract at that time (early 1929). My salary was 7,500 dollars a week. I knew that unless I proved I could talk before my contract expired, I would be a dead pigeon. I went after every Paramount big-shot in Hollywood demanding a voice-test. Finally it was arranged. . . . What a painful experience that was! I came out of the projection room a chastened man. Only one thought consoled me: the test proved that I could talk; there was nothing wrong with my voice. . . . So I knew there was still hope for me if Paramount would fit me into a picture. But that was something of a hurdle, for Paramount were busy making pictures with people who had stage experience. The pictures weren't very good, but they talked and that was all the fans wanted. I sat around drawing my salary for quite a while before somebody decided that I was an expensive item of overhead and that, good or bad, I ought to draw at the box-office.'†

Even after Menjou's first talkie, *Fashions in Love* (1929), received good notices, Paramount was still silent. 'It was buying stage

* Ibid., 15th August 1928.
† *It Took Nine Tailors*, by Adolphe Menjou (Sampson Low, Marston & Co., Ltd) pp. 184–5.

stars very cheaply, so it had decided that if it waited long enough it could get me back at a reduced salary.'* Menjou's suspicions were well based. Many other stars felt neglected, unwanted, cold-shouldered and disorientated inside their own studios precisely because of the marvellous opportunity that talking pictures gave producers for cutting down salaries which had reached an all-time peak just at this time. It was felt that insecurity would persuade stars to take cuts, or re-sign at a lower figure, in order to hang on to their stardom.

To create attention, to literally get a hearing, movie stars were being forced to fend for themselves. Many vaudeville agents by mid-1928 were reporting a flood of requests for bookings from film actors and actresses on the Coast who wanted to establish themselves as having stage experience when the talking-picture avalanche finally came. 'Agents getting the chill from picture stars for seasons announce they now have more clients than they can handle and that the big-shots of the silent screen are usually too late applying to dive into vaudeville for a few weeks between pictures.'†

Some actors even took the step of financing shows for a few weeks so as to get across the fact that they had adequate speaking voices. Nearly all the stars installed dictating machines and practised elocution, or rehearsed their lines, in the privacy of their own homes in order to detect the snags in their diction before coming on the set. Feature players, who had less prestige to lose, enrolled at voice production schools. Dozens of these sprang up almost overnight. Before the talkies there were about ten legiti-mate drama academies in the Los Angeles area; when sound came in, their number rose to over fifty.

Radio stations were besieged by actors seeking to 'air' their voices. The Big Broadcast from the United Artists studio was only the most spectacular of many. Studios owning their own broadcasting stations now had no trouble getting their contract stars to give an hour or two each week, without fee, for special programmes about the movies. Paramount's weekly broadcast

* Ibid., p. 186.
† *Variety*, 13th June 1928.

over Station KNX comprised a two-hour programme on Sunday
nights for which there was sharp competition among the contract
artists – to the extent of their employing professionals to write
their dialogue.

The close association between film stars and radio throughout
the next decade, plus the cycle of 'Big Broadcast' pictures,
derives from this traumatic frenzy to get a hearing on the air and
the popularity it created for film stars among the radio fans.
And the entry into films of comedians, singers and instrumentalists,
like Bob Hope, Bing Crosby, Jack Benny and others who started
their careers in radio, suggests how successfully the voice was
established in these years as a paramount attribute of talent and
the star personality.

It is perhaps a sign of how the talkies increased the chronic
insecurity of film stars that a great influx of fortune tellers,
palmists, astrologers and crystal gazers was reported taking place
in the Los Angeles area at the start of 1929. It was noted dryly that
their predictions often spanned seven years – the period coming
to be established as the term of a star's contract.

*   *   *

The talkies had hardly hit Hollywood with anything like
hurricane force when, three years earlier, Warner Brothers had
gambled their corporate fortunes on the novelty value of sound
films to get their own product a screening on the cinema circuits
controlled by their rivals. If Jack Warner's account is to be believed, even the Brothers failed to appreciate just what they were
starting. 'But don't forget you can have actors talk,' Sam (Warner)
broke in. 'Who the hell wants to hear actors talk?' Harry (Warner)
asked testily. 'The music – that's the big plus about this.'

Don Juan (1926), the first feature-length film with a full synchronised sound track, contained no dialogue at all when it was
premièred on 6th August 1926, but simply music which was
designed to save exhibitors the expense of a cinema orchestra.
This was the bait to get it into the cinemas. It was the story of

* *My First Hundred Years in Hollywood,* by Jack L. Warner (Random House)
p. 168.

Don Juan's fight against the Borgias; and John Barrymore doubled as the Don and his dying grandfather. His athletic stunts have a lot of Fairbanks' *brio*: at one point he holds a dozen or more swordsmen at bay in ones and twos while his beloved, played by Mary Astor, perches in precarious safety on a tree. Sturdily directed by Alan Crosland, it is in all respects but its music essentially a silent film.

Even the short film preceding it, in which a slightly out of 'synch' Will Hays delivered a talk anticipating what he called 'the speech-film', could hardly have seemed revolutionary. The night was made notable, though, by a programme of songs and music on synchronised film, and of variable quality, in which the tenor Martinelli made the biggest hit and Marion Talley, dubbed 'the Kansas City canary', was not too well favoured by her close-ups. ('Long shots – and good long ones – were just invented for that girl,' said one ungallant reviewer.)

The film generally credited with precipitating the talkie revolution is, of course, *The Jazz Singer* (1927). It is often incorrectly called the first all-talkie film. It was not: it had only snatches of dialogue and songs between silent-film sub-titles. (The first all-talkie was *The Lights of New York* (1928).) It has even been asserted that *The Jazz Singer* made Al Jolson into a star. But Jolson was already a very big vaudeville star before the film. In the early 1920s his phonograph royalties for one month alone amounted to 120,000 dollars; his musical, *Big Boy,* grossed 1,419,000 dollars in forty-three weeks and Jolson was paid not less than 150,000 dollars plus half the net profit which could well have totalled another 150,000 dollars. *The Jazz Singer* owed far more of *its* success to the celebrity he already possessed.

It is ironical, however, that George Jessel, not Jolson, had been the first choice of Warner Brothers. Jessel was then appearing in the stage version of the show. He had signed a contract for 2,000 dollars a week and film publicity about it had already been prepared when he pointed out that since he would be expected to make two or three records for Vitaphone, the sound system Warner Brothers were using, to accompany the picture, he ought to get an additional fee. Negotiations with him were abruptly broken off – and opened with Jolson. Jessel is also believed to have claimed that he could get two more years out of the stage version of *The Jazz Singer* and he did not want to see the Vitaphone discs sold in competition with himself!

Al Jolson had already made one attempt at a screen career – and had abruptly dropped the idea as soon as he saw himself in the rushes. 'I thought all along I was an actor! Why, I'm only a song and dance man,' he was quoted as saying. This painful illumination occurred in 1923. The film had been entitled *Black and White* and Jolson was cast as a young lawyer who masquerades as a Negro to solve a murder. (It was a natural way of exploiting his fame as a blackface vaudeville artist.) It was to be directed by none other than D. W. Griffith – and Griffith, it is worth recording, believed even after this false start that Jolson would be as successful in films as he already was on the stage.

But if *The Jazz Singer* in no sense *made* Jolson a star, it amply confirmed his stardom in a new medium. Heavy-lidded, dark-eyebrowed, a skull-cap of hair, a lean, streaky, ever-eager look and a style that punches his personality over a row of imaginary footlights – Jolson plays the part like one who knows he is the star of the show. But what must have been striking at the time was the new dimension that sound could add even to this star personality. May McAvoy, as the singer's girl-friend, sums it up in one line when she tells him, 'There are lots of jazz singers, but you have a tear in your voice.'

The tear trickles through three of the most emotionally charged themes round which any film has been built – Jewish traditions, showbiz sentiment and mother love. All three are interwoven in a mawkish, yet crudely effective story of how Jackie Rabinowitz, the cantor's son, rebels against his faith and his father, wins Broadway fame (and of course mother's joyful approval) as 'Jack Robin' the song-and-dance man, and then has to face surrendering his part in the Big Show in order to take his ailing father's place and sing *Kol Nidre* in the synagogue on the Eve of Atonement. It is undoubtedly this calculated pitch to the basic sentiments of an audience which makes the film's poorly recorded sound so emotionally effective even today and which, in its day, gave it what one might call a heart-start over the other part-talkies on the screen.

The famous semi-prescient lines, 'Wait a minute, wait a minute. You ain't heard nuthin' yet,' occur early on in the film between Jolson's lyric *Dirty Hands, Dirty Face* – the first of several songs plugging mothers, sons and the love between them – and the *Toot-Toot-Tootsie* number he launches into in the Ragtime restaurant. But far more important and, perhaps, more affecting at the time is the long dialogue sequence between Jolson and Eugenie Besserer, as his mother, in which he plays her *Blue Skies* on the parlour piano and asks, 'Did you like that, mother? ... I'd rather please you than anyone I know,' and so on for a minute or two until his vows of affection stop short just this side of the Oedipal danger line.

The appeal of lines like 'If I'm a success in this show, mother, you're going to move from here,' has been deadened because they, or countless variations of them, have been repeated so often in films since then. But on unsophisticated filmgoers in 1927 their sentimental impact must have been like the bursting of a sound barrier. It is surely not accidental that the first notable addition that sound made to a star's performance should be linked with mother love. The theme is maintained right to the end where Jolson, in blackface make-up, renders *Mammy* to his mother in the front row, having previously done his duty and sung *Kol Nidre* while his father dies happily. One may be pardoned for the irreverent thought that the only trick the film-makers missed was having Jolson sing *Kol Nidre* in blackface, thus achieving an unbeatable concentrate of racial sentiment.

The Jazz Singer was influential in starting the rush into talking pictures because the other studios saw how much money Warner Brothers were making out of it *with the few exhibition outlets open to them*. (There is an analogy here with the 'sexploitation' pictures imported from Europe by small American distributors in the 1960s whose enormous success convinced the major film-makers of the box-office potential waiting to be tapped by more and more permissive sex themes.) The lesson of the fairly modest business being done by the silent version of *The Jazz Singer* was not lost on Warner Brothers' competitors, either. Some cinemas not wired for sound and forced to play the non-talkie version were able to boost their takings by playing non-synchronised Jolson records along with the film; but even their receipts were far below those of the talkie. The lesson was blindingly clear: the great draw was the human voice, *talking*.

In artistic terms, though, *The Jazz Singer* could not have brought much in the way of comfort to the apprehensive stars of other studios who saw the omens for themselves in this novelty. James Agate's contemporary review of the film neatly indicates the flaw in its conception of dialogue which was then characteristic of the general ignorance about how to use sound. Writing of the scene between Jolson and his mother, Agate says: 'Al Jolson . . . forced his voice upon the ear . . . gave us illusion coupled with admiration that a machine could do so well. Eugenie Besserer, who played the old woman, was content to mumble, and here the illusion was perfect and unmannered. Every flesh-and-blood actor knows that he must not speak as an actor, the essence of theatrical illusion being that the actor is overheard. The same applies to films, the essence of film illusion being that the film actor shall be overheard'.*

Actually Agate is drawing the right conclusion from the wrong facts. Eugenie Besserer was simply poorly recorded and her few, probably improvised interpolations into the middle of Al's spiel would in any case lack the sock-it-over impact of the vaudeville man's technique. But the effect she makes is indisputably more naturalistic; and this was the hardest lesson that the silent stars had to master when they took to sound. So long as the voice took priority in a performance, the naturalness of the acting was bound to suffer.

*   *   *

Variety ran two reviews, side by side, of *Tenderloin* (1928), a gangster film about a cabaret dancer's redeeming effect on a bank robber, which the paper described as 'virtually the first try at character-talking from the screen'. (It followed *The Jazz Singer*

* James Agate, op. cit., p. 28.

into the Warner Cinema and had been publicised by a fifteen-minute talkie trailer.) One review reported reactions among the 'hard-boiled first-night audience seeing it too cold-bloodedly', the other the reception by 'a wholly lay audience' on the third night.

The film ran eighty-five minutes and had, all told, between twelve and fifteen minutes of dialogue distributed in four or five bursts, notably a third-degree scene that went down well on both nights: 'The slight voice of the girl' – played by Dolores Costello – 'is pitted against the harshness of the males, the dialogue is consistent and a rather good impression is received.' Less favourable was a later bedroom scene 'with the man threatening, the woman appealing and resisting . . . her voice and the dialogue could not hold pace with the situation. The audience on the first night laughed.' The reviewer concluded that 'stripped of its mechanicals, *Tenderloin* is a very ordinary crook meller' that would probably make 'a good small-town picture'.

The review is important because it shows even at this relatively early date that the writer – identified variety-style simply as 'Mori' – could accurately predict that 'unless the novelty of screen talking is strong enough to overcome the picture itself, the talking picture appears to be a matter of the voice and the calibre of the dialogue to be employed, together with the situation involving both.' (This was written, remember, before the first all-talkie, *The Lights of New York,* was premièred a few months later.) The same reviewer added, not quite so accurately, that 'vocally the talking picture will [draw its] appeal from the trained voices of the stage'. He praised Conrad Nagel and Mitchell Lewis, two of the crooks, for having the best voices and emphasised that both were stage-trained.

Of the film's star, Miss Costello, he wrote: '[She] is not an elocutionist, nor does she evince more vocal instruction than may have been given her for this film. That she falters at times when speaking cannot be unexpected from Miss Costello, or any other of the picture players who find themselves unable to speak in action through not having control of their voices. In fact Miss Costello's main fault in talking is the very lack of sympathy between her emotional expression and speech that is the basic

Gloria Swanson: glamour
was the first rule of life

Joan Crawford collected
generally unfavourable
notices when she played
Sadie Thompson, the
prostitute in *Rain*, in 1932.
Critics found the part
beyond her range, fans
found the character
'common'. Viewed today,
though, her ability to create
and sustain the part, her
drive and strength of
emotion, even her
ruthlessly unflattering
appearance, were ahead of
her time. Unfortunately it
was a performance from the
gut in an age that preferred
glamour

Invisible Negro: Sidney Poitier in *The Slender Thread* shows the colour problem can be kept out of mind if the Negro is kept out of sight. The white would-be-suicide on the other end of the line does not know that the man trying to help her is black

principle of the Vitaphone's projection. . . . Chances are that the director, Michael Curtiz, was but one of many. Perhaps a dozen or more of the Warner people were watching and suggesting during this experiment. It may be believed that a picture director realizes but little more of what may be required, so far, for a motion picture with dialogue than the actors in it. And for that matter, who does know at this stage? Perhaps the Western Electric's engineers would be the best directors of the talkers.'*

The reception that industry critics gave *The Lights of New York* was a cool one, too. Directed by Brian Foy, this story of gangsters, gunmen, bootleggers, cons, muggers and chorus girls ran for fifty-seven minutes. While Richard Griffith has called it less stagey than many early talkies, its cinematic quality was marred by the fact that nearly all the cast came from vaudeville and showed nervousness all round with the notable exception of Eugene Pallette who had stage raining. Helene Costello was judged to be 'a total loss – for talkers, she had better go to school right away.'†

But the cast in many early talkies had to fight the success of the sound effects and at the same time the handicap of their dialogue. One suspects the reason why many talkies were gangster melodramas was not simply the genre's popularity which had been initiated by von Sternberg's silent film, *Underworld*, in 1927, but the way that screaming tyres, rattling machine-guns and 'speakeasy' orchestras registered with impressive naturalism on the sound track. As Gilbert Seldes remarked, 'in the gangster picture, the talkies found themselves, and . . . all pictures made after the gangster cycle was finished are more terse in speech and vigorous in action because of the imagination which this type of picture brought to the screen.'‡

Actually the impact made by the first all-talkie was not great. Richard Griffith points out that *The Jazz Singer* had preceded *The Lights of New York* by several months; cinemas which re-opened wired for sound tended to book Jolson's next film, *The Singing*

* *Variety*, 21st March 1928.
† *Variety*, 11th June 1928.
‡ Gilbert Seldes quoted in *OK for Sound*, by Frederic Thrasher (Duell, Sloan & Pearce), p. 105.

Fool (1928), and play *The Lights of New York* as second feature.

Hardly a single film actor who made a debut in a talkie in 1928 gained stardom as a result – Jolson, as has been pointed out, was a star name in entertainment before he went into films – and the quotes and opinions of contemporary reviewers show why. Technically so much was primitive, artistically so much was unknown. The big stars prudently held back. Most of them, including Garbo, Fairbanks, Mary Pickford, John Barrymore, did not essay the talkies until the following year, 1929, by which time a lot more was known about the innovation and the public's reaction to it.

In the first ten months of talkies, in 1928, eight companies presented or had in course of production thirty-one all-talking films. Over 220 players had been seen and heard in them, sixty-eight of whom had come directly from the stage and had taken the leading parts in fourteen, or nearly half, of the pictures. *Variety* commented that 'the proportion would probably have been greater were it not that seven out of the 31 features were made primarily as silent pictures and given the customary silent film casts; and the decision to make all-talking versions was not made until they were either completed or well under way as silents.*

What this first flush of talkies did was not to make unknown actors into overnight stars, but to facilitate a comeback for some stars whose ratings had been slipping. In nearly every case this was as a result of the good vocal impression they made. One of them was Betty Compson. She had been getting 3,500 dollars a week when she quit Paramount in 1926. It had dropped to 500 dollars a week and after co-starring in von Sternberg's *The Docks of New York*, which failed to repeat the box-office success of *Underworld*, it was reckoned she was finished. But she did so strikingly well in the first talkies, especially in George Fitzmaurice's *The Barker* (1928), that she was again in demand at a salary of 2,500 dollars a week.

Conrad Nagel, formerly a feature player, jumped into star prominence in Archie Mayo's bank robbery drama, *State Street Sadie* (1928). And when Warner Brothers, who made the film, were

* *Variety*, 2nd January 1929.

testing other stars for their vocal qualifications it was Nagel who sat with Jack and Harry Warner in a sound-proof booth and appraised his fellow artists' chances of switching to the talkies while they performed in front of a microphone.

Edward Everett Horton had had a fair, but not outstanding success in films before the talkies. He had gone back to the stage, apparently for good, when Roy Del Ruth's mystery thriller, *The Terror* (1928) re-established him with a strong comedy perform-ance as a detective in disguise. This film was Warner Brothers' second all-talkie, produced after *The Lights of New York,* and was rated 'more than a novelty. . . . *Bona fide* picture entertainment. . . . Through the medium of the talking picture it is here shown pos-sible to lend greater power to the simplest dialogue and the most inconspicuous action. . . . Even the butler, Frank Austin, scores strongly though limited to only three or four speaking lines. His intonation as he says merely, "I am the butler" sounds as preten-tious [*sic:* portentous?] and awe-inspiring as a confession of murder in a silent sub-title.'*

It was a lucky film for more than the butler. John Miljan, who was often to play a suave villain, was rated highly on account of his 'smooth delivery'. Miljan proved to be the year's out-standing talkie actor, though perhaps one reason for this was sheer numbers: he appeared in twelve talkies in 1928, four of them all-talkies and eight with dialogue sequences. It shows how hot the demand was for a proven talent.

Lois Wilson ranked second only to him with three all-talking features and two all-talking shorts which had boosted her fortunes sensationally. It was noticed that 'the male voice regis-ters better than the feminine in talking pictures. It is of signifi-cance that of the 220 players who have appeared to date in the new standard of the film business, the all-talker, only 14 are women'.†

*   *   *

By October, 1928, no fewer than 300 talkie pictures had been scheduled for production. Yet although the players may not have

* Ibid, 22nd August 1928.
† Ibid., 2nd January 1929.

realised it at the time, the popularity of the talkies was beginning to swing round in favour of the silent stars who, because they wished to or because their studios had ignored them in the rush to sign up stage stars, had held off committing themselves to a talkie until the teething troubles had been more or less solved.

Public enthusiasm for the all-talkie was on the wane by the end of 1928. The reason was simply that people had had a surfeit of talk. The novelty value of the talkies vanished very quickly. Warner Brothers, the pioneers, announced in December 1928, that they planned to include 'no more than 75 per cent of talk' in their films. It was claimed that experience showed that 'all-talk' slowed the action down and necessitated confining a large part of the picture to close-ups of the stars which caused filmgoers to get tired. 'Pictures comprising half-dialogue and half-action have been far superior, it is said. *The Singing Fool* is offered as an example.'

Universal, too, was having second thoughts and deciding on a fifty-fifty ratio of talk to action. 'Fans are bound to miss the action on which screen entertainment is based and will not permanently accept the slowed-up movement that prevails with dialogue unless the latter is of exceptional character.' It was noted that Joan Crawford's silent movie, *Our Dancing Daughters* (1928), which had only a couple of dialogue sequences, was doing every bit as well as *The Singing Fool* which had Al Jolson and full sound. 'The sound picture,' *Variety* concluded, 'has failed to increase the bulk gross in the majority of downtown picture theatres.'*

By the end of 1928 the reviews in the trade papers had become far less tolerant of talking pictures: judgments were harsher and reflected this economic disenchantment. A good example is Paramount's film about society blackmail, *Interference* (1928), described as the company's 'first all-talking picture on release and the first dialogue film to be done in the drawing-room manner'. The production qualities were praised, the gowns, the smooth camera work, the gorgeous sets 'which make it the first talking production as a production' – yet it was finally dismissed as 'indifferent entertainment'. As well as being clumsily adapted, it

* Ibid., 19th December 1928.

had 'characters [who] talk with precise diction which achieves very little realism'; and while Evelyn Brent got praise 'considering her total lack of experience on the speaking stage', and William Powell and Clive Brook 'know their stuff thoroughly [and read] lines with the easy naturalism of the stage-trained', the total verdict was unfavourable. 'Earlier in the epoch of dialogue pictures, *Interference* would easily have been a clean-up at the box-office. Now it's dubious.'*

What was now reasserting itself was the quality of the picture and in many cases this depended not on the novelty of the spoken words, but on the talent and personality of the stars who spoke them. The balance of power began to swing back to the old-established film favourites between the fall of 1928 and the spring of 1929. The prediction that a complete change in film personalities would occur with the talkies simply failed to come true. Box-office returns, coupled with the grass-roots reports of cinema managers, began to show up the weaknesses in the importation of stars from the Broadway drama, musical comedy and vaudeville. It was found that such 'legitimates' as Ruth Chatterton, Richard Bennett and Jeanne Eagles were not known to the majority of film fans and their popularity could not be built up quickly to the point reached by the money-makers of the silent cinema since talkies took much longer to make and distribute.

The only exception seemed to be Al Jolson. (Jolson was paid 75,000 dollars for *The Jazz Singer*, 150,000 dollars for *The Singing Fool* and then went to United Artists for 500,000 dollars and ten per cent of the profits: big money, proving big drawing power.) Out of 200 players cast in some fifty films released between January and mid-March, 1929, fewer than a dozen were estimated to have come from the stage and an equally small number from vaudeville. Dramatic and musical comedy names starred in only six of the pictures.

Some of the feature players in the talkies were conceded to have stage experience before making films, but they were already screen personalities in their own right when they appeared in talkies. In fact the box-office decline that really bit hard in 1930,

* Ibid., 21st November 1928.

when attendance fell by 40 per cent, was partly blamed on the failure of the stage recruits to deliver at the box-office with anything like the consistency of the old silent stars. 'Even poor films,' *Variety* commented bitterly at the end of 1930, 'could count on some box-office reaction if the star names were there, but when the favourites passed out it meant the drawing power was left to the story-telling element alone. . . . Looking over the present list, the producers find few names that, since the talkers, carry anywhere near the weight of the bread-and-butter earners of the silent regime. Of the hold-overs, fewer than a dozen mean box-office today. Outside of [names like] Barthelmess, Greta Garbo, Gloria Swanson, Joan Crawford, William Haines, Clara Bow, George Bancroft, Charles Farrell and Janet Gaynor, the number is negligible. And few of these are considered as powerful for straight "name" draw as in the silent era.'*

But as recording and reproduction methods improved in the studios and cinemas it was found that most of the silent stars and feature players had better recording voices than anyone had suspected – in some cases better than the imported Broadway stars. The silent stars noted with malicious satisfaction that on some occasions the Easterners had trouble registering emotions without an audience to react to. Sometimes the old studio orchestra had to be revived to get the Broadway star in the mood. In addition cinema managers' reports indicated that fans would rather hear a weak-voiced favourite than an unknown with a cultured delivery. Impeccable diction did not mean a damn in the sticks.

The mistake had been made in imagining that Broadway's lordly amusement at 'twangy' accents would be shared by out-of-town audiences. It was not. The natural voice in the right role produced, if anything, a bond of identity with regional audiences – the Americanisation of manners and morals which the movies were to promote during the 1930s owed a great deal to the vocal impact of the stars. But what had not been appreciated until well into 1929 was that personality still swayed audiences and speech was only one of the factors contributing to it.

* Ibid., 17th September 1930.

Nevertheless, as Adolphe Menjou had observed, speech was a great disciplining weapon for studios to wield over stars who were 'difficult' or over-priced. And confidence was slow to return among the stars who had to make their delayed debuts in the talkies. Some reports of what happened when their films were shown could not have been very reassuring either. Mary Pickford's first talkie, *Coquette* (1929), got off to a disastrous start at the Rivoli Theatre, New York, when a fuse blew two minutes after the start and the film had to be begun again. Even then the amplification system was so distorted that Pickford's voice sounded weak compared with the male players' voices and this made an accurate impression of her success impossible. 'If further showings fail to substantiate the early reports [of an outstanding voice],' said one commentator, 'then it simply emphasises the wide difference between projection-room and auditorium showings.'*

If this happened to a star of Mary Pickford's prestige and power, and at the Broadway première, what were things like when a film was shown in its out-of-town play-off? In the end, of course, Pickford's voice, with the Southern drawl she assumed for her role in *Coquette,* proved quite competent and she even won an Oscar for her performance. But such première incidents were numerous. *Bulldog Drummond* (1929), starring Ronald Colman, also suffered a breakdown and the last twenty-five minutes were run as a silent movie; but Colman, too, made the transition to sound without trouble.

Garbo delayed her talking debut till March 1930, when *Anna Christie* was premièred. It had been immediately apparent from the ten-minute sound test she had made in mid-1929, using the *Anna Christie* script, that her surprisingly low, husky voice with its under-notes of melancholy increased her mystery. Added protection came from choosing a heroine who was a Swede like herself, although she later said, 'Did you ever hear any Swede talk like that?'

John Barrymore delayed almost as long, then made *General Crack,* premièred in December 1929, a historical potboiler about

* Ibid., 10th April 1929.

a mercenary who hires his armies out to the Emperor of Austria till he hears his gipsy wife has been regarded as part of the deal. The star was rapped for 'squandering his talent on bedroom twaddle', but his voice was so satisfactory that it aroused less comment than his lower limbs which he had shown up to good advantage in tight breeches. (At least it was a change from Barrymore's non-costume films which give an overpowering feeling that the set has been built around his profile, not his thighs.)

Sound put Chaplin in a dilemma. He risked sacrificing the Tramp's universality the moment he opened his mouth, and he delayed doing so till his nonsense song as the singing waiter in *Modern Times* (1936). But early in 1933 he seriously considered what kind of voice he might give the Tramp and decided on a near-Oxford accent, since he always had the idea of the Tramp as a once-aristocratic figure now on his uppers. To make filmgoers accept this, he first thought of appearing as himself in a talkie in the hope that his own English accents would transfer more naturally to the Tramp in a later film.

Clara Bow's brittle voice suited the talkies, once she had got over her restlessness in front of the microphone which, in these early days, had not the mobility to follow her around. Norma Talmadge practised elocution for a year before making a successful debut in *New York Nights* (1929) where her nasal tones were at home in the big-city milieu. But then she plunged into a stilted costume story, *Du Barry, Woman of Passion* (1930), where her combination of silent-movie grimaces and twangy accent proved disastrous. 'Leave them while you're looking good and thank God for the trust funds Momma set up', her sister, Constance, cabled her.

Douglas Fairbanks Sr's main trouble with his voice was keeping it within bounds. Shakespeare's verse imposed its own discipline on him in *The Taming of the Shrew*, but relieved of it in *The Iron Mask* (1929), his voice carried so dramatically that the microphone had to be moved thirty feet away from him. Lon Chaney's premature death prevented one from discovering whether 'The Man of a Thousand Faces' could muster a thousand voices for the talkies. His one talkie in 1930, a remake of his 1925 horror movie, *The Unholy Three,* showed a shrewdness in using sound for dramatic denouément when the villain, disguised as a white-haired old woman, gives himself away in the witness box by letting his voice drop to its normal male register. But Chaney's handling of dialogue throughout the female impersonation was thought by some not to be skilful enough to make the character as plausible as in the silent version.

Chaney relapsed during his fatal illness into a contorted posture and apparently suffered a loss of voice: a bizarre end for a man who was the child of deaf-mute parents and whose mother had been afflicted by a life-long rheumatoid complaint which made all movement painful for her. If Chaney experienced some sense of sympathetic identity with his parents' afflictions by playing the grotesquely handicapped parts in which he specialised, then the need to talk like a normal person may have posed its own psychological as well as artistic problems.

*   *   *

To sum up: the idea that the coming of the talkies ruined the careers of many stars is a false one. Sound gave some fading stars a new if brief lease of life; it increased the artistry of some of the established stars once they had proved they could 'talk'; and it helped create new stars from among some, though by no means many, of the stage players whom Hollywood had recruited.

George Arliss is an interesting example of the last category – and himself quite a phenomenon. For sound gave this fastidious English actor a pre-eminence in Hollywood he could never otherwise have achieved. His sudden success is symptomatic of the awe that attached to a stage player who could handle dialogue – and also of the studios' yearning to see the new invention add to their status as well as their profits. The old hunger for prestige which had impelled Adolph Zukor to recruit stage names in 1912 now attached itself for a brief, but earnest period to actors with recognisably 'superior' speaking powers. When Arliss was awarded a gold medal for diction from the American Academy of Arts and Letters, he said in reply, 'What we actors should do is to set a worthy example which the youth of today may be inspired to follow. And with the advent of the talking picture, our responsibility becomes far greater than it was before: not that the masses go to the movies to learn how to speak; but young people are inclined to be very imitative, particularly of those actors whom they especially admire.'*

Arliss was given power to approve the director, select the cast and supervise the production, and was generally indulged by his studio, Warner Brothers, though for less philanthropic reasons than his effect on the elocution of American youth. His pictures were believed to be profitable as well as prestigious; and so at first they were. His *Disraeli* (1929) was the first 'starring vehicle' as such to be equipped with sound and, for all its staginess, it made Arliss into the mouthpiece of the new medium, the prestige equivalent of John Barrymore or Emil Jannings in the silent days. Barrymore was in fact explicitly chided with the comparison after the 'bedroom twaddle' of *his* first sound venture: '*Disraeli* is demonstrating that film audiences can be exhilarated without aphrodisiacs,' sniffed *Variety*. And the remark was echoed in the survey of the year 1930 written by one of *Variety*'s chief correspondents, Sidney Silverman, who said: 'Another instance that the public is able to appreciate something other than a man, a girl and a couch is the success of the George Arliss pictures. Allowing that none of the English star's films may have been dynamic successes, nevertheless it may be said that the Arliss releases were an opening wedge and many a film will profit by the pioneering of this English actor and his type of work.'†

A box-office survey published in the same paper a year later showed this to be an accurate prediction. Arliss was declared to be the top money-making male star of 1931, leading Wallace Beery, Maurice Chevalier, Clark Gable, Edward G. Robinson and Will Rogers. And he kept his stature as a culture product of the talkies till the mid-1930s. Though it is easy, and sometimes just, to take a less than reverent view of the great historical personages he played, from Disraeli and Richelieu to Alexander Hamilton and Roths-

---

* *George Arliss, by Himself* (John Murray), pp. 127–8.
† *Variety*, 31st December 1930.

child, all in the same sly, ironic manner with the looks of an eminent weasel, there is no mistaking the care he took in creating them. His steely egotism, plus the drawing power of his stage reputation, gave his talking pictures an air of intelligence that impressed audiences with the potential of the talkies.

Conrad Nagel may have been slightly overstating it when he said at the end of 1930, 'Illusion, which was 50 per cent of the old silent pictures, is now gone.' But he was on firmer ground when he added, 'In talkers even the most ardent fan and every type of audience can consciously or unconsciously recognise a good performance and an able actor. George Arliss proved this.'*

*   *   *

But had 'illusion' gone? And if it had, what had taken its place? A 'loss of illusion' was certainly one of the first effects that the talkies had on audiences. Richard Schickel defined 'silence' as the most valuable attribute of the pre-talkie stars. 'A godhead is supposed to be inscrutable. It is not expected that he speak directly to us. It is enough that his image be present so that we may conveniently worship it.'† Once they had dialogue on their lips, the once-silent idols suffered a serious loss of divinity. They ceased to be images in human shape personifying the emotions through the delicately graded art of pantomime. Their voices made them as real as the audiences watching them.

Marshall McLuhan has already drawn attention to how sound disturbed the sensory relationship of the spectator to the silent movies by adding an ear to an eye. It brought a new perspective into the relationship. Each person in the audience at a talkie could no longer 'hear' what he or she wanted to hear – paradoxically this was possible only on the silent screen. There is less 'talking' in a silent film because the sub-titles are only meant to sum up what the 'dialogue' has been about – to give a snappy, humorous or emotional *précis* of it. Consequently, although there are more lip movements than the sub-titles warrant, there are also far fewer words to 'listen' to with the inward ear than if the film

* *Variety*, 17th September 1930.
† Richard Schickel and Allen Hurlburt, op. cit., p. 13.

were a talkie and unable to take advantage of the short-cut of sub-titles.

During the 'dialogue' of a silent film, when the characters' lips were moving, filmgoers projected their own feelings on to the characters on the screen in order to give a sense of closure to the relationship between them until the sub-title flashed up and clinched it. The talkies reversed this process. They made film-goers the recipients of the feelings, thoughts and intentions of the characters as they gave voice to them – there was far less room for spectator interpretation.

There was also less active participation. By comparison with the involvement of audiences in a silent film, the sound cinema was a fairly passive place where most of the work was done for the spectators. This is not contradicted by the complaints which were frequently made during the early months of the talkies that they had destroyed the sense of relaxation to be experienced from going to a silent movie because they forced filmgoers to con-centrate on the new-fangled dialogue. All that this signifies is that filmgoers were going through a period of adjustment. By 'relaxa-tion', they probably meant unconscious participation. What the talkies did was to *fix* the audience's attitude towards the people and the situation on the screen. The feeling of the dialogue working on a filmgoer to this end is what probably caused the sense of disturbance suggested by these complaints.

The French critic Jean Keim has described the phenomenon very well in his book *Le Cinéma Sonore*. 'Sound has generally deeper resonances where a person is concerned than sight; the impres-sions which the eye receives touch the senses rather than the depths of the mind; whereas it is through the ear that deeper and more lasting impressions are received, which trigger off the mental apparatus with more force. Formerly the impressions received did not last long; now they are invariably prolonged . . .'* Anyone can test the truth of this by trying to recall a silent film even a few hours after seeing it. Its details have faded from the mind in a dismayingly short space of time, leaving only a vague residual

* *Le Cinéma Sonore*, by Jean A. Keim (Editions Albin Michel), p. 43. Translation by the author.

image; but precisely because this is so unfocused it sometimes acts like a spell on the emotions. In a talkie, on the other hand, though the dialogue is a firm aid to recall, it also tends to confirm one in one's attitude to the actors and the characters they are playing.

All this helps to explain why the talkies so greatly altered star values. The mythical power of the silent stars was diminished by the addition of their voices – which is why many of them, even while giving excellent acting performances in the talkies, suffer a loss of magic. We see them too plainly.* Garbo is the outstanding exception. Her voice actually intensified the air of mystery which already surrounded her – her persona was sound-proof. Others were not so fortunate. Parker Tyler has written, 'If one sees the extraordinarily talented Lillian Gish in Griffith's *Way Down East*, wherein her performance told everything in pantomime and very good pantomime, one can realise that the shifting of part of the acting responsibility from pantomime to voice entailed laziness in the craft of screen acting, a deterioration in gesture and in everything that makes the actor an eloquent moving image. Indeed in Miss Gish's late acting days, when she must use a voice . . . she seems commonplace.'†

One can quarrel with Tyler's verdict on Gish, but the rest of what he says has a large element of truth. Sound made acting, if not lazier, then certainly more naturalistic. It took away the plastic mobility of the silent pantomime and began a process in which eventually the sense of acting, or people playing parts, is diminished to a stylised naturalism that requires a dominant personality

---

* This is only too true. The low-definition imagery in the best of the silent movies was the result of photography and lighting which supplied the emotional ambience in lieu of audible dialogue. It compelled the filmgoers to take a participant role in the action by stimulating the imagination. With the talkies, dialogue usurped the function of photography which quickly lost, for a time at least, its atmospheric qualities. The talkies had crisp, bright photography which concentrated the players' personalities, whereas the silent-movie photography had diffused them. Clear photography complemented clear sound, but both diminished the audience's participation in the mystique of the stars.

† *Magic and Myth of the Movies*, by Parker Tyler (Henry Holt & Co.), pp. 8–9.

to make it endurable from film to film. One gets less and less chance as the cinema approaches contemporary times to write about *acting* performances as distinct from personality traits which are repeated in role after role until ultimately they tell us more about the audience which finds them fascinating than the actor or actress who exhibits them. The silent stars were mythical figures in their own right: today's stars are ikons possessing the utilitarian properties of go-betweens.

Sound made it essential to present a more authentic description of life on the screen. And quite a few of the silent-film archetypes withered away in the glare of this realism. One has already seen the fate of the 'Great Lover'. Clara Bow's flapper-girl was another victim, relegated to limbo by the cynicism of the Depression years and the more mature interest in sex, but also unable to meet the competition from the new breed of screen ladies like Joan Crawford, Norma Shearer, Ann Harding, Jean Harlow, Ruth Chatterton and Bette Davis whose voices contributed so much to the definition of their roles as worldly women of the new decade. The influx of journalists and newspapermen, brought to Hollywood to write dialogue, accelerated the loss of fantasy.

To see what a damaging effect the new social realism of sound could have on the old relationship with the audience, one has only to look at the moment in Paul Fejos's part-talkie *Lonesome* (1928) when dialogue suddenly breaks out between the young factory worker and the telephone girl who have fallen in love. Up to this moment the detail of their background in New York tenements and amusement parks has been presented with an intelligence that makes one attribute a like degree of maturity to the silent hero and heroine. Suddenly the pair start to speak – and at once their sentimentally banal natures become distressingly obvious. 'All my life I wanted a little white house in the country with blue shingles,' says he. 'Pink,' says she. 'Blue, the colour of your eyes,' he drools.

A moment before they had only been responsible for their actions – and we, the audience, had done the rest. The moment they opened their mouths, the quality of their minds, lives, thoughts and aspirations revealed them as silent-film stereotypes of Boy and Girl, protected from our contempt by a wall of silence.

As sound reproduced the social scene in dialogue, it brought into prominence stars with personalities and voices that fitted the milieu and were themselves projected by it. 'Motivated by the knowledge that headlines are sure box office, the screen took on a truly journalistic flavour after the advent of sound,' Frederic Thrasher noted, and quoted the gangster cycle as creating new movie types – Cagney, Edward G. Robinson, Joan Blondell, Harlow, Lee and Spencer Tracy – whom he called 'stars made by journalists'.

But while sound increased the variety of stars, it indirectly entrenched type-casting. Actors whose voices fixed them precisely in some social role found it as hard to manoeuvre into another kind of part as some of the silent stars had done. A voice print was as identifiable as a finger print. And the new stars had to submit to roles that were chosen to exploit the distinctive qualities of their voices as well as their looks.

Yet when all was said and done – and when it was appreciated that, in terms of entertainment, less needed to be *said* and more to be *done* – sound humanised and democratised the stars. In an astonishingly short space of time, measured almost in months, the vocal proficiency, striking naturalism and strength of personality had been blended together to form the Hollywood idiom. And those who mastered it became themselves part of the American idiom – people whom millions of filmgoers admired and imitated.

Sound found the stars with the aspects of gods: it left them with the characteristics of their fellow men.

CHAPTER FOURTEEN

ALL WORK AND
LESS PAY:
STUDIO RULE

Only recently have stars again become as free as they were in the days before the talkies. And significantly Hollywood has had to lose much of its power as a production centre for them to regain their freedom. Sound did not kill the established stars of the 1920s, but it clamped constraints around them, as well as the newcomers arriving off the train from Broadway, which were far more fettering than some of the early dialogue all of them had to cope with.

The movie industry had been held to ransom in the 1920s by the very creatures it had created. The financiers who came into studio management when they invested fresh capital for the switch over to sound from 1928 on, simply added their economic determination to the vows already being taken by the film executives that never again would they put themselves at the mercy of their employees.

The star system in the 1930s gradually took on the reality, if not the appearance, of a star serfdom. Glamour was its camouflage and fame its dazzling illusion. But behind the grandeur of being a movie star in these years lay all the gradations of servitude. Stardom may have looked the most enviable attribute a film actor could hope for; but when it was achieved at last, it generally turned out to be something else again. The first change that sound made in the old silent studios was ominous. It killed the festive atmosphere, almost a mood of carnival, which prevailed on the sets when the making of silent movies took place in anything but silence.

This transitional period did not last long, which is probably why accounts of it by visitors to Hollywood are hard to come by.

(Hollywood natives have been for the most part notoriously poor observers of their own scene.) But two English reporters with exceptionally sharp sensibilities, and the occasional phrase to match, did register the unfriendly vacuum in which the stars now had to perform when they visited Hollywood in 1928-9. 'Here, where the actors were still feeling nervous in experimenting with an almost untested technique, the atmosphere was charged with an amount of subconscious dislike [of the visitor] that almost amounted to a smack in the face. . . . Here was none of the bustle and jollity that ruled on the normal [silent-movie] set. It seemed a ceremony almost religious, church-like in a sense of awe that oozed from the operators. I could never imagine the script-girl here perched on the director's knee. The influence of "Silence" seemed to have turned even the stage-hands into ghosts; the director spoke his instructions in a lowered voice, not a megaphone on the premises. . . . No gay music burst out to stimulate the stars to an emotional brilliance; they must suck it all from their own entrails.'* Even when the stars grew used to working in sound pictures – and they soon did – the old friendly atmosphere never returned. The techniques and economics of sound imposed a discipline on the play world before even the front-office executives did.

The new mood was felt off the set, too. To re-equip itself for the talkies, the film business had had to turn to financial interests which had escaped the Stock Market crash or had the funds to invest in Hollywood's future. Though much of America had slumped into the Depression, the future of the film city looked bright by contrast. The box-office continued to enjoy a boom for two full years after the market crash; and the bankers hastened to buy into an industry apparently able to sell dreams lucratively to a nation that was short of money to buy bread.

But once Wall Street moved its representatives into the film studios, the artists and executives there lost a great deal of the autonomy that 3,000 miles of land had created between them and the East Coast offices of their companies. And when the financial crisis began affecting even impregnable Hollywood in 1932, as the

* Jan and Cora Gordon, op. cit., pp. 278-9.

deepening Depression showed it meant to stay around for years, then the financiers began to insist on studio economies. These weakened everyone's morale. The shake-up retired some executives and brought others into prominence; and this mattered significantly in a tight-knit community based on one industry where social status was determined by studio ranking.

The cut-back and slackening of production that ensued in 1932 left only six major studios making films that year in the month of January: they were Paramount, Universal, R.K.O., Warner Brothers, M-G-M and Fox. Columbia was temporarily eliminated because it had to close down for several weeks; and United Artists had to suspend operations until the spring. Stars were made rudely aware, if they did not already know it, that temperament could not longer be indulged. 'If an actor has had a falling out with one studio,' said one, 'that doesn't leave too many to go to instead. If two studios are sore at him, he is probably a has-been.'

In the same year the studios began to axe the cohorts of feature players and character actors. Anyone who had not got star status was simply regarded as an overhead who had to be carried between pictures. Thirty second-magnitude stars were 'released' from their contracts in the month of January alone. Foreign-born stars found themselves especially vulnerable. The House Committee on Labor was supporting the 'America for Americans' demand that inevitably sprang from a shortage of jobs and it was examining the high proportion of foreign talent in Hollywood. It was resolved that unless such talent was extraordinary and unique, it should not be imported. This mood obviously encouraged studios with foreign talent already working for them to insist that unless the foreigners toed the line, they risked being deported.

Throughout 1932 the studios buttressed their shaky economies by putting more and more controls round the freedom of their existing stars and the recruits whom they were hopefully building into stars. The preponderance of new or lapsing contracts in this period facilitated their policy. One plan considered was to adapt the waiver system widely used in baseball to fit film-star contracts. It would have meant that a star who had been in one studio's service could be retained under contract until the studio cared to exercise its waiver. It ruled out the option system which had been brashly used by agents to get higher fees for their clients. In baseball, the system worked like this: if a player and club failed to agree on a salary when making a new contract, the club was empowered either to suspend him from organised baseball or trade him to any other club that was willing to meet his price. The film chiefs envied the stability they felt such a system would bring into their business. An additional advantage was that it would outlaw raiding by other studios. Only the fact that, as so often happened, the studios could not agree among themselves on its practical working prevented stars being treated in the same proprietary way as baseball players.

*   *   *

By the middle of 1932 the box-office was falling off so alarmingly that the major companies actually considered forming a studio coalition to pool their star talent. Garbo and Joan Crawford might be lent by M-G-M to Paramount in return for Chevalier; Lew Ayres could cross the border from Universal to star in an M-G-M picture with Norma Shearer. This would mean more work for every big name: a distinct advantage to studios who estimated that their stars spent 40 per cent of their time between productions in studio-subsidised idleness. It would also keep up a much better continuity of production. Above all it would soothe the aggrieved feelings of the major cinema cricuits which were being forced to play the films of studios other than the ones they were linked to simply in order to stay in business.

Joseph Schenck, of United Artists, publicly backed this plan for greater (and cheaper) flexibility in the loan-out of stars: 'The opinion that the public will tire of stars who are not conserved by their studios does not apply. . . . Fans like to see their favourites. Companies by keeping their stars in judicious circulation are rebuilding public confidence and interest in the industry as well as in their own studios.'* Sceptical stars could be forgiven if they recalled the remark about the old showbiz maxim, 'The show must go on' – it was first said by a theatre-owner.

* *Variety*, 30th August 1932.

As things turned out, Schenck's experiment got nowhere. Where studios did loan out their stars it was at the old high price, always well in excess of what the star was being paid on the home lot. Or else it was used as a disciplinary measure to curb an uppity artist by sending him or her to work at a less prestigious studio for a spell. Free and frequent loan outs foundered on mutual jealousy. Studios guarded their prizes and answered requests for one star by demanding another in return which the first studio rated even more highly.

The economic slump put the stars in weak bargaining positions when it came to seeking higher salaries. The studios enlisted the plea of national emergency to enforce salary stringency. When a pay cut of 35 per cent was proposed at M-G-M the stars discovered that it would apply not only to the current crisis but to the balance of their contracts if their options were taken up in the better times ahead. Long-term contracts up to seven years, with suspension time capable of being added on, virtually ended the bargaining power of the independent artist. Stars no longer signed for two or three pictures only. They were the property of their studio till their term expired or their options were dropped.

The economic shake-out meant that star salaries rarely recovered to the extravagant level of the silent films. In 1927 over forty stars were said to be earning from 5,000 dollars a week upwards. By the end of 1931 the salary scale, and the numbers of those on it, had shrunk. Conrad Nagel, then president of the Motion Picture Relief Fund which levied a tax of 1½ per cent on *all* artists' fees, announced that out of 25,000 registered actors only twenty-three earned 'large salaries from 3,500 dollars a week upwards'. In the same year the U.S. Commissioner of Inland Revenue permitted such fading stars as Betty Compson and Bebe Daniels to regard their loss of popularity as a 'depreciation of good will' and deduct it from their tax returns.

As the industry strove to preserve its corporate image many other kinds of pressure were brought to bear on the stars 'for the good of the business'. The Hays Office instituted some of these. It recommended in October 1931, that stars should no longer be allowed to lend their names, faces or voices [*sic*] to endorse

commercial products. Such discretion in future was vested in the
'employing producers', not the individual star. Even then it was
only to be used for charitable purposes and for 'the distribution,
exhibition, advertising and exploitation of photoplays or...
any other phase of the business of the producer'. The reason
given was the injury some stars were said to have done to their
drawing power by indiscriminate advertising. But it is doubtful if
this was the only reason. The loss of the sizeable 'pin money' of
this type made stars even more dependent on their studios.
Moreover the Hollywood chiefs had never forgotten how Valentino had kept his name before the public, and fought them with
his own publicity, by linking his fame to a commercial product
for the better part of a year when Paramount had suspended him
and he was not allowed to make films for any other studio.

Commercial radio had come in since then. Television was being
tested and found practicable in the Los Angeles area, with a radius
of up to 200 miles, as early as mid-1928. Contracts in the early
1930s were far-seeing enough to forbid artists to appear on television. And the Hays Code recommendation on advertising closed
even the loophole of broadcast commercials. The fact that it was
sporadically observed after the industry's fortunes picked up
does not contradict its usefulness at the time as a means of resisting
the independence of those under contract. And there were other
means. . . .

*   *   *

Hollywood adopted in 1930 its own self-administered censorship in the shape of the Motion Picture Production Code, a list of
'thou-shalt-nots' for producers which was supported in public
and subverted in practice. Under its wide and hypocritical
shelter, other codes sprang up. If the studios had to make a show
of bowing to public morality then the stars must subscribe to
studio morality. The 'morality clause' which became a feature of
contracts in the 1920s was now stretched to cover almost everything a star might do professionally or privately. Companies took
the view that a star turned over his or her reputation, character
and physical well-being when a contract became effective. Stars

were regarded first as corporate property, only then as human beings.

It is significant that Hollywood's relations with the press reached the lowest point around the same time. The real establishment of the Hollywood press corps had begun around 1928 when newsmen poured in with the East Coast celebrities, writers, actors and Broadway talents lured west by contracts for the talkies. In mid-1928 Hollywood was second only to New York as the most-written-about place in the United States. A town of 250,000 people, in short, became a contender for news interest with a city of seven million.

The new reporters' mood was very different from their silent-era colleagues. News services and fan magazines had decided, rightly, that their readers were fed up with stories and gossip planted by the studios. They sent their reporters out to compete for the 'inside dope', the 'real dirt', or to conduct 'knocking' interviews and take excessively candid pictures. The studios were soon complaining of the 'army of movie chatterers' which had invaded them, seeking favours, using studio transport, trying to break into films, twisting arms for private gossip, exploiting grievances and even blackmailing stars with lightly veiled threats. Sightseeing visitors had already been barred by most studios when sound came in and in the early 1930s one studio after another closed its gates to the free entry of newsmen who by 1932 numbered hardly fewer than 200. Louis B. Mayer eventually had to mediate personally and help re-establish an edgy truce.

But the chief danger remained in the star interview which could reveal embarrassing aspects of a studio's investment in a personality and be used by a ruthless or cunning star to gain public sympathy and turn it against his or her employers in some wrangle over pay, scripts or casting. So it became a feature of long-term contracts to stipulate in their preamble that 'the average artist is not well qualified by experience to talk unguidedly for publication . . .'. The studio publicity department had for years been friend and comforter to the stars: the 1930s confirmed its function as censor.

The financial crisis deepened in 1933. This was the worst year in Hollywood's memory. Paramount and R.K.O. both went into receivership in January. So did many of their theatre subsidiaries and those owned by Fox on the West Coast. Only a break in the European market and the unexpected success of Mae West's films at home enabled Paramount to refloat itself with its own resources at the end of the year. M-G-M and Warner Brothers escaped bankruptcy mainly because their star cadre helped them turn out superior pictures with great regularity, so that their chains of cinemas were not forced to play the movies of independent producers which thus cut down on the home studio's screen time. M-G-M in particular owed its salvation to the star system. Before an M-G-M picture began shooting it was estimated that casting alone gave it a box-office head-start over any other studio.

But fearsome economies were made by M-G-M all the same. Making a film cost the studio an average of 450,000 dollars in 1932, at a time when a film was doing well to gross 500,000 dollars. After Nicholas Schenck visited Hollywood the order was given to cut every budget by at least 100,000 dollars, though such economies failed to work in the long run and by mid-1934 an M-G-M picture was costing 50,000 dollars more than in 1932. But they fell heavily on the stars, again depressing their economic power.

Assembling an all-star cast for one picture was a way of not only boosting its box-office appeal and making one production do the work of two or three, but it also hammered down the price of the individual stars in it. *Mata Hari* (1932) starring only Garbo, Ramon Novarro and Lionel Barrymore cost 850,000 dollars. But *Grand Hotel* (1932) with its all-star cast of Garbo, John and Lionel Barrymore, Joan Crawford, Wallace Beery, Jean Hersholt and Lewis Stone, was made for only 120,000 dollars more. M-G-M followed it with *Dinner at Eight* (1933: Jean Harlow, John Barrymore, Wallace Beery, Marie Dressler and Billie Burke) and *Night Flight* (1933: Clark Gable, Robert Montgomery, Myrna Loy, John and Lionel Barrymore, Helen Hayes), and Paramount followed the trend with *Alice in Wonderland* (1933: Gary Cooper, W. C. Fields, Cary Grant, Charles Ruggles, Edward Everett Horton, Jack Oakie).

In the end the all-star stratagem rebounded. Exhibitors reported that the public were expecting supercasts in every major picture and were turning away disappointed if only one or two names topped the cast. Soon there was neither profit nor safety in numbers.

*   *   *

If stars worked harder at the box office, they worked themselves harder to keep where they were. Personal appearances were one way of doing so and these really got into their stride in the 1930s and kept on into the war years of the next decade when they could be associated with patriotism as well as self-preservation. Not till television later blurred the high-definition personality of film stars did personal appearances become sporadic or confined to celebrating the movie industry's own rites on Oscar nights or at premières.

The stars in the early 1930s were unsure of their pictures and concerned about their security. They had been rudely awakened from the Hollywood play-world of the 1920s where silence ringed them round with its own isolating mystique that kept audiences in awe of them. Now the stars wanted to make contact with their public and beguile it with their personalities. But over and above this they wanted to impress the studio with their popularity and importance. Once the need to prove they could talk had been satisfied, the need to prove the reality of their status remained. Actors wanted to read lines and show they could face an audience as well as they could a camera. One commentator wrote, 'The picture performer wants to show he is just as good as the imported legitimate player, claims as much attention, merits as large a salary. He finds his best chance to impress the studio through P.A. tours.'

Such tours were just one way, though an important one, of humanising the stars of the new decade. Once quicker transport could bring them to their public they lost the exoticism of being remote. Many P.A. managers significantly advised their stars to shun all mention of Hollywood in case it was considered patronising. The emphasis was to be on the warm, democratic qualities of stardom. There was a strong drive to identify with audiences.

Stars played a comedy routine, if possible, with the local M.C.: the audiences already knew him, it was figured, and he would help them like the visiting stars. Once contact had been established and the idea implanted that 'film stars are people', the stars launched into their speciality acts: a song, a monologue, a playlet specially written to tie in with the mood or theme of their latest film. This re-established their uniqueness – the skills, dramatic abilities or personality traits that made them who they were. For after all, 'film stars are special people'. When it was all over, and if all had gone well, the audience had felt that stars were folk like themselves projecting ordinary human qualities, yet endowing them with a heightened enjoyment. The film that followed confirmed the feeling of the star as a magnified representative of the people.

This populist role is far more characteristic of the stars of the 1930s than of their predecessors. The silent movies probably touched the unconscious dream world of the audiences more powerfully than the talkies; but once sound had perforated the envelope of silence, it let in the audiences' consciousness. And the new stars became representatives of this collective consciousness, men and women exemplifying not only private dreams but the 'American Dream'; beings of fantasy all right, but beings whose personalities were moulded by the system to project the heightened characteristics of millions of their countrymen who recognised the homely body and the familiar speech at the heart of the fantasy.

One trend which was minor in itself nevertheless suggests how the image of the star was becoming humanised. Family life became a sanctioned part of stardom. Hollywood had previously been a place where, as far as the fans knew, no babies ever got born; for it was feared that fans would find it difficult to associate motherhood with film stars or, at least, with the kind of romantic or worldly roles with which the film stars were identified.

Like most Hollywood taboos, this one was quite irrational; yet apprehension did not begin to fade till the advent of an infant to Norma Shearer and her husband Irving Thalberg. Miss Shearer had only recently switched from playing a demure and gracious type of role to ones in which she was a neurotic society girl or a

vengeful *divorcée*; and it was feared at M-G-M that public knowledge of her baby would confuse her fans about the type of person
she was and generally hurt her popularity. Actually her motherhood only increased the interest her fans took in her. And Hollywood soon had further proof that while a double standard might
persist in sex, there was none in parenthood; for the news that
such heavily romantic stars as John Barrymore and Robert
Montgomery had become fathers without damaging their appeal
to female filmgoers confirmed the studios in their realisation that
fans liked to feel their idols were human like themselves and, with
a few exceptions, undergoing the same human experiences.

Before long this showed up indirectly in a cycle of motherhood
films. For while pictures had glamourised the ruthless career girl,
and thus implicitly disapproved of babies, stars had been careful to
relegate motherhood to the background of their public lives. Now
that they discovered it actually enhanced their popularity, films
appeared glamourising motherhood or justifying a star's sacrificing herself for the sake of her child. (It was also, of course, a useful
sop to the censors: a mother who took to the streets to feed a sick
infant could count on sympathy, while a babe in arms prudently
insured that she did not get very far in her profession.)

The gap between stars and fans was narrowed by deliberate
policy, too. It is not generally realised how unpopular the fan
clubs had made themselves with the studios at the end of the
1920s. Fan mail had increased so rapidly that by 1928 it was a
costly burden to be borne by studios or freelance stars. It was
calculated that 32,250,000 fan letters were received in Hollywood
each year; and the cost of replying, with a photo, ran to around six
cents each or a total of nearly two million dollars simply for maintaining public goodwill. Only a quarter of the letters were
regarded as having any value in sustaining a star's popularity or
affecting box-office returns. The trouble was separating them from
the mass of casual mail. Paramount at this time was the only
studio that handled the correspondence addressed to all its
contract artists: which shows what a high nuisance value the rest
placed on fan clubs. Most studios even forbade club organisers
to enter their gates. And at the start of the 1930s it became the

practice to charge members up to a dollar for photos of their favourites.

But by 1934 the picture had changed. Instead of getting the brush-off, fan clubs were having the welcome mat laid down for them. They had become invaluable pressure groups through which the studios could sell their stars' films via block bookings once the loyalists in the grass roots had put the squeeze on the local box-office. A census taken in August 1934, revealed 535 official fan clubs with a membership of 750,000. Joan Crawford, Jean Harlow and Clark Gable – all M-G-M stars – topped the list, the two women having about fifty clubs between them and Gable over seventy. Harlow's clubs totalled 16,000 members, Gable's nearly four times that.

Significantly this was the year in which the Legion of Decency was formed to take the crusade for a more moral Hollywood right up to the box-office by threatening a boycott of dubious movies or the pictures of stars who had got involved in scandal. Fan clubs became the Hollywood studios' troops in the field who were called on, in such situations, to throw their weight behind the dubious movies or the damaged stars. Keeping the fans' loyalty thus became a political move instead of a personal chore. It was never more zealously performed than in this era.

But of course it added innumerable extra hours to the amount of 'on duty' time the stars had to put in. A P.A. tour was reckoned to involve eighteen hours' work a day while it lasted. And the exposure had its psychological strain too. Fan worship was a public furnace that annealed the film image, but often burnt out the individual psyche. One wonders how the stars of this decade found relief from it – a thought that does not occur so readily with regard to the stars of earlier or later decades. The interviews they gave, with few exceptions, were done under surveillance and are inevitably guarded or officially ingratiating. When they did rebel against the system it was to insist on their dignity as human beings capable of free choice – usually expressed as a revolt against type-casting. Or else they struck back with their employers' own weapon, money – usually by holding out for more of it. They did not always get it; and when they did there was usually some humiliating concession extracted from them in return.

*   *   *

Apart from such sensational outbursts, the stars did their suffering where it could do least harm: inside the studio gates. The studio is the key concept of Hollywood in this era. It was concentration camp and entertainment factory. The way it was run depended on the personalities of the men who ran it quite as much as on the way it was geared to making pictures and profits. And for the most part they were not descended from the more benign patriarchs.

The economic slump actually ended by increasing the power of the studio bosses. For as the financiers discovered that film-making was not the fabulous exception to the capitalist debacle, they also discovered they were ill equipped to look after the human investment that the stars represented. They retained their seats on the board, but left the nurse-maiding and stick-threatening to the showmen. The latter brought film-making to a pitch of industrial efficiency unmatched before or since. At its height M-G-M was turning out one picture every nine days. But this was possible only because the human element had surrendered all freedom of choice. It was the price the stars had to pay for the durable moulding of their images.

How ruthless this process could be is revealed in possibly the last outspoken interview given by Clark Gable before the iron curtain of studio-imposed silence dropped around him. 'I have been in show business for twelve years,' he said in 1932. 'They have known me in Hollywood but two. Yet as picture-making goes, two years is a measurably long time. Nevertheless, my advice has never been asked about a part in a picture. . . . I found out I was going into *Susan Lenox* [1931: starring Greta Garbo] in Del Monte. Read it in the paper. . . . When I walked on the set one day, they told me I was going to play *Red Dust* [1932: co-star, Jean Harlow] in place of John Gilbert. . . . I have never been consulted as to what part I would like to play. I am paid not to think.'*

* *Photoplay*, December 1932.

Many other artists who became stars in the 1930s would endorse this complaint. The pressure to put them into one picture after another was tremendous. When Hortense Powdermaker made her famous anthropological sortie among the Hollywood natives in 1950, she recorded to her surprise that 'while most executives swear by the star system, it is not a part of Hollywood custom to plan coherently even for the stars'.*

Economic necessity twenty years earlier left even less time for rational star building. Personality manipulation, hit or miss, was then at its most intense. Likely stars were given a screen exposure in much the same way that novice swimmers might be thrown in at the deep end. Gable in his first year at M-G-M was put into fourteen films, sometimes having to go from set to set on the same day to play different roles. Bette Davis made eight films for Warner Brothers in 1932, her first year there. Even Jean Harlow while not under long-term contract to any studio appeared in five films during her first year as a potential star.

The player was exposed to the public as if on a spit, and his or her personality was rotated until a physical feature or character trait got a significant response at the box-office. This could then be repeated and manipulated to give an appearance of variety. Such had always been the economic rationale of stardom. But in the 1930s it was a singularly oppressive method.

The players then were generally a more sophisticated and intelligent generation than the stars of the silent screen. Many thought they were valued for the dramatic abilities they had shown on the legitimate stage. Instead they found themselves being turned into film stars by having an imbalance deliberately created in their personalities.

Bette Davis detected other reasons than economic ones behind this affront to human dignity. 'The insecurity of most of these moguls made them wary of a literate group of kids from the theatre. They wanted ganglings they could mould. They wanted to create personalities, not be challenged by them.'† Either way, the

* *Hollywood The Dream Factory*, by Hortense Powdermaker (Little, Brown & Co: The Universal Library), p. 246.

† *The Lonely Life*, by Bette Davis (G. P. Putnam's Sons), p. 139.

new stars had few of the consolations of their predecessors. They had to serve contracts measured in length of years, not numbers of pictures. Hardly any of them were able to use their established stardom to promote themselves into becoming their own producers. With rare exceptions they could not ask for a percentage of their pictures' profits with any hope of getting it.

Some studios guarded this privilege with patriarchal obduracy. Clark Gable stayed on a salary basis at M-G-M from the day he came in 1930 to the day he left in 1954. 'I asked (them) if I could go into partnership in some of my films, but they said no. So I left,' he said bitterly a few years later. And even to leave he had to take advantage of a California law passed to protect underpaid workers from unfair labour practices.

The relationship of the stars of the 1930s to their bosses was basically manipulative. Once the public hailed them as stars, they ceased to be regarded as artists and became art objects. They were type-cast. Resentment at the loss of individuality is the commonest neurosis of the period. In some cases the vehemence directed against it practically suggests a loss of identity. 'My comedy role in that one successful movie (*She Married Her Boss:* 1935) was a saleable commodity; they began exploiting what was supposed to be the comic Melvyn Douglas. . . . I earned what became an international reputation for being one of the most debonair and witty *farceurs* in Hollywood. I was cut off from the world I knew.'*

The same complaint was made even more forcefully by a star hardly regarded as possessing the same sensitivity as Melvyn Douglas. Barely a year after the erotic impact of her appearance in *Hell's Angels* (1930), Jean Harlow was saying: 'There are two distinct people: the Jean Harlow that's me and the Jean Harlow I see on the screen. I'm tired of being that girl. Fans, particularly feminine filmgoers, hate her. I'm beginning to hate her myself. I wore a low-cut gown and overnight I became a hussy. . . . I've played a series of abandoned wretches whose wickedness is never explained, never condoned, never accounted for. How can I expect audience sympathy when I have none for the parts I've

* *The Player*, by Lillian Ross and Helen Ross (Simon & Schuster), p. 19.

been forced to play? . . . Women are the back-bone of box-office popularity. Why should I deliberately alienate them by enacting creatures that all women loathe? It is foolhardy to invite their criticism and contempt. A sordid heroine can be sympathetic only when she is clearly a victim of circumstances.'*

The rage and despair over type-casting is a cry that echoes through this decade. One wonders how many frustrations would have been eased if those afflicted by them had been able to trade roles. The type that proved traumatic to one star was the role that another coveted. In tones very similar to Harlow's, Joan Crawford expressed just the opposite sentiments. 'I portrayed so many girls and women who went from rags to riches that Louis B. Mayer thought I represented Cinderella to the public. My audience was composed of women. I began to long to play bitches . . .'† Crawford was more fortunate than the Platinum Blonde. Harlow never really escaped from her hoydenish allure. But once Crawford was in a part, her identification with it was total. She did not feel dissociated from her roles, only dissatisfaction at the time it took begging for a different kind of part. It is a facet of her that will be examined in a later chapter.

For Bette Davis, on the other hand, the need to challenge the moguls created far more difficulties in the way of self-fulfilment; and the treatment she received when she tried to break away from type-casting was calculated to mortify her ego. Her chief consolation was appealing directly to her public. The personal appearance tours were like a holiday after Warner Brothers' inhospitable regime. 'I was almost grateful for the long list of garbage I had been made to play. . . . It exposed me to the public.'‡

*   *   *

Once the talkies defined the kind of life depicted on the screen as specifically American, social forces were of help to the studios in creating new stars. Three of the latter may be briefly examined.

* *Variety*, 22nd December 1931. It was an interview Harlow gave *before* she signed her M-G-M contract. She was far less outspoken afterwards.

† *A Portrait of Joan*, by Joan Crawford and Jane Kesner Ardmore (Doubleday & Co. Ltd), p. 69.

‡ Bette Davis, op. cit., p. 164.

The players who took the great gangster roles in films like *The Public Enemy* (1931), *Little Caesar* (1931) and *Scarface* (1932) became instant stars because they fitted dynamically into the pattern of expectation that the public had already formed from its knowledge of the real-life gangsters. The incisive characteristics of Cagney, Robinson and Muni were sharpened by the wider social references of their roles.

Cagney and Robinson were new hard-boiled types cast as much for their quick, clipped, unsentimental snarls as for their appearances. Otherwise they were very dissimilar. Cagney possessed a feminine relish for aggressiveness: the famous moment in *The Public Enemy* when he hits Mae Clark with half a grapefruit has a bitchy petulance behind the male muscle-power. His scorn of women, treating them as object-molls, made them secondary to his pursuit of power; and his appreciation of power had a decadent sweetness quite new on the American screen. Add to this his puckish smile, twinkling eyes, dainty hands and feet that forever itched to dance on his victims' bodies. (Cagney's six years as a vaudeville hoofer knitted him rhythmically together, even in non-dancing roles.)

Such traits projected him vividly on to the American consciousness at a time when it was alternately excited and appalled by the reports of gangsterdom. And even the unrelentingly moral ending of *The Public Enemy* – one of the few films that successfully squared the criminal code with the Production Code – could not obliterate Cagney's glamour. Filmgoers sensed an affinity with this on-the-make example of young America – and the gangster *gestalt* into which he fitted only gave it a perverted relevance. Even in his non-criminal parts like the cab driver in such a routine picture as *Taxi* (1932) his star appeal is generated by his rough courtship of his girl-friend, his readiness to pick a fight at any provocation and by dialogue that always derived from the tough vernacular of the streets. In such a role Cagney typified the new, humanised star of the talkies who closely approached the ways that the average American guy would have liked to act in moments of everyday stress.

Edward G. Robinson's *Little Caesar,* on the other hand,

One-eyed Matriarch: Bette Davis in *The Anniversary*

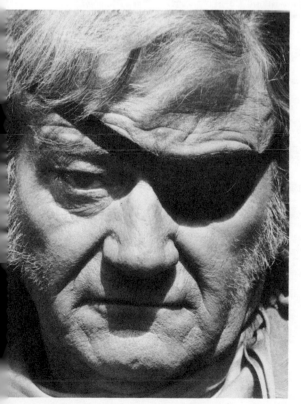

One-eyed Patriarch: John Wayne in *True Grit*

The old guard of Hollywood stars guarded their screen images and rarely altered them from film to film. The new generation of anti-stars do not hesitate to play character parts and lose their identities in a role. Dustin Hoffman as he appears in two films made the same year: *Above: Midnight Cowboy* (1969) as the little crippled Bronx conman Ratso Rizzo; and *Below: John and Mary* (1969) as the self-sufficient bachelor boy

differed from Cagney's criminal type in the satisfactions that crime brought the character. In Robinson's case they were associated with possession of a wider business empire, in Cagney's with a sharper mental exhilaration. Cagney's great moments were those in which he realised himself to the full: Robinson's great moments arrived when he realised his empire had collapsed. 'Mother of God, is this the end of Rico?' became on Robinson's dying lips the bemused query of a Caesar seeking his place in criminal history. Cagney, one feels, would have scorned history and expired with the egotistical question '. . . is this the end of *me*?'

Thus the two stars who appeared almost at the same time in criminal roles were able to complement each other. Neither ran the risk of blurring his image by having to compete with an already established star of the same type. This was Paul Muni's problem when he entered the talkies in 1929 with a voice he had proved to the satisfaction of Hollywood talent scouts at the Yiddish Art Theatre, New York.

But this was just the moment when Lon Chaney was having to face the rigours of sound and the possibility that it would narrow the range of roles available to his genius at make-up. Muni made a strong, humane impact in *The Valiant* (1929), his first talkie, in which he played a drifter who commits a murder and tries to hide it from his family. But then he starred in *Seven Faces* (1929) and was instantly dubbed 'another Chaney' for his virtuosity in playing seven roles including a man of seventy. He protested, 'Chaney likes to play grotesques. I take my characters from the street, real types everyone recognises.'

Chaney's premature death would have settled the succession, but by then Muni had created a sensation with his ruthlessly deglamourised gangster in *Scarface*, a criminal Golem turned against the society that had created him. Muni, however, never felt comfortable with his film stardom. He retained the impersonator's compulsion to hide his self: it went with his shy nature. And the roles he used as a cover for it are interesting reflections on the liberalism of the New Deal period when this actor personified the reassuring and benign liberalism which, in films anyhow, ultimately proved victorious. Roles like Pasteur, Zola or Juarez were saviour figures for the children of the Depression; while others like the convict in *I Am a Fugitive from a Chain Gang* (1932) or his striking miner in *Black Fury* (1935) or his Chinese peasant in *The Good Earth* (1937) touched the social conscience of the nation by picturing the plight of the exploited and the oppressed.

Something of the Yiddish stage's patriarchal traditions determined his predilection for playing characters considerably older than himself. Such a flair was also a kind of defiant anti-stardom, since it involved sinking his identity untraceably into a character and projecting his own personality only when it was a means of clarifying a dramatic point. He never gave himself wholeheartedly to a film career, and consequently escaped many of the degradations that lay in wait for those who did.

At first he had had to fight the damning image of having 'no image' – for he attributed the mediocre reception of *Seven Faces* to being sidetracked into pulling off a stunt as a Protean make-up artist. And then he had to battle for roles whose validity appealed to him on political or ethnic grounds: his intellectual make-up ultimately proved stronger than the greasepaint variety. Before *Scarface* was released he called the star system 'an outworn device, a worthless inheritance and a shortsighted policy'; and even after its tremendous success he only returned to Hollywood from Broadway on a picture-to-picture basis.

*   *   *

But whether social or economic pressures, or both, assisted the rise of some stars, all those who embraced the system surrendered some part of their artistic or personal liberty to the absolute monarchy of their studio bosses. The relationship of men like Mayer, Zukor, Harry Cohn of Columbia, or the Warner brothers to their stars is a treacherously documented area of studio history. Many reports about them simply project the writers' subjective hopes, fears or suspicions. But their personalities, often primitive and always powerful, shaped the daily, even hourly routine of their studios; and impelled them to realise their satisfactions, or work off their inadequacies, through the stars they created.

The paternal tyranny of Louis B. Mayer has been admirably analysed by Bosley Crowther and Philip French. He had a Judaic sense of his position. He saw his stars as members of a family in which love, honour and obedience were venerated and rewarded, while the neglect of them earned self-righteous retribution. His relations with his stars were well summed up by what he himself innocently said to the director of his beloved Andy Hardy series: 'A boy may hate his father, but he always *respects* him.' The spy system he maintained was the most efficient of any Hollywood studio – and every studio had one. If Hedy Lamarr is to be believed, Mayer's plainclothes-men even followed his stars after studio hours. He doted upon those who paid him the compliment of seeking advice from him about their careers. Some stars did this quite genuinely. Others made a stratagem of it and played up to the Yiddisher poppa side of him: needless to say, his 'daughters' found it easier than his 'sons'. He had a high regard for orthodox virtue. He never could abide Jean Harlow, despite the money she made, because of her flamboyant sex appeal: Harlow was only hired by the studio when the nod had come from the East Coast accounting end of the business.

Mayer knew the value of sex in motion pictures; but by temperament and faith he was compelled to endow it with a worshipful attitude which sometimes resulted in hypocritical relationships. 'Of course we shall have sex in pictures,' he said in one early interview, 'but it will be normal, real, beautiful sex – the sex that is common to the people in the audience, to me and to you.'* He signed Hedy Lamarr to an M-G-M contract after seeing her sensational nude appearance in *Extase* (1933) and then loaned her out for her American debut to Walter Wanger who was producing *Algiers* (1938) with the hint that it would be in order for her to appear in the nude again, provided it was not under M-G-M auspices. This attitude reinforced the sexual unreality that surrounded the screen images of many M-G-M female stars. They were always more glamourised than their earthier sisters at other studios.

After Irving Thalberg's death M-G-M showed a trend towards

* *The Lion's Share*, by Bosley Crowther (Dutton), p. 106.

producers' units which has persisted to this day. The producers maintained Mayer's view of stardom as a transcendent American ideal. Philip French has underlined the attractiveness to him of being able to transmute his east European Jewish origins into an industrial image that influenced the look and goals of gentile American society. His admiration for the Andy Hardy films starring Mickey Rooney and featuring all the homely American virtues is a significant part of his make-up. He badgered Clark Gable into playing Parnell, the Irish patriot, because he identified the tribal wrongs suffered by the Irish with the persecution of his own religious sect in Russia. (Such re-identification is not unusual in the film industry. Racial sympathy for the Indians in post-war westerns manifested itself around the same time as the Zionist struggle to set up their own state of Israel. To espouse the redskin cause was an acceptable way of backing racial identity without being un-American.) To have so complex and ruthless a character as Louis B. Mayer imposing his rule on a studio was a fact of stardom that had to be lived with by all and suffered through by some.

Fear and degradation were even more brutally imposed at Columbia, a studio which Harry Cohn had pulled up from being a 'poverty row' outfit to one which successfully challenged the Hollywood majors for prestige and profit. But Cohn worked on the theory that, 'If you're soft, you won't amount to anything.' His most recent biographer, Bob Thomas, has said, 'Aggressiveness was the only tactic Cohn understood or respected.' Any actor who achieved stardom under his aegis – and he was the only Hollywood mogul to be chief of production as well as company president – was regarded as a personal possession. He was autocratic to a degree and vulgar to a calculated extent since he felt that those who riposted in kind were brought safely down to his own level where dealings with them could comfortably begin. Changing the names of artists he signed up was one way of imposing his authority, wiping out the identities they brought to Columbia and making them over into an image he himself dictated. Having 'created' them, he then expected obedience and compelled it where he did not get it. 'He informed himself of the most intimate details of their personal lives and attempted to prevent them from committing mistakes that would endanger their careers and hence Columbia's investment in them.'* What he said in reply to an interviewer's apparently ingenuous question about close-ups illuminated his whole approach. 'Close-ups? We don't like them in our pictures. Only on very rare occasions do we use single close-ups. When action takes place between two or three people, we show them all in the close-up. . . . We don't have temperament in our studio. We don't tolerate it. There is no reason why an actor should be more temperamental than a doctor or lawyer or teacher or preacher. . . .'†

The lure that Cohn offered the stars to come to Columbia from other studios was the chance of playing in some of the wittiest, most sophisticated and topical scripts of the decade. Paradoxically he attracted liberal-minded directors and writers, many of them ex-newspapermen, who extracted the irony and optimism out of the Depression scene. Since Cohn's own tastes leaned towards the types and interests he felt easiest with, the studio's pictures reflected these tastes and so did the stars who passed through his hands, like Jean Arthur, Cary Grant, William Holden, Claudette Colbert and, on a loan-out from M-G-M, Clark Gable. The style of pictures that other studios preferred might not have made the tough, irreverent, laconic subjects so easily available to them. The fortunate ones whose Columbia films were box-office hits returned to their home studios with their prestige enhanced – but nearly all of them, whatever the result, returned chastened.

*   *   *

Given all the factors at work in Hollywood at this time, artistic, economic, social and personal, stardom takes on a new appearance. It can be seen as not just a rewarding and glamorous end product, but as a process for survival in a situation which any normally adjusted person would have found untenable in a short time. Before the studio system became so impregnably entrenched as

---

* *King Cohn*, by Bob Thomas, (Barrie & Rockliff) p. 215.
† Ibid., pp. 47–8.

the Hollywood way of life, the profitable 'life' expectancy of a top
star was estimated at between five and seven years. Paradoxically
the most rigorous system ever devised for controlling the personal
and professional aspects of an artist resulted in extending a star's
life-time by six to eight times that figure. Gable, Cooper and
Tracy remained stars till death, an average of over thirty years;
James Stewart and Henry Fonda have also lasted as long; while
Joan Crawford, Bette Davis and Katharine Hepburn are billed
over the titles of their films after nearly forty years of stardom.
With all its afflictions, the star system evoked a response that
sustained and preserved such individuals as these for many more
years than they might have hoped for in more human, democratic
or rationally ordered careers.

The psychologist R. D. Laing makes some observations in his
book *The Politics of Experience* which may be highly relevant to
this view of stardom in which a person 'cannot make a move, or
make no move, without being beset by contradictory and para-
doxical pressures and demands, pushes and pulls, both internally
from himself, and externally from those around him. He is, as it
were, in a position of checkmate.'* Laing was writing, as it
happens, about 'the experience and behaviour that gets labelled
schizophrenic'. He and his researchers took a more perceptive
view of it, not as an 'illness' but as a 'special strategy that a person
invents in order to live in an untenable situation'.

Now it is not being suggested that film stars are subjected to a
pathological process by the whole situation they inhabit inside and
outside the studio, though certainly some of them have been and
this book has touched on examples which tend to show a 'schizophrenic' reaction to it. But it would be facile to view stardom only
as a glamour concept and overlook its more painful reality as the
individual star's reaction to, and reflection of, the whole system of
incompatible pressures which create and sustain him, which give
him idolatry but demand obedience, which insist on his uniqueness but enforce conformity. The feeling of 'checkmate' that this
produces can be hideously damaging to the individual artist's
psyche. But it can also preserve those who adapt themselves to it,

* *The Politics of Experience*, by R. D. Laing, (Pelican), p. 95.

either going along with it docilely or else inventing stratagems to allow them to live and flourish within it. Even resisting it can be sustaining for an artist of the right will-power and temperament.

The studio system was a harsh regime: a form of twentieth-century slavery. But like earlier systems of servitude, those whom it did not destroy were preserved by it for marvellous spans of time.

PART SIX
ENDURANCE

'You manufacture toys, you
don't manufacture stars.'
— JOAN CRAWFORD

CHAPTER FIFTEEN

ACTION OF
THE TIGRESS:
BETTE DAVIS

Every picture is a test of stamina for those who work on it. For some of the stars it can also be a battle for power. The need to stay in charge can be a fatiguing and self-destructive passion. But for a few it can actually be a source of inexhaustible energy and in fact preserve the human personality in the way that scar tissue protects an old wound.

Hollywood has always offered plenty of testing opportunities to those who have the will to stand and fight the system of which they are part. And two of the most indestructible stars the system ever produced, Bette Davis and Joan Crawford, have seldom ignored a chance to accept the challenge even when the outcome was never in doubt for a moment. What they have had to endure in the course of their careers has given them a quality of endurance in the sense of staying power which they have been able to convert into a very real sense of star power. Each of them has gone on long enough in films to warrant the gossip-writers' cachet of being a 'Hollywood immortal'. In fact, the title that would be more justly applicable to each of them is a 'Hollywood indestructible'. Whatever else they have achieved, no one can deny them one thing – they have lasted.

'That wasn't one of my best pictures,' Bette Davis once said, adding by way of explanation, 'I didn't have to fight to get it.' The flip sarcasm is a self-comment on the bellicose stance she has always taken up towards life in general and her career in particular. Acting meant power to her long before it meant Hollywood. She first savoured the authority it brought with it as a child when a beard she was wearing as Santa Claus caught fire at a children's party she had been asked to – and she pretended that the flames had blinded her. 'I was in complete command of the moment. I had never known such power,' she wrote years later with no penitent regret but only a rueful reflection that Santa's sack was a burden she had to continue to carry through life for the benefit of all those in the movie industry who depended on her or exploited her, or did both.

Davis's autobiography, *The Lonely Life*, is one of the most obliquely revealing of recent star memoirs. It is perhaps unremarkable that she should have been born in a thunderstorm – a more conscious artist might have counterpointed the event with clear skies and tranquil days – but as she unconsciously describes the elements in terms of the stage it begins to look as if she came into the world from the wings, not the womb: 'I happened between a clap of thunder and a streak of lightning. It almost hit the house and destroyed a tree out front.'* (For anyone but a born actress, the tree would simply have been 'outside'.)

Acting for her has always had the same connotation of elemental power and she has been shrewd enough to perceive, through the way she has played her assigned or chosen roles, that what the women who make up her audience identify with is this very power for action. It might seem odd that someone with this temperament could desire to play Alice in Wonderland: a passive character if ever there was one in literature, who initiates little and to whom everything happens. But Davis saw Alice as 'a little spitfire . . . rebellious, ferocious, both innocent and cynical, spiritual and intemperate. Alice isn't sweet, she's salty.'† She might be suspected of reading her own character into Lewis Carroll's heroine. She ultimately did get to play Alice, but it was under the name of Jezebel.

Davis was brought up a Yankee and an Episcopalian in a family from which her father vanished when she was about seven. In Sunday School she was taught by Una Merkel, who later became a film actress with something of the same emphatic manner as Davis. The name 'Bette'‡ derived from Balzac's *Cousine Bette* and

* Bette Davis, op. cit., p. 13.
† Ibid. p. 19,2.
‡ In spite of its literary origins, Miss Davis insists that her first name be pronounced as if it were 'Betty'.

was adopted at the suggestion of a family friend along with the dangerous advice to a child that it would 'set you apart'. Her strong will was already doing that. When she and her mother swapped clothes and personalities for a party masquerade, the older woman tried, vainly, to teach Bette a lesson in making herself agreeable by miming her surliness. Her mother was also an excellent photographer: so that although the daughter was later made angry by the inadequate preparation allowed her for a screen test, she was well versed in posing for the home camera sessions. The awfulness of her screen test probably arose from seeing her perfectly familiar features *in motion:* for the first time she found how lop-sided her mouth was when she spoke.

In common with many stars of vivid screen presence, dancing was another early influence on her: she was instructed by a pupil of Isadora Duncan, the apostle of free expression in which bodily movements mimed the emotions. Davis's films, the early ones in particular, show the characteristically restless energy she could wring from her whole body. (And in the light of this early training the skips and swoops displayed so disturbingly by her at the end of *What Ever Happened to Baby Jane?* (1962) and throughout *Hush, Hush . . . Sweet Charlotte* (1964) suggest an Isadora Duncan run to seed and far into madness.)

What Hollywood did when she got there with a contract from Universal was to confirm her temper after raping her dignity. In these painful years was laid her craving for stardom and her contempt for its processes. The sarcasm and mistrust she vents on the male sex in many of her best performances perhaps draws its energy from these years, too. It cannot simply be due to the competition, fair and unfair, she later suffered from male co-stars: Alec Guinness, Paul Muni, Erroll Flynn and Robert Montgomery have been blamed at one time or another for trying to upstage or otherwise 'sabotage' her scenes with them.

Typical of the hurts her pride suffered in those early days was a screen test in which she had to withstand a series of players 'vamping' her: 'The camera was concentrated exclusively on the men as they ravaged this anonymous being.'* Davis took to heart the common Hollywood experience of a newcomer, that of being invalidated as a person – and it hardened her heart.

*   *   *

What particularly baffled her first employers at Universal was the type she represented. How should she be cast? They implied she lacked sex appeal. To them, said Davis years later, 'this meant *sympathetic* sex appeal, the kind that collects its man at the fade-out'. Something they sensed in Davis seemed to disqualify her for this chore. Perhaps it was her voice, for otherwise one shares her bafflement that anyone could watch her sensual performance in *The Cabin in the Cotton* (1932) and not consider her sexy. But she was one of the very first of the 'personality' voices in the talkies; and the roles she was assigned jarred on her personality, just as her voice jarred on them. Mostly they were 'sisterly' parts.

The turning point came when George Arliss, at Warner Brothers, picked her for his production of *The Man Who Played God* (1931). Arliss was then 62, Davis 23. Though professionally a martinet, his manners were practically courtly compared with the Hollywood boorishness she had experienced; and this courtesy, coupled with a fatherly concern that her family life had lacked since childhood, made her feel wanted and appreciated. 'Universal had asked to see my legs, Mr Arliss was examining my soul.'

It is a strange reflection on the reach of Anglo-Saxon patronage that Arliss and Elinor Glyn, both born in the 1860s, within four years of each other, should have excelled at the Hollywood game of personality grooming. Just as uncultured producers bowed to Madame Glyn's power of protocol, a sensitive actress like Davis warmed to Arliss's sense of propriety. His considerateness went further: it extended to changing the style and colour of her hair, shortening and lightening it, and seeing that she was well photographed. The film's photographer, Ernie Haller, became, along with Tony Gaudio, the favourite cameramen on Bette Davis films: which suggests it was about this time that she began laying

* Bette Davis, op. cit., p. 134.

the star's first strategy for long-term survival: sympathetic photography. Arliss's famous concern with diction* left its mark on her own emphatic enunciation.

Though her part was small – a girl in love whose happiness is promoted by Providence, otherwise George Arliss – the film was indeed a turning point. She was taught about film acting and how to preserve the continuity of mood and emotion essential to creating a character who is a jigsaw of edited shots. She saw Arliss wield power. And her own later concern over every detail of her films, from the screen test of a co-star (Paul Henreid) to the hair-cut of a leading man (Glenn Ford), reflects the lessons of those early days as an autocrat's apprentice.

But the most valuable thing Arliss gave her was self-respect. Subsequent directors like Michael Curtiz and Mervyn LeRoy hardened her determination to protect it against all future assault. Both men embodied in their art the cynical, heartless, fast-paced Warner Brothers films about tough, low-life *milieux*. Both put the accent on male supremacy, if not in the picture then on the set. Curtiz in particular was a tyrant to many of his actors. Yet it was in *The Cabin in the Cotton*, a rural drama of exploited Southern sharecroppers and as such an untypical Curtiz film, that Bette Davis found her authentic style playing the first forthright bitch of her career. Such directors seemed to 'set' the style of the stars that laboured under them. It was the same when Davis worked with William Wyler, a man who gives no leeway to his players.

A long and scarred Hollywood apprenticeship like this establishes patterns in a star's work and one of them is the compulsion to fight a new director, to test his fortitude, gauge his breaking point, perhaps even invite reprisals just to prove that he is enough of a professional to handle the well-matured and highly-priced material that the star represents. Film acting for some stars is the time when pent-up resentments can be released in the security that the enormous cost of the film, the perpetual crisis of the production and even the fact that *prima donna* behaviour is actually expected from a first-magnitude star will all nourish the

* See Chapter 13 for a fuller account of Arliss's influence in Hollywood.

stars' sense of power and assuage their sense of grievance. Such lessons are learned early, but they are generally retained for life.

*   *   *

The Cabin in the Cotton was Richard Barthelmess's last big picture, but it was the first Bette Davis one in which her inner characteristics gelled with her outward trademarks. It was the film that defined her. She plays Madge, a Deep South example of nymphomania in bud, who seduces a conscience-bowed share-cropper's son (Barthelmess). Her voice, pitched between a taunt and a whine, radiates a selfish spoiltness. Her obtruding eyeballs, ogling Barthelmess from under that globular forehead, the way her fingers clutch his hand as he lights her cigarette, the flirtatious sag of her body against the shop counter, and especially the breathy little ballad of Willie the Weeper which she croons to the em-barrassed Barthelmess as she strips to slip into 'something more restful' and then calls him enticingly to his seduction: every detail adds provocativeness to a confidently assembled impression of a woman in heat.

It is almost unbelievable that Warner Brothers refused to see the value of the property they had on their hands and relegated her to more sympathy-getting roles. Having defined her screen character, the lack of opportunity to use it in the right roles was maddening. She had to wait until *Of Human Bondage* (1934) before her bitch incarnate was again seen effectively on the screen in the person of Mildred, the neurotic self-destructive tramp; and the loss of the Oscar she deserved for the performance was attributed by her to the studio's attempt to curb her growing temperament and cut her down to size.

One rarely quoted piece of evidence illustrates the humiliating chores to which stars at this time could be assigned. Warner Brothers in 1933 was a large shareholder in General Electric. The electrical appliance company had paid part of the expenses con-nected with the personal appearance tour by train (The 42nd Street Express) of Warner Brothers stars which was undertaken with more sense of showmanship than political tact at the very height of the Depression. In return the stars were pressed into doing advertising stints in General Electric showrooms, and Dick Powell and Bette Davis even had to appear in an advertising short where they played a married couple extolling garden floodlighting and kitchen dishwashers. The cheaply slick commercial – 'Oh, if I had to wash dishes for a hundred days three times a day!' sighs Bette at the sink – is a disenchanting exhibit of the grooming and grovelling that went on inside Hollywood studios at the time.

Poor pay was another source of constant irritation on the Warner lot. Stars in other studios shared in the same complaint and 1933 was not only the worst year of the Depression as far as cinemas were concerned, but also the one when talented names were desperately making a stand against the attempt to enforce a cut-back in pay, or battling with the tight-fisted hierarchy (in most cases vainly) for some solid acknowledgement that their drawing power entitled them to a slice of the profits. Warner Brothers paid less, sometimes much less than any other studio of its size.

Davis in desperation left the country in 1936 to make a film in England and was promptly sued in the English High Court for breach of contract. At the hearing some interesting facts emerged about her star status and, by implication, that of other leading players. Jack Warner in evidence said that any Warner Brothers film starring her could be worth 600,000 dollars to 700,000 dollars gross in the world and the number of films she made was entirely at the discretion of her employers. Yet if she were to serve the term of the contract entered into on 27th December 1934, she would be earning only 3,000 dollars a week by 1942. Moreover Clause 23 of her contract – a 20-page document which was referred to as incorporating 'the whole collective memory of mankind' – claimed that if she failed, refused or neglected to perform her services under it, her employers had the right 'to extend the term of this agreement and all of its provisions for a period equivalent to the period during which such failure, refusal or neglect shall be continued'. Her counsel in the London action, Sir William Jowitt, declared that if Bette Davis 'walked out' of a film, 'the specified period [of her contract] could be suspended by the plaintiffs and would never come to an end at all. The bar against Miss Davis working for anyone else would never come to an end either. It is a life sentence.'*

Yet a clause like this was common in nearly every star's contract in the 1930s: it was known in Hollywood as the 'hangman's loop'. Any struggle simply tightened it: the only relief was passive obedience. The High Court upheld Warner Brothers in their action against Bette Davis; and the iniquity of the never-ending suspension was not ended until Olivia De Haviland won an action in the California courts in the 1940s. Davis said about her legal defeat, 'I was made to seem greedy and high-handed. . . . In an attempt to protect themselves against this rising class [of discontented stars] Warners . . . cast me in the role of a spoiled brat, an intractable infant who needed a good spanking.'†

Actually this accusation contains slightly more irony than she perhaps appreciated. For the 'role' in which Warners had cast their recalcitrant actress, so that they could make an example of her, was hardly different from some of the screen roles in which they made a star of her. Perhaps a 'good spanking' is too frivolous a retribution for the damage done by some of her screen bitches; but otherwise the terms 'greedy', 'high-handed', 'spoiled' and 'intractable' are perfectly applicable to the heroines of films like *Of Human Bondage*, *Dangerous* (1935) and *Jezebel* (1938) and their later, more heartless sisters in *The Letter* (1940) and *The Little Foxes* (1941). When it came to protecting their own economic interests, Warner Brothers had a pretty shrewd idea of casting. It was only in the matter of meeting their stars' artistic aspirations that they proved slow learners. It was a battle to get the two to meet by design, rather than accident.

*   *   *

The link is close, then, between the personal image that Bette Davis's best-known screen roles established of her and the embattled existence she felt compelled to lead off screen in order to get them or have her way in them. The neurotic energy she

* *The Times*, 16th October 1936.
† Bette Davis, op. cit., p. 195.

unleashes in such parts is a symptom of her will. Of course she has played many dissimilar parts, a wider range of comedy, pathos, farce and even historical drama than one at first glance appreciates. But the public tends to hoard one or two special films in its collective memory and it is these which become the basis of a star's image. Bette Davis so forcefully created Mildred, the shrewish Cockney waitress in *Of Human Bondage* who drags her lover down with her, that, as she noted, 'many people believe . . . it was my first picture although I had made 21 films before it.'

Many filmgoers, as fan letters are constantly proving, do believe that the star is the character she portrays. But Davis's art is not to be explained by such a naïve, or libellous, an equation. What she does is draw inspiration from the true adjustment of herself to her material. Her own individuality is artistically re-expressed. And the roles that give it greatest play are the ones in which her own will to take command interacts most completely with the character she is playing.

The title of *Dangerous*, in which she won her first Oscar, is applicable to many of these parts. She is generally a woman with a jinx on her – she attracts and destroys without falling into what could be conventionally called love. What she is in love with is the power drive. The little Cockney, Mildred, with her fanatical eyes is the prototype of such a bitch. Joyce Heath, the ex-alcoholic in *Dangerous* who is rescued from Skid Row by Franchot Tone, sneers, nags, betrays and nearly ruins him, gaining a masochistic fulfilment from the rough time she gives him and herself.

Indifference to guilt is common to all the roles – except when a happy ending is unwarrantedly dictated by the studio and even it tends to vanish as Davis gains artistic power. Nor is compassion ever asked for: in its place is an obsession with power or a compulsion to pull others into her own neurosis. A man who meets Davis in a bitch role gets the rough edge of her tongue before she shows him, if ever, any softer feature. She is beset in *Jezebel* by an inability to give in to her husband-to-be, even when she really wants to. ('Like Julie in *Jezebel*,' she once said in explanation of a marriage that had gone wrong, 'I had to remain in charge. And when the man allowed it, I lost all respect for him.')

The adulterous wife she plays in *The Letter* shoots her lover and then perjures herself in court. It is arguably her best study in neurotic compulsion. Deceit becomes her. It sharpens her femininity. She never seems so desirable as when she is lying her way out of a crisis and falling back on wiles and pleas that are pitched towards the male whom she basically despises and mistrusts. A similar dilemma in *In This Our Life* (1942), as a spoilt Southern girl involved in a hit-and-run accident, produces the same seductive dissimulation.

Both stories, incidentally, are set in communities – Asian in one case, Southern negro in the other – where her flagrant disregard of guilt have racial undertones which give her performance a decadent resonance. This is what is missing in *The Little Foxes*. She is basically a mercenary woman; and the exercise of power for an end outside itself robs the character of its interior flux of emotions. Moreover William Wyler, who directed the film, made her subdue her own neurotic power to the more ordinary theatrical intentions of the play. Her exercise of pure power is better served in the two films about Elizabeth Tudor, a part that has a strong pull for strong-willed Hollywood actresses. Katharine Hepburn always regretted that it was the other queen she got to play in John Ford's *Mary of Scotland* (1936). 'I prefer the type of woman who doesn't lose her head,' she quipped.

Davis might have phrased its attraction differently – causing people to lose *their* heads is the ultimate sanction of the part. (If she were casting herself in Alice in Wonderland today, she might have second thoughts about the part she would pick.) Watchful, proud, jealous, intriguing, distrustful, ruthless, her monarch in *The Private Lives of Elizabeth and Essex* (1939) maintains her absolutism in ways that have affinities with Davis's own experience that human relationships are treacherous and work is the only sure satisfaction. Statecraft, too, is a kind of stardom; and the court setting parallels a film studio in ways too obvious to need stressing.

Both 'royal' films – the second is the darker, sourer *The Virgin*

Queen (1955) – give full rein to another of the star's inherent characteristics. This is her sarcasm, her talent for public rebuke. She displays it crushingly in other films. But these two institution-alise it in the person of a Tudor queen who is by protocol 'unanswerable'. (When Errol Flynn does answer her back – she wanted Laurence Olivier for the role – she exercises another royal prerogative and boxes his ears.)

On meeting Davis in the flesh one is uncomfortably aware that she needs no film script to manifest this particular quality. It is prudent to stand still, as one is instructed on safari, and let her do the approaching. For Hollywood has bred in her a psychic aware-ness of people: which is maybe why that memorable line in *All About Eve* (1950) – 'Fasten your seat belts, it's gonna be a rough evening' – is uttered with a matchless sense of someone used to sniffing blood on the wind.

Bette Davis has an uncommon ability to absorb physical make-up psychologically into whichever part she is playing. The outer realism has always an inner logic. Mildred the waitress's pale, unsunny complexion has an occupational reality to which her mascaraed eyes and voracious mouth stand out in contrast as the self-applied marks of her carnal nature which grows stronger as she grows weaker from consumption. Davis insisted on doing her own make-up for the death scene, suspecting that here, if anywhere, the studio would try to soften her unflinching delinea-tion of the part. The realism of it alarmed the front office, an additional source of gratification to her. Her remarkable make-up for Elizabeth I obtains the effect of a living effigy by thinning her mouth to a Tudor lip-line, shaving the eyebrows and painting out the eyelashes. The Davis eyeballs are objects to juggle with: their thyroid-like effect can be effortlessly simulated when the intensity of the scene requires it; but make-up often emphasises it and turns the eyelids into veritable snowploughs when a high-definition piece of acting is wanted. (The effect is sometimes most noticeable when another 'strong' actress is co-starred with her in the film.)

No other star can 'age' as well as Bette Davis. Usually 'ageing' roles to a glamour star are what a slumming expedition is to a rich man: an act of self-indulgence, seldom edifying to watch. But Davis excels at it. Too confident an actress to need to *feel* she is acting when she puts on the grey hairs, she makes the most of the drama without upsetting the metabolism of the character. She has been very shrewd at gauging the moments in her career when she needs to make 'sympathetic' pictures. She has gone so far as to admit that her career has been quite consciously based on this change of pace. Ageing helps her achieve it, since the women who go to her films are themselves passing through the middle-age of the emotions at a roughly similar time of life. The identification is very close.

The most notable films of this type also exploit with some finesse the character's sense of being deprived of something – generally something of common importance to women. In *The Old Maid* (1940) it is motherhood – for over twenty years she has had to bear the sight of her sister (Miriam Hopkins) playing surrogate mother to her illegitimate child. In *Old Acquaintance* (1941) it is love – the younger man with whom she has fallen in love is himself in love with the daughter of her old school chum (Hopkins again). She makes such soap-opera sacrifices seem true and touching, at the time anyhow, since the woman she presents is a more likely creature than the 'woman's picture' rigged up around her.

But it is *All About Eve* that links her own film-star personality most poignantly to her skill in suggesting the ageing spirit of a woman. All her sarcasm, exhibitionism, bitchiness and well-founded distrust of human relationships, especially in the film-theatrical set, find their marvellous expression in a larger-than-life portrait of the Broadway star Margo Channing. It is a role created in her own image of a maverick Mother Goddam. Yet when her treacherous protégée, Eve, pushes her off her throne and she opts for marriage, she humanises Margo by the unexpected grace of her decision to abdicate before she is forced to concede defeat.

At the time of the picture she was 42, nearing the age when the prospect of staying a star is determined by a diminishing number of roles available to her. Youth, beauty and sex appeal, the qualities at the heart of stardom, are all quickly depreciating qualities, which explains why female stars generally live shorter, more fraught lives than male ones who can rely on a diffused personality that can even show a profit as they grow old, maturing like a good endowment policy. Davis herself has acidly noted the unfairness of a double standard that allows male stars to 'see themselves as permanently appealing and [not to] think it at all strange that they are making love to actresses who could well be their grand-daughters'.* (The 'love scene' seems to hold particular resonances for her, as she frequently refers to it in a variety of contexts – her first screen test, the give-away scene for a male player's vanity, etc.)

Fortunately for her, one can carry the will to dominate into maturity and beyond with unimpaired vigour and it is this that has sustained her star appeal though sometimes at the price of a melodramatic heightening of her characteristics. In films like *What Ever Happened to Baby Jane?* and *Hush, Hush . . . Sweet Charlotte* this was abetted in no very kind fashion by director Robert Aldrich's attitude, gloating and surgical, towards the haggish aspects of freakish female characters in his films – though, to be fair, Davis did conceive the Gothic make-up which made Baby Jane look as if she had been pickled and bottled. Aldrich has described her first sight of the finished film and how he heard 'this quiet but kind of desperate sobbing . . . "I just look awful," she wept. "Do I really look that awful?" '†

Make-up has played a weightier part than usual in recent performances, though not to conceal but to emphasise. As the half-blind maternal tyrant in *The Anniversary* (1968) she affected an adhesive eye-patch that looked like a swollen red eyelid and intensified the glare-power of the one remaining eye: it was in other respects too, a suitably rampant performance. Her subtlest acting has drawn on the ambiguity of her own disturbing nature and also on her compulsion to alternate between 'unlikeable' and 'sympathetic', 'sour' and 'sweet' roles. (To hear her talk about

* Bette Davis, op. cit., p. 241.
† *Sight and Sound*, Winter, 1968–9.

'being so sweet I almost nauseated myself', one feels that acting for her could almost be an emetic.)

The Nanny (1965) held the character's real nature in intriguing suspension right to the end so that one never knew whether she was acting the tyrant for everyone's good or for her own sadistic satisfaction. In fact she vibrated, rather than acted, as if the actual striking of the precise note had taken place a split-second before the camera began shooting. Only a star like Davis could have sustained so well, or so long, the doubt about her real motives in the middle-class English household. (On accents, incidentally, she is very good.) Though in a minor key, *The Nanny* is one of her most masterly performances and one can see how well she absorbed Arliss's training in preserving the continuity of the character, even if here the continuity resides in the ambiguity.

Sometimes the gear shift between good and bad has not been achieved between films, but within one. *Dead Image* (1964: American title *Dead Ringer*) was a dichotemised melodrama of good and evil with the star in a dual role of identical twins – the virtuous, mousy one accidentally killing and then taking the place of the rich, wicked one in a re-working of her earlier film *A Stolen Life* (1946). And *Connecting Rooms* (1970), follows the same pattern and presents her, after the maternal dragon of *The Anniversary*, as a pity-worthy cellist pretending to be part of a symphony orchestra but actually earning a living as a street musician.

One wonders when and in what kind of role the see-saw feeling of someone alternately getting sympathy or else giving hell which these latter day roles convey will be find its own equilibrium. 'Give me a nice, normal woman who just shoots her husband,' Margo Channing cracks in *All About Eve*. Maybe it requires a part as ironically well-adjusted as this to reconcile her nature and her art: if so, it would be an ideal solution. And then, again, on reflection, would it? Being a star involves an imbalance precipitated by the way that circumstances have of reacting upon personality and bringing into prominence aspects of the individual that are reinforced by her film roles and the appeal she makes to the public. The whole career, artistry and personality of Bette Davis exemplify this process to a degree that is uncommonly vivid even among her film-star peers. She is a star who not only survives but actually thrives under stress, off screen and on, and to this end life will always co-operate with art in her profession. Battle is what has shaped her, will-power is what has preserved her. Take away the one and you inevitably weaken the other. The only martial sound that has probably never thrilled her is the bugle call for a truce.

CHAPTER SIXTEEN

ALL FOR LOVE: JOAN CRAWFORD

At no time in her career, if her account of it is to be believed, did Joan Crawford ever say to herself, 'Now, *after this,* I will be a star.' Her professional life is characterised by the total certainty that she was a star right from the start and that in a very short time, at some opportune moment for believers, the quality of her stardom would be revealed to them like the revelation of another person's sainthood, though without the need to have it confirmed by a higher source. When she talks of entering a film studio for the very first time, she makes it sound as if she were taking a vow.

From the very first she has spoken about stardom as if she knew no other way to live. Her ambition had – and has – an almost holy zeal to it. 'I want to do some really fine things to be remembered by, and then I shall say goodbye, thanks a lot, it was lovely. But how to know it when the time comes?' – she was speaking in 1932 – 'That's why I'm always groping, seeking to learn, trying to improve myself. I want so much to fight off conceit. I must never allow myself to become self-satisfied. But I don't think I ever will. My ambition is too driving – too relentless to permit me to grow complacent. I would never, for instance, talk over the radio – "When I did this, when I did that" – those silly stupid interviews all about oneself. Who cares? If you're important enough, people will talk about you. You don't have to do it yourself.'*

The quality of very few stars burns through to the printed interview; but this one, thanks to some anonymous reporter whose shorthand was fast enough to keep up with the subject and literal enough to transcribe her clenched phrases, seems to

* *Variety,* 12th July 1932.

seize the essential Joan Crawford so well that it might fit into any of the career-women parts she has played without changing a word – though, to be sure, before she came on the set she might have thought of a few words to change just out of habit. For, according to some of her own reports, she established an early reputation for having dialogue altered to suit her. After all, the writer's words 'were dead words. They were brought to life by me.'*

Her career was built on a desire to earn people's gratitude, even if they were writers – but really *earn* it. Like Bette Davis she has a compulsive need to feel in charge of her career or of the part she is currently playing. And why not? she might ask – isn't it for the good of the picture, if she is? Unlike Davis, though, she evinced from the very start a desire to please everyone, from the highest to the lowest, who might have anything to do with her part, her picture or her career.

It is not a sentimental explanation to suggest that this shows how strong is her need for love. It is simply a condition of her kind of stardom. A star, to her way of thinking, is one who is loved – period. She has never stopped trying to please the first people who loved her to the point of actually bestowing a name on her: her vast audience of fans. When she got an M-G-M contract in the mid-1920s, largely on the strength of her dancing talent, she was known professionally as Lucille Le Sueur. The studio wanted to change it and the readers of *Movie World*, in 1925, voted for a new one. She became Joan Crawford.† She had found 'that incredible thing, a public. . . . From this moment on, I had sense of audiences as warm, loving people who would care for me in direct proportion to the energy and talent I would give to a public to whom I owed a loyalty and from whom I've always received loyalty.'‡

She was doubly lucky in going to M-G-M. Mayer's patriarchal rule, treating his stars like children to whom he meted out rewards and punishments, answered her own need for the kind of father

* Joan Crawford, op. cit., p. 68.
† Actually she first became Joan Arden, but this turned out to be the name of another actress, so the second choice of 'Joan Crawford' was adopted.
‡ Joan Crawford, op. cit., p. 64.

figure that her parents' broken marriage – they had separated before she was born – prevented her from acquiring inside her own family. Mayer had had predecessors, though. Even the president of the small college she worked her way through as a waitress – thus laying down experience for the archetypal Crawford role – was 'Daddy' Wood to her. And the advice he gave her sounds like the strategy for the continual renewal she was to apply to her screen career: 'When you find you can do one thing, Joan, stop doing it and do another.'

Such 'older' studio executives as Paul Bern and Carey Wilson also supplied paternal comfort, but 'Mr Mayer' most of all. To this day Crawford will not hear a word against him, or even have books that are sharply critical of the M-G-M overlord inside her house. 'He knew how to build and protect his "properties" and he had considerable regard for them as people,' she recalls; though a slightly cooler recollection of Mayer by the M-G-M scriptwriter Salka Viertel suggests that Mayer's protectiveness had at times a markedly one-way flavour: 'He went on telling me that Joan Crawford blindly followed his advice and had fared very well by it, and that "poor little girl, Judy Garland, she always does what I tell her; even Norma [Shearer] listens to me – only Garbo is difficult. I am her best friend. I want her to be happy – she should come and tell me what she wants – I'd talk her out of it".'*

The important thing, however, is that the set-up at M-G-M corresponded to Crawford's emotional needs and satisfactions to a quite exceptional degree once she learned to find her way around it. She came with the usual six-months option contract: she stayed over twenty years. Though her looks were striking from the first – 'Your face is *built*,' a cameraman told her – it was for her vitality she was valued. The action pictures popular with newspaper picture-desks now that the Speed Grafics had come into fashion radiated this vitality.

Her early parts deployed it in energy in the chorus line or on the dance floor, for she was at first asked to do no more than play

* *The Kindness of Strangers,* by Salka Viertel (Holt, Rinehart & Winston) p. 271.

the showgirl type she had been. Dancing had given her an early taste of stardom; she had won over a hundred cups for dancing the Charleston in exhibition contests. Vitality was thus a direct pathway to her ambition. But even in straight roles one notices Crawford's electric contact with the ground she is walking on, the way she might be drawing power from it.

Her ramrod straightness shows her inner discipline and makes her look much taller than her 5 feet 5 inches. And her wide collar-bone and square shoulders, on which Adrian's shoulder-pads became epaulettes of power, intensify her masculine drive. She did not present the look of tailored gauntness from the first; but quite early on she stopped trying to feminise her features by diminishing them and instead based her facial impression on what she remembered of a photograph of her real father – 'eyes . . . prominent cheek-bones . . . bold eyebrows.' Her skin gave her bones a covering as classic as the canvas on a prairie-wagon: it was made to withstand all weathers.

*   *   *

But the very vitality which shaped her movements and trans-fused the character she was playing also, at first, imposed limits on her acting – and on her writers. 'Writing for Joan Crawford is difficult,' Scott Fitzgerald said, 'She can't change her emotions in the middle of a scene without going through a sort of Jekyll-Hyde contortion of the face, so that when one wants to indicate she is going from joy to sorrow, one must cut away and then back. Also, you can never give her such a stage direction as "telling a lie" because if you did she would practically give a representation of Benedict Arnold selling West Point to the British.'

Though a sizeable overstatement itself, this contains a modicum of truth; yet essentially it is irrelevant. Crawford has to be taken at face value, literally so. For her face invariably carries total conviction in whichever moment or whichever part she happens to be playing. Fans tell themselves, 'Joan believes it' and do not require her to make them believe it, too. Garbo deliberately withheld a part of herself from an audience and compelled them to penetrate her inscrutability. Crawford leaves nothing to be guessed at, but projects herself generously towards the loyal troops. Each part she plays seems performed on a saluting base. 'Eyes right!' There she is, God bless her! *Acting!*

She admits she acquired a few talents from watching others. Co-starred with the 'rather frightening' Lon Chaney who played the armless knife-thrower in *The Unknown* (1927), she was awed by his on-camera concentration and taught herself to do the same. A sense of continuity, such as that which Bette Davis acquired from George Arliss may serve a film actress better in the long run than the habit of concentration, but Crawford's energy needed to burn itself up on something, and concentration served her well: continuity soon followed as she watched other stars and directors on the set and saw the results on the screen. Her vitality was kept topped up to strength after she experienced the undiluted ardour of John Gilbert – then at the peak of his off-screen affair with Garbo – as the bootlegger who hijacks her in *Twelve Miles Out* (1927).

She has never made a secret of these male stars' influence; but it is not in her nature to define herself by reference to a female star. 'I admire Garbo,' she said when both of them were starring in *Grand Hotel*. 'I think she's a great talent, and because I said so they started whispering; "She's imitating Garbo – ah, ah!" That's so unfair, so untrue. I don't have to imitate anybody. I don't – I'm my own personality.' (Years later she boasted that no one could imitate *her*.) 'You don't know what I suffered when I first learned what they were saying. I cried, I raged, for I have worked so hard. I wish I could harden myself against criticism, rise above it, but I can't. I take my work seriously – too seriously. At least with my temperament, I can never become static.'*

The last word is a well-chosen one. For constant change is an overriding need with her. She has been continually re-defining herself in terms of the parts she plays: not simply to stretch herself, to see if her reach exceeded her grasp, but chiefly to renew her welcome with the great matrix of the audience she exists to please and which, in turn, gives her a secure place in their affections.

* *Variety*, 12th July 1932.

Of course such role-switching cuts right across the 'public like what they know' basis of the star system. If she had not been able to give such constant proof, so sincerely, of her high regard for 'Mr Mayer', one guesses that Crawford might have been classed as another dissatisfied ingrate like Garbo who did not know what was good for her. But her driving ambition was expressed not in terms of how much it meant to her, but of what she meant to those millions of filmgoers who were also part of the M-G-M family.

This kind of selflessness always touched Mayer on his sentimental nerve. The rest was a matter of persistence. 'Mr Mayer accused me of camping outside his front door. The truth is, I kept an eye on the back door as well.' Mayer at first seems to have seen her, off-screen anyway, as the working girl who makes good. His studio intelligence system relayed to him the very details of her 'private' life that earned most marks by his patriarchal standards. She was Joan the breadwinner to him, keeping her family together, maintaining her mother, playing Big Sis to her kid brother, being careful about the dimes and wary about her dates.

But unlike Bette Davis, she never thought of herself from the start as a straight actress: nor did Mayer think of her in that way. She was valued for her dancing talent; and most of her early roles in the silent films were the ones she had filled in real life in ballrooms and night clubs or on the stage – high-kickers, taxi dancers, star-struck showgirls, jazz babies – so that the habit of drawing on her own experience was fixed early. Her switch to dramatic roles did not break her of the habit – the roles simply permitted her to invent new experience.

So intensely did she do this that each new script she schemed and intrigued to get her hands on offered her a fresh sensation in autobiography. 'I remember every one of my important roles the way I remember a part of my life,' she has said, 'because at the time I did them, I *was* the role and it *was* my life for 14 hours a day.'* Such conviction is her professional armour plating. Even a bad Joan Crawford film stays horribly watchable because, where

* Lillian Ross and Helen Ross, op. cit., p. 64.

another star would manifest her disinterest in it all, Crawford never exhibits a second's disbelief in herself.

*   *   *

Our Dancing Daughters (1928) was the last, definitive film of her jazz baby period and shows no stern-jawed Joan. From the opening shot of her legs doing an impatient dance while she puts on her undies to the time she loses her man to another girl, the impression is one of spoilt exuberance and of a little tease who takes a sip out of each of the Martinis held by her dance partners. Finding herself encumbered by her skirt in the Charleston she whips it off and finishes the dance in her slip. 'You want to take all of life, don't you?' her boy-friend says, and the reply comes, 'Yes – all. I want to hold out my hands and catch at it.'

What she held out her hands for after this film was star billing. She was awarded it 'in the field', so to speak, on the basis of its fantastic box-office, by cinema managers more in touch with the public than studio executives. With stardom came fan mail and the presentiment of an audience that had to be kept loving her with each new film. In the same year she married Douglas Fairbanks Jr, over reported objections from his family. This intensified her desire to switch to straight acting, get the higher cachet that went with dramatic roles and so improve her standing with her socially conscious in-laws.

At this time, too, she fell under Garbo's spell and her physical looks changed in sympathy, if not in imitation of the other star. She became gaunter. The vulpine hollows appeared in the previously rounded cheeks. Adrian began impressing his tailored look on her. And a film called *Paid* (1930), about a shop-girl falsely jailed and bent on revenge, provided a dramatic part that defined her image in terms of feminine will-power, the girl who makes her own way in the world, the woman who insists on the right to lead her own life. She had pleaded for hours with Mayer for permission to play the part. After taking a night to think it over, he told her she had got it.

Film after film in the next couple of years set the new image hard in emotional plaster. Again and again she was placed in the gratifyingly invidious dilemma of having to choose between two men, whom she made look positively selfish for wanting her to love them both at the same time: Robert Montgomery or Nils Asther? (*Letty Lynton:* 1932); Franchot Tone or Gary Cooper? (*Today We Live:* 1933); Tone or Gable? (*Dancing Lady:* 1933); Gable or Otto Kruger? (*Chained:* 1934); Montgomery or Gable? (*Forsaking All Others:* 1935). A male star's life in these years must have resembled a relay race in which the last lover, as he dropped exhausted on the track, passed on a Joan Crawford script to the man ahead.

But Mayer knew the value of exposing one kind of sex appeal to another, to their mutual benefit, and the image of the strong-willed woman whose will faltered over a *choice* of lovers paid off compound interest. In *Grand Hotel,* as Flaemmchen the stenographer on the make, her creamy yoke of collar-bone and deep-cut dress foiled John Barrymore's attempt to steal the scenes, while her acting of a working girl using sex appeal to seek economic security is sharp enough to lend likelihood to the rumour at the time that if Garbo had not renewed her M-G-M contract the balance of interest in *Grand Hotel* would have been shifted from her to Crawford. And then she made *Rain* (1933).

Crawford intended *Rain* as her graduation exercise to big-league acting and was shocked by the dislike her fans showed towards her performance as Sadie Thompson, the prostitute in Samoa whose salvation undermines the minister's own righteousness. Her fans thought her vulgar and common. It was a fearful lesson and when she played the bitch in future films she took care to do so with a residual style. The critics were hardly kinder.

In retrospect one wonders how the film and its star could have been so undervalued. Both must have been ahead of their time. Next to Mildred Pierce, Sadie Thompson is Crawford's strongest, most successful performance. The sudden increase in a star's horsepower which it represents is amazing, for even her Flaemmchen had not suggested she could create and sustain from start to finish so unsparing a character. Even the physical change in her is surprising: she has developed the high, protruding bosom, the flat waist, accentuated hips and ramrod stiffness that belong to roles nearly fifteen years later.

Her first appearance in the film is done by the director, Lewis Milestone, in graphic, staccato one-shots of her gaudy appurtenances – a bangled arm, ringed hand, white high-heeled shoes almost stamping defiance at convention, *and there she is,* giving a rakish salute to the Marines, lolling against the doorway with the negligent, casual posture of a woman who knows thoroughly what men are after. Make-up gives her face a blowsy heaviness. Her nose looks in profile like the prow of a ship. She is direct in her dealings with life and her voice sounds as if it was made for transacting business on her terms.

It is a superbly controlled impression of a woman who has been battered by life and cannot be hurt by any more knocks. She has learnt to handle a long monologue almost as well as Walter Huston's minister handles self-inflammatory sermons. (Though not called 'Rev', Huston has an evangelist bleat in his voice, an imperative tone that takes the Lord's name arrogantly.) As he prays at her while Milestone's camera looks down at her from the angle of his holy aloofness, Crawford lets her voice catch on to his like someone at a revivalist meeting and she in turn begins to follow his hysteria up the scale while the camera duplicates the effect in a crane shot that carries it to roof level and leaves the two small figures locked in prayer far below.

Sadie's 'conversion' is a shade less successful, though Crawford refuses to rely on the face tissues and cleansing cream to take away the taints of her 'profession'; and by the way she substitutes a still, very still composure where previously she had been restive and jerky, she shows how carefully she has thought the character through.

Crawford has said, by way of explaining the film's box-office disaster, that Milestone was an 'actors' director!' Maybe so. But he does not fall down on the job of directing the star of *Rain*. It was probably the way he revealed the male will inside Sadie's assertively female body – a conjunction that fascinates many of Crawford's male followers today, even when they do not find her sexually stimulating – which proved too unexpected a charge for contemporary fans to accept.

Technically, she was now ready for the most exacting roles. Milestone's labyrinthine camera movements, involving a 360-degree travelling shot and at least one unbroken take more than six minutes long, compelled her to sustain the character without the relief of cutting, quite a feat for a film star with no stage work behind her. Her unrecognised triumph is all the sadder considering the emptiness of the M-G-M glamour roles she reverted to over the next seven years.*

*   *   *

A new marriage to Franchot Tone, in 1935, contributed to a new image. Some film stars have a way of using the characteristics of each new husband as a way into another kind of identity: marriage is an extension of professional experience. Tone was a politically active actor, with left-wing sympathies and Moscow Art Theatre interests, although his Hollywood career suffered from his being continually cast as the emotional 'stooge' in 'women's pictures'. Encouraged by him to seek 'valid' parts, Crawford again petitioned Mayer, this time to let her play Peggy O'Neal, the tavern-keeper's daughter in *The Gorgeous Hussy* (1936) who marries a Secretary for War and indirectly influences America's political future. She got the part and Tone, ironically, was handed a twenty-six-line role as her husband in the film. Mayer explained, 'We can't have you walk off into the sunset with just any actor – it's got to be an important one.'

The graph of Crawford's career after 1936 is a falling one. Irving Thalberg had died in that year. She had never been as close to him as to Mayer. But the way that 'production values' were now allowed to usurp the creative energy he had generated at M-G-M was bad for a studio's vitality – and for Crawford's.

---

* She had been loaned out for *Rain* to United Artists, whose president, Joseph Schenck, seems to have favoured it as a vehicle for determined actresses. He presented the silent version of the story starring Gloria Swanson.

Adrian's tailor-mades were soon the sturdiest vehicles she was appearing in. It was her 'glamorous clothes-horse' period that ended with her leaving M-G-M and opting for marriage to a little-known actor, Philip Terry, and what looked like retirement. In fact it was only a rest pause, a refuge from the accumulating sense of deceleration in her career. She became a housewife, cooked, cleaned, gardened and stayed at home with her husband; but inside her, the left-over energy that sends other women back to work after home-making and child-raising was building up its creative force. It was finally unleashed in the film *Mildred Pierce* (1945).

Her performance won her an Oscar but, on her own admission, was the easiest role she had ever played. For Mildred, a Californian housewife who uses energy, brains, nerve and ruthlessness to grab wealth and position while losing her family and a chance of love, harnessed Crawford's ambition like an oil strike.

The time, the studio and the director were also beautifully opportune. For with male stars in uniform, the 1940s brought the women stars into dominance as the embodiment of the tenacity that their sex was showing on the home front. Women got a cathartic satisfaction from films like *Mildred Pierce* which made them feel that they, too, were fighters in a man's world. Moreover at the very time the Allies were crushing Germany, Hollywood was under the influence of the Teutonic strain of *emigré* directors, like Wilder, Lang, Preminger, Siodmak, etc., who set the tone of the era's dark and violent melodramas in which women played dominant but often ambivalent roles.

When Crawford went to Warners, after seventeen years at M-G-M, she found herself in a previously male-star stronghold and inherited in Michael Curtiz a director with a callous disregard for any star's sex or status. He treated her pitilessly, for he had wanted Barbara Stanwyck for the role; and though she finally broke down his resistance in the scene where her screen daughter slaps her on the face and real tears jetted from the Crawford ducts, the steel he drove into her stiffened every subsequent role she played. When she made *Mildred Pierce* she had just turned forty. She emerged annealed by the experience.

Crawford exemplifies the American phenomenon of the career woman who analyses life while it is happening to her. She shows how a determined individual, given a particular kind of society, can rise above her origins, change her identity, make the running and feel she has earned the material rewards of it all. There is a feeling of biological overdrive about her in a film like *The Damned Don't Cry* (1947) when she turns on the curt but sensible employment bureau lady who has advised her to learn a trade and snaps desperately, 'I can't wait that long.'

Her films ensure that she does not have to. If she starts off as a housewife in a two-dollar work-frock from Sears-Roebuck, one can be sure her clamber up the economic footholds in American society will soon land her in afternoon gowns with someone teaching her social graces and *savoir-faire*. There is never any feeling of economic guilt in her films, only emotional guilt expressed in terms of the career mother who works hard for her children and sees them turn out spoilt, disobedient or ungrateful. 'Get out before I kill you!' she snaps at her uppity daughter in *Mildred Pierce*. Children in her films are like the pelican's brood – they eat their mother's heart out while she is cherishing them.

Crawford can be an extraordinarily convincing mother, as *The Story of Esther Costello* (1957) proves. With four adopted children of her own, it is as if they had permitted her to invent the whole experience of motherhood. No one else can play the maternal instinct so brilliantly against the masculine grain of her character. When Dana Andrews in *Daisy Kenyon* (1948) offers to give up his wife and family in order to marry her, she recoils in horror: 'Marriage can't be all over if children are a part of it still.' Inside every career woman is an imprisoned mother and Crawford knows just the moment to let us hear her beating to get out.

In her career-woman pictures the men are practically emotional dependents. Love is mistrusted. If she feels its stirrings, she instantly fears it will 'mix me up'. If a single man professes to be in love with her, she is 'being used'. If a married man does so, he is 'running away from responsibility'. After the car accident in

Daisy Kenyon, which is introduced merely as an extreme means of clearing her head, what a good shaking does for other women, she warms her stockinged feet at the fireside while her two lovers quarrel over which will make her his wife. The cool spectator look on her face, that of a woman who never gets into a mood she can't fight her way out of, signifies that there is nothing like a crisis to show what is inside other people.

Her 'bitch' roles are fed from the same stream, only now richly polluted with melodrama. *Queen Bee* (1955), written and directed by the same Ranald MacDougall who had scripted *Mildred Pierce,* pushes her compulsive domesticity to cannibalistic extremes. Her unfortunate family is now her career and she manages them with a smile that nearly cuts her face in two, disposing of relationships that have served their purpose the way other women empty ash-trays after a party. 'Now you can go back to your drinking,' she purrs at her husband, 'it'll make you feel at home.'

But if it imputes such lack of feeling to a lack of love, *Queen Bee* also offers her the self-indulgence of atonement the minute she feels wanted again, followed by the positive luxury of suffering retribution in a car crash the minute she starts to lead her new life while still clad in the old style of mink wrap, evening gown and diamond bracelet. As Paul Dehn wrote, 'She compels our credulous enjoyment of an unbelievable plot by so manifestly enjoying her own villainy.'*

Crawford, like Bette Davis, has shown great skill in keeping in step with her audience's own insecurities. She has grown old along with them – the ultimate allegiance of star to fans. And as she has done so, the cracks in the self-reliance of the woman she plays have opened wider. What could be called her 'panic' roles exploit her emotional dependence, usually on a younger man who gives her love but treats her roughly, treacherously, even murderously. *Humoresque* (1947) probably began this class of menopausal melodrama, with John Garfield as the musical protégé whose fidelity to his art proves so unshakeable that she sinks her own competitive demands, along with herself, in the Pacific.

* *For Love and Money,* by Paul Dehn (Reinhardt) p. 112.

Sudden Fear (1952) and *The Female on the Beach* (1955) put her in peril of her life from gigolo-types.

A scared Crawford is an awesome sight: her stretched face holds fear the way a sponge holds water. *Autumn Leaves* (1956) is the masterpiece of this kind, with its carefully graduated revelations that the crew-cut lad she has married after years of caring for Father is a liar, a thief, an ex-convict, a near-bigamist, a potential killer and, in addition, is rapidly reverting to infantilism. Even so, she will not accept that anything or anyone is beyond her love. She has him committed to a mental asylum and from then on is frenetically depicted by director Robert Aldrich revolving in her mind the last question one would have expected had cause to be there: Will the cure kill *his* love for her?

In *I Saw What You Did, I Know Who You Are* (1965) the cure for love is indeed lethal, administered to *her* with a carving knife by yet another psychotic young stud with whom she is infatuated. To end up as someone else's neurotic need or commercial prey or murder victim are extreme cases, with a nice sense of progression about them, of what happens when one is not loved for oneself alone. Crawford in such films taps the latent fear of women fans who are finding that life is turning into loneliness. The films capitalise on this as age separates her from the roles available to her. The young male symbol to whom she attaches herself helps boost her screen appeal; while the agony of mind or body which his treacherous nature puts her through keeps her image from being cheapened and permits her female audience to suffer along with her.

*   *   *

Insanity is another device for giving her later performances a jagged edge of interest. *The Caretakers* (1963), *Straitjacket* (1964), *Berserk* (1967): the very titles trace the ascending line of lunacy. Yet even here, in spite of playing a patient on parole in *Straitjacket*, a kind of axe-murderess *emerita*, she is usually the victim of other people's madness. The theme of the ungrateful child gets a more sinister twist in two of these films where her own daughter is revealed as being the certifiably insane killer all along.

Suffering in adversity becomes her even better than some of the melodramas in which it is implanted. How shrewd the casting is in *What Ever Happened to Baby Jane?*: Aldrich's heartless exploitation of the harridan angle in his film is almost pardonable for the sense of fitness that pinions Joan Crawford, passive and masochistic, in her wheelchair while Bette Davis, busily malevolent, turns her life into a daily series of nasty happenings. The sight of stars who are said to be real-life rivals playing ex-film stars condemned to life in vengeful propinquity to each other gives the Punch and Judy show a dimension of reality and illusion that would have interested Pirandello. For reality interacts with illusion, and both combine with the stars' personalities to produce an indelible impression of a couple of indestructible women who know of no other way to live except as film stars.

Crawford, much more than Davis, has always insisted on film stars being accorded their dignity and, in turn, fulfilling their duties. She believes that Hollywood's decline began when the break-up of the contract system gave actors power beyond their destiny as film stars by turning them into film-makers, too, which is rather like Royalty wanting to run the country as well as rule it. There may be more percentage in the new deal, but there is a lot less mystique.

Crawford has preserved the mystique by attention to detail as well as will-power. The latter is seldom openly manifested in the process of film-making, but wherever she has made a film she has left a gathering legend of the pains she has taken and the favours she has extended to the lowliest members of the film unit. For those who give her love and loyalty, no trouble is too much for her to take. Even as director of the Pepsi-Cola Co., whose late chairman was her last husband, she conducts herself as a star rather than a tycoon. 'What did she get out of making films?' she was once asked, and replied, 'Joy. Expression. Outlet. Creativity.' And what did she get out of business? 'Joy. Expression. Outlet. Creativity.'*

The value of a long life as a star lies in the feeling she conveys

* *The Sunday Times Colour Magazine*, 2nd April 1967, interviewed by Philip Oakes.

that there was no time when she was not a star. And with her, one
has to believe it. Though there may be many Joan Crawfords, all
of them are her own invention and she herself is no one's. Nobody
else could make her but herself. How could they have done so?
she enquired on one occasion, genuinely puzzled that such a
question should have been asked. 'You manufacture toys,' she
reminded her interviewer. 'You don't manufacture stars.'*

* BBC TV, 29th June 1967, interviewed by Philip Jenkinson.

CHAPTER SEVENTEEN

KING AND
COMMONERS:
CLARK GABLE

The 1930s were the last decade when Hollywood produced screen heroes who were forces for moral good. A remarkable handful of male stars came to the fore as confidence returned to post-Depression America, defining in their persons the ideals of the New Deal society. Gary Cooper, Spencer Tracy, Henry Fonda, James Stewart, Clark Gable: all of them represented a society which still had a place for the individual and where he could exert power to get things done or prevent other things from being done. Against the complexities of today's America, the very simplicity with which they were able to match ends and means makes them appear supermen. Possibly very few of them started out intending to become 'Hollywood democrats', but then few stars anticipate how their private personalities will crystallise and lock them into their public images.

They moved quickly from role to role, for leading men were scarce in every studio at the start of the 1930s. This and the high-definition acting required by simply written scripts in quickly made films accounts to some extent for their swift popularity. Their physical stature helped: it lent their moral stature height, weight and punch. Their accents and even the way they moved suggested the breadth of America. The city did not seem to have bred them, so much as the rural community, the small town, the farm and the prairies.

None of them was cast in the mould of the Great Lover. This occupation did not survive the realism of the talkies, nor the cynicism of the new breed of good-bad girls in the screen. All of them appealed to both male and female filmgoers, though only in the case of one of them was sex appeal the dominant 'draw'. The exception was Clark Gable. The rest defined themselves, or were defined by their most memorable roles, in relation to society rather than to the opposite sex. They made good husbands, not good lovers.

But the aspect of them that appealed to their public and helped make stars of them was not always the first one they displayed on the screen. Spencer Tracy for example, typecast by his huge stage success in the gangster play *The Last Mile,* for some years took tough-guy screen parts, racketeers, brutish convicts, even on one fortunately unmemorable occasion a psychotic husband trying to feed his wife, Joan Bennett, to a cage of Great Danes. The studios saw him as the talkies successor to George Bancroft, the massive underworld type created by von Sternberg's silent gangster films. It took a film like *Fury* (1936) to establish Tracy for good as essentially a gentle man, slow to anger though terrible in avalanche. The revenge he set out to take on the mob that had tried to lynch him in this film had to be modified into retribution before it merged acceptably with the classic Tracy hero.

Again with the exception of Clark Gable, all these heroes are slow to meet violence with violence: it takes a lot to rouse them and the suspense often comes from watching a slow fuse burn down under provocation. James Stewart profits from what is almost a speech defect – his stammering, apologetic way of swallowing his words as he utters them – which delays his physical reaction to insult or injury. Such stoicism gives them a kind of piety. Gary Cooper made silent suffering into a chivalric quest for purification: a healthier version than Brando's masochistic quest for humiliation.

But even in Cooper's case the image was carefully adjusted over the years. He made an immediate hit in Sam Goldwyn's drama of land reclamation, *The Winning of Barbara Worth* (1928), playing the 'brotherly' cowboy type while the romance was reserved for Ronald Colman; but subsequent parts left it an open question as to which aspects of him might dominate his image. The showy extrovert looking up from under his white Stetson and giving the camera a ladykilling look at the start of *City Streets* (1931) has a Cagney-ish rakishness, especially in the show-off moments when he plucks a gangster's hanky out of his breast pocket and, throwing it in the air, drills a hole through the monogram. The first gesture utterly typical of the taciturn 'Coop' he turned into is struck when his girl friend, Sylvia Sidney, loses her temper in the film, flails away at him and he just stands there and lets her wallop him till she wears herself out. Cooper's silence, however, according to Howard Hawks, worried some of his early directors. 'There was always the problem that his silence in a love scene might suggest that he would get violent with the girl.'*

Along with the feeling of still waters, the 1930s heroes gave the impression of deep roots: although here again an exception has to be made for Clark Gable. The city, almost synonymous with Wall Street, was the asphalt villain in many of the Depression-era films, to which their own contact with the honest labour of the soil or the simple decency of small-town folk stood in shining contrast. But, Fonda's early American face and lanky limbs retained the look of rural America no matter how many sophisticated parts he played. And roles he came to in mid-career, like *Young Mr Lincoln* (1939) or Tom Joad in *The Grapes of Wrath* (1941), sum up his rural integrity so definitively that they colour all the films he made before then. One finds it hard not to attribute the dryness of his characteristic tones to some of the same dust from the blighted farmlands of *The Grapes of Wrath*. It was as if he had not cleared his throat since playing Tom Joad, so strongly does one role encapsulate a career.

Guile, self-reliance, stubbornness – the countryman's virtues – mark most of these stars. Gary Cooper in *Sergeant York* (1941), would make a less easily laudable hero if he had not enticed the Germans to pop their heads over the trench top and look into his gun sights by his imitation of a turkey's gobbling call. Curiosity kills them, we are able to tell ourselves, as the old huntsman's ruse turns slaughter into an acceptable equivalent of a rough shoot.

Instinctive misgivings about the men in charge was another trait of the post-Depression hero. Usually it was City Hall, the bankers or the landowners, though occasionally mistrust went higher still. When James Stewart, in a late film, can hardly bring

* Hawks to the author in an interview, London, 1966.

himself to thank the Lord for the harvest, since it is obvious that more thanks are due to the human labour expended on it, he says a lot about the Godfearing and unfrightened character of this group of men. If ever a country got the film heroes it needed, it was the U.S.A. in the decade up to World War Two.

*　　*　　*

Clark Gable was to be found among this company, but not quite of it. A hero he certainly was, even to his peers who dubbed him 'The King' – a title he carried lightly, yet liked others to treat respectfully. But what differentiates him from them is his attitude to sex – the attitude that gave him so powerful an appeal to male and female filmgoers in his day and has preserved his fascination right up to our own day when the screen is populous with heroes whom Gable might have sired though not necessarily wished to legitimise.

Every generation which re-discovers *Gone With the Wind* (1939) finds Clark Gable its most 'modern' character. If his looks have dated romantically, his outlook where women are concerned is refreshingly contemporary. Only the total absence of self-doubt in his make-up, the confident, cocky assurance that he knows who he is and where he is bound for, keeps the Rhett Butler image anchored in pre-war Hollywood.

Gable's ascent to box-office stardom was so quick that it caught M-G-M by surprise. Film exhibitors in 1931 said in a poll that they could underwrite a week's net with a Gable picture; yet at the time he was the cheapest drawing card in Hollywood's hand. He was getting only 650 dollars a week. To have Gable in a film cost a producer about 4,000 dollars: to have Will Rogers cost, by comparison, 150,000 dollars. Having been signed up at rock-bottom rates, it took Gable years before he gained financial parity with stars like himself. He was receiving only 2,500 dollars a week in 1933, whereas Gary Cooper was getting 5,000 dollars and Frederic March 7,000 dollars.

The disparity rankled a long time and was recalled over twenty years later at the time of his far from genial separation from M-G-M. But the studio thought it had good reasons at the start for mistrusting Gable's star potential. Hollywood was full of promising leading men who were quickly signed up and just as quickly dropped from contract. The wastage of talent being tried out for the scarce virile type was particularly heavy, and Gable's one visible advantage was his physique. He had been an oil rigger, telephone linesman, lumberjack and reporter: trades where a man had to use muscle, stand on his own feet and make out with other males. His visible defect was, of course, his prominent ears which, reportedly, cost him at least one contract.

At the time he was looking for film work he was married to drama coach, Josephine Dillon, who was fourteen years his senior and who had groomed him socially and taught him to project his personality. Somewhere in this relationship was formed the essential Clark Gable: but where, or how, must be a matter of conjecture. Gable always glossed over the marriage and Miss Dillon was equally discreet about it. It has been said, and it seems likely, that her attraction for him had something maternal in it. His own mother had died a few weeks after his birth; and Josephine Dillon's ambitions for Gable had the stern affection which some mothers reserve for the sons they wish to see do well. The tones of the few guarded comments she made years later recall a woman resigned to the inevitable loss of a grown-up son, rather than an ex-husband.

Gable had acquired a chronic restlessness from his father, a roving oil-rigger. He was complaining as early as 1932 about the time he spent 'doing nothing' between film takes; and the long agony of enforced inactivity he had to put up with during the ill-fated filming of The Misfits (1960) was physically onerous and, it was said, helped shorten his life. This impatience made him a highly professional actor with whom to work. He was intolerant only of co-stars who wasted time and ran down his energy. It showed up in every part he played: he started like a man whose engine was already running.

His roustabout youth and the confidence he had in his own brawn and energy could also be sensed in his acting. A minor peculiarity enhanced his appeal. He hated personal uncleanliness. This went back to his days as a teenager, helping his father on the oil rigs and getting coated with greasy slick. The memory of it promoted a spick-and-span appearance, wherever the screen part suited it – and it generally did. And because his furrowed forehead, quizzical brows, half-shut eyes, tom-cat grin and genial cocksureness were all visible proof that he had seen life, the trimness of his appearance, plus the ladies' man flake of moustache he added to his lip around 1932, did not look like mere film star grooming, but the polish of a once-rough nugget.

Gable made twelve films in 1931, sometimes acting in two at once. 'Screen time, that's what you need,' Louis B. Mayer told him, 'screen time.' It was the old practice – Hollywood knew no other – of forcing a promising beginner into a personality, finding his type by trial and error, market-testing it and then patenting the result. Gable's complaint a year later that 'my advice has never been asked about a part in a picture' can be sympathised with, but is largely irrelevant. The system he had committed himself to was not one that consulted the players. He got the right answer when he concluded ruefully, 'I am paid not to think.'

But his activity in that year had also a less dispiriting cause. Women stars, in need of leading men, wanted him badly. The silent names like Gilbert, Novarro, William Haines and John Barrymore, were all in eclipse. Chevalier was the only male star listed in the six top box-office films of 1930; while the scarcity of rivals helped George Arliss become the leading male draw the next year. Gable, whose career had scarcely begun, actually came fourth in 1931, preceded by Arliss, Wallace Beery, Chevalier and followed by Edward G. Robinson and Will Rogers.

It was an amazingly rapid ascent. The women stars of some of these twelve films he made contributed to it. Out of the seven top box-office actresses in 1931, four were teamed with Gable; Constance Bennett, Joan Crawford (in no fewer than three films), Garbo and Norma Shearer. Established female stars helped his popularity by drawing in women filmgoers; and he, in turn, soon became a sought-after guarantor of *their* audiences. The mutual aid that stars can render each other has seldom been more clearly illustrated. M-G-M also co-starred Gable in two films out of these twelve with actors like Richard Barthelmess (*The Finger Points:* a newsman-exposes-gangster story) and Wallace Beery (*Hell Drivers:* a Naval Air Force setting) who were solid draws with male filmgoers. So he got exposed to both audiences.

By the time Gable's last film of 1931, *Polly of the Circus*, was released the exhibitors were putting his name above the title and leaving its titular star, Marion Davies, to be guessed at. By April 1932, M-G-M was reported to be dubious about letting Gable co-star in Marion Davies' next film: apparently the front office had awakened to the risk to Gable's drawing power by using him in support of waning female stars. When such protective reservations begin to hedge in an actor, especially one on Gable's pin-money salary, one thing is clear – his stardom is an acknowledged fact.

Even with this help, Gable's essential personality did not emerge quite so quickly or confidently as such high-pressure exposure suggests. Some of the casting he suffered actually impeded it. In *Polly of the Circus* the role of the ordained minister had been intended for Johnny Mack Brown, and Gable, who replaced him, thus had a part meant for another type of actor grafted awkwardly on to his personality. He was equally unconvincing in *Laughing Sinners* (1931) as the Salvation Army man who reforms Joan Crawford. In *Susan Lenox, Her Fall and Rise* (1931) he was obliged to show priggish revulsion at the idea of Garbo as a kept woman. In *Strange Interlude* (1931) he could not be made to look elderly enough to be convincing as O'Neill's aged hero – even after eighteen make-up tests. In *Night Nurse* (1931) he had to play a despicable character, a chauffeur whose plan to murder two children and marry their rich mother is foiled by Barbara Stanwyck.

*   *   *

Neither parts nor pictures established Gable's appeal so much as an attitude he struck in his fifth film, *A Free Soul* (1931). Its director was Clarence Brown, a film-maker with an instinct, it seems, for constructing a scene that would allow the player's screen personality to split open and show its cinematic grain. Gable was playing a racketeer, Ace Wilfong, in the film; Norma

The 'violent' star: Lee
Marvin shambling like a
rough beast into the world
of the crime syndicate in
Point Blank

The 'cool' star: Steve
McQueen concealing his
feelings behind a cop's
steely professionalism in
Bullitt

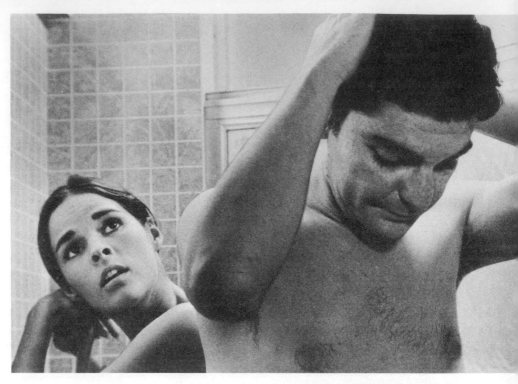

Above: The 'permissive' stars: Ali MacGraw and Richard Benjamin repre-
senting on-screen in *Goodbye, Columbus* the life-style of their youthful fans.
Below: The 'instant' star: Jon Voight as Joe Buck (with pick-up companion)
in *Midnight Cowboy,* a film that showed today's new stars need no build-up
if their films find immediate favour with youth audiences

Shearer had the role of a famous lawyer's spoilt daughter who was infatuated with him. At one point in the film Gable, at Brown's direction, slapped her face to show her who was who and then slammed her down into a chair. 'You make no more bargains with anyone but me,' he barks at her in a rough voice. 'You're mine and I want you.'

Audience reaction to this was electric. Not just because Gable had manhandled a woman – this was Cagney's party trick, too – but because he had manhandled a *desirable* woman and not one who was a gangster's moll and rated no more courtesy than having a breakfast grapefruit pushed into her face. The rough treatment, moreover, was meted out by a *desirable* man. Gable manifested none of Cagney's barely concealed contempt for the opposite sex. (Power is what attracts the hero of *The Public Enemy:* the only woman who counts with him is his mother.) Gable's gesture was unchivalrous. But this was not the novelty, either. John Gilbert had been just as unchivalrous, just as brutal, in another Clarence Brown film, *The Cossacks.* The difference is that Gable offered more than, not less than love: he offered sex. He dominated women. He wanted them on his terms – terms his sex appeal dictated. And the confidence he inspired in his own power to enforce them was both audacious and attractive. 'A new kind of man,' Norma Shearer murmurs in *A Free Soul,* 'a new kind of world.' It was indeed.

Gable's sex appeal in subsequent films was frequently backed up by violence or the threat of it. He was startlingly cold-blooded in going after what he wanted in some of those early movies. The cigarette smoke blown coolly, sardonically, into a woman's face showed how his mind was working. Words made sure there would be no confusion. 'You're a spoilt silly brat in need of a hair brush,' or 'Better listen to what I'm saying or I'll knock that smile off your face.' The action followed. 'Now beat it,' he says, slapping the woman's rear. 'Thank you,' she says, though this was not an invariable reply. To a woman who shoots him in one of his films, he gives a flippant blessing, 'All right, if it'll make you feel any better.' He kept the upper hand, dead or alive.

Another side of the same appeal was indicated, quite unin-

tentionally, by a contemporary reviewer of *A Free Soul*. Mordaunt
Hall, in The *New York Times*, wrote: 'Clark Gable is all very well
as a gangster, but it is problematical whether a young woman of
Miss Shearer's type would ever become enamoured of an individual who behaves as he does here.' Although Hall wrote
'type', what he meant was 'class'. But it was characteristic of
Gable's sexual assurance to be able to ignore class barriers. If he
noticed them at all, they drove him on to storm them with greater
relish. The woman he could not immediately get for one reason or
another was, of course, the most desirable one. Class sharpened
his appetite, attack and tongue. Sex for him was the great leveller –
in this sphere of operations at least he was a good democrat.

Frank Capra found no more successful exponent for conducting
the class war in terms of the sex war in his comedy *It Happened
One Night* (1934). Capra had already made what was essentially
the same film about a newspaperman and a spoilt heiress three
years earlier, in 1931, as *Platinum Blonde*. But whereas Robert
Williams, as the foot-in-the-door reporter of that film, left Jean
Harlow's nympho-heiress to her own style of idle life and went
back to his kind of simple girl, Gable provided the perfect sexual
weapon in *It Happened One Night* to beat the nonsense out of
Claudette Colbert's stand-offish society girl. The class barrier was
appropriately represented in terms of a sex barrier by the blanket
hanging between their beds in the 'Walls of Jericho' scene; and
just as appropriately it proved vulnerable to Joshua's horn.

It should have surprised no one that Gable could play a relaxed
sex-comedy part well enough in *It Happened One Night* to win an
Oscar, for in his 1931 film, *Susan Lenox,* he had deftly and wittily
welcomed a runaway Greta Garbo to his up-state cabin with an
urbane offer of 'Caviare? . . . coffee? . . . a little port?' and later
seen her well provided for the night with his own pyjamas, the
favourite garment of lady fugitives in 1930-ish comedies. But
Gable himself preferred a leading lady whom he could treat like a
man in all but sex. 'In his face there is cruelty. So maybe that is
what they like,' a critic wrote in 1931. Filmgoers applauded *Red
Dust* (1932) when he dunked Jean Harlow under water for using
the drinking supply as a bath-tub. When she surfaced, spiky wet

and spitting like a platinum alley-cat, he did it again. More applause. And he made sexual capital out of the scene where he lets Harlow pull off his plantation boots, then strips off the rest of his clothes himself (off-screen) and chucks them at her before climbing into bed alone and pulling the sheets coquettishly up to his chin. To leave the girl out of bed was the measure of this man's insolence! In the same film he cut across class lines again to furnish Mary Astor with a sexual awakening, though it was with Harlow that he ended the film.

He preferred, he said, speaking of his off-screen attitude to women, 'the one who has seen more, heard more, knows more'. Harlow was the leading lady he liked best on these grounds. It has been noted that his personal life repeated the same pattern. Of his four marriages after the divorce from Josephine Dillon, two were to socialites (Rhea Langham, Lady Ashley) and two were to down-to-earth, companionable types (Carole Lombard, Kay Williams), and it was with the latter that he was happier.

Once he had accepted studio rule, Gable gave little trouble over the parts he was cast in. He had no burning ambition to be known as a 'great actor'. He knew his limitations very well indeed. Better, in fact, than those he worked for. His bitterest set-back was playing the title role in *Parnell* (1937), and he was forced into this by Louis B. Mayer who had hoped to find in the Irish patriot a sentimental equivalent for his own racial sympathies which the casting of his studio's cherished male lead would make into highly rewarding box-office.

The film, both as art and box-office, was a disaster. The reasons throw interesting light on Gable's limitations. For one thing the director, John Stahl, having scored a success in casting Irene Dunne against type in *The Magnificent Obsession* (1935), tried to make Gable act a role rather than display a personality. But the role of Parnell was that of a man who is defeated and ends up a martyr, not a hero. The final scene showed Gable on his death bed, his natural virility resisting all the semblance of mortality that the make-up department could lay on, delivering with his last breath the injunction, 'Carry on my fight for Ireland, I charge you. See that Ireland is never defeated.' It was an unhappy, unconvincing sight. If the Gable hero has to die, he must end up with his work done: it is not his style to ask someone to carry on the fight for him by proxy.

Though he never analysed his acting, Gable kept a sharp eye on his public image and was quick off the mark to protect it. The gravest threat to it was any situation which subordinated him to a woman. This is why he was particularly riled by the publicity slogan, 'Gable's Back and Garson's Got Him,' unwisely devised by M-G-M to announce his first post-war film. Even as early as 1932 it was no consolation to him to have a strong, virile role in *Red Dust*, since the property had been bought for Garbo who had dropped out when Gable had replaced John Gilbert. It had been bought to star a woman, he figured, and therefore unless the script were changed it was a woman's picture. The script *was* changed. Twenty-one years later virtually the same one was used for Gable's film *Mogambo* (1953), in which Ava Gardner and Grace Kelly took the original Jean Harlow–Mary Astor parts. Otherwise Gable deemed no further changes necessary. After all, it was already a man's picture.

*   *   *

Even such outwardly confident and assured stars as Gable protect their images and transform their star power into very real behind-the-scenes power when they do so. Probably the main reason for the replacement of George Cukor as director of *Gone With the Wind* with Victor Fleming, after shooting had started, was budgetary: Fleming was a fast, efficient worker. But Gable's influence played a part, too. He was concerned in case the masculine impact of his Rhett Butler portrayal be compromised by a director with a reputation for enhancing his women stars. It was doubly important this time, for he was starring for once in a film whose heroine, Scarlett O'Hara, was already established in the minds of filmgoers, a heroine who preceded him on to the screen and outlasted him in the story, and who exhibited a fiery stubbornness that was a match for his own obstinate hall-marks. The appointment of Victor Fleming, who had directed him in *Red Dust*, offered certain guarantees to Gable which tipped the balance in his favour, though it is to Fleming's credit that Gable and Vivien Leigh gave such fairly matched performances.

It is ironical in retrospect that Gable was at first reluctant to play Rhett Butler. The role was to be the culmination of his career; but at the time it presented him with a curious crisis. For some stars suddenly find that a newcomer's popularity, or even appearance, is so close to their own that it prejudices their uniqueness and can supersede their popularity. Publication of the book of *Gone With the Wind* posed a similar kind of problem for Gable. In spite of Margaret Mitchell's disclaimer that she had based Rhett Butler on him, people identified the fictional character so closely with Gable that it became something like a matter of national importance to ensure that Gable was cast in the film as Rhett Butler. Gable thus experienced the unsettling feeling that his screen image had got separated from him as the hero of a work of fiction – and he could not hope to satisfy their expectations by playing the part in another work of fiction. He would virtually be in competition with himself.

It took persistent argument from David Selznick, the film's producer, before he gave in with the admission, 'I couldn't escape him [Rhett Butler].' When the film was seen, of course, the dislocation of identity proved a baseless fear. Gable and Rhett fitted each other's outline perfectly because the former's screen characteristics, which the latter had confiscated in the public mind, were now being fed back into him like a booster current with all the accumulated power of fictional amplification behind them. The feeling of closure which this adds to Gable's outstanding performance is what makes it such a permanent satisfaction to watch. (Bette Davis in *All About Eve* is a similar case: the star *is* the role to an uncommonly close degree and there is no space between her and it for critical doubts to be insinuated.)

Gone With the Wind has been reissued half a dozen times since its première, keeping Gable's personality on semi-permanent exhibition long enough for two generations to have made its acquaintance before his death in 1960. His masculinity being the type that weathers well, no unsightly discrepancy crept in between the ageless image on the screen and its ageing owner in the flesh.

He even improved into social significance. The cynical, amoral, brutal, reluctantly chivalrous, sexually bold, professedly un-gentlemanly Rhett Butler, the outsider who watches Southern society dig its own grave and then profits out of the burial, the rebel who radiates such an existential will that he needs no climate of permissiveness to operate in beyond the censor's approval of the then audacious insult to Scarlett of 'Frankly, my dear, I don't give a damn!' – all these qualities made Gable a precursor of the post-war anti-heroes. They were to be men of much less charm, humour and reliance – hard men often driven by a neurotic need that would have seemed contemptible to the King. But the family strain in this unromantic off-shoot is plainly traceable in Clark Gable's Rhett Butler – or is it Rhett Butler's Clark Gable?

Disenchantment of a subtle kind was not spared Gable, how-ever. It filtered in towards the end, at first with a change in his attitude to acting. He began expressing disdain for it, calling it an ignoble occupation not worthy of a real man. Other emphatically virile stars have said the same thing, of course, and it usually leads to their insistence on proving themselves by doing their own stunts and action scenes, or else in taking a disdainful (and costly) attitude to the whole business of acting for the screen. But some felt that Gable's disgust was traceable to his mortification at the 1940 Academy Awards where *Gone With the Wind* garnered nine Oscars, plus two citations, but his own superhuman performance as Rhett Butler lost the 'Best Actor' award to a character in every way its antithesis, Robert Donat's Mr Chips.

Then again he felt keenly M-G-M's rejection of him when he asked for a share in his pictures' profits. As a contract star, he got between 7,500 and 10,000 dollars a week: as a freelance he was to get over 500,000 dollars a picture plus a percentage of the gross profit. *The Misfits* (1960) came along at just the right moment, however, to save him from facing the inevitable decision of coming to terms with supporting roles or character parts by giving him the chance to play a role on the screen which was what he had in fact become – the last of a vanishing breed of uncom-plicated, un-neurotic, manly heroes.

And yet it turned out to be not quite so simple. For Gable's old masculine ethics no longer worked against a sex goddess like Marilyn Monroe. This was a woman he could not clout on the jaw – maybe earlier in her career, he might have, but not now – for in the film she is hardly corporeal. Monroe's Roslyn is less of a sex symbol than a nature symbol – a species that offers few hand-holds for a determined man of action. She exists in the moonlight she dances in, in the leaves of grass Gable walks on, in the suffer-ing wild life that he, in his Hemingway outlook, has thought to be only good for pot shots. When brute force meets the life force, it is the former that has to yield. The aspects of a woman which make her lovable in the abstract often turn disturbingly into neurotic reflexes that are unliveable with in practical life. Arthur Miller's screen play which has been taken as a celebration of his wife, sometimes has more the flavour of an attempt to exorcise her – and Gable was the body on whom all her ethereal qualities were projected, bewitchingly at first, then perplexingly, frustrat-ingly, maddeningly – till he gave in.

Instead of having his ego boosted, Gable's character finds his spirit being broken in the way that he once broke the wild horses. The heroic man had met his match in the neurotic woman. When his consort starts to rule the King, it is time to quit. Death saved Clark Gable the pain of abdication.

CHAPTER EIGHTEEN

GO WEST AND
TURN RIGHT:
JOHN WAYNE

The male heroes of the 1930s, to judge them by their screen images, were all good democrats, personifying the New Deal brand of liberalism – pledges for the nation that was struggling out of the Depression. Their best-known roles emphasised unquestionable virtues and the non-controversial attributes which pioneer Americans had brought with them as they pushed the frontier west: in short, human values that were too broad to be classified as political. At this time it was also assumed by the general public that Hollywood stars had no 'politics'. They were folk heroes, not political representatives.

The for-or-against attitudes that quite a few of the stars took up at the time of presidential elections do not contradict this – they were simply exercising their rights under the constitution, were they not? In any case their own party allegiance to 'the next president' was apt to be quickly forgotten in the publicity for their next picture. The war effort put many stars into uniform as servicemen or as touring morale-boosters; and again political affiliations were not to the fore. Not till after the war, with the coming of 'the Communist scare', was Hollywood's own loyalty to the constitution called into question; and this, in turn, threw into relief the political configurations of stars previously known almost exclusively by their facial ones.

A fascinating study still waits to be made of the politics of the film capital: not the industry-studio politics, but the radical-reactionary brand which probably came west with the politically conscious talents recruited for the talkies and also with the growth of the totalitarian studio system and its answering response from the craft unions. The hearings of the House Committee on Un-

American Activities in 1947, produced some fine ironies when it took evidence from Hollywood figures like Jack Warner and Louis B. Mayer who were called on to rebut the accusation that their studios might have been 'soft' on Communism because of such war-time productions as *Mission to Moscow* (1942) and *Song of Russia* (1943).

Although it is now easy to smile at this kind of political *naïveté*, the aftermath of the Communist purge of Hollywood was tragic: the blacklisting and the indictment of 'the unfriendly ten' witnesses who refused to testify to the committee all created enmities that are still active. But so far as the general public were concerned, the most surprising aspect was not the putative Left-wing views of numerous writers and directors, but the openly right-wing attitudes adopted by some of the stars whose screen images scarcely prepared one for it. Gary Cooper said in evidence: 'I have heard tossed around such statements as "Don't you think the Constitution of the United States is about 150 years out of date?" and ... "Perhaps this would be a more efficient Government without a Congress" – which statements I think are very un-American.'*

Again this is naïve to the point of being fatuous; but such utterances, and many more like them, expressed an active political outlook among numerous Hollywood stars. They had begun to take up a militantly right-wing position as early as 1944, the year in which The Motion Picture Alliance for the Preservation of American Ideals was founded. Its work does not concern us. But its membership was characterised, with acid-spray asperity, by Carey McWilliams, the noted sociologist and author of *Southern California Country*, as being 'shot through with self-hatred ... blind mole-like fear of chaos ... deep-seated social envy and sense of personal inadequacy ... cheap cynicism ... pseudo-hard-boiled know-nothingness.' Such are scarcely the epithets that the mass public would have applied to office holders and founder members of the Alliance like Clark Gable, Gary Cooper, Robert Taylor, Ward Bond or John Wayne. The popular image of them,

* Gary Cooper, quoted in *Hollywood on Trial*, by Gordon Kahn (Boni & Gaer), p. 57.

as the previous chapter has suggested, was in direct contradiction to this list of unheroic defects.

Even granted that the McWilliams view is a partisan one, it still leaves an interesting problem in reconciliation. For a star seeks or accepts screen roles which seem to reflect the image he has of himself and which he knows his public have come to share. Usually the role is physical or sexual. Sometimes, though, it is political. The star of professedly liberal to left-wing views who appears in films that reinforce his outlook is commonplace today, though perhaps more so in Europe than in America. But how far can a star's right-wing bias be made consistent with a truly popular image? And how far is such a star the captive of his own image when he comes to propagandise for his political bias?

In the names listed above that of John Wayne offers the most complete example of a star who has taken his politics with him into his films and his public image. Others have adopted a right-wing stance off screen, Wayne has done so on screen – and he has been able to do so without forfeiting his box-office power. He was at the top of the exhibitors' poll in 1969 even after he had delivered the 'inspirational address' in support of George Wallace, the extreme right-wing candidate for the U.S. presidential nomination, and in addition had produced his own 'hawkish' pro-Vietnam film *The Green Berets* (1968). How Wayne has reconciled the image of right-wing propagandist with his other image as a western hero – and with what degree of consciousness in his own mind – is a paradox worth examining.

*   *   *

The Wayne hero is a westerner whose physical presence is practically the extent of his moral conscience. Someone has said that one cannot imagine Wayne philosophising about his lot as one could Gary Cooper. Though Cooper's hero was a man of fewer words than Wayne's, his silences were more than hiatuses between 'Yup' and 'Nope'* – they were the intervals in which he confronted himself. Only Randolph Scott, at least in Budd

---

* Cooper, in fact, took care to have such words as 'yup' and 'nope' deleted from his scripts in case he fell into self-parody.

Boetticher's films, shares Cooper's knack of turning momentarily into a totem – but a *thinking* totem.

Dialogue in Wayne's scripts is minimal, but this very fact gives his utterances a menacing purposefulness. When he says something, it means something. His flat voice is not only incisive, it is curled at the edges. A good voice for contempt. His acting, too, is largely a matter of reacting. Again the effect is deliberately aimed at. 'We evolved a system,' says one of his scriptwriters, 'of making John a sort of bystander so that he could avoid taking part in situations, and thus avoid having to act.' When he does intervene at length, it seems to be with brutal decisiveness. While invariably on the side of right (in its lower-case appelation), Wayne's hero has few moral or legal scruples when he gets down to business. It is James Stewart in *The Man Who Shot Liberty Valance* (1961) who hesitates over fitting means to ends when his pacifist conscience inhibits him from drawing in a gun duel. It is Wayne who takes aim and kills Valance and Stewart who takes the credit for it. The newspaper editor in the film comments dryly, 'When the legend becomes a fact, print the legend' – and does so. Nevertheless this is all the glory that the Wayne hero expects. He is not a romantic, but a stoic and a cynic.

It was not always so. In John Ford's *Stagecoach* (1939), the film whose success pulled Wayne out of the B-picture rut, his Ringo Kid was so innocent that he could mistake a prostitute for a decent woman: in this respect the Wayne hero's sight has got clearer with age. He has also got more brutal in his attitude to women whom he once treated with chivalrous courtesy. In more recent years he has, as likely as not, exposed the more uppity females to the test of a running fight with him or the indignity of a spanking.

The fiction that love comes with a slap serves a film star well who is on the wrong side of the age gap to make it come credibly any other way. One qualification has to be made, however: it is the woman who forces the issue with Wayne. Unlike Gable, he does not first provoke her affection by his own aggression. This strategy has to some extent been dictated by Wayne's physical prowess: for at 6 feet 4 inches, he is not just big – he is outsize.

Temperamentally, too, it is agreeable to be a woman-tamer, and his more recent knockabout westerns, in which punches are flung as ritually as fans are waved in *The Mikado*, have had to furnish him with a shrewish-tempered partner whom he can break in. Direct confrontation is at the heart of his hero's code, as it is in the western's, though in Wayne's case such directness is not limited to the 'Old West' indeed it is not specifically western.

'My father used to tell me, "If you tell a lie, admit it." I have always believed that – I always believe in facing everything directly,' he said in an interview while making the Pacific War film *In Harm's Way* (1965). 'Kirk Douglas in this film,' he added, 'has a rape scene with a girl who is engaged to another soldier. Douglas gets killed in action. Now if I were playing the part, I would want the girl's boy-friend to return and kill me. I don't mind dying in a film, if the confrontation is direct.'* Self-reliance, not co-operative alliance, is Wayne's way and also very much that of one of the two directors whose own outlook has sparked off mutual sympathy. This is Howard Hawks: the other is, of course, John Ford.

Hawks often elaborates his films from the characters in them and undoubtedly many characteristics which Wayne has taken over as his own, off screen as well as on, were first defined in this way. (Another procreative source is, ironically, published inter- views with the star. Wayne tends to scoff at them, but, on the evidence offered by subsequent interviewers, he often absorbs the views into his own voiced outlook.) The blunt belief that a man should stand on his own feet is a Hawks axiom that compelled the director to make a rebuttal to one of the most famous of all the western parables of mutual aid in the defence of civilisation – Fred Zinnemann's *High Noon* (1952). The film Hawks made in answer to it was *Rio Bravo* (1958).

According to him, the creative process 'started with some scenes in ... *High Noon* in which Gary Cooper runs around trying to get help and no one would give him any. And that's rather a silly thing for a man to do, especially since at the end of

* *Daily Mail*, 23rd July 1964, interviewed by David Lewin.

the picture he is able to do the job himself. So I said, we'll do just the opposite, and take a real professional viewpoint: as Wayne says when he's offered help, "If they're really good, I'll take them. If not, I'll just have to take care of them." '* The 'real professional viewpoint' of this kind makes sense in a western like *Rio Bravo*. But Hawks leaves the disturbing feeling that he would apply it to other choices in life than simply how a man defends himself at the show-down. It has an uneasy identity with the Right-wing position that government is something too important to be left to the will of the governed.

Wayne once said, 'Instead of going in and running his office the way he should, the politician . . . appeals to the popular vote, that being the mob vote. Believe me, this is ruining America.'† He uttered these words five years after *Rio Bravo*, but Hawks's 'real professional viewpoint' has transferred itself to him with ominous facility. One is reminded how often in the west, as in the westerns, the township's sheriff was a hired gun, lawless under the law, sanctioned because he did the job he was paid to do, but always a dubious democrat and sometimes hard to vote out of office unless one had a quicker trigger-finger.

The truth seems to be that the 'ethics' of the western lie at the back of all John Wayne's political thinking – and on those occasions when control of the film is his entirely, they have been used to express this thinking. It is really not surprising that much of his reactionary outlook comes from this source. Film after film, especially the ones directed by Ford and Hawks, associated Wayne with every institution, event and tradition of the 'Old West': the Indian wars, cavalry government, great cattle drives, the home-made entertainment of homesteaders, range feuds, lawlessness and bar-room brawls in frontier towns, sudden justice under the marshal's gun, migrations and massacres. . . . No other actor has formulated a whole American saga so fully in his films or looked so perfectly adapted to the wear and tear of epic labours. His film *McLintock* (1963) may be a low-comedy western, but when Wayne tosses his stetson in a mighty arc clean over the

* *Movie*, December 1962, interviewed by Peter Bogdanovich.
† *Esquire*, May 1963: 'God and Man in Hollywood' by Thomas B. Morgan.

bull's horns on his ranch-house weathervane, he is achieving the humorous hyperbole of the *chanson de geste*.

But equally no man could be exposed to such an American heritage for forty years in the movies without coming to regard himself as the custodian of it. The preservation of American ideals is so well wrapped up in western folk-lore that for much of the time Wayne's political bias is not visible. Yet scriptwriters and directors who have worked with, or for, him have helped form his political character – and so have the pictures in which he has scored a great success.

Red River (1948) was one of them. A story of the great cattle drive that beat out the Chisholm Trail, it was directed by Howard Hawks and scripted by Borden Chase who, four years earlier, had helped found the right-wing Motion Picture Alliance for the Preservation of American Ideals. The story switched Wayne away from roles in which he had been the chivalrous, romantic cowboy and into a part in which he was a domineering cattle baron, a kind of prairie Captain Bligh – Hawks makes no secret that the film is a landbound version of *Mutiny on the Bounty*. Wayne's word is law, like Bligh's, and he brooks no questioning of his authority 'Get down off those horses – I don't talk up to the likes of you,' he barks at two deserters from the cattle-train, on whom he proceeds to execute summary justice, halted only by his adopted son (Montgomery Clift) who picks this moment to play Mr Christian and start the mutiny.

Wayne in *Red River* is a deeply abivalent figure: the kind of lovable bastard who puts men through hell and earns their respect but also their hatred. Their sacrifice is sanctioned because he has established himself as their leader: the relationship is common enough in certain wartime commanders. Wayne showed how well he understood it when, in reference to *In Harm's Way*, he said, 'In this film I must show that I care about other people – otherwise when they go off and get killed on my orders, people would hate me. I don't mind audiences hating me – they did, perhaps, in *Red River*, but they understood my point of view.'

The comradeship or the quality of caring is something Wayne has always associated with the sacrifice or the quantity of slaughter. Provided it is glorious, defeat is acceptable; frequently, though, the commander comes through it better than his men, for he at least finishes the film alive. If defeat is inglorious, like the humiliating evacuation of the Philippines in *They Were Expendable* (1945), then ways are found to reconcile Wayne's position with his country's. At his insistence a tiny scene was included in this film when the U.S. forces are being air-ferried out showing him ready to disobey orders and sneak off as a jungle guerrilla, until a superior officer orders him back aboard. Not quite a *geste*, but certainly a gesture.

The new Wayne of *Red River* found immediate public favour. In 1948 he had been sixteenth in the box-office listing; in 1950 he was number one. The character of Wayne the hard man, re-appeared memorably in John Ford's *The Searchers* (1956), the story of the hunt for a white girl abducted by Indians and – her searchers find – inducted into their tribe. Again not a 'political' film, for Ford's loving re-creation of a bygone period would pro-bably render him incapable of a contemporary political parallel – yet the Wayne character is a more extreme example of Americanism than any of his earlier western heroes. His search is a defence of the purity of the race he belongs to and it is accompanied by his continuous taunting of his travelling companion for being a quarter-Cherokee, as well as a readiness to shoot his own niece when he hears her calling the Indians who kidnapped her 'my people'.

For all the warmth of hearth and home in Ford's poetic opening and closing sequences, *The Searchers* has a bitter core. And the core is Wayne – his character's inbred hatred of non-Americans. The role, tailored for him by the writer Frank Nugent, takes care to establish right at the very start the man has fought for his values, which happen to be those of the losing side in the Civil War, and, having been beaten, he does not show up at the surrender of his values but makes tracks back to the homestead bastion of the American family.

*　　　*　　　*

Wayne's super-patriotism had manifested itself strongly in the work of the Motion Picture Alliance during the McCarthy era;

but it also formulated itself on the screen in the most outspoken piece of propaganda he has yet made, not excluding *The Green Berets*. This was in a film called *Big Jim McLain* (1952). (Note incidentally the concept of 'bigness' so attractive to Wayne's sense of he-manship. Even adversaries have to be 'big' to be worthy of him: when he was cured of cancer in the mid-1960s, he referred to the disease, which had hit his pride almost more than his body, as 'Big C.'). *Big Jim McLain* was co-produced by Wayne and starred him as the two-fisted flail of the Communist left. He played a special agent of the House Un-American Activities Committee tracking down a cell of disloyal Americans – suave society types, sinister scientists, turncoat trade-union leaders – only to see them escape justice, if not his own bunched fists, through the bolt-hole of the Fifth Amendment.

As film-making, it was unconvincing; as propaganda, it was hysterical. By implication it gave its nod of approval to informers and offered its pardon to Communists who confessed their errors. The ex-party member in the film, self-accused of crimes against humanity, atones for them by working in a leper colony. Left-wing film people who recanted under pressure from the Motion Picture Alliance were shown slightly more mercy: they did not have to leave the movie colony.

At the box-office the film did nothing for Wayne, though he later claimed it had done a lot for the re-election of Senator Joe McCarthy. 'McCarthy was a friend of mine. Whether he went overboard or not, he was of value to my country. A number of liberals think he started the witch-hunt. I think that he was witch-hunted himself.'* Wayne was an active Republican throughout the 1960s, supporting Eisenhower's two presidential campaigns and the unsuccessful one of Richard Nixon in 1960. In this year, too, he brought out his own spectacular political statement, neatly timed for the election, in his film *The Alamo* which he produced, directed (with John Ford's occasional help) and in which he starred.

The Alamo was of course a historical adventure film for Wayne before it was a patriotic manifesto; but the latter concern was a

* John Wayne to the author, London, October 1960.

close second and in later years, as the film crawled slowly into profit, he tended to give patriotism pride of place among his motives for making it. It is symptomatic of the extreme views he holds that 'to show this living generation of Americans what their country really stands for' he should have picked the story of a glorious massacre. The hundred odd Americans who held up the armies of Santa Anna, dictator of Mexico and ruler of the province of Texas during the thirteen-day siege of the Alamo mission hut in 1836, exemplified the belief that it was better to be dead than Mexican. Such a message was easily convertible into the 'cold war' slogan that it was better to be dead than 'red'. Not that Santa Anna was totally equated with the Kremlin imperialists: the desire to see the film do well at the Mexican box-office added a shade of nobility to the character that it might have lacked if he had been a Communist. But in an interview given a few years after the film, Wayne explained – and regretted – this touch of benevolence in terms of his contemporary political views. 'Santa Anna,' he told Thomas B. Morgan, 'got a charter of freedom for the Mexican people that was a lot like ours. But then, when he took over, *he pulled a Kennedy* and started grabbing power.'*

The early box-office receipts came in slowly and Wayne put this down to the type of role in which he had cast himself. He played the straightforward, uncomplicated Davy Crockett who turned up at the Alamo with twenty-three ragged patriots to die for the idea of a free Texas. Wayne felt, looking back, that he would have done better by the film to cast himself, instead of Laurence Harvey, in the part of Colonel Travis who commanded the garrison and died breaking his sword over his knee. Harvey made him a stiff-necked, snake-eyed fanatic, talking like the Act of Independence one minute, ranting like Hitler the next, impatient to sacrifice everyone to his own messianic zeal. One can see that Wayne would have kept him in the low register and made him an obstinate bastard; and this departure from the *Red River* image of himself probably did hurt the film, though the fact that it was sluggish, mawkish and long-winded hardly helped either.

* *Esquire*, May 1963: 'God and Man in Hollywood,' by Thomas B. Morgan, italics are the author's.

But consolation came a few years later. The film had originally been released during the early part of President Kennedy's administration when relations between the United States and the Soviet Union were at their warmest for a decade. Such a time, said Wayne, had hardly been a propitious one in which to 'remember the Alamo'. Russo-American relations had frozen over again fairly solidly by the end of 1962; and Wayne now commented, 'If we'd released *The Alamo* this year instead of last, we'd have done better. America's mind is more intelligent now. It makes a difference, you know.'*

*   *   *

Plenty of examples have already been quoted to suggest the insidious ways in which film-making can blur a star's perception of life, so that it seems to be an extension of what goes on around him on the screen. John Wayne has not escaped this influence. But in his case it has resulted in a two-way process which maintains an extraordinary equilibrium between his own nature and the nature of the world as he views it. With the exception of a directly propagandist piece like *Big Jim McLain*, he tends to restructure his extremist politics in terms of the western for his roles on the screen; and when he actively engages in off-screen political work he injects into it the beliefs that are a guide to action in his western roles.

Obviously it is not necessary to wear six-guns and a wide hat to be behind the principle of direct confrontation as the basis of a country's foreign policy. But when Wayne urges it, when he announces that he still wants to unleash Chiang Kai-Shek's troops against the Chinese mainland, it is the unmistakable reflex of a man who has so often forced a show-down with the villain at the other end of the boardwalk. When he decries negotiations with the 'reds', it is with the contemptuous conviction that it did no good, either, to parley with the Indians – as he sneers in *The Searchers,* 'I don't stand talkin' to the wind.' And when he preaches the need for 'the world's free people' to find 'new heart and faith' in face of the enemy, the text he takes is 'Remember the Alamo!'

* Ibid.

During the 1960s Wayne moved even farther to the political right. He backed Barry Goldwater's campaign for the Presidential nomination as well as that of Ronald Reagan, an ex-Motion Picture Alliance member, for the Governorship of California; and he gave the inspirational address on behalf of George Wallace at the 1968 Republican National Convention, telling his listeners, 'I want my daughter to be as grateful as I am grateful for every day of my life I spend in the U.S.A.' And on the screen he directed and starred in *The Green Berets*.*

This highly pro-the-war view of Vietnam again demonstrates how thoroughly he conceives his political statements in terms of a western. The film is set in North and South Vietnam; but it is a starkly over-simplified morality play with events and characters, gestures and platitudes more reminiscent of the American Badlands in the 1860s than South-East Asian political complexities in the 1960s. That this concept was deliberate was freely admitted by Wayne's producer son Michael. 'In a motion picture you cannot confuse an audience . . . I'm not making a picture about Vietnam. I'm making a picture about good against bad. I happen to think that's true about Vietnam, but even if it isn't as clear as all that, that's what you have to do . . . It's the same thing as the Indians. Maybe we shouldn't have destroyed all those Indians. I don't know, but when you're making a picture, the Indians are the bad guys.'†

The character Wayne played in the film differed substantially from his counterpart in Robin Moore's novel on which the screenplay was based. In the book he is a Finnish-born ex-Nazi surrounded by an all-Anglo-Saxon team of Special Force men; as Wayne plays him, he is Captain Kirby commanding a melting-pot squad of Kowalskis, Muldoons and assorted Negroes – just like any cavalry troop – and the advance camp in the jungle plants the film still more firmly in western territory by calling itself Dodge City. The massacre by 'the Indians' is the central Alamo-like event of the first half – dying is still the best thing one can do for one's country. The figure of the liberal journalist, a conscience-ridden

* Ray Kellogg also took a director's credit.
† *Variety*, 1st November, 1967.

doubting 'dove' who is finally convinced by the sight of his own eyes, represents the callow 'easterner' in a western film who owes his life to the commonsense of the professionals in the saddle.

Wayne's philosophy is characteristically contemptuous of legal niceties about the conduct of the war in the way that a lynch party used to resort to execution first and justice afterwards. To the journalist's protest at the treatment of Vietcong prisoners not being in accord with due process of law, he returns an answer straight from his frontiersman's heart: 'Out here due process of law is a bullet.' Against the appalling actuality of the Vietnam war, which television broadcasts at the time were bringing *live* into millions of American homes, a film like *The Green Berets* is offensively simplistic.

Yet simplistic is how it is meant to be. 'Simple themes,' says Wayne, 'save us from the nuances.' That is the original formula for his success. It is also the one he applies to his politics. In his mind at least there is no distinction between the star vehicle and the political statement. What is good for John Wayne is good for the western and, by extension, good for the country.

His latest film, *True Grit* (1969), presents him as a one-eyed, fat-bellied marshal, Rooster Cogburn, who hires himself out to pursue a 'passel' of badmen. He is now like a stoic grandfather in the saddle. But the same fierce self-reliance is there: and he has stood so long in the dwindling forest of American screen heroes that his seasoned eminence is undeniably splendid. It even has to be admired by those who mistrust the soil it is rooted in. The film is not directly 'political', but its law-and-order theme connects directly with the shifting bias of American society under the Nixon administration. And the same hard line on vanquishing your enemy with justice untempered by mercy is inherent in Rooster's willingness to shoot a man between the eyes so long as he had *judged* him before he drew a bead on him. 'He's simply trying to make life habitable for the most people in his territory,' says his creator. The role won Wayne an Oscar in 1970.

Evidence of Wayne's popularity after thirty years of stardom, and ten more as a film actor, is certainly impressive. After only eleven weeks in U.S. theatres, *True Grit* had earned 3,500,000 dollars and was leading all other current releases at the box-office. *The Green Berets* ran into the heaviest critical flak that any post-war picture has had to take, but its gross domestic receipts between July 1968 and the end of December were 8,700,000 dollars and it was tenth in the year's list of top box-office films. But whether people came to see it for Wayne the film star and said 'Damn his politics' is something such figures cannot indicate. The likelihood is that they did. For what he represents – 'the big tough guy on the side of right' – is luckily more viable in terms of stardom than politics, and probably more durable, too. But just as the other Hollywood heroes expressed something of the decades they flourished in through the way they constructed their screen personalities and their attitudes to society, so Wayne has used the concept of the western to mould his own star personality and his attitude to politics.

The political facts of life, as he sees them, derive from the experience of the essential western hero of history and, even more, of legend. It is certainly not Wayne's fault if people insist on separating the two, the politics and the heroics, in their allocation of preferences. The newspaper editor in *The Man Who Shot Liberty Valance,* however, turned out to be a wiser judge of public preference when he remarked, 'When the legend becomes fact, print the legend.'

PART SEVEN

EMANCIPATION AND AFTER

'One producer, in New York, last
week detailed a roster of "so-called
million-dollar stars I've been offered
and for whom I wouldn't give a nickel
if I didn't have the right property,
and if I had the right property I
don't need them." '

            – *Variety*, 10th September 1969

CHAPTER NINETEEN

STARS GO FORTH: WHAT PRICE INDEPENDENCE?

Stars setting up as the producers of their own pictures are no new phenomenon. They flourished, as we have seen, during the 1920s when huge, largely untaxed salaries gave them the means to protect and promote their careers by making films over which they had complete control. The regimenting studio system of the 1930s ruthlessly repressed this economic self-aggrandisement with long-term contracts and the threat of suspension in perpetuity.

The war years, with their box-office boom, postponed the day of liberation, though there were signs of the old system loosening its bonds: Olivia de Havilland gained a significant victory in the California courts where she got a declaration that the time spent on suspension must not be added on to contract time. But stars who were aiding the war effort on screen or battlefield obviously had little chance to take advantage of this. The studio crack-up began about 1947, and it has been well chronicled in the red ink of company balance sheets and the black ink of headlines announcing that one star name after another had turned 'independent'. It is a chilling experience to turn through the last thirty-odd years of a publication like *Variety* and see the principal agent of this revolution growing from a bland news item in 1928 about television tests in the Los Angeles area to the point where the small screen's inroads into movie profits had driven practically all the film news off the front page. It is like a Biblical curse coming inexorably to fruition.

Television forced the studios to cut back production and very quickly there were more stars on the pay-roll than there were movies for them to star in. The care and maintenance of artists not earning their keep, and having to be paid contract fees from dwindling box-office receipts, gave them their independence more speedily than any previous acts of defiance or supplication. The superstars who had been established in the 1930s took their leave gradually: in some cases it was a form of face-saving, for their post-war films were doing badly.

Others were put on contracts that required them to make only one or two films yearly: a utilitarian way of having the use of a star without the cost of upkeep. But the effect was to force the price of talent up whenever it *was* used. For the agents who had maintained a running battle with the studios almost from the beginning of the Hollywood moguls' empire, being tolerated, banned, reprieved, solicited, cursed or otherwise manipulated, now obtained the power to negotiate for their clients on individual pictures and not simply on long-term contracts and options for their services. And so fees shot up. Instead of being in so many thousands of dollars per week as under the contract system, they soared into hundreds of thousands of dollars per picture. For the stars who proved their worth at this price, the budget was not simply the limit – the future earnings of the film could be raided by taking a percentage of the net, or, better still, of the gross profits.

All the same, high taxation had to be reckoned with, or else there was no point save egotism – a not unimportant factor, of course – in negotiating such rich rewards. Consequently stars incorporated themselves, preserving their fees-plus-profits deal in the shape of capital gains which were less stringently taxed. It was a short step from this arrangement to the actual production of pictures by and starring the artist. Among the first to do this was Burt Lancaster, who, significantly, was among the very last group of stars – Elvis Presley, Rock Hudson, Tony Curtis, Kirk Douglas were some of the others – to be given anything like the traditional studio build-up by their agents or the producers who had signed them to personal contracts.

In many cases the agent became a producer. Hal Wallis is the outstanding example of a producer who followed the Goldwyn pattern of signing some of the already named stars to a personal contract and then attempting to build up their careers through his own and other studios' productions. But even he found that the attraction of being an independent power was irresistible to some of his stars who settled their contracts with him. Consequently the predominant pattern became, as Richard Dyer MacCann put it, that of 'the agent [who] is not necessarily a producer. He has power over individual stars ... but that power may be fleeting, for an artist can change his agent. ... He has the power of ideas, or preparing "packages" for independents, but these are usually "one-shot" deals. Although there are many responsible agents who are smart enough to worry about their clients' long-term interests, the agent – by nature and by function – is not a responsible film-maker. It is not his business to worry about whether the box-office receipts will cover costs and profits. ... He does not have time to think about an actor's development as part of a programme of production.'*

*   *   *

The practice of agents turning producers for the stars they represented was at first encouraged by the Screen Actors' Guild. It was a way of giving agents the necessary edge to cut their members into the boom in television production. If they controlled the talent, agents could produce the shows for TV. The result was that from the mid-1950s the outpouring of filmed series for television was largely what kept the big Hollywood studios going.

The series replaced the old B-pictures which had played such a staple part in studio economics and provided a seedbed for future stars. The effect on stardom was to depress it and lead to the curious hiatus one sees in looking back on these years when the old stars are desperately hanging on but, apart from some phenomenal discoveries, few potential stars are in evidence and even their careers have a hesitant and vulnerable look. Stardom lost its high-definition image as a distinct product of the motion-picture industry. Stars' images became blurred by over-exposure

* *Hollywood in Transition,* by Richard Dyer MacCann (Houghton Mifflin Co.), p. 57.

on such disenchanting media as the television networks. Stars found there was now no sense of continuity to their careers, nor even the momentum which the studio publicity machine had provided; and they were thrown back on their own frequently inadequate resources or those of their agents and producers.

When the Department of Justice, in 1961, required the agencies to separate their star-owning functions from their star-producing ones, the situation took a new turn. Stars were compelled either to resort to producers who were more or less expert in the 'packaging' of assorted film deals – wrapping up a pre-sold property like a hit play or a best-seller, along with a writer, a director and a couple of star names and taking the whole package to a studio for backing – or else the stars became producers of their own movies and themselves learned to 'package' deals on the strength of their corporate names. 'The long thin line of independents,' wrote Richard Dyer MacCann, 'is made up of men who are all trying bravely to think like studios.'*

This neatly sums up the paradox of post-war stardom. On the one hand the stars achieved a freedom of economic and artistic choice denied to all but the most successful few in earlier decades. On the other hand they fell victim to hazards and burdens that their temperament or training left them ill-equipped to cope with. These now seemed in retrospect to have been borne with enviable stoicism by the often reviled front offices of the old movie studios. The transition from studios who owned stars to stars who owned pictures was accompanied by so many unforeseen problems that it seemed less like emancipation than slavery by other means. But possibly the greatest problem was not the changes in the structure of picture production, but the deeper changes taking place in American society which violently disturbed the relationship between stars and their audience. Hitherto the stars had set the goals and images for society; from now on it was society, or at least the part of it which still went to the pictures, which set the style for its stars.

* Ibid., p. 61.

HEROES FOR
THE UNDER-30s:
LIFE-STYLE
STARS

It is no longer possible to apply the alluring epithet 'Hollywood' with the same old assurance to the phenomenon of stardom. For the truth is that the major new stars who have risen in recent years do not correspond to any studio-created image. How could they? The studios have abandoned the means, as well as the desire, to build stars to public specification: it has become too costly and too risky. What today's new stars, many of them anyhow, do correspond to is the life style of the predominant section of society, the young.

Teenagers were, of course, always the largest audience for film stars. But as Edgar Morin, the French critic, observes, 'it is only recently that adolescence has become conscious of itself as a particular age group, opposing itself to other age groups and defining its own imaginary range and cultural models.'* The power of this generation has already changed the look of the American cinema. In 1969 it was reliably estimated that seventy per cent of those who still go to the movies were between the ages of 16 and 24. And the potential power of the generation to change society was unmistakably manifested in mid-August of the same year when over 400,000 young people, mostly between the ages of 16 and 30, swarmed to the three-day rock festival at Bethel, N.Y. 'With surpassing ease and a cool sense of authority,' said a writer in *Time,* commenting on the festival, 'the children of plenty have voiced an intention to live by a different ethical standard than their parents accepted. The pleasure principle has been elevated over the Puritan ethic of work. To do one's own

* Edgar Morin, op. cit., p. 123.

thing is a greater duty than to be a useful citizen. Personal freedom in the midst of squalor is more liberating than social conformity with the trappings of wealth. Now that youth takes abundance for granted, it can afford to reject materialism.'*

The stars whom this age group has turned to in order to define its 'counter-culture', as Theodore Roszak called it, are the very ones whose life off screen and roles on it correspond to the group's confusion, vulnerability, rebellion, alienation, freedom and anarchism – all qualities that are not susceptible to studio promotion without causing an instinctive suspicion of manipulation and betrayal among the adherents of the new youth-directed stars.

The life style of the latter has to be seen or felt to echo that of the community who have turned on or dropped out. The stars who have come into prominence over the last fifteen years exhibit characteristics that get progressively closer and closer to the life style of the young, as they in turn define their rebellion with a surer sense of identity, until there is scarcely any distinguishable distance between them. The star has in fact become a kind of superfan. Instead of being worshipped for himself, it is he who worships the values of his followers.

It is the lack of any sort of agonised contact with a specific section of mass society which has kept the last wave of studio-made stars – Burt Lancaster, Tony Curtis, Rock Hudson, Kirk Douglas, etc. – from getting the responsive recognition of the alienated film audience. Such stars are conservationists by nature, not nonconformists. They cater to the exterior needs of comedy or adventure and rarely try to express the troubled inner conflicts of the audience in their roles. (It is notable, though, that on the occasions they do undertake anti-social roles they become better actors, if not more popular stars.)

Of all the great studio-bred male stars of the 1930s and 1940s, only one achieved a close identification for a time with the generation of the mid-1960s. He was Humphrey Bogart and it was a posthumous influence he exercised. Bogart became a cult hero for the under-30s nearly ten years after his death, from cancer, in

* *Time*, 29th August 1969.

1957. The fashion for camp nostalgia that was prevalent around 1965 partly helped his fans define their fondness for him. The trenchcoat he wore so belligerently was an amusingly dated prop; his sibillant lisp was easy to copy and appealed to the mynah-bird side of one which seeks to transfer some of the star's charisma on to oneself by mimicking the well-known accent; and lines of dialogue, actual or apocryphal, which he uttered in his films, like 'Drop the gun, Louie,' or 'Play it, Sam,' or 'I don't risk my neck for anybody,' provided an all-purpose phrase book of Bogartisms.

But identification with him went deeper than these attributes. Bogart's films from *The Petrified Forest* (1936) onwards developed a character whose attitude to life he gradually, probably grate-fully, assimilated and improved on in his own off-screen persona. Nonconformism was an important part of this. Bogart was anti-Hollywood, for a start. Without it occurring to him to annihilate the studio system that made him a star, he resisted it by turning down roles and going on strike. The Holmby Hills Rat Pack, his association of friends and allies whose sardonic slogan was 'Never rat on a rat,' was one of his ways of expressing scorn of the film industry. It all contributed to the credibility of his screen self, though he took care never to let it actually harm his career. There was the occasion, for instance, when he and other film celebrities flew to Washington, in 1947, to protest against McCarthyism and the Un-American Activities Committee's investigation of Holly-wood. But having made his protest in the marching line, the revelation of some of his fellow artists' views on Communism caused him to pull back swiftly and issue a statement regretting his action as 'ill-advised, foolish and impetuous'. The Bogart myth fortunately effaced this uncharacteristic climb-down: he is remembered for the protest, not his apology.

Bogart developed a characteristic which nearly everyone who knew him intimately agrees on – as they do on few other things about him. This was his malicious relish for provoking people, for offering or inviting insult. One's first introduction to him usually drew an abrasive personal observation designed to test one's flashpoint. Experience had maybe taught him the star's self-protective reflex of considering all-comers as potential enemies till proved otherwise. But his pleasure in needling people contributed to the scepticism of his screen character. His rasping voice was perfect for this; so was his stiff upper lip. (His lip wound, incidentally, apparently formed no impediment to his speech.) As Louise Brooks once said, referring to his quite conscious elaboration of his acting technique, 'he decided to exploit his mouth'.

Joseph Mankiewicz probably did not know how prescient he was, in view of the campus revolts of the 1960s, when he observed about Bogart, 'He had that rather intellectual disrespect for authority which, I think, is why the average college student would sooner identify with (him) than, say, with Sinatra.' It is hardly accidental that the establishment of the Bogart cult coincided with the rise of the campus militants.

He has other aspects that made him attractive to the same age group. At a time when confusion and uncertainty was spreading among young people of draft age, Bogart's screen character offered a basic security. His heroes did not suffer identity crises every ten minutes. Duke Mantee in *The Petrified Forest,* in which Bogart first struck stardom, has his gangster's glamour and the uncertainty of a wavering gun to give him suspense; but he also has a defiant sense of his own identity. Of all the people in that petrified play, he alone has defined himself by action, by an act of will.

If there is a measure of envy in the way we look back at how the Hollywood stars of the pre-war period filled their roles, it springs from the secure sense of personal identity which the repetition of their personalities in role after role seemed to confer on them. Bogart had this, improved on it with the aid of writers and directors, and bequeathed it to a generation that was having to think things out afresh and find its own centre. Most important of all, he did not represent idealised virtues. As various writers have pointed out, his most popular roles in films like *The Maltese Falcon* (1941), *Casablanca* (1943), *To Have and Have Not* (1945) and *The Big Sleep* (1946) threw him into relief as a man committed only to himself ('I mind my own business.'). It is circumstances which force him into taking sides. He is the loner, the criminal gone straight, the private eye who trusts nobody. His impulses are conditioned by who he is, not what he ought to do. His performance in *The African Queen* (1952) won him his only Oscar, yet it remains with good reason one of the least liked by his admirers. For chivalry and patriotism are not the obligations Bogart was destined to fulfil on the screen. His hard-edged acting as Sam Spade, Philip Marlowe or Harry Morgan gave his existentialist stance a sense of dynamic involvement that belied his basic aloneness. Richard Schickel summed it up best when he said, 'Bogart could get interested in a fight for justice or principle only when his own, direct stake in the outcome was made painfully clear to him.'

At an agonising time in America's history, when doubt was being cast on established values and ideals as the Vietnam War divided the nation, Bogart's example seemed to many young people to be the only responsible one to follow.

Probably the earliest move towards reflecting the anguished sensitivity of the audience, as if it was also his own, came from Montgomery Clift and even he was not so much in rebellion against society as in flight from it. Its stigmata were not so visible on him at the start of his career. When he played the U.S. soldier looking for a lost child in Fred Zinnemann's *The Search* (1948), he himself was a symbol of the same care and protection he later came to look in need of. He once said that he only felt secure, unthreatened when he was with children: a revealing remark in this context. Yet in the same year he stood up to John Wayne's despotic cattle king in *Red River* without any of the flinching that became his characteristic trademark. It is Howard Hawks who takes the credit for this. 'I took Monty out to the wilds of Arizona before we got the movie under way,' he said. 'I sat him, protesting, on a horse for three weeks. I said to a cowboy, "Take him up into the hills and don't treat him as if he was at a riding school." There was nothing but cowboys in that part of Arizona and he couldn't talk to *them* about his psychological hang-ups. He was his own worst enemy. After *Red River* I never wanted to use him again.'* It was left to directors more sympa-

* Howard Hawks in interview with author, London 1967.

thetic than Hawks is to the mind's delicate stresses to draw out of Clift the anguished concern they detected.

To look at his films in sequence is to see a haunted personality gradually appear in those almost too handsome features that were to be painfully yet forcefully transfigured by his appalling car accident in 1957. The hunching shoulders as if he were about to draw his head in like a tortoise to shelter in his shell; the voice that sounded parched from spiritual drought; the eyeballs popping out with the 'don't hit me' supplication; the impression of a man who has seen in daylight the sort of nightmares that other people only see when asleep: this was the later Clift who came to represent so well the man of concern cut off from others by his own impotence. He was the priest in the confessional who is a prisoner of other people's sins (*I Confess:* 1953), the author of the agony column tortured by other people's pleas (*Lonelyhearts:* 1959), the analyst by the couch-side who is burdened by his own neuroses (*Freud:* 1963). It was a calculatedly successful irony that John Huston should cast such a troubled star as the father of psycho-analysis. But on second thoughts, Huston was absolutely right in *his* analysis. For Freud found the key to relate his private neuroses to the larger condition of man. And Clift also found a way to release, more delicately than did some of his fellow stars, his own inner tensions and relate them to his acting in a way that made it possible for the growing numbers of mixed-up youth to feel that the star was one of them. A symptom as well as a symbol of the times.

*   *   *

James Dean, being an even younger representative of the 'beat' generation, was still more spontaneously their screen hero. He enshrined what Pauline Kael has called 'the glamour of de-linquency'. 'When the delinquent becomes the hero in our films, it is because the image of instinctive rebellion expresses something in many people that they don't dare express.'* Dean gave expression to the unformulated need of the young people who wanted to see their own growing pains reproduced in films. An inability to find a meaningful affection in his parents, a self-hugging loneli-

* *I Lost It at the Movies,* by Pauline Kael (Cape), p. 46.

ness, a secret hurt in the eyes, 'the face of James Dean,' wrote Edgar Morin, 'is an ever-changing landscape in which can be discerned the contradictions, uncertainties and enthusiasms of the adolescent soul.'*

Dean's sudden emergence as a star in many ways anticipated the appearance of Dustin Hoffman fourteen years later and confirms how stardom has been moving closer and closer to social and emotional involvement with the section of filmgoers who are growing younger and more decisive in the election of their stars as the older age group has deserted the movies for television. Dean was a tragic hero for this generation because he was a victim of the same lack of love, or emotional alienation, which was straining the American family group. Hoffman in *The Graduate* (1968) rode with the comedy, but became a hero to his generation because he rejected both the predatory designs of the older Mrs Robinson, who would have exploited him sexually, as well as the economic goals of his parents who would have made him conform socially. Dean was a rebel, Hoffman a drop-out: both focused the loyalty of the age group which had rejected the love and authority of *their* parents.

The basis for such stardom obviously did not exist in pre-war Hollywood since adolescents were not then a separate group with a sub-culture antagonistic to the family and society; but neither would it have emerged in any studio system run on lines which tried to make artistic uniqueness compatible with social conformity. It is no accident that stars like Dean and Hoffman emerge when the disintegration of the studios coincides with the fragmentation of society.

The special quality which the new stars have in common is that they do not act for the satisfaction it gives them – in their audience's eyes, this would be a suspect indulgence – but for the relief. They need to act the way other people need to sleep. Acting for them has become the way to self-knowledge, whether or not it is supplemented by the more professional services of a psychiatrist. This often expresses itself in a desire to know, in detail, the motivations of the character they are playing.

* Edgar Morin, op. cit., p. 124.

The Method system of acting, which started out as a search for the role has often ended up uncovering the self. Marlon Brando was the forerunner and most dynamic exemplar of the introverted star. His physical appearance assists every aspect of it. His eyes are the first thing one picks out in seeking the personality inside the physical man: they are slits which do not look out at one so much as force one to look in at him. His bulk fills his clothes and gives the impression of bursting physical force that his acting supplements powerfully. Dean and Clift invited feelings of protectiveness: Brando makes one feel like a trespasser. He never wastes energy: often he does not need to move at all to make his effect. For much of the time in *The Chase* (1967) he is doing nothing, simply standing there as the sheriff with his head lolling on one side in quizzical suspicion of the corrupt townsfolk. Yet he gives Arthur Penn's film a core of stored-up energy more powerful than all the violence erupting around him.

Brando's parts reflect the rising graph of violence in society; and violence plays a deeply ambivalent role in his acting. He has a compulsion to play men who undergo a moral awakening, who start the film against law and order or human decency and then end up fighting for these very values. His uninvolved docker in *On the Waterfront* (1954) eventually accepts and suffers the penalties of moral responsibility; so does his Nazi in *The Young Lions* (1958) who finally turns against all Hitler stands for. Yet the feeling persists that he accepts the physical punishment that is almost invariably meted out to him a bit too readily; that he relishes the suffering, the savage beating in *On the Waterfront,* the flogging and maiming in *One-Eyed Jacks* (1960), the protracted death from burns in *Mutiny on the Bounty* (1962) and the especially bloody battering he gets in *The Chase.*

An extravagant indulgence in simulated pain seems to some actors the most intense part of their performance; and a masochistic streak is a dark, but probably necessary one in Brando's screen personality. His mutilated hero is initiated into the violence that post-war adolescence has accepted and created. His anarchic motor-bike bum in *The Wild One* (1954) combines speed with hostility to the world: a 'world' whose Main Street is peopled almost exclusively by the over-40s – today it would be the over-30s. And his reply to the exasperated query of what was he rebelling against – 'What have you got?' – became the Beat Generation slogan. Though the film drooped like the trajectory of a spent bullet, hitting earth with a sentimental thud, it transferred on to Brando the intoxication of the age group that needed no cause, only a leader to rebel.

Brando's early films gave him the leadership of the alienated young who found a mutual sympathy in his mumbling, stumbling, glowering, confused rejection of social values. The verbal inarticulateness of his characters invited identification with them – just as in the 1960s the very silence, the coolness of certain screen heroes was to attract those who had formulated their own sub-culture and become both vocally articulate and at the same time turned-off as far as the rest of society was concerned.

*   *   *

If identification with alienated heroes who are *in control* of themselves, is the later phenomenon, then Paul Newman stands at the cross-over point. At first he was judged to be a Brando imitator. As Rocky Graziano, rising from grade 'A' delinquent to middle-weight champion in *Somebody Up There Likes Me* (1958),
Newman certainly had Brando's shambling, mutinous look of an athlete ordered to turn out for training on a frosty morning; but he was far from annihilated by the comparison and it was a coincidence in the choice of source material rather than any conscious copying which prompted the comparison in the first place. For Brando was a close friend of Graziano and had studied the boxer's mannerisms for his role as Stanley Kowalski in *A Streetcar Named Desire* (1952). When Newman came to play Graziano, he naturally went to the same model, not copying him but simply keeping him company for a time and so achieving an empathy with him.

The film's bloody digest of the six rounds that Graziano fought with Tony Zale suggested that Newman, like Brando, was a candidate for fulfilment through suffering. This may be nearer the mark. The films that have done him most good with his audience share an ever-emphatic taste for degradation and pain. Of course there are possibly various reasons for this. Where the range of parts available to American film actors is narrower than in the European film industry, violent suffering is the quickest way to increase a star's status. Pauline Kael has noted that European film heroes are far more complex creatures than their Hollywood counterparts; and physical suffering is a handy way of suggesting spiritual depths in the Hollywood hero. Again the self-disgust that sometimes overtakes stars of integrity continually forced to compromise with Hollywood materialism may demand to be purged in the choice of masochistic roles. Whatever Newman's motivation, the list of his roles from the Graziano film through *The Hustler* (1962), *Sweet Bird of Youth* (1962), *Harper* (1966: retitled *The Moving Target* in Britain) and *Cool Hand Luke* (1967) adds up to a devastating multiple injury report.

Now the acceptance of pain by these heroes is a strong point of contact with a teenage audience. It gives them a physical bond with the most painful age of life. Montgomery Clift's terrible car injuries in real life seemed to his fans to be proof of his integrity. James Dean's death in his racing Porsche made his mythic status secure. Newman's trial by pain has only taken place on the screen. But it has spared hardly any limb or feature of him; and in *Cool Hand Luke,* in particular, it approached a stage of compulsive martyrdom in which the character was less the protagonist of the drama than its punchbag.

Newman's best-known roles have left him with other stigmata that guarantee him the sympathy of a young audience, even though his own age puts him outside the trusted under-30s. The compulsion of *The Hustler* is that of an addict, hooked on gambling as a junkie is hooked on dope. As someone remarks, he is a born loser. His wan, alcoholic girl-friend, played unsentimentally by Piper Laurie, compounds his own crippled capacity for living. His ultimate victory enlarges this capacity. The hero of adolescents is always someone who, through his own endurance, enlarges the capacity of his fellow-men to enjoy life.

Other Newman roles exhibit a solidarity with the drop-out.

Cool Hand Luke is a middle-class drop-out, without home-ties or anything more companionable than a liquor bottle, who expresses his rejection of society's regimentation by chopping the tops off parking meters. Thirty-five years earlier a hungry belly was the motivation of Paul Muni's chain-gang fugitive and the theft of a hamburger was the cause of his monstrous incarceration. Paul Newman's modern hero is condemned for a 'motiveless' act and in the age of affluence his starvation is not in his stomach. The word 'cool' in the title plays a significant part in the picture: it is the convict's assertion of his apartness. It is present again in the daunting equality, almost verging on contempt, with which Newman as Harper, the private eye, treats his rich employers. And it is knotted even more tightly into *Hud* (1963) in the form of a rugged individualism gone wrong. 'Look after yourself,' is Hud's creed, 'for the only helping hand you'll get is the one that lowers you into the grave.'

This extreme form of cool self-reliance appears again in *Hombre* (1966). Newman's study of an Indian and his place in a white mans society does not stop short at portraying an outcast. It is more important that his hero is isolated. For a long stretch of the film he does nothing but watch what goes on. The conception of the character is rooted in his physical immobility. He meditates. Newman spent some time in an Indian reservation before shooting started and 'borrowed' the physical postures of the people there for his part in *Hombre*.

He is clearly an interpretative artist, not simply a personality performer; yet he calls himself a 'cerebral' actor, working from the outside in, and claims that it is only when directing a film like *Rachel, Rachel* (1968), starring his wife Joanne Woodward, that he feels his emotional instinct is readily available to him. But what he interprets in his acting, how he honours in performance the specific emotional nature of a character, has connected with the loyalty of an audience that no longer judges its needs fulfilled by an actor's personality, but needs to have its way of life defined by a star's interpretation of it.

*   *   *

To an even sharper degree this is true, too, of Steve McQueen. What his roles embody on the screen is cool professionalism. His characters all have a thorough understanding of what they are doing, be it catching a criminal or organising a bank robbery. Such self-reliance is so extreme and manifested in ways that absorb the whole energies of the character that the social purpose behind it, be it the committal or the prevention of crime, hardly matters in the audience's enjoyment of the man behind it. Machinery plays a preponderant part in the creation of some of McQueen's most popular roles. Well-publicised off-screen as an automobile buff, a mania that combines a high degree of risk and skill, and the ever-present possibility of mutliation or death to guarantee his integrity, McQueen has taken roles that keep him moving at speed, facing death or quite simply manipulating the complexities of inanimate things to his own advantage.

The car chase in *Bullitt* (1968) exemplifies this appeal: his car becomes an extension of him to the point that he is simply the thinking part of a machine, with no nerves showing and hardly more emotion. The sequence recalls not only the exhilaration of his motor-bike flight from the Germans in *The Great Escape* (1963) – itself a challenge that *Bullitt*'s director, Peter Yates, and the star deliberately set out to surpass – but also an earlier film in which Steven McQueen Jr, as he was then known, was waved down by a speed cop and linked adolescent rebellion directly with acceleration in his aggrieved query, 'Is it a crime to be seventeen?' The mechanics of *The Thomas Crown Affair* (1968) are those of inter-locking crime schedules; but fast cars and the lurching sand-cruiser, that leisure-wagon for a rich beachboy, give a flip, sportive air to McQueen's millionaire who is still antisocial enough to rob a bank for kicks. There is no machinery in *The Cincinnati Kid* (1968), but the mechanics of card-playing in big-time poker reinforce the image of the loner who has it all at his finger-tips.

In *The Sand Pebbles* (1967) he plays the engineer of a rusty U.S. gunboat who nurses his wheezing boilers as if they were ailing buddies. Again there is an instinctive feeling for machinery – a feeling reciprocated by today's adolescent audiences whose assurance in mechanical skills has an easy-going intimacy peculiar to their generation. The scene in *The Sand Pebbles* where McQueen initiates an unskilled Chinese coolie into the mystery of steampower has an affectionate patience that describes the man who is master of himself and his environment.

Though McQueen's sexuality is unmistakable – 'a none too subtle effluence of tomcat' is one critic's accurate if none too subtle description of it – he swerves aside in recent films from committed relationships, preferring to remain free or, rather, mobile. He lives dangerously, in a way that accepts impermanence as a condition of life and precariousness as a prelude to death; yet his own compact vitality is continually charging and recharging his appetite for experience.

Lee Marvin is a more atavistic star. Whereas McQueen treats machines as if they had an identity of their own and melts his own identity into them, Marvin treats human identity as if it were a piece of machinery in the hands of an ape. When its usefulness or curiosity value lapses, he smashes it to pieces. He has burlesqued his own rangy villainy in *Cat Ballou* (1965), but it is in roles like those in *Point Blank* (1968), *The Dirty Dozen* (1968) and *Hell in the Pacific* (1969) that he has made his star status secure. In these he is called on to suppress his humanity and act like a rogue Caliban: there is something only half-human in his aspect. He stands out in violent contrast to civilisation and even the corrupt sophistication of modern life.

It is like a rough beast that he shambles into the world of the Syndicate in *Point Blank*, to retrieve his share of the loot, and finds the money has been absorbed into a criminal society so sophisticated that it uses credit cards instead of ready cash. His rage is marked by a trail of broken bodies that have been shaken like money boxes and mangled underfoot when no pennies drop out. In *Hell in the Pacific*, as an American airman forced to share the same atoll with a Japanese, he behaves with elemental ferocity so that the film seems at times more a lesson in evolution than a sermon about neighbourly love. And in *The Dirty Dozen* he is set to work brutalising the already criminal to turn them into killing machines. In all of which the actor's primitive looks and aboriginal movements exemplify his nihilism. He has a will to destructiveness on screen that no other actor has so far equalled.

Point Blank is filled with fights of a primitive directness rare even in today's cinema – the punch that someone gets in the genitals constantly hits audiences in their most sensitive parts, too. And it also has one extraordinary and unmotivated moment when Marvin sweeps the contents of a woman's cosmetic shelf into an empty bath-tub with sadistic relish at seeing the flagons crack and the porcelain stained with a psychedelic-hued mishmash of crystals, perfumes and lotions. It is like a psychotic making his own Rorshach blot. Without a doubt Marvin offers audiences a gratification that derives from the escalating violence of life in general and the particular attitude to life of those subgroups who live by violence. Unlike James Dean, Marvin is not the victim but the perpetrator; and in a world where the former finds it harder and harder to come by sympathy and the latter expresses something that many people find grossly exhilarating, he was bound to reinforce the identity of a significant section of society.

The earlier stars were the ideals of a dream, says Edgar Morin, and he adds, 'the modern stars are models and examples'. It is hardly for us to deplore this and cry, 'What models! What examples!' The new gods would not have been breakaway ones if society itself had not produced the dissidents who are their most fervent worshippers – the alienated young.

CHAPTER TWENTY-ONE

BLACK IS
BOX-OFFICE:
ETHNIC STARS

Apart from stars who symbolise the most militantly conscious age-group in America today, the adolescents, only one other new category of stars has appeared in recent years: those who symbolise the most militantly conscious ethnic group in America today, the negroes. Not till Black America threw up its social revolutionaries did Hollywood admit the possibility of numerous coloured stars. Only one black actor, Sidney Poitier, had any claim up to then to be called a film star, which had resulted in the familiar quip around the studios, 'If you can't get Sidney Poitier, rewrite the part for a white man.'

It was a joke, though, that was often taken seriously and acted on. Hollywood has always been a white man's cinema, its pictures embodying the white man's fantasies and aspirations, notwithstanding the social consciousness and racial sympathies of the numerous anti-prejudice movies it has produced. These have reflected the white liberals' view of black America: the idea that the harmonious interdependence of the two races is desirable and practicable and can be made to work given good-will and mutual understanding and respect.

Intermarriage has even found Hollywood sponsorship in recent years, but generally in films that are themselves integration fantasies like *Guess Who's Coming to Dinner* (1967) in which the negro becomes an eligible husband for the white girl only after he has been idealised into *her* class and practically out of *his* race. The only thing he retains which is specifically negro is his skin. And in the film he was played, of course, by Sidney Poitier. One says 'of course' reluctantly; but it remains a fact that for a long time no other negro actor who is not also a show-business entertainer has been acceptable to black *and* white audiences.

Poitier has been sardonically dubbed a 'showcase negro'; and though the taunt is grossly neglectful of his skill as an actor, it contains a certain amount of truth. The dark notes in the black American's make-up have been deliberately lightened in Poitier's screen personality and in the roles he has played in many of his films. Almost without exception they are roles which are re-assuring to white audiences and also gratifying to black ones – at least before the recent negro revolution ensured that the black man no longer had any problem of identity.

Poitier is handsome and still boyish-looking in his early forties. While sexually attractive, he does not look sexually aggressive; and there is nothing about him that might invite the jealous resentment of white male filmgoers or indeed feed the old but still potent racial fear of the over-endowed negro. Poitier operates in areas of conscience, not sex. He is usually presented as a charac-ter with a high degree of intelligence and manual skills. And because he is so emotionally true and honest an actor, he is some-thing of an example as well as a reproach to white filmgoers. He emphasises in a comforting way some of the uncomfortable facts of interdependence between blacks and whites. This is what gives his films their liberal thrust, but also their essential compromise.

The Defiant Ones (1958) chronicled the manhunt of two manacled fugitives and showed the growth of understanding between a black man and a white one who start off loathing each other, but in attempting to save their own skins come to ignore the fact that their skins are different colours. The film had verbal bite and graphic performances, but these actually helped conceal its total irrelevance to the real issue. It did indeed demonstrate that black and white can co-exist, but ignored the fact that co-existence *in society* is what the race problem is all about. By making both the protagonists outcasts from society, on the run from the law, it evaded the real issue and turned itself into a placebo for middle-class white consciences; while many of the dialogue sequences had Poitier speaking lines like the one to Tony Curtis, just after saving him from drowning, 'I didn't pull you out, I kept you from pulling me in', that were guaranteed to assuage any suspicions among black filmgoers that their racial integrity was being got at. Nowadays the last scene where Poitier cradles the white man in his arms and pumps out his defiance in the ringing ballad *Long Gone* tends to arouse the derision of black separatists.

The scene is virtually a reprise of one in an earlier Poitier film, *Edge of the City* (1957: retitled in Britain, *A Man is Ten Feet Tall*), though this time it is the white man who weeps for his black buddy. Directed by Martin Ritt, its novelty was to portray the urban black American as not only the white man's equal, but actually his superior in every way – optimistic, adaptable, intelligent, skilled and economically secure compared with John Cassavetes's white social misfit. A clever reversal of racial stereotypes, it made its pitch for the black man's dignity by intimating that he could well spare a few feet to enhance the white man's stature.

Edge of the City was sincerely acted, particularly by Poitier, but nowadays such a thesis rather takes one's breath away by the enormity of its presumption. *Something of Value* (1957) is a poorer film in every way, but Poitier's soured nobility as a Mau-Mau rebel leaves a slightly better taste in the mouth: at least it *implies* the case for separatism, even if what it *argues* is the case for assimilation.

The virtue of Poitier the actor lies in his ability to give individual humanity to a racial stereotype; and one sympathises deeply with his often-expressed wish to play a role without reference to the character's colour. Once or twice he has done so. In *The Bedford Incident* (1965) he was a news photographer and in *The Lilies of the Field* (1963) a hesitant good samaritan who is pressed into service by a colony of none-too-gentle nuns. His race does not matter in such roles because in the first he is a relatively passive observer and his colour simply serves to give variety to an all-male cast, while in the second he is active only within the perimeter of the nuns' divinely inspired society whose Utopian nature is camouflaged by the amusingly worldly way in which they put the screw on their hapless helpmeet.

The disturbing thing about Poitier is that he sometimes has seemed genuinely unable to distinguish between the intention of a film and its actual effect – possibly because the former is usually so good, so safely liberal. Two curious examples of this blind spot are films in which he played, in effect, the negro who presents no problem at all to society because no one sees him. It is one of the commonest neuroses of the black race in America that because a negro is often 'ignored' by white people, either out of shame or antipathy, he begins to feel he is not there at all, that he is an invisible man. In *The Slender Thread* (1966) Poitier institutionalised this phenomenon without perhaps being aware that he was doing so. He played a social service volunteer manning an S.O.S. telephone post which kept would-be suicides hanging on the line till help reached them – and of course the suicidal whites on the other end of the line had no idea they were talking to a negro. It is another example of a well-meaning film that 'solves' its problem by shutting its eyes to it. The telephone 'gimmick' might have rung with a more sardonic truth had it relayed the message 'Tell Your Troubles to a Negro – He Understands.'

In *A Patch of Blue* (1966) the pathos came from the fact that the young girl befriended by a stranger in the park stays literally blind to the fact of his blackness. The result certainly promotes racial tolerance. But the lesson that 'None are so well integrated as those who can't see' seems a high price to pay for it.

*   *   *

Poitier said about one of his most popular recent films, *To Sir, With Love* (1967): 'People are not coming to see me [but] to be exposed to a feeling, a reassurance that love is a force in human affairs . . .' It was a perceptive comment and one supported by the poll taken by the distributors who were so astonished by the success of a modestly budgeted movie that they attempted to find out what people *liked* about the film. Its setting in London's East End, where a black teacher with problems eventually wins out, was an advantage for American audiences. It removed the film a safe distance from their own racial tensions in the classrooms, although Poitier's problems barely touched on his own colour: an omission that threw doubt on the film's picture of the English social scene, but also permitted British audiences to enjoy it for the 'reassurance' – i.e. unreality – of its sentiments.

Guess Who's Coming to Dinner appealed to the same integrationist groups as *To Sir, With Love* and for much the same reason. Though race was an issue in the intermarriage story, Poitier's world-famous doctor was eminent enough to be a social catch for any family; and the old race-prejudice angle was snidely shifted on to the coloured maid who had absorbed what would have been the outlook of her employers in a less enlightened Hollywood era.

In the Heat of the Night (1967) appeared at a time when Civil Rights were getting legal sanction in many areas of life, and the film even improved on this theme. The Poitier character in it was not only given the support of the Law, but he *was* the Law. His tenacious Northern detective operating in the cotton country, despite the embittered discouragement of Rod Steiger's 'poor white' sheriff, was like a black bloodhound on the scent of the Deep South's old prejudices. It is the best of all the films in which Poitier has played the white man's superior, for he was allowed, or insisted on having, his moments of race resentment when the negro stops showing his silver lining on the outside and looms like a dark cloud on the white man's territory. Poitier for once gave signs of identifying with his own hue and race and not the opposite pigmentation. And in doing so he anticipated the crucial element in the breakthrough of other black film stars – and indeed in his own evolution. Henceforth anyone who has black stardom as his aim will have to define his relationship to his own people – to the new consciousness that black Americans have acquired in the ferment of the last four or five years.

The negro revolution in America, coupled with political assassinations and urban violence, has violently altered the assumptions of the past and is ruthlessly setting new values and goals for the future. No longer is integration of the races the imperative solution: for a sizeable part of the black community it has become a free option to be taken up or not. The traumatic pressure of events has created a new identity for black Americans which can exist independently of the white man's world; and they will wish to see their own dreams and aspirations similarly reflected in culture and entertainment as well as politics. There are plenty of signs that this is making its impact on Hollywood. And once a socio-cultural pattern of this kind has been formulated, new stars will be found emerging to fill it and old ones adjusting their images to match it.

*   *   *

It would be reassuring to imagine that racial and political sympathies were the principal considerations behind Hollywood's new policy of giving other black actors besides Poitier the chance of stardom. But it is unlikely that this was the case. The same considerations apply to black stars as to white. They are *accepted* by filmgoers for a variety of social and individual reasons: but they are *created* for relatively simple economic ones. Black becomes even more beautiful in the eyes of a Hollywood producer when it is also box-office.

The value of the black box-office was not really recognised till 1967 when market surveys showed that although negroes comprised only ten to fifteen per cent of the population, they accounted for nearly thirty per cent of the total patronage of first-run cinemas in the big cities. Readers of *Ebony*, the most influential negro magazine, reported that they spent nearly half-a-million dollars a week in filmgoing; and the grosses running into eight figures for Poitier's two films, *To Sir, With Love* and *In the Heat of the Night*, brought the lesson unmistakably home to Hollywood. 'The Negro is important to distribution and exhibition', said a *Variety* editorial. 'This must in turn increase the case for a more open-minded use of Negro actors in the production side of the industry.'*

Signs that Poitier was responding to the altered racial consciousness of Black America, and Hollywood's economic reappraisal of it, came swiftly with his film *For Love of Ivy* (1968), the first to be produced for his own company. From the 7,500 dollars he had got for his first film, *No Way Out* (1950), he had climbed to 300,000 dollars after his Oscar-winning role in *The Lilies of the Field*. With his box-office power confirmed by his recent successes, he was free to exercise power over his pictures. *For Love of Ivy* was based on a story of his own. Its theme seems

* *Variety*, 29th November 1967.

cosily conventional at first glance: a love affair between Ivy, a negro maid in a white household, and a wheeler-dealer businessman (Poitier) who runs a mobile craps game when the store is closed. The film even patronises the blacks in several ways. The romance is 'promoted' by the two spoilt brats of the white family Ivy works for so as to keep her happy and stop her quitting her job; for except that she is female and coloured, Ivy is not very different from Hollywood's old stereotype of the English butler in prewar comedies who bosses his boss and his boss's terrible family.

To even up the score, though, the white family was satirised as a group which had all the ulcerated marks of its individual members' success drives and hang-ups. The film's claim to reflect the new black consciousness rests on the attention it devotes to the sex life of its two black stars, Poitier and Abbey Lincoln, which is examined with a warmth and candour hitherto reserved for white or white-and-black relationships. Black filmgoers must have found it a fairly novel experience to see love and sex develop between black characters in a film that had not got an all-negro cast. Poitier has said, 'I thought I would like to make a film that was in a way a recognition of the negro woman's existence, and to say that I think she's beautiful.'* It was also an attempt to make good the shortcomings of his earlier film roles which had limited him very drastically to fulfilling the plot function, leaving out of the characters he played those personal interests like love, marriage or sex life which might have interfered with his acceptance by white filmgoers. Even in the South, which accounts for fourteen per cent of the domestic film market, a Poitier picture has seldom run into this kind of trouble.

But Poitier did not make the decisive break with his own screen image until his next film. It was in *The Lost Man* (1969) that he laid his racial sympathies militantly on the line. Carol Reed had used the novel on which it is based, *Odd Man Out*, for his Irish thriller in 1947; and writer-director Robert Alan Aurthur, whose collaboration with Poitier embraces the screenplay of *For Love of Ivy* and goes as far back as the script for *The Defiant Ones*,

* *Newsweek*, 11th December 1967.

re-located the story in the Black Power struggle and projected Poitier, in dark glasses, as a kind of Malcolm X planning to rob an all-white factory in order to feed the children of soul brothers languishing in jail. The motivation is overly senti-mental. But the film's emotion is separatist and revolutionary. Poitier clinches it at one point when he says, 'Non-violence is one thing, passive dying is another'.

The same ability to humanise and personalise the negro, which saved many of his goody-goody roles from being stereotypes, serves him well in the opposite extreme. The thoughtful and well-adjusted negro who competed with whites by his skilled labour, or showed them up by his moral superiority, has been replaced by a wised-up enemy of white society who looks on violence as a self-justifying act of rebellion. It is too early to say what effect this may have on his box-office popularity. The question may be not: Will it eliminate the white audiences? but rather: Can he align black ones behind it? For if Poitier's early image of the well-adjusted negro assuages white guilt at the wrongs that had been done to black Americans and fed the wrongdoers' need for atonement with a consoling and even entertaining character, the transference of this good-will may still make the kind of black activist in *The Lost Man* a palatable figure *so long as he is played by Poitier*. Familiarity also breeds respect. But to get himself accepted as a negro militant by black filmgoers, Poitier may need to go in for a more radical change of image off screen, too. And this is hard, now that he has taken his place in the superstar Establish-ment: a producer of his own and possibly other people's films, a partner of Paul Newman and Barbra Streisand in their own production outfit, First Artists, and a star who gets a million dollars a picture and possibly participates in the profits when he works for other companies.

To reproach Poitier with not making Black Power films earlier is irrelevant: for until society changed, that genre of film did not exist. All his skilful energy was being used to create a film star who was also black. And that was a hard enough labour. Now that he has proved it possible, it may be up to others to give the colour a more definite application to racial upheaval, aided by the film industry's appreciation that now there is also a good box-office reason for social change.

*   *   *

By the end of the 1960s several major film companies had hired black publicists or public relations firms specialising in the negro market; black character actors were appearing more frequently in pictures; and a couple of the studios seemed to be 'running' a particular black player as a candidate for the more militant breed of black star whose roles are shaped to make it easy and attractive for the average black American to identify with him. Calvin Lockhart, Raymond St Jacques and Jim Brown all had pictures built round them projecting these new elements.

One of them was an emphasis on the black man's sexuality, the quality that Poitier had played down until recently in favour of a more generalised virility. Though violent sex between the races, like the rape scene between Brown and Raquel Welch in *100 Rifles* (1969), was toned down by such old ploys as making the white actress a half-caste girl in the script and darkening her body tan during the semi-nude clinch, there were also love scenes between blacks like those of St Jacques in *If He Hollers, Let Him Go* (1969) designed to put black passions on an emotional parity with those of the whites. (*For Love of Ivy* had shown how well this paid off at the box-office.)

Poitier had nearly always steered clear of roles which cast him as the 'heavy'. St Jacques has had no need to be so cautious. He passed from the vicious Haitian chief of police in *The Comedians* to personifying Black Power on its own turf in Jules Dassin's *Up-Tight* (1969) in which his black separatist leader equated the death of Martin Luther King with the end of passive resistance and the birth of armed revolt. He defined the negro in terms of his own 'negritude'. Roles like these have obviously more of the quality called 'gut and soul' for the actor playing them than the earlier range of parts which related the black man to the white community.

It is the former Cleveland Browns football star, Jim Brown, who has been most conspicuously groomed to follow Poitier's success on the screen. Brown's image is that of the cool man of action, not specifically lined up with either blacks or whites though inevitably claimed by the former, especially when a screenplay presents him as the hero-victim of white violence. In both *Dark of the Sun* (1967: U.S. released in Britain as *The Mercenaries*) and *The Dirty Dozen* (1967) he was killed by Germans. Such killers would first of all be regarded as white men by a negro audience and only then as Nazi mercenaries or the wartime enemy. There is an obvious parallel here with the numbers of black casualties among American forces in Vietnam. The negro is on the white man's side, runs the implicit argument, but he is the one who is most frequently being bayoneted or shot.

An excellent example of 'injustice' occurred in *Ice Station Zebra* (1968), a submarine adventure about the Cold War appropriately set above and below the Polar ice cap. Brown played a U.S. Marines captain. The role allowed him to project those cold qualities he has abstracted from other contemporary screen heroes – the gangster part he played in *The Split* (1968) had been meant for Lee Marvin – by pulling his captain's rank on the white lieutenant and vowing that no officer whose men liked him could be worth a damn. A British intelligence agent, played by Patrick McGoohan, believes there is a Russian counter-spy aboard the submarine and suspicion settles round Brown. Actually the real spy is Ernest Borgnine, as Brown discovers at the very moment Borgnine has stunned McGoohan with a baling hook. In the ensuing fight the negro gets hold of the hook, only to be shot dead by the reviving McGoohan who assumes that *he* was his assailant. Once again it is the black man who is the victim.

The Mexican western, *100 Rifles*, also managed an oblique comment on the contemporary position of the two races. Brown plays a Texas deputy sheriff, though it is made plain he has the job because no one else – i.e., no white man – wanted it. And when he unpins his badge at the end and releases his half-breed prisoner to lead the peasants' revolt instead of taking him back to jail, the law's conventional surrender to the cause of freedom is backed by the negro's implied distaste for doing the white man's work for him.

Brown has insisted that he does not want to be thought of as a specifically negro actor. But he and his fellows will find it hard to resist the pressures – not all of which come from the box-office – to relate their roles to social upheaval. Poitier's films described the place of the negro in a white society; and the values of the society were instinctively understood by the white men who made the pictures even when they did not figure explicitly in the stories. Now that such values are challenged, something more than black stars is needed to embody alternatives. The need is for directors, producers and writers of the same colour and racial consciousness as their stars. The good intentions of white liberals are no longer enough. Jules Dassin's *Up-Tight* was a fatally confused and over-wrought film, very much the work of a white man looking in from the outside. And *If He Hollers, Let Him Go!* was patronisingly false to all but a few aspects of its coloured hero-victim.

Negro stars will emerge and, like all stars, contribute powerful new personalities to the screen. But personalities will not be enough to ask for from these stars. They will have to contribute a far more complex entity to the process of projection and participation that goes on between the star and his audience. This entity is the new consciousness of their own race.

CHAPTER TWENTY-TWO

OUTLOOK:
FADING STARS
AND
ANTI-STARS

As the American cinema enters the 1970s one of the most frequently pondered questions is, have the stars had their day? It is
ironical to hear such doubts being voiced at the very moment
when the stars have been drawing rewards in the shape of fees
and percentage deals which would have seemed in the realm of
fantasy to their studio-reared predecessors. In trying to answer
it, one has to be careful not to fall into the trap referred to by
Paul Mayersberg and assume that the end of the star phenomenon
is at hand because we mistake a stage of transition for a terminal
point. 'The history of Hollywood,' says Mayersberg, 'has covered
the lifetime of a human being or star. We have not yet got used to
the comings and goings of stars that in a hundred years will
probably seem natural.'*

Nevertheless the increasing hazards facing a film industry no
longer underpinned by the star system have been accompanied
by a rising scepticism about the value of having stars at all.
'Established stars no longer bring any insurance to a film production,' a top executive of California's Bank of America, one of
Hollywood's two main sources of finance, affirmed at the start of
1969. It would have sounded like heresy to Mayer, Thalberg,
Zukor, Cohn or the Warner Brothers. But to the newer breed of
studio boss, it is only sound business sense. Stars have lost their
power at the very moment they have cashed in on their profits.

The reasons for this are exceedingly complex and embrace every
aspect of film-making and social change; but a few of them at

* *Hollywood The Haunted House*, by Paul Mayersberg (Allen Lane, The
Penguin Press), p. 82.

least can be specifically identified and others can be deduced from the evidence. One major cause has been simply the increased difficulty in remaining a film star. With far fewer films being made, there have been correspondingly fewer opportunities, such as the old formula pictures used to provide, for keeping oneself prominently in view on the screen. Except for specific markets, the formula picture is a thing of the past. The B-picture, once the testing ground for star potential, was killed off by television – or, rather, it was absorbed into television via the filmed series, a format that has certainly produced stars, but type-cast them even more ruthlessly than a Hollywood studio did in its days of power. Instead of playing one 'type', such stars play simply one 'part'.

The fewer films that do get made are assembled with far greater anxiety over their need to succeed in order to recoup their cost. The proliferation of talents that now work on major movies has stretched out the shooting time to the point where the stars can virtually drop out of public sight for the better part of a year or more. William Holden said in 1967: 'Where I used to work thirty to forty days on a picture before the war, I can now count on six months per picture. I spent eight and a half months on *The Bridge on the River Kwai*.' For blockbuster movies, schedules of a year for the major stars have not been uncommon.

One of the factors adding to the shooting time has been the power that a star can now exercise during the shooting, either because the picture is for his own company and he has hired the director or because the necessity of protecting his box-office power compels him to intervene whereas under the old system he would not have risked suspension. 'The star today works more closely with the director and needs at least to be a consultant in the production,' said Gregory Peck in 1966. The words 'at least' signify a starting line, not an agreed perimeter. Even when his office as president of the Screen Actors' Guild prohibited Charlton Heston from producing his own films, the star had director approval and certain rights that extended to the way the film was edited.

This is nothing new in itself. Power was exercised in similar ways by the stars who turned producers in the 1920s. But in those days the production system had the resiliency of a growth industry. Nowadays the 'hit' that a film makes has got to be as spectacular as the time, money and hopes consumed in making it. And if a 'miss' is recorded instead, whatever the possible reasons it is the old shibboleth figures of the stars who suffer most of the recriminations.

*   *   *

The backlash against the stars has always been fiercest at periods in Hollywood's history when the industry is embroiled in economic crisis. It happened towards the end of the 1920s when the stars' escalating salaries threatened the producers' prosperity until the arrival of the talkies providentially gave the latter back the upper hand. It happened again at the end of the 1930s, as evidenced by the notorious red-bordered advertisement placed by a group of exhibitors in a trade paper which listed the stars who were deemed to be 'box-office poison'. The war came just in time to keep Hollywood going full blast till well into the 1940s.

Fresh evidence of the industry's disenchantment with the stars was recently provided by a long analysis, published in *Variety,* of the American stars who were alleged to be poor investments for the money they were paid. The animus this time came from 'exhibitor organisation spokesmen complaining that the performers' "outrageous" salary demands unwarrantably inflated the terms that theatres must pay for films.' All the stars under scrutiny were said to 'command fees of 250,000 dollars or more per picture, all were at one time or for a long time box-office magnets, and all have at least four recent consecutive flops.'* The names included those of Marlon Brando, Yul Brynner, Tony Curtis, Glenn Ford, James Garner, William Holden, Rock Hudson, Anthony Quinn and Natalie Wood. Miscasting, poor quality films, unwise attempts to break their image, the problem of ageing gracefully into later middle-age: these were some of the reasons suggested for their decline.

But a more generally significant reason is probably the change in the filmgoing audience. It used to be securely based on the

* *Variety,* 15th May 1968.

wide spread of middle age, middle income and middle class values. It liked to see its stars embodying appropriate qualities and to have instantly recognisable traits that did not vary greatly from one picture to the next. Paul Mayersberg was thinking of this kind of audience when he wrote, 'We like to see our heroes over and over again in the same situation. . . . Reproduction of the performances on film and repetition of the performances from film to film are both part of the same process.'* But the new audience for American films is vastly different. Not only is it younger and more complex, as a previous chapter has shown, but it is apathetic to the whole idea of movie stars as creatures of a separate breed or more mysterious charisma than all the other 'stars' – protest leaders, politicians, pop artists, polemical writers, singers and underground talents, notable drop-outs, revolutionaries and martyrs – whom the mass media project with an immediacy and intimacy that makes the style of older Hollywood stars look *passé* and remote.

The members of this audience do not want film stars who embody their dreams: they go for stars who provide sanctions for their own behaviour, attitudes and philosophy. The sanction role of the star is one that he or she must play if the loyalty of the new audience is to be secured; but it is one that most of the traditional stars are least well equipped to fill. They lack the sense of identity with their audience. They are the wrong age. They do not see the world in terms that win sympathy from the new generation. They have commitment all right, but it is usually to their own careers and ego satisfactions. They lack the aptitude for taking up a life style that is foreign to them, even when a film role is specially designed to supply this deficiency.

Only exceptionally in recent years has a well-established star broken through to the new young audience in a way that makes him, temporarily at least, their representative. Anthony Quinn was one who managed it. The character he played in *Zorba the Greek* (1964) evoked a spontaneous response because it represented a free spirit unfettered by convention, taking life as it turned up and living each moment to the full regardless of consequences.

* Paul Mayersberg, op. cit., p. 70.

For the complexities of life, Zorba had an engagingly simple philosophy: 'To dance, one must be a little mad.' Zorba was a spiritual guru well before such holy men became part of the scene and, as such, an uncannily prophetic embodiment of the life style of the hippy generation which was at least twenty-five to thirty years younger than the star. No subsequent role of Quinn's has got through to the same audience, though an attempt was made in a film aimed so calculatingly at the youth market that it was called *The Happening* (1967). He played a Mafia boss who teaches his teenage kidnappers how to get a superior ransom for him. But a movie that set a high price on an adult's self-esteem was a poor bet with adolescent filmgoers from the start. When Zorba danced, nothing jingled in his pockets.

The life-style stars, in contrast, represent a sharp break with the established conception of a leading man. The complexities of living, which they sanction in their respective ways, allow little room for the old 'ideal' qualities of stardom. They are in fact stars who have come near to being character actors – and this is another reason why the traditional identity marks of the film star are fading. The star today is having to trust as much in varying his roles as his predecessor did in repeating his personality in film after film.

Rod Steiger is the leading example of someone who has emerged as a major actor *and star* without resorting to any single audience image of himself. None could have been successfully created, for his roles have been so varied and his performances so chameleon. Steiger himself would have resisted the standard star build-up from the outside; for if anything links all the parts he has played it is not a specific theme, but a general approach. It is the use he makes of acting to explore himself.

Steiger was once asked in an interview: 'What relationship do you see between the psychiatric treatment you have received and the theme of isolation in your acting?' In reply he refused to narrow things down so precisely, but said; 'I think it's obvious that psychiatry, the study of human behaviour, is therefore very close to the art of acting ... it has made me more aware of myself, and therefore helped me to be more aware of my fellow

men. Now I observe little things and idiosyncracies in people I
might have overlooked in them, because I refused to recognise
them in myself before that. . . . As far as isolation is concerned, I
understand more why I'm an autonomous personality than I did
recently. I understand why I like to be alone more than I did.'*
The increase in self-awareness which Steiger alludes to has come
at the same time as audiences are wanting to know more about what
is going on inside their screen heroes. Private need thus coincides
with public demand.

Now although Brando has used acting for similar therapeutic
purposes, as has already been noted, some deep protectiveness in
his nature, a wish perhaps to insulate himself against the hurts he
has suffered in his career, whether at the hands of others or self-
inflicted, seems to have grown a skin round the characters he has
created on the screen in recent years. His performances remain
extraordinarily skilful, but do not manage to touch the painful
quick of life as Steiger's do. Perhaps the Brando that the younger
generation could fully respond to belongs in films like *The Wild
One* and *On the Waterfront* which are now on the wrong side of the
age group. He casts a deeper spell nowadays when he takes part
in protest marches and civil rights campaigns which give direct
sanction to sentiments he embodied in his early films.

*   *   *

It is partly fear of the younger generation's apathy towards
them that has encouraged some of the established stars to take on
character parts that hardly fit their accustomed images. This
applies particularly to the last wave of conventional stars signed
up by producers or studios between 1946 and 1948. Thus Rock
Hudson, a laconic playboy in the Doris Day sex comedies,
appeared as the middle-aged businessman† in *Seconds* (1966)
rejuvenated by miracle surgery to become a free-living member of
the Big Sur artist set. Kirk Douglas adopted a heavy set of
character traits including a thick moustache – the Zapata model

---

* *Cinema*, December 1968.

† Actually the ageing Hero at the start of the film was played by a
different actor.

was then hanging on every hippy lip – to play a veteran Mafia boss in *The Brotherhood* (1968) who cannot compete with the new breed of assassin-accountants moving in on him. In Elia Kazan's *The Arrangement* (1969) Douglas played a successful executive disenchanted with the same values of society as were being rejected by the younger generation of Americans. Burt Lancaster had already a couple of anti-Lancaster roles behind him – as the *Birdman of Alcatraz* (1961) and the Sicilian prince in *The Leopard* (1963) – but he sought a more specific identification with the contemporary mood when he played the drop-out hero of *The Swimmer* (1967) who is dazed by the reflection of his own failure in every ex-urbanite's swimming-pool.

It is scarcely accidental that all three stars accepted roles which dealt with fears of inadequacy, uncertainty about the future and anxiety over growing old. But it was Tony Curtis who took the most dramatic step to realign his career with a contemporary youth audience after a severe bout of rejection at the box-office in a string of farces. He switched to a new agent and reportedly took a cut in salary to 100,000 dollars in order to secure the title role in *The Boston Strangler* (1968). He sacrificed quite a number of his star attributes. The film required him to alter his familiar looks; it did not even show him on the screen till an hour of running time had passed; and it played down the strangler's physical violence in favour of analytical scenes that would allow Curtis to profit from the audience's interest in the in-depth reporting of present-day folk figures, whether they were presidential candidates or multiple killers.

Curtis could hardly have gone further in sincerely trying to avoid the traps of star casting, yet some critics complained that by comparison with the film *In Cold Blood* (1968), which used two unknowns to impersonate the real-life murderers, *The Boston Strangler* was guilty of exploiting its grisly material for the greater glory and advancement of Tony Curtis. However shakily based this criticism is, it demonstrates that stardom is no longer a quality that transfers acceptably to all manner of roles. It can now be a handicap, even a stigma in some parts. No one attacked the film *I Want to Live* (1957) because Barbara Graham, the B-girl

convicted of murder and sent to the gas chamber, was played by
Susan Hayward. In those days such a part was invariably called
'unsympathetic' – i.e., the star risked her popularity by playing
it – even though Susan Hayward in fact remained highly 'sympathetic'. But nowadays it would almost be considered unethical to
cast such a role from the ranks of established stars, especially if the
film itself had no bias against, say, the death penalty but simply
confined itself to analysing the convicted man or woman's personality. The star's personality would be considered harmful to
this enquiry and raise doubts about the makers' integrity. Only a
very 'committed' star like Steiger might have undertaken the
Strangler role without fear of reproach.

Such attempts by established stars to remould their images have
scarcely been breakthrough successes: in Hudson's case it was
nearly disastrous. But their reverses were just part of a more widespread scepticism about the value of having stars at all in view of
the fact that pictures without stars were doing better business
than those with them. Evidence of this began piling up from 1968
onwards in the shape of the huge box-office profits made by
films whose 'stars' were either relative unknowns or else played
inconsiderable parts. *The Graduate*, released in January 1968, had
grossed 39 million dollars in North America by the end of the
year; *Rosemary's Baby* released in June 1968, made 12,300,000
dollars over the same period; *2001: A Space Odyssey*, released in
April 1968, made 8,500,000 dollars; *Valley of the Dolls,* released
in December 1967, made 20 million dollars.* Yet not one of these
phenomenally successful movies was sold on the strength of a
single star name. No one had heard of Dustin Hoffman, and only
television's *Peyton Place* fans knew Mia Farrow before *The
Graduate* and *Rosemary's Baby*. Instead it was the 'total concept' of
their films which constituted their appeal for predominantly
young audiences. Beneath the sardonic satire of the first half of
The Graduate, which reproduced the Mike Nichols–Elaine May
style of cellar cabaret in the seduction of the college boy by the
older sophisticate, there was a solid rejection of hypocritical
adult values. At the same time the second half of the film was a

* Such grosses are still climbing at the time of writing.

confirmation of youthful rebellion and belief in a relationship based on true love.

Rosemary's Baby is harder to relate to its audience's life-style. But the psychologist Rollo May put forward a plausible explanation by relating the attractiveness of its witchcraft theme to 'the disintegration of familiar myths that leaves individuals alienated and adrift'.* *Bonnie and Clyde* (1967) anticipated both these films. Its story of doomed youth united in a hail of machine-gun bullets after a brief exhilarating career as rebels with charmed lives, and the freedom from convention which distinguished Arthur Penn's style of telling it: such elements mattered far more than the one name, Warren Beatty, which had previously meant anything at the box-office.

The success of *Goodbye, Columbus* (1969), whose young lovers fought and lost against the constrictions of family and racial traditions, was further evidence that youth goes for the picture, not the people in it. Stanley Kubrick's awesome conception of space was what made *2001: A Space Odyssey* so successful financially, not Keir Dullea or Gary Lockwood as the astronauts: their human interest was in any case less than that of HAL 9000 the all-too-human computer. (Kubrick had become absolutely set against 'star' names for the film when one second-magnitude Hollywood star with whom he had opened negotiations began the bargaining with a demand for his name to precede the picture's.) *Valley of the Dolls* may have depended less on a specifically youth appeal than on its best-seller origins. But it certainly did *not* depend on anyone of importance in it.

What reinforced this general trend against the stars was evidence suggesting how other pictures that were built solidly and expensively around star talent were proving box-office disappointments. *The Comedians,* starring Elizabeth Taylor and Richard Burton, released in December 1967, was quoted as grossing a meagre 2,800,000 dollars by the end of 1968 in North America. *Boom* (1968), with the same stars, and *Reflections in a Golden Eye* (1967), where Brando was Taylor's co-star, have also been less successful than they ought to have been with such stars,

* *Time,* 7th February, 1969.

judged by the extent of their fame and the amount of their fees.

No less an authority than Darryl F. Zanuck conceded, in mid-1969, that both *Doctor Doolittle* (1967) and *Star!* (1967), two costly musicals built round their stars, were proving box-office disappointments. Yet one of them starred Rex Harrison, the other Julie Andrews, artists commanding fees of at least a million dollars and probably a percentage of the gross profits. Even with conventional filmgoers – not simply those in the 16- to 24-year-old bracket – the power of stars was on the wane.

*   *   *

Stars once guaranteed the profitability of routine, even mediocre films: now they can no longer be banked on to recover the enormously increased cost of today's films to which their own swollen salaries as well as the escalating fees of others on the production side have contributed. 'The movie companies have lost control of their product,' the then president of M-G-M, Louis 'Bo' Polk, was quoted as saying in mid-1969. 'They don't develop their own actors any more, don't develop directors, don't develop writers. Instead of using packagers, they're at the packager's mercy.'* This complaint was simply an updated version of the sarcastic old welcome given to the stars' own company, United Artists, just fifty years earlier, by the president of Metro Pictures Corp., Richard Rowland; 'So the lunatics have taken charge of the asylum.' The only difference now is that the lunatics include just about everyone who is anyone on a picture.

Yet it is the discredited gods and goddesses who feel most threatened by the rise of new powers and dominions inside the film industry. One of these has been the steady ascent to star status of the film director. Until recently this has been a factor foreign to Hollywood tradition. American films generally have not expressed the viewpoint of one distinguishable maker, or *auteur*, as in Europe, but have been popularly regarded as studio-made assemblies of talent grouped prominently around the stars. But as American directors, as well as stars, have gained their independence of the studios, they have been granted control over

* *Newsweek*, report by Joseph Morgenstern 30th June 1969.

many of the elements in the pictures. Public recognition has taken the form of putting the director's name above the title, where the stars' names used to be.

Perhaps the point of the accolade is missed by the mass public: inside the industry, though, the new ascendancy it signals is increasingly recognised by the actual power the director is given from first concept to final cut, so that the stars have to compete with him as equals, rather than rely on their power as potential tyrants, while filming is in progress. The director's new celebrity creates an envy which is no longer satisfied by the star simply setting up as his own producer; and it may explain the trend of stars expressing a dissatisfaction with their careers very early on and trying to set up as directors. The old type of star wanted to Be Someone; the new type wants to Fulfil Himself. The old type coveted better parts; the new type covets different skills.

But hardly has one noted the trends tending to devalue the stars than one must take account of a paradox. The phenomenal success of films with no stars in their cast has shown how unnecessary they are; yet this same success has resulted in the relative unknowns in the cast turning into celebrated stars. They do so far more spectacularly than any established star of the older group could ever have dreamed. They become instant stars on the strength of one movie and develop a charismatic power in proportion to the picture's financial success. They are in immediate demand to do the same for other films. If the film industry is aware of the contradictions in this, it does not pay much attention to them. The contribution made by other talents, the accident perhaps of hitting a public nerve when it is exposed to the picture's theme or mood, are ingredients that are not so easily identifiable or repeatable as the sheer bodily presence of Mia Farrow, Dustin Hoffman, Ali MacGraw, Jon Voight or whoever the next instant star may be.

The success of such stars cannot be moderate; it has to be immense. It cannot be gradual; it has to be instantaneous. The cost of the film has to be recouped so quickly that there is no time to allow the stars to mature. Instant stars have become an economically viable way of tackling the enormous hazards of an inflated film industry in which a movie that may take eighteen months to two years to make, and cost upwards of ten million dollars, has to gross two-and-a-half times this figure before a profit begins to be seen. The need to create stars as big as the required successes still mesmerises Hollywood.

At the same time the process has a hopeful corollary. It is the professed reluctance of such instant stars to regard themselves as stars in the accepted sense. They have become known as anti-stars and some of them have laboured, sometimes with suspicious ostentation, to make it plain that they reject the old styles and appearances of Hollywood stars. They do not live in Hollywood: more important, they do not invariably make their movies in Hollywood studios, or, indeed, in any studio if need be. They take on the coloration of a non-Hollywood background both at work and between pictures. They do not go in for conspicuous glamour, though they do go in for conspicuous casualness. They often dress the role of rebels as well as play it. They are immune from the fear of scandal in a way that probably no stars before them were, because they often sanction and set the style for the permissive behaviour of their audiences.

They have defence in depth if attacked by pressure groups; for the mass media, which also confront their audiences with far greater candour than ever before, are available to the anti-stars to propagate their views, four-letter words and all. Nor are they at all easily vulnerable, for most of them have a deep mistrust of acquiring material possessions that could represent a style of life they would fear to lose. Above all they have a horror of getting hung up in contractual obligations to make pictures that would limit their freedom. This is not to say that their careers are managed in an amateur flush of self-expression. Self-interest plays as steely a part as ever, though it is probably more subtly expressed since the overnight success is nowadays analysed as soon as day breaks and programmed to repeat the success by the time the sun sets again.

But one feature of the anti-star's life has definitely the solid hallmark of Hollywood on it, even though it may be deliberately left inconspicuous in contrast to the older stars who used to blazon it all over their persons. This is the money that these same anti-stars demand for appearing in pictures. If only one film returns a profit of phenomenal proportions, the anti-star is well on his way to asking for rewards to match in easy stages of a quarter of a million dollars or a sizable percentage of the film.

It is at this point that the posture adopted by the newcomers towards Hollywood begins to crumble into gold dust. The economic imperatives of the film industry are the hardest to escape from; its economic rewards are the hardest to resist. The anti-star posture may turn out to be just as much a fashion of the times as the old type of committed stardom was a reflection of the industry. The old fable of the emperor who convinced himself and his subjects that he had new clothes on, whereas he was nude, may yet acquire an appropriately contemporary twist if those who believe that they have cast off the trappings of stardom and go around boasting of their nakedness gradually discover that all they have done is alter the cut of a very old costume. Time will show.

APPENDIX ONE

To calculate just how much the stars of any particular decade were worth in real money and purchasing power, one needs to know just how much the dollar and the pound sterling were worth over the same period. It is hoped that the following tables will provide the reader with a rough but revealing guide to the value in wealth and power of the star salaries, production costs, etc., mentioned in the text·

	Official dollar-sterling rates of exchange (end of each five years)		Equivalent sterling purchasing power of 100 dollars
1915	$4.75	1967	£42
1920	$3.54	1965	£38
1925	$4.87	1960	£45
1930	$4.87	1955	£52
1935	$4.93	1950	£68
1940	$4.03	1945	£58
1945	$4.03	1940	£75
1950	$2.80	1935	£77
1955	$2.80	1930	£72
1960	$2.80	1925	£65
1965	$2.80	1920	£63
1967	$2.40	1915	£94

APPENDIX TWO

Florence Lawrence was the most prominent among the early contract players who were publicised by name from 1910 onwards. The article reprinted below is probably the first substantial interview given by such a star. It appeared in the Sunday Magazine section of the St Louis Post-Dispatch, 20th March 1910, about a week before Florence Lawrence's personal appearance in the city of St Louis. (A shorter interview with the film actress was published a week later, 27th March in *The St Louis Star*.)

The article is not by-lined; and it may have been intended as a trailer for the visit 'inspired' by Carl Laemmle's film company which owned Miss Lawrence's services. Nevertheless the interview gives a remarkably candid and detailed, if necessarily popular, account of movie-acting at that date; and in its natural reliance on terms in use on the legitimate stage, it catches the movie medium at just the point before it gained self-confidence as a separate art. Its emphasis on moving-picture actresses working as hard as, if not harder than, those on the stage is an important point in this context.

THE GIRL OF A THOUSAND FACES

Florence Lawrence, Three
Times Reported Dead but
Still Very Much Alive, Is
the Highest Paid Moving
Picture Actress – An Adept
in Pantomime She Rehearses
300 Rolls [*sic*] a Year, or
One for Each Working Day

An actress whose face is known to millions of people in the United States, but whose name is known to few, if any, is the girl whose lissom figure flashes through the comedies and dramas that are exposed on the screen in the thousands of moving-picture theatres in this country controlled by the independent film manufacturers. Her face is as well known, almost, in Europe, wherever American films are shown, as it is here.

This girl is known to the throngs of steady moving-picture show patrons who, like Elbert Hubbard, are known as 'moving-picture fiends', as 'The Girl of a Thousand Faces', and her stage name is Florence Lawrence.

Miss Lawrence, who is only 20 years old, has the distinction of being the highest-salaried moving picture actress in the United States, as well as the one who has been pictured in motion oftenest, whence her name 'The Girl of a Thousand Faces', but it might well be 'of a million faces'.

Miss Lawrence comes from Hamilton, Ontario, and like a great many Canadians who have come to 'the States' [she] made good quickly. Her name at home was Florence Solter, but when she went on the real stage she took the name of Lawrence.

Thousands of readers will readily recognise her pictures, herewith published for the first time in a newspaper, and will be sure to recall the many comedies and dramas in which they have seen her expressive features, which are so mobile that she is constantly expressing with them, in a manner that is quite as telling as spoken words, the emotions she is depicting.

Miss Lawrence suddenly leaped into newspaper publicity by the persistent reports of her violent death in New York on three different occasions. Each time the report was denied by her employers, the Independent Moving Picture Co., who vouchsafed the information that a rival film company had started the reports in the hope that her admirers on hearing of her death and believing that they would never see her again on a moving-picture screen would desert the independent theatres.

But the canard fell flat for to the thousands who read the report the name of Florence Lawrence meant nothing, but when they see her picture here they will recognise her at once and will rejoice that she is still living and at work playing in new 'canned drama' for their edification.

Quite recently Miss Lawrence signed a life contract to act exclusively for the 'Imp' company at a yearly salary of 15,000 dollars which is a pretty large stipend for a girl of her years, but not excessive when her popularity and drawing power to the theatres in which the films she is pictured on are shown is considered.

Miss Lawrence is now known as 'The Imp Girl' and every night when she appears on the screen in five or six thousand darkened 'nickelodeons' her pictures are cheered by the humble lovers of the silent drama, who have come to have a very high regard for the young girl who labours so hard to please them. There is no question that she is the most popular of the moving-picture players in this country.

To realise how hard Miss Lawrence must work to earn her 15,000 dollars a year, it needs to be known that she learns and rehearses 300 roles in one year, which is about 75 per cent more than the average hard-worked stock actress is compelled to assimilate. This means that she must accomplish about six a week – or one for each working day in the year.

This accomplishment is almost beyond belief, but there is a demand for the films and so long as the demand exists there must be a way of filling it.

Of course if Miss Lawrence had to commit to memory the dialogue of 300 plays a year the task whould be impossible, but she does not. She learns the roles she plays in pantomime. Maud Adams may charm an audience when she asks: 'Do you believe in fairies'? and the words carry her as far as her acting, but Miss Lawrence must make her pantomime do the work of both.

A movement of the lips, a glance of the eye, a contraction of the facial muscles, a gesture of arm or hand or a swaying of the body must take the place of speech, they are her only vehicles of getting the meaning of the play 'across the footlights'. She must make you see the laugh or the sigh or the sob in the story without a word to help her. This is the consummation of the art of acting.

'Do moving-picture performers speak while posing before the camera in the plays they are interpreting?' Miss Lawrence was asked.

'Some do and some do not,' she answered. 'I do even when I have to improvise speech that seems reasonable to the action. I simply must talk. Otherwise I find myself acting mechanically and without spirit and emotion.'

This is another feature of the intensity of the work imposed upon this girl in learning her 300 roles a year.

'How many rehearsals are necessary for the average film play?'

'Usually two are enough for me,' answered Miss Lawrence. 'The first is called a rehearsal for "mechanics". That is, we just go through the pantomime which the stage director tells us is necessary for that particular situation. Next we go through it "with feeling", as the saying is. Then we are ready for the camera. It often happens that in the same morning or afternoon, we are called upon to rehearse comedy, drama and tragedy one after the other. This is one of the most trying experiences that happens to the moving-picture performer who conscientiously tries to "feel" his part.'

'Did you ever feel stage fright in facing the moving-picture camera?'

'Oh, no. As a matter of fact I didn't realise the importance of the work I was doing. I was totally unaware that the time would come when this sort of acting would be criticised and judged as severely as that of the regular stage. I have seen many performers lose their nerve in front of the camera – old-timers, at that, who think nothing of acting before a vast throng of people. Others can't help from looking into the camera while they are performing, which is bad acting in this business, and something we are never supposed to do unless we have a situation that requires us to look directly at an audience.

'Moving-picture performers have much to contend with – even more than their brethren on the regular stage. Upon one occasion, which is but an instance of many, I saw a moving-picture actress collapse purely as a result of the strain caused by a defective camera. She had "gone through" the emotional rehearsal to the satisfaction of the stage director, and the scene was then begun for the camera. While she was at the height of her dramatic situation the film in the camera "buckled" and the whole scene had to be done over. This happened a second time, then a third. It was more than highstrung human nature could stand. The result was a swoon, not of the stage variety.'

'Do you ever go to the theatres and see yourself on the screen?' she was asked.

'Oh yes, most certainly,' was the smiling response. 'I like to go there, get off in a corner and listen to the comment. And when they applaud—you've no idea how strange it all seems and how much real happiness it means to me. I do not believe any artist glories more in the plaudits of an audience to which she is visible and can acknowledge than I do in the applause of the people who see me only in pictures. Once I was recognised by someone in the audience while I was watching my own pictures and it was simply awful. The word spread that I was in the theatre, and I was fairly mobbed for autographs. The first time I ever saw myself in a moving-picture was terribly disappointing. I looked clumsy to myself. My work seemed full of faults. It was annoying. I felt like going up to the picture on the screen and saying, "You goose, why didn't you do it this way instead of that way?" '

'In what sort of pictures do you like to appear?'

'I love the ones where I can ride horseback. I was born in Hamilton, and from the very earliest time [I] can remember I was always riding. The folks used to say that they never waited meals on me if they knew I was on horseback, for I'd rather ride than eat. When I am riding before the moving-picture camera, I really forget the picture and everything else. And I always act better in such scenes because I am not acting at all. I am just having fun.'

Another of the difficulties of the moving-picture actors is the public performance of their plays in public places, in the streets of large cities and small ones, in vacant lots, on the steps of public buildings and other places where crowds congregate and laugh or applaud or jeer as the spirit moves them.

'Do the idle crowds that gather about when you are performing in the open annoy you?' Miss Lawrence was asked.

'Oh, no, not particularly,' she replied. 'Children often delight in getting in front of the camera but I have found that grown-ups generally regard the proceedings with good nature and a good deal of interest. Sometimes, however, they are inclined to laugh and say and do things that would "rattle" a nervous actor, and then it is hard to forget the surroundings and play the part as called for.'

When she was asked if she received 'mash' notes such as are written to vaudeville performers and the women of the dramatic theatres and the musical shows Miss Lawrence flushed and laughed.

'Do I!' she exclaimed. 'Just look at these!' She produced from a large box bundle after bundle of letters, notes, picture postcards and what not. There were a lot of letters from boys and girls who were stage-struck for moving-picture show acting, who wanted to know what school of dramatic art she would advise; notes from dazzled youth and moneyed bachelors and fickle married men and merry widowers pledging everlasting love and devotion; a surprising number of requests from autograph hunters, even offers of marriage from men who claimed enough combined wealth to pay the national debt. There were letters from coast to coast, from Canada, from France, England, Germany, Australia and from Russia where, by the way, American moving-pictures are extremely popular.

'It may seem foolish, but I keep them all,' said Miss Lawrence. 'They are the direct evidence that out of the hundreds of thousands of people who see me on the screen every week there are many who regard me as a real, live human being and not just an automaton or a phantasy.'

As for being the most-photographed woman, Miss Lawrence claims the palm. For example, every moving-picture film contains 14 separate pictures to the foot, and the average film of a picture drama is 1,000 feet long. This means that Miss Lawrence is actually photographed 14,000 times six days a week, or in 300 films a year, which means that her picture is taken more than 4,000,000 times annually.

APPENDIX THREE

Role playing for the Hollywood stars of the 1920s did not stop when the day's filming ended. Fancy-dress parties characterise the play-world of the stars of this decade in a way that makes it seem the extension of the fantasy world of the silent screen. The following account of one of these events appeared in *Photoplay,* April 1926, and conveys the extraordinary social atmosphere of Hollywood at this time and the way in which the world's entertainers endeavoured to entertain themselves.

Hollywood society has talked of very little else recently but Marion Davies' costume ball held in the Ambassador ballroom and attended not only by all the most celebrated stars, but by a large number of titled and distinguished foreigners as well.

The big ballroom was turned by a decorator's art into a lavish and beautiful Hawaiian scene, two orchestras played the most enticing dance music and at midnight an elaborate supper was served at small separate tables scattered among the coconut palms.

Miss Davies herself appeared in the costume of a 19th century belle and I don't believe she has ever looked so pretty on or off the screen. . . . It was great fun to see Mr and Mrs Douglas Fairbanks enjoying themselves, dancing together like a couple of youngsters. They so seldom go to big parties. Mary was Lillian Gish, she said, and wore Miss Gish's little seamstress costume from *La Bohème* and Douglas was *Don Q.* in a dashing black Spanish costume. Mr and Mrs Charlie Chaplin were the Emperor Napoleon and the Empress Josephine. Charlie has always wanted to play Napoleon and he is always saying that when he gets ready to retire he will make one last picture of the 'Little Corporal's' life, playing the title role himself. He had a very lavish costume made of the Emperor's white uniform. Mrs Chaplin looked particularly lovely in an empire gown of sapphire blue velvet, and a lovely diamond coronet in her dark hair, which was piled high on her head.

Norma Talmadge was a Russian ballet girl, in a strikingly individual little dancing dress in scarlet and blue, with high black patent leather boots and a stiff little patent leather helmet. And Constance was a Dutch boy in bright blue satin pantaloons, her blonde hair worn straight and short like a little Hollander's. Buster Collier, who accompanied her, wore the outfit of a Bowery tough, topped by a brown derby

Tom Mix wore a pure white vaquero's outfit trimmed in silver, and Mrs Mix was a Victorian court lady, in purple velvet and ermine. The dress of that period and the hair dressed high gave her an opportunity to wear some of her most beautiful jewels, including a diamond tiara and a diamond collar of exquisite workmanship.

The costume voted by everyone the most beautiful was that designed for Florence Vidor by Banton, the Parisian designer. It was a Venetian affair of pure white tulle, with a tight fitting satin bodice above the frothy skirt, a tiny velvet hat with a black lace mantilla draped about it, and touching the oval of her face. George Fitzmaurice and Ronald Colman, who accompanied her, came in regulation clothes, as did Joe Schenck. Jack Barrymore was a tramp, with a large putty nose painted red and the most realistic suit of clothes that ever draped rags and tatters about a famous actor. But the hit of the evening among the men was Jack Gilbert, who came as 'Red Grange', his football togs topped by a flaming red wig of gigantic proportions.

Miss Lillian Gish looked like one of Jane Austen's heroines stepped straight from the pages of the book, in a little white frock and old-fashioned hair-dress. The Princess Bibesco, who is the house guest of

Mr and Mrs Fairbanks and the daughter of the Earl and Countess of Oxford and Asquith, came in the full court dress of Roumania. Her husband is the Roumanian minister to the United States. Her brother Anthony Asquith, was a toreador and Madame Elinor Glyn was a Spanish grande dame, in black velvet with a huge comb and graceful mantilla draped about her lovely red hair.

One of the most stunning costumes there was that of Bebe Daniels as Joan of Arc. Bebe had a suit of armour made of cloth of silver. Her high boots were of silver leather, over white silk tights. On her breast hung a flashing cross of diamonds and she carried a silver cross with a lot of diamonds outlining it. She wore a short black wig.

Colleen Moore was the cutest thing imaginable in blue satin overalls, an enormous straw hat, and a bright red wig.

The comedy sensation of the evening was Marshall Neilan and Alan Dwan as the Smith Brothers. They made up to look exactly like the well-known pictures on the boxes of cough drops, beards and all, and they were a riot everywhere they went. Norman Kerry was in the uniform of a French officer.

Mr and Mrs Charles Ray wore elaborate Spanish costumes and Lilyan Tashman was stunning in a ballet costume of black velvet and tulle, with very short skirts and full length black silk tights. She also wore a small, heart-shaped black velvet hat over a white silk wig. Anna Q. Nilsson was in peach velvet pantaloons and Renée Adorée was a French peasant girl. Corliss Palmer wore a hoop skirt of the Louis XVI period, in apricot satin with gold lace. Jack Pickford was a bellhop, Claire Windsor an Eton boy and Ann Pennington wore a white ballet outfit.

It will be a long time before this party is topped.

ACKNOWLEDGEMENTS

A complete bibliography of all the works consulted for this study would be too long to print here. But the author wishes to acknowledge his indebtedness to the writers and publishers of the following works quoted in the text:

Around Cinemas, by James Agate (Home & Van Thal, London, 1946)

The Autobiography of Cecil B. DeMille (Prentice Hall, New York, 1959; W. H. Allen & Co., London, 1961)

Behind the Screen, by Samuel Goldwyn (George H. Doran Co., New York, 1923)

Behind the Screen, by Kenneth Macgowan (Delacorte Press, New York, 1965)

Charlie Chaplin: Early Comedies, by Isabel Quigly (Studio Vista-Dutton Pictureback, 1968)

Le Cinéma Sonore, by Jean A. Keim (Editions Albin Michel, Paris, 1947)

Doug and Mary and a Few Others, by Allene Talmey (Macy Masius, New York, 1927)

Douglas Fairbanks: The Making of a Screen Character, by Alistair Cooke (Museum of Modern Art Film Library Series No. 2, 1940)

Film Technique and Film Acting, by V. I. Pudovkin, translated and edited by Ivor Montagu (Memorial Edition, Vision Mayflower, 1958)

George Arliss, by Himself (John Murray, London, 1940)

A Girl Like I, by Anita Loos (Hamish Hamilton, London, 1967: Viking Press Inc., New York, 1966)

Hollywood in the Twenties, by David Robinson (A. Zwemmer, London: A. C. Barnes & Co., New York, 1968)

Hollywood in Transition, by Richard Dyer MacCann (Houghton, Mifflin, Boston, 1962)

Hollywood on Trial, by Gordon Kahn (Boni & Gaer, New York, 1948)

Hollywood Rajah: The Life and Times of Louis B. Mayer, by Bosley Crowther (Holt, Rinehart & Winston, New York. 1960)

Hollywood The Dream Factory, by Hortense Powdermaker (Little, Brown & Co., Boston, 1950: Secker & Warburg, London, 1951)

Hollywood The Haunted House, by Paul Mayersberg, Allen Lane, The Penguin Press, London, 1968)

Hollywood: The Movie Colony, The Movie Makers, by Leo Rosten (Harcourt Brace, New York, 1941)

The House That Shadows Built, by Will Irwin (Doubleday Doran & Co., New York, 1929)

I Lost It at the Movies, by Pauline Kael (Little, Brown & Co., Boston, 1965: Cape, London, 1966)

The Italian Comedy, by Pierre Louis Duchartre (Dover Publications Inc., New York, 1966)

The Italians, by Luigi Barzini (Hamish Hamilton, London, 1964)

It Took Nine Tailors, by Adolphe Menjou (Stephen Low, Marston & Co., London, 1950)

The Kindness of Strangers, by Salka Viertel (Holt, Rinehart & Winston, New York, 1969)

King Cohn, by Bob Thomas (Putnams, New York, 1967: Barrie & Rockliff, London, 1967)

King of Comedy, by Mack Sennett as told to Cameron Shipp (Garden City, New York, Doubleday & Co., Inc., 1954)

The Life and Adventures of Carl Laemmle, by John Drinkwater (Heinemann, London, 1931)

The Lonely Life, by Bette Davis (G. P. Putnam's Sons, New York, 1962)

The Memoirs of Will H. Hays (Doubleday, New York, 1955)

A Million and One Nights, by Terry Ramsaye (Frank Cass & Co., Ltd, London, 1964)

The Movie Moguls, by Philip French (Weidenfeld & Nicolson, London, 1969)

The Movies in the Age of Innocence, by Edward Wagenknecht (University of Oklahoma Press: Norman, 1962)

My Autobiography, by Charles Chaplin (Simon & Schuster, New York, 1964: The Bodley Head, London, 1964)

My First 100 Years in Hollywood, by Jack L. Warner (Random House, New York, 1965)

O.K. For Sound, edited by Frederic Thrasher (Duell, Sloan & Pearce, New York, 1946)

The Parade's Gone By, by Kevin Brownlow (Knopf, New York, 1968: Secker & Warburg, London, 1968)

The Player, by Lillian Ross and Helen Ross (Simon & Schuster, New York, 1962).

The Politics of Experience and The Bird of Paradise by R. D. Laing (Penguin Books, London, 1967)

A Portrait of Joan, by Joan Crawford with Jane Kesner Ardmore (Doubleday & Co., Inc., 1962)

The Public Is Never Wrong, by Adolph Zukor (G. P. Putnam's Sons, New York, 1953)

The Rise of the American Film, by Lewis Jacobs (Harcourt, Brace & Co., New York, 1939)

Romantic Adventure, by Elinor Glyn (Ivor Nicholson & Watson, London, 1930)

Star-Dust in Hollywood, by Jan and Cora Gordon (George G. Harrap Ltd, London, 1930)

The Stars, by Edgar Morin (Transatlantic Book Service, London, 1960)

Sunshine and Shadow, by Mary Pickford (Heinemann London, 1956)

A Tree Is a Tree, by King Vidor (Harcourt, Brace & Co., New York, 1953)

Two Reels and a Crank, by Albert E. Smith (Doubleday & Co., New York, 1952)

When the Movies Were Young, by Linda Arvidson (Mrs D. W. Griffith) (E. P. Dutton & Co., New York, 1925)

Grateful acknowledgement is made of quotations from articles in the following publications:

Evening Standard, Daily Mail, New York Times, Sunday Times Colour Magazine, St Louis Post-Dispatch, Variety, Photoplay, Picturegoer, Time, Newsweek, Esquire, Sight and Sound, Cinema, Films in Review. The stills used in the illustrations come from the following companies or private collectors to whom the author expresses his thanks for their use here.

Hammer Films, Metro-Goldwyn-Mayer, Paramount, Twentieth Century-Fox, United Artists, Warner-Seven Arts; The Kevin Brownlow Collection, The Leslie Flint Collection; the two stills from *Broken Blossoms* are reproduced by the kind permission of Raymond Rohauer, formerly Film Curator and Programme Director of the Gallery of Modern Art, New York City, Copyright holder of an interest pertaining to films and publications by Mack Sennett. Mr. Rohauer is also thanked for permission to quote from Mack Sennett's *King of Comedy*.

In addition to those named in the Introduction, the author wishes to express his thanks to the following people for the personal assistance they gave him in researching this book:

Miss Elizabeth Tindall, Reference Department, St Louis Public Library; Mr Roy T. King, Reference Librarian, *St Louis Post-Dispatch:* Mr Paul Myers, Curator, Theatre Collection, Library and Museum of the Performing Arts, Lincoln Center, New York; Mr Robert Hawkins, London Editor, *Variety*; Mr Ernest Lindgren, Curator, The National Film Archive, London; Miss Brenda Davies and Staff, Reference Section, British Film Institute; Mr David Meeker, Chief Booking Officer, British Film Institute; Mr A. G. Collard, Midland Bank; Miss Sally Williams; Chief Librarian and Staff, British Museum Newspaper and Periodical Library; Studio Corot and the National Film Archive who prepared the frame enlargements.

INDEX